WISDOM IN ISRAEL AND IN THE ANCIENT NEAR EAST

SUPPLEMENTS
TO
VETUS TESTAMENTUM

VOLUME III

LEIDEN
E. J. BRILL
1969

WISDOM IN ISRAEL AND IN THE ANCIENT NEAR EAST

PRESENTED TO

PROFESSOR HAROLD HENRY ROWLEY

M. A., D. D., Theol. D., F. B. A.

BY THE SOCIETY FOR OLD TESTAMENT STUDY IN ASSOCIATION WITH THE EDITORIAL BOARD OF VETUS TESTAMENTUM

IN CELEBRATION OF HIS SIXTY-FIFTH BIRTHDAY, 24 MARCH 1955

EDITED BY

M. NOTH AND D. WINTON THOMAS

SECOND, PHOTOMECHANICAL REPRINT

LEIDEN
E. J. BRILL
1969

PRINTED IN THE NETHERLANDS

CONTENTS

[1]) These two contributions, though they deal primarily with matters other than Wisdom, are included in this volume in the belief that they will be of interest to many readers (M. N., D. W. T.).

Prof. H. H. Rowley

HAROLD HENRY ROWLEY

ZUM FÜNFUNDSECHZIGSTEN GEBURTSTAG

Die internationale alttestamentliche Wissenschaft gedenkt des 65. Geburtstages von H. H. ROWLEY mit besonders grosser und lebhafter Anteilnahme. Denn H. H. ROWLEY nimmt in ihrem Kreise eine ungewöhnliche und singuläre Stellung ein. Wenn gegenwärtig zwischen den Alttestamentlern vieler Länder eine sehr erfreuliche wissenschaftliche und menschliche Verbundenheit besteht und auf den internationalen Alttestamentlerkongressen eine Atmosphäre des Vertrauens und der Bereitwilligkeit zur sachlichen Zusammenarbeit herrscht, so ist das zu einem guten Teil den Bemühungen von H. H. ROWLEY zu verdanken. H. H. ROWLEY war es, der nach dem zweiten Weltkrieg als erster die abgerissenen Fäden nach allen Seiten hin wieder anknüpfte, sobald sich die Tore zwischen den Ländern der Welt wieder geöffnet hatten; und er ist bis heute derjenige, der die Verbindung zu den Mitarbeitern auf dem Gebiete der alttestamentlichen Wissenschaft und auf den Gebieten der benachbarten Wissenschaften mit einer Treue pflegt, die nur bewundert werden kann. Er tut dies in einem Geist vorbildlicher Gerechtigkeit und Weitherzigkeit, die auch den Vertretern von Auffassungen, die von seinen eigenen abweichen, Achtung entgegenbringt und ihr volles Recht zuteil werden lässt. Damit bereitet er den Boden für eine Gemeinsamkeit internationaler wissenschaftlicher Arbeit am Alten Testament, auf dem gute Früchte wachsen können und hoffentlich noch auf lange Zeit hinaus wachsen werden. Die internationale alttestamentliche Wissenschaft ist ihm für das alles zu aufrichtigem Danke verpflichtet.

Er konnte und kann das mit umso grösserer Autorität tun, als er selbst in der alttestamentlichen Wissenschaft einer der fleissigsten und produktivsten Arbeiter ist. Von der geradezu bewundernswerten Fülle seiner wissenschaftlichen Arbeiten, die sich auf die verschiedensten Gegenstände im weiten Bereich der alttestamentlichen Wissenschaft erstrecken, gibt das Verzeichnis seiner Schriften, das dieser Festschrift beigegeben ist, ein eindrucksvolles Bild. Es ist nicht nötig, seine Arbeiten im einzelnen zu charakterisieren; denn sie sind in aller Welt bekannt. Aber auf gewisse Grundsätze seiner Arbeit darf hier doch hingewiesen werden, da sie vorbildlich und nachahmenswert für alle wissenschaftliche Arbeit und besonders für die Arbeit in der alttestamentlichen Wissenschaft sind. Da ist zunächst zu erinnern an die Gewissenhaftigkeit, mit der er seine eigene Arbeit in den Zusammenhang der gesamten Wissenschaft hineinstellt. Diese Gewissenhaftigkeit besteht in erster Linie ganz schlicht darin, dass er alles, was zu einem bestimmten Gegenstande veröffentlicht worden ist, liest und ernst nimmt und sich damit auseinandersetzt. Fast alle seiner Publikationen sind zugleich bibliographische Fundgruben ersten Ranges zu dem betreffenden Thema. In diesem Zusammenhang muss mit Dankbarkeit der Sorgfalt gedacht werden, mit der er im Auftrag der Britischen Society for Old Testament Study die jährliche "Booklist" herausgibt, die zu einem unentbehrlichen bibliographischen Hilfsmittel der gesamten internationalen alttestamentlichen Wissenschaft geworden ist. In dieser Weise macht er nicht nur mit Worten, sondern mit der Tat wirklichen Ernst mit dem Grundsatz einer echten Zusammenarbeit. Damit hängt zusammen die ebenfalls vorbildliche Vorsicht und Umsicht, mit der er sich seine wissenschaftlichen Urteile bildet. Es dauert oft längere Zeit, bis er in einer bestimmten Frage zu einem begründeten Urteil gelangt ist, und erst dann äussert er sich zu dieser Frage. Als Beispiel mag seine Stellungnahme in dem wissenschaftlichen Streit um die Datierung und Beurteilung der neu gefundenen Texte von *chirbet ḳumrān* gelten, in dem so viele vorschnelle und nicht ausgereifte Thesen öffentlich vorgetragen worden sind. Er hat in diesem Streit lange gezögert, ehe er seine Stimme erhob. Erst dann ist er mit einer wohl überlegten und gründlich fundierten Meinung hervorgetreten. Diese Grundsätze eines hohen wissenschaftlichen Ethos sollte die gesamte alttestamentliche Wissenschaft sich als Beispiel vor Augen halten.

Möge H. H. Rowley diese Festschrift als ein Zeichen herzlicher Dankbarkeit entgegennehmen, die die Alttestamentler aller Länder für ihn in aufrichtiger Gesinnung empfinden.

M. Noth
D. Winton Thomas

THE tribute paid to H. H. ROWLEY by Professor Martin NOTH and Professor WINTON THOMAS will be felt by all British Old Testament scholars to express admirably their own sentiments. Nevertheless, it is entirely fitting that there should also be a further tribute in the English tongue from H. H. ROWLEY's own British colleagues who yield to none in their esteem for his person and their appreciation of his work.

For some years before the Second World War it had become clear that H. H. ROWLEY had moved into the front rank of British Old Testament scholars. There were books of high quality to cite as evidence, and none who heard him read a paper to a congress in Göttingen in 1935 will forget the impression he made on his audience by the exhaustive thoroughness of his treatment of his chosen theme. Yet few perhaps could have foreseen then the extraordinarily influential, and indeed central, position in the world of Old Testament scholarship which he was to achieve immediately after the war. It was an inspiration on his part to recognize, as he did, the challenge of the hour, and, without waiting to see what others would do, to take the initiative in bringing together again those whom war had divided. How right he had been in his judgment was shown by the remarkable response his action called forth. The fruit of what was done then is to be seen in many lands and in many of the friendships which have been made possible. His British colleagues recognize his leadership in these matters, and have been proud to follow him and abet his efforts.

Not only, however, in such practical ways has H. H. ROWLEY set an example. He has himself reached an astonishingly high standard of scholarship. These last ten years have been his *anni mirabiles*. An unending stream of books, articles and reviews has flowed from his busy pen, and readers must have marvelled at his tireless industry, the range of his interests, the width of his reading, the brilliance of his documentation, and the sobriety and soundness of his judgment. The languages, literature, history, archaeology, religion and theology of the Old Testament have all received his attention. His colleagues have come to expect every now and again a survey of some particular field which is as exhaustive as it is illuminating, and yet seems at times to have been tossed off as a parergon. But for his enthusiasm and energy the Book List which he edits on behalf of the Society for Old Testament Study would not be the valuable aid to scholars everywhere which it now is, while many another project has his eager, restless mind behind it.

There is, however, still another side of H. H. Rowley's work which should not be overlooked, namely the help and encouragement he has given to others. If he sets a high standard for other men and challenges them to reach it, he never asks of them what he is not prepared to do himself. There is to be sure something of the gadfly in him, and he is no admirer of those who fold their hands when there is work to be done. Few men have as much right to chide the idler as he has, but the twinkle in his eye takes the sting from his rebuke.

In offering H. H. Rowley this volume, which is remarkable for the fact that he has not contributed to it, his many friends would thank him for all he has been and has done, and would wish him many more years to further the studies he and they have so much at heart and to continue to exert that unselfish and brotherly influence which has meant so much to others and which only his largeheartedness can explain.

A. Guillaume
(President, Society for Old Testament Study, 1955).

N. W. Porteous
(President, Society for Old Testament Study, 1954).

SELECT BIBLIOGRAPHY OF THE WRITINGS OF HAROLD HENRY ROWLEY

COMPILED BY

G. HENTON DAVIES
Durham

Abbreviations: *AJSL* = *The American Journal of Semitic Languages and Literatures*; *BJRL* = *The Bulletin of the John Rylands Library*; *BO* = *Bibliotheca Orientalis*; *BQ* = *The Baptist Quarterly*; *CQ* = *The Congregational Quarterly*; *ET* = *The Expository Times*; *HJ* = *The Hibbert Journal*; *HTR* = *The Harvard Theological Review*; *HUCA* = *Hebrew Union College Annual*; *I* = *Interpretation*; *JBL* = *The Journal of Biblical Literature*; *JQR* = *The Jewish Quarterly Review*; *JRAS* = *The Journal of the Royal Asiatic Society*; *JTS* = *The Journal of Theological Studies*; *PEQ* = *Palestine Exploration Quarterly*; *TH* = *Theology*; *VT* = *Vetus Testamentum*; *ZATW* = *Zeitschrift für die Alttestamentliche Wissenschaft.*

1924:
"The Belshazzar of Daniel and of History", *The Expositor*, 9th Series, ii, p. 182-195; p. 255-272.
1926:
"The Interpretation and Date of Sibylline Oracles iii 388-400", *ZATW*, N. F., p. 324-327.
"The Text and Interpretation of Jeremiah xi. 18-xii. 6", *AJSL*, xlii, p. 217-227.
1928:
"The 'Chaldaeans' in the Book of Daniel", *ET*, xxxix, p. 188 f.
1929:
The Aramaic of the Old Testament: A grammatical and lexical study of its relations with other early Aramaic dialects.
1930:
"The Historicity of the Fifth Chapter of Daniel", *JTS*, xxxii, p. 12-31.
1932:
"Prophetic Ministry", *BQ*, vi, p.1 -13.
"The bilingual problem of Daniel", *ZATW*, NF., ix, p. 256-268.
1933:
"Early Aramaic Dialects and the Book of Daniel", *JRAS*, p. 777-805.

1935:
Darius the Mede and the Four World Empires in the Book of Daniel: A historical study of contemporary theories.
Review: *An Introduction to the Books of the Old Testament* (W. O. E. OESTERLEY and T. H. ROBINSON), *HJ*, xxxiii, p. 313-316.
1936:
"Some Problems in the Book of Daniel", *ET*, xlvii, p. 216-220.
"The Semitic Sources of 'Cipher' and its Cognates", in *Werden und Wesen des Alten Testaments* (*ZATW*, Beiheft 66), p. 175-190.
Review: *An Introduction to the Books of the Apocrypha* (W. O. E. OESTERLEY), *JTS*, xxxvii, p. 88-90.
1937:
"The Interpretation of the Song of Songs", *JTS*, xxxviii, p. 337-363.
"The Riddle of the Song of Songs", *BQ*, viii, p. 411-416.
Review: *Das Buch der Psalmen übersetzt und erklärt* (H. HERKENNE), *JTS*, xxxviii, p. 66-68.
Review: *A Fresh Approach to the Psalms* (W. O. E. OESTERLEY), *BQ*, viii, p. 341-343.
Review: *Daniel* (A. BENTZEN), *JTS*, xxxviii, p. 425-427.
1938:
"The History of Israel: 3. Political and Economic", in *Record and Revelation* (ed. H. WHEELER ROBINSON), p. 160-186.
"Some Hebrew Prepositional Forms", *Zeitschrift der Deutschen Morgenländischen Gesellschaft*, xcii, p. 53-59.
"The Song of Songs: An Examination of Recent Theory", *JRAS*, p. 251-276.
"Israel's Sojourn in Egypt", *BJRL*, xxii, p. 243-290.
Review: *The History of Israel: Its Facts and Factors* (H. WHEELER ROBINSON), *BQ*, ix, p. 186-188.
Review: *A Critical and Exegetical Commentary on the Book of Ezekiel* (G. A. COOKE), *JTS*, xxxix, p. 183-186.
Review: *Recensio und Restitutio: Eine Vermuthung über die früheste Geschichte des alttestamentlichen Texte* (P. RUBEN), *JTS*, xxxix, p. 182 f.
1939:
Israel's Mission to the World.
"Introduction to the Old Testament", in *A Companion to the Bible* (ed. T. W. MANSON), 31-77.
"The Meaning of 'The Shulammite' ", *AJSL*, lvi, p. 84-91.
"Zadok and Nehushtan", *JBL*, lviii, p. 113-141.
"The Eisodus and the Exodus", *ET*, l, p. 503-508.

Review: *Prophetengestalten des Alten Testaments* (P. VOLZ), *JTS*, xl, p. 396-398.

1940:

"The Herodians in the Gospels", *JTS*, xli, p. 14-27.

"Ras Shamra and the Habiru Question", *PEQ*, p. 90-94.

"Jewish Proselyte Baptism and the Baptism of John", *HUCA*, xv, p. 313-334.

"The Changing Emphasis in Biblical Studies", *BQ*, x, p. 185-190.

"The Chinese Sages and the Golden Rule", *BJRL*, xxiv, p. 321-352.

"The Danite Migration to Laish", *ET*, li, p. 466-471.

"The Inspiration of the Old Testament", *CQ*, xviii, p. 164-177.

"The Structure of Psalm xlii-xliii", *Biblica*, xxi, p. 45-50.

Review: *Development of the Canaanite Dialects* (Z. S. HARRIS), *PEQ*, p. 124 f.

1941:

"The Text and Structure of Psalm ii", *JTS*, xlii, p. 143-154.

"The Date of the Exodus", *PEQ*, p. 152-157.

Review: *The Bible in its Ancient and English Versions* (ed. H. WHEELER ROBINSON), *JTS*, xlii, p. 125-127.

Review: *The Gospel of the Infancy and other Biblical Essays* (E. BURROWS), *TH*, xlii, p. 374 f.

Review: *The Study of the Bible in the Middle Ages* (B. SMALLEY), *BQ*, x, p. 458 f.

1942:

The Relevance of the Bible.

Submission in Suffering.

"Jericho and the Date of the Exodus: A Rejoinder", *HJ*, xl, p. 207 f.

"Habiru and Hebrews", *PEQ*, p. 41-53.

"The Exodus and the Settlement in Canaan", *Bulletin of the American Schools of Oriental Research*, No. 85, p. 27-31.

"Sacrament and Sacrifice: A Protestant View of the Lord's Supper", *HJ*, xl, p. 181-185.

Review: *The Throne of David* (A. G. HEBERT), *HJ*, xl, p. 199-201.

Review: *The Book of Isaiah, Vol. i* (E. J. KISSANE), *JTS*, xliii, p. 77 f.

Review: *The Historic Mission of Jesus* (C. J. CADOUX), *BQ*, xi, p. 60-63.

Review: *The Prophets and their Times* (J. M. POWIS SMITH, 2nd ed., revised by W. A. IRWIN), *BQ*, xi, p. 125 f.

1943:

"The 'Prince of the Covenant' in Daniel xi. 22", *ET*, lvii, p. 24-27.

Review: *The Origin and Significance of the New Testament Baptism* (H. G. Marsh), *JTS*, xliv, p. 79-81.

Review: *Jesus in the Light of History* (A. T. Olmstead), *PEQ*, p. 110-113.

Review: *The Christian Philosophy of History* (S. J. Case), *BQ*, xi, p. 188-191.

Review: *Proto-Septuagint Studies* (H. M. Orlinsky), *JQR*, xxxiii, p. 497-499.

Review: *The Old Testament in the World Church* (G. E. Phillips), *JTS*, xliv, p. 78 f.

Review: *Archaeology and the Religion of Israel* (W. F. Albright), *CQ*, xxi, p. 71 f.

1944:

The Relevance of Apocalyptic: A Study of Jewish and Christian. Apocalypses from Daniel to the Revelation.

"Early Levite History and the Question of the Exodus", *Journal of Near Eastern Studies*, iii, p. 73-78.

"*Hattorah wehannebi'im*", in *Melilah*, i, p. 185-191.

"The Significance of Moses and his Work", *Religion in Education*, xi, p. 63-67.

Review: *A Pilgrim's Further Progress* (C. J. Cadoux), *JTS*, xlv, p. 117 f.

Review: *The Book of Isaiah, Vol. ii* (E. J. Kissane), *JTS*, xlv, p. 206-211.

1945:

The Missionary Message of the Old Testament.

An Outline of the Teaching of Jesus.

"The Origin and Meaning of Baptism", *BQ*, xi, p. 309-320.

"The Nature of Old Testament Prophecy in the Light of Recent Study", *HTR*, xxxviii, p. 1-38.

"The Figure of 'Taxo' in the Assumption of Moses", *JBL*, lxiv, p. 141-143.

"Criteria for the Dating of Jubilees", *JQR*, xxxvi, p. 183-187.

Review: *Studies in Divine Kingship in the Ancient Near East* (I. Engnell), *JTS*, xlvi, p. 80-82.

Review: *Isaiah, Chapters xl-lv* (S. Smith), *JTS*, xlvi, p. 215-217.

1946:

The Re-Discovery of the Old Testament.

"The Unity of the Old Testament", *BJRL*, xxix, p. 326-358.
"The Religious Value of Sacrifice", *ET*, lviii, p. 69-71.
European Scholars and Publications chiefly relating to the Old Testament during the War Years.
"Britische Literatur zum Alten Testament in den Kriegsjahren 1939-1945", *Theologische Zeitschrift*, ii, p. 241-265.
Review: *The Westminster Historical Atlas to the Bible*, (G. E. Wright and F. V. Filson), *PEQ*, p. 49-51.
Review: *Israel: its Life and Culture III-IV* (J. Pedersen), *PEQ*, p. 51-55.
Review: *The Relevance of the Prophets* (R. B. Y. Scott), *BQ*, xii, p. 43-45.
Review: *The Apocryphal Literature* (C. C. Torrey), *JBL*, lxv, p. 217-221.
Review: *Inspiration and Revelation in the Old Testament*, (H. Wheeler Robinson), *BO*, iii, p. 65 f.
1947:
"The Relevance of Biblical Interpretation", *I*, i, p. 3-19.
"The Marriage of Ruth", *HTR*, xl, p. 77-99.
"The British Society for Old Testament Study", *JBL*, lxvi, p. xxvii-xxxi.
"Was Amos a Nabi?" in *Festschrift Otto Eissfeldt*, p. 191-198.
"The Prophets and Sacrifice", *ET*, lviii, p. 305-307.
Review: *The Old Testament and the Future Life* (E. F. Sutcliffe), *TH*, l, p. 156 f.
Review: *An Outline of Biblical Theology* (Millar Burrows), *JBL*, lxvi, p. 221-224.
Review: *The New Bible Handbook* (ed. by G. T. Manley, G. C. Robinson and A. M. Stibbs), *BQ*, xii, p. 286-291.
Review: *An Aramaic Approach to the Gospels and Acts* (M. Black), *BO*, iv, p. 35 f.
Review: *Studies in the Book of Nahum* (A. Haldar), *BO*, iv, p. 60 f.
Review: *The Hebrew Book of Psalms* (B. D. Eerdmans), *BO*, iv, p. 110-114.
Review: *The Religion of Israel* (B. D. Eerdmans), *BO*, iv, p. 152-154.
1948:
"Jeremiah", in *The Westminster Study Bible.*
"The Voice of God in Apocalyptic", *I*, ii, p. 403-418.
"The Chronological Order of Ezra and Nehemiah", in *Ignace Goldziher Memorial Volume, Pt. i*, p. 117-149.

"The Chinese Philosopher Mo Ti", *BJRL*, xxxi, p. 241-276.

Review: *Geschichtliches und Übergeschichtliches im Alten Testament* (O. Eissfeldt), *BO*, v, p. 100.

Review: *The Early Traditions of Israel* (C. A. Simpson), *BO*, v, p. 138-140.

Review: *In the Beginning* (S. H. Hooke), *PEQ*, p. 68-71.

Review: *The Jewish New Year Festival* (N. H. Snaith), *Theologische Literaturzeitung*, p. 534-536.

1949:

The Authority of the Bible.

"The Manifest Splendour of God: A Study of Biblical Thought on the Media of Revelation", *CQ*, xxvii, p. 248-264.

"Recent Discovery and the Patriarchal Age", *BJRL*, xxxii, p. 44-79.

Review: *How Came our Faith*? (W. A. L. Elmslie), *BQ*, xiii, p. 39-41.

Review: *The Suffering Servant in Deutero-Isaiah* (C. R. North), *JTS*, l, p. 76-78.

Review: *Old Testament Commentary* (H. C. Alleman and E. E. Flack), *BO*, vi, p. 60 f.

Review: *Islam and Christian Theology* (J. W. Sweetman), *BO*, vi, p. 66 f.

Review: *The Book of Daniel* (C. Lattey), *TH*, lii, p. 183-185.

Review: *Studies in Daniel* (H. L. Ginsberg), *JBL*, lxviii, p. 173-177.

Review: *The Inspiration and Authority of the Bible* (B. B. Warfield), *BQ*, xiii, p. 133-136.

Review: *The Targum of Isaiah* (J. F. Stenning), *BO*, vi, p. 159 f.

1950:

The Biblical Doctrine of Election.

The Growth of the Old Testament.

From Joseph to Joshua: Biblical Traditions in the Light of Archaeology (Schweich Lectures, 1948).

(Editor) *Studies in Old Testament Prophecy presented to Professor Theodore H. Robinson by the Society for Old Testament Study.*

"The Prophet Jeremiah and the Book of Deuteronomy", in *Studies in Old Testament Prophecy, etc.*, p. 157-174.

"The Suffering Servant and the Davidic Messiah", *Oudtestamentische Studiën*, viii, p. 100-136.

"The Antiquity of Israelite Monotheism", *ET*, lxi, p. 333-338.

"Melchizedek and Zadok (Gen. 14 and Ps. 110)", in *Festschrift für Alfred Bertholet*, p. 461-472.

"The Gospel in the Old Testament", in *The Enduring Gospel* (ed. R. Gregor Smith), p. 19-35.

Articles on Biblical Criticism, Daniel, Ezra, Job, Nehemiah, and Song of Songs, in *Chambers Encyclopaedia*.

"The Meaning of Sacrifice in the Old Testament", *BJRL*, xxxiii, p. 74-110.

Review: *The Mosaic Tradition* (F. V. WINNETT), *JTS*, N. S., i, p. 193-195.

Review: *The Ancestry of Our English Bible* (I. M. PRICE: 2nd revised ed. by W. A. IRWIN and A. P. WIKGREN), *BQ*, xiii, p. 278 f.

Review: *The Jews from Cyrus to Herod* (N. H. SNAITH), *BO*, vii, p. 109 f.

Review: *Histoire de la littérature hébraïque et juive des origines à la ruine de l'état juif* (A. LODS), *BO*, vii, p. 110-113.

Review: *History of New Testament Times with an Introduction to the Apocrypha* (R. H. PFEIFFER), *JQR*, N. S., xl, p. 303-305.

Review: *Studies in the Name Israel in the Old Testament* (G. A. DANELL), *Symbolae Biblicae Upsalienses*, xii, p. 42-53.

1951:

Submission in Suffering and Other Essays in Eastern Thought.

(Editor) *The Old Testament and Modern Study.*

"The Istanbul Congress of Orientalists and the Old Testament", *VT*, i, p. 313-318.

"Moses and the Decalogue", *BJRL*, xxxiv, p. 81-118.

"A Note on the Septuagint Text of I Sam. xv. 22a", *VT*, i, p. 67 f.

Review: *The Wisdom of Koheleth* (R. GORDIS) and *Studies in Koheleth* (H. L. GINSBERG), *JQR*, N. S., xlii, p. 87-90.

Review: *Essays and Studies presented to Stanley Arthur Cook* (ed. D. WINTON THOMAS), *JTS*, N. S., ii, p. 188-190.

Review: *The First Book of Maccabees* (S. TEDESCHE), *BO*, viii, p. 238.

Review: *Die Nachtgesichte des Sacharja* (L. G. RIGNELL), *JTS*, N. S., ii, p. 190 f.

Review: *Het Hart (Leb, Lebab) in het Oude Testament* (E. H. VON MEYENFELDT), *BO*, viii, p. 192 f.

Review: *The Old Testament against its Environment* (G. E. WRIGHT), *JTS*, N. S., ii, p. 186 f.

1952:

The Servant of the Lord and Other Essays on the Old Testament.

The Zadokite Fragments and the Dead Sea Scrolls.

"The Unity of the Book of Daniel", *HUCA*, xxiii, Pt. i, p. 233-273.

"A Year's Work on the Old Testament". *I*, vi, p. 79-98.

"The Internal Dating of the Dead Sea Scrolls", in *Ephemerides Theologicae Lovanienses*, xxviii, p. 257-272.
"The Historical Background of the Dead Sea Scrolls", *ET*, lxiii, p. 378-384.
"The Covenanters of Damascus and the Dead Sea Scrolls", *BJRL*, xxxv, p. 111-154.
Review: *De Derivata van de Stam* 'mn *in het Hebreeuwsch van het Oude Testament* (J. C. C. van Dorssen), *BO*, ix, p. 144.
Review: *Het offermaal in het heidendom en in de Heilige Schrift* (L. Zielhuis), *BO*, p. ix, 20.
1953:
The Unity of the Bible.
"The International Old Testament Congress at Copenhagen", *VT*, iii, p. 423-428.
"Marcel on Infant Baptism", *ET*, lxiv, p. 361-363.
"The Book of Ezekiel in Modern Study", *BRJL*, xxxvi, p. 146-190.
„Menelaus and the Abomination of Desolation", in *Studia Orientalia Ioanni Pedersen ... dicata*, p. 303-315.
Review: *David Ḳimḥi's Hebrew Grammar* (*Mikhlol*) (W. Chomsky), *ET*, lxiv, p. 263 f.
Review: *The Book of Psalms, Vol. i* (E. J. Kissane), *ET*, lxiv, p. 366 f.
Review: *De Molochdienst in het Oude Testament* (K. Dronkert), *BO*, x, p. 195 f.
Review: *Lachish III*: *The Iron Age* (O. Tufnell, *et al.*), *ET*, lxv, p. 10 f.
Review: Josue (B. J. Alfrink), Spreuken (J. van der Ploeg), and *De Kleine Profeten* (*Osee ... Micheas*) (D. Deden), *BO*, x, p. 227 f.
1954:
"The Literary Growth of the Old Testament", in *The Times Bible Supplement*, p. 6.
"The Servant Mission: The Servant Songs and Evangelism", *I*, viii, p. 259-272.
Review: *The Meaning of* zar *in The Old Testament* (L. A. Snijders), *BO*, xi, p. 64 f.
Review: *Die Erwählung Israels nach dem Alten Testament* (Th. C. Vriezen), *JBL*, lxxiii, p. 116 f.
Review: *A Theology of Salvation*: *A Commentary on Isaiah 40-55* (U. E. Simon), *JTS*, N. S., v, p. 83-85.
Review: *Essays presented to Leo Baeck*, *ET*, lxvi, p. 8 f.

Review: *Prediker* (J. VAN DER PLOEG), *BO*, xi, p. 64.
Review: *The Mysterious Numbers of the Hebrew Kings: A Reconstruction of the Chronology of the Kingdoms of Israel and Judah* (E. R. THIELE), *VT*, iv, p. 446-448.
"Recent Foreign Theology", *ET*, lvii, 79-81, 109 f., 136 f., 163, 220 f., 250 f., 304-306; lviii, 26 f., 54 f., 137 f., 164 f., 192-194, 219-221, 248-250, 276-278; lix, 22-24, 51 f., 108-110, 164, 193 f., 334 f.; lx, 54 f., 109 f., 138 f., 168, 190-192, 252 f., 289 f., 352-354; lxi, 29 f., 60-62, 93-95, 123 f., 154-157, 189-191, 220-222, 253-255, 316-318, 380-382; lxii, 62 f., 93-95, 125 f., 157-159, 190 f., 222-224, 286-288, 318 f., 349-351, 380-383; lxiii, 29 f., 61-63, 90 f., 127, 194 f., 223-226, 258, 355; lxiv, 29 f., 61-63, 93 f., 157 f., 189 f., 219-221, 254, 284 f., 316-318, 350 f., 380; lxv, 27-29, 91-93, 126 f., 189 f., 222 f., 253-255, 317-319, 350 f.; lxvi, 28-30, 62, 93-95, 126 f., 157-159, 190 f.
(Editor) *The Book List of the Society for Old Testament Study*, 1946-

SOME CANAANITE-PHOENICIAN SOURCES OF HEBREW WISDOM

BY

W. F. ALBRIGHT
Baltimore

In recent years the importance of Canaanite and Phoenician civilization for proper understanding of the culture of Israel has been increasingly recognized [1]). Occasional denials may generally be credited to a reluctance to abandon cherished positions of the recent past. After all, it was not until 1932 that the flow of Ugaritic illustrations of biblical literature began, carrying with it completely new insights into the already known Canaanite and Phoenician data. Published and unpublished data are already so extensive as to dwarf the significance of most other cultures of the Near and Middle East, in so far as direct service to biblical scholarship is concerned. Of course, nothing can change the overwhelming importance of Egyptology and Assyriology (*sensu stricto*) for our general knowledge of ancient Eastern civilization, and I am the last to deny that these two subjects remain more important in the last analysis for biblical scholarship.

There has been much misunderstanding of the nature of Canaanite-Phoenician culture [2]). It must be emphasized that this was a relatively homogeneous civilization from the Middle Bronze Age down to the beginning of the Achaemenian period, after which it was swallowed

1) There is now a rich literature on this subject. Since I am here concerned chiefly with biblical parallels, I shall limit myself to a very few references: my *Archaeology and the Religion of Israel* (third edition, Baltimore, 1953); "The Old Testament and Canaanite Language and Literature", *Catholic Biblical Quarterly* (1945), p. 5-31; "The Psalm of Habakkuk", in *Studies in Old Testament Prophecy* (T. H. Robinson Festschrift, 1950), p. 1-18; "A Catalogue of Early Hebrew Lyric Poems (Psalm LXVIII)", *HUCA* XXIII (1950/51), p. 1-39.

2) For a general historical survey see my chapter in *Historia Mundi*, II (1954), especially p. 340-348, 354-357, and 362-365. EDUARD MEYER's account of Phoenician history and culture (*Geschichte des Altertums*, II, 2 (1931), p. 61-186) was by far the best that had appeared until then, but it has been thoroughly antiquated by Ugaritic and other discoveries since. My long paper "The Rôle of the Canaanites in the History of Civilization" (*Waldo G. Leland Volume*: *Studies in the History of Culture* (1942), p. 11-50) is now unobtainable.

up in large part by much more extensive cultures. Chronologically speaking, it is certain that "Phoenician" is simply the Iron-Age equivalent of Bronze-Age "Canaanite" [1]). Recent numismatic discoveries prove that the Phoenician script and language were still used on coins as late as the reign of Gordian (A.D. 238-244) [2]), a fact which indicates that Phoenician culture did not finally expire until the triumph of Christianity in the fourth century. From the geographical standpoint, there was a homogeneous civilization which extended in the Bronze Age from Mount Casius, north of Ugarit, to the Negeb of Palestine, and in the Iron Age from north of Arvad (at least) to the extreme south of Palestine [3]). This civilization shared a common material culture (including architecture, pottery, etc.) through the entire period, and we now know that language [4]), literature [5]), art, and religion [6]) were substantially the same in the Bronze Age. From the twelfth century on we find increasing divergence in higher culture, but material culture remained practically the same in all parts of the area. The differences (except in the case of

---

[1]) Cf. B. MAISLER (MAZAR), *BASOR* 102, p. 7-12.

[2]) *Israel Exploration Journal*, 4 (1954), p. 208.

[3]) How far some scholars are from appreciating this fact might be illustrated by many citations from centres of learning in both Europe and America. In 1951 an eminent American biblical scholar declared at a public meeting which I attended that there was no more relation between Ugaritic and Hebrew culture and literature than there was between the cultures of the Plains Indians and the Aztecs!

[4]) See especially R. DE LANGHE, *De taal van Ras Sjamra-Ugarit* (1948); W. F. ALBRIGHT, *BASOR* 89, p. 8, and *CBQ* (1945), p. 14 ff., 22 ff. The relation between Ugaritic, Amarna Canaanite, and early Hebrew has also been studied in three unpublished Johns Hopkins dissertations by G. E. MENDENHALL (1947), W. L. MORAN (1950), and HORACE D. HUMMEL (1955).

[5]) There can be little doubt any longer that the Ugaritic epics were all composed in Phoenicia proper and its hinterland, from which they were transmitted orally to all parts of the Canaanite continuum, including Ugarit in the north and Palestine in the south; for evidence see particularly my remarks in *HUCA* XXIII (1950/51), p. 3, n. 3, and *BASOR* 130, p. 26 f. Additional material for this localization may be found in published and unpublished papers by various scholars; e.g., M. H. POPE has shown that the home of the god El in the Baal Epic was primarily in the underworld near the famous sources of Afqā above Byblos. Any scholar who remains sceptical has only to recall the similar situation in the early Hellenic world, where the Homeric epics were diffused through areas occupied by speakers of many different dialects (and were sometimes modified dialectally in the process).

[6]) See especially *ARI*, ch. III. Note that there was a temple of Anath at Gaza (B. GRDSELOFF, *Les débuts du culte de Reshef en Egypte*, Cairo, 1942, p. 35 ff., dealing with an ostracon from the end of the 13th century B.C.), temples of Dagon at Ashdod and Gaza, and a temple of Ḥaurôn at Jamnia—all in the extreme south of the coastal region of Canaan, later occupied by the Philistines.

Israelite religion) were no greater than they were in different parts of the Mesopotamian area of culture, which was geographically much more extensive. The situation in Canaan is in a number of ways comparable to that in Egypt, where the distance down the Nile is just about twice the distance along the coast from Gaza to Ugarit—and yet the civilization of Egypt was much more homogeneous than even I would maintain with respect to Canaanite culture.

Since Israel emerged from the same Northwest-Semitic background as the Phoenicians and other Canaanite groups which continued to exist down into the Iron Age, one would expect to find extremely close relationships in both material and higher culture. It is true that Israelite ties with Egypt were very strong, both historically and geographically, but it is doubtful whether Canaanite and Phoenician bonds with Egypt were any less close. Quite aside from the close ties of reciprocal trade, it must never be forgotten that Palestine, Phoenicia, and Egypt were as a rule part of the same political organization, in which Egypt generally played the controlling part. So far as we know, the only exceptions, during the period which interests us particularly, were during the 18th century B.C., again at the end of the 13th, and from the middle of the 12th to the late tenth. After the early ninth century B.C. Egyptian political influence in Asia decreased greatly, but was compensated by the steady development of reciprocal trade relations.

It would be very strange if the Northwestern Semites [1]) of Syria and Palestine did not share in the high appreciation of didactic literature in all important categories which we find in Egypt and Mesopotamia. In his admirable survey of "The Wisdom Literature" in *The Old Testament and Modern Study* (ed. H. H. Rowley), W. Baumgartner has briefly surveyed the material available in 1949, with a good bibliography; there is no object in traversing this ground again in the present paper. The most important additions to our available material for comparison during the past five years should, however, be mentioned. In the first place, our knowledge of Sumerian didactic literature, and especially of Sumerian proverbs, has been increased enormously by the latest discoveries and publications by S. N. Kramer, A. Falkenstein, and others [2]). Though our extant copies

---

[1]) I am using this term of the speakers of related dialects from northern Syria to southern Palestine, including the "Amorites" and the proto-Aramaeans.

[2]) The material available before 1952 has been well summarized by J. J. A. van Dijk, a pupil of Falkenstein, in his excellent monograph *La sagesse*

from Nippur date mostly from about the 18th century B.C. (low chronology), there can be no doubt that the original compositions come in the main from the third millennium, being thus fully as old as the earliest recorded didactic books from Egypt. Secondly, we may mention the valuable collection of translations of didactic and wisdom literature by John A. Wilson, R. H. Pfeiffer, and H. L. Ginsberg which was published by James B. Pritchard in *Ancient Near Eastern Texts Relating to the Old Testament*, 405-452 [1]).

It is most unreasonable to assume that didactic literature appeared any later in Syria-Palestine than in any other cultural area of the ancient East, relatively speaking. It is, however, true that Canaanite, Phoenician and Israelite wisdom books might be expected *a priori* to share in the syncretistic aspect of all Syro-Palestinian cultures which are now known to us. We should expect influences from Egypt and Mesopotamia to be represented in all periods and in all important literary categories. Following the analogies of these lands, as well as of Asia Minor and Greece, we should expect to have long compositions as well as short at any given period. We should, accordingly, reject the evolutionary strait jacket imposed on early literatures by H. Gunkel and some of his successors, according to which short compositions are generally earlier than long compositions in the same category [2]).

For want of space we shall limit ourselves to the Book of Proverbs, with a few comments on Job and Ecclesiastes, merely to indicate that the latter two also draw heavily on traditional Canaanite-Phoenician didactic sources.

In the course of the past century a curious myth has arisen: that of the Age of Wise Men, who are supposed to have flourished in the Achaemenian and early Hellenistic period, about the fifth-third centuries B.C. [3]). We may freely admit that the Book of Proverbs was

---

suméro-accadienne (Leiden, 1953). The Nippur collection of about 212 proverbs, pieced together from 446 tablets and fragments by S. N. Kramer and his pupil, Edmund I. Gordon, has been described by the latter in his paper "The Sumerian Proverb Collection: A Preliminary Report", *JAOS* 74 (1954), p. 82-84.

1) A new edition, revised throughout, is scheduled for 1955.

2) Cf. my discussion of this question in "Some Oriental Glosses on the Homeric Problem" (*Amer. Journ. of Archaeology*, 54 (1950), p. 162 ff.). It may be observed that my approach to the Homeric question is being confirmed with wholly unexpected speed by the results of the 1953 decipherment of the Mycenaean-Minoan Greek script.

3) This myth will be found most drastically stated in popularizations of modern critical scholarship of the Wellhausen school. R. H. Pfeiffer's remarkably

not edited in approximately its present form until about the fifth century B.C. without assuming that any material of post-exilic date is included in the Book [1]). But the content of Proverbs is considerably older, and it is entirely possible that aphorisms and even longer sections go back into the Bronze Age in substantially their present form. CULLEN I. K. STORY has shown in a Johns Hopkins study [2]) that the metric style of Proverbs often agrees entirely with that of the Ugaritic epics as analyzed by C. H. GORDON [3]). STORY has given numerous examples of different categories; the number might easily be increased several times. We content ourselves with two examples, both given by STORY; the translations are new:

The final unit of a tricolon may be different from the two preceding cola, thus producing a climactic effect, as in the following,

"As vinegar to the teeth	"Like the feeling of a wild cow for her calf,
And as smoke to the eyes,	Like the feeling of a wild ewe for her lamb,
So is the sluggard to them that send him." [4])	So (was) the feeling of Anath for Baal." [5])

The second half of a bicolon may omit a word parallel to an outstanding word in the first colon, as in the following,

"Let a stranger praise thee, and not thy mouth,	"From his mouth let the message go forth,
A foreigner and not thy lips." [6])	From his lips, the word." [7])

These, and many other poetic forms which are common to Proverbs

complete account of the literary composition of the Book, occupying only fifteen pages (*Introduction to the Old Testament*, p. 645-659) does not make this error. However, I do seriously object to his tendency to date the contents of Proverbs as late as possible, and his overemphasis on Edomite and North-Arabic wisdom, combined with total neglect of possible Canaanite-Phoenician sources. According to ROBERT GORDIS (*HUCA* XVIII (1944), p. 77-118), there were schools of wisdom resembling contemporary Greek schools of the sophists. He dates this period of wisdom teachers between about 500 and 200 B.C. and derives them chiefly from the "patrician" class.

[1]) In *JBL* 61 (1942), p. 123 (review of PFEIFFER's *Introduction*), I wrote: "There is no need to date any of the contents [of Proverbs] after the fifth century B.C. at the latest, though the final redaction may come down as far as the third century." I should now change these two centuries to the sixth and the fifth (possibly fourth) respectively

[2]) Published in condensed form as "The Book of Proverbs and Northwest-Semitic Literature" (*JBL* 64 (1945), p. 319-337).

[3]) *Ibid.*, p. 321-324. [4]) Prov. x 26.

[5]) Baal Epic, I AB (GORDON, No. 49), ii, lines 6 ff., 28 ff.

[6]) Prov. xxvii 2. [7]) I Aqhat, i, 113.

and Ugaritic literature, are totally absent in the Aramaic Aḥîqar, which was probably composed in or about the second half of the seventh century B.C. As recognized by an increasing number of scholars, including MEISSNER [1]), DOSSIN [2]), and BAUMGARTNER [3]), the Aramaic Aḥîqar goes back to Mesopotamian sources for most of its wisdom; OLMSTEAD has made out a very plausible case for an historical setting in early seventh-century Assyria [4]). We must, accordingly, date the content of Proverbs, as a whole, well before Aḥîqar [5]), and look for earlier Canaanite sources of its metric and stylistic structure as well as for direct Canaanite prototypes of many individual proverbs and bodies of material. The famous demonstration by ERMAN and others that the Maxims of Amenemope are the ultimate (orally transmitted) source of much of Prov. xxii-xxiv, shows how whole bodies of aphorisms could be taken over. It must be pointed out that scholars have been misled by the lateness of the hieratic copy which we possess (belonging to the Bubastite or Saite period, between the tenth and the sixth centuries B.C.) into dating the Egyptian text late. Actually, the name of Amenemope is most common in the New Kingdom, particularly in the 20th Dynasty, while the name of his father, Kanakht, is recorded by H. RANKE for the New Kingdom, but not later [6]). In view of the otherwise complete drying up of Egyptian literary inspiration with the fossilizing of the classical tongue after the end of the Ramesside Age, it is very risky to date the composition of the Maxims of Amenemope after the end of the second millennium. On the other hand, the spelling of loan words, etc., precludes a date before the twelfth century B.C. at earliest. It is probably not accidental that these chapters of Proverbs do not seem to contain any specific Canaanitisms, either in style or in vocabulary. Since the order of borrowed passages is seldom the same as that of the Egyptian original, the borrowing must have taken place orally, and I see no reason why this cannot have occurred as early as the tenth century B.C.

Proverbs contains numerous words, word parallels, and expressions which appear also in Ugaritic literature. The late UMBERTO CASSUTO

---

[1]) *Babylonien und Assyrien*, II, p. 423, 430, including a reference to my observations in *JAOS* 38 (1918), p. 64 f.

[2]) *Revue d'Assyriologie*, 29 (1932), p. 123-129.

[3]) *The Old Testament and Modern Study*, p. 211.

[4]) *JAOS* 56 (1936), p. 243.

[5]) See the discussion by STORY, *op. cit.*, p. 333 ff.

[6]) See H. RANKE, *Die ägyptischen Personennamen*, p. 27, No. 18, and 338, No. 7.

had isolated some forty pairs of words in parallelism which appear both in Hebrew poetry (or prose going back to verse originals) and in our recently recovered Ugaritic texts [1]). Since his death his pupil MOSHE HELD has brought together about thirty more [2]). Even if we omit a few which are too general or not quite certain, we still have at least sixty such pairs of parallel words. Many of these occur in Proverbs, as first pointed out by STORY. Since we do not possess any didactic literature from Ugarit, we are dependent on the Amarna Letters for direct proof of the antiquity of proverbs among the Northwestern Semites. Two good ones are known, and there are suggestions of others. The prince of Byblos quotes four times from an obviously familiar aphorism: "My field (territory) is likened (*mašil*) to a woman without a husband, because it is not ploughed" [3]). Over a decade ago I pointed out that a previously obscure passage in a letter from Lab'ayu of Shechem must be read as Canaanite, not as Accadian: *kî namlu tumḫaṣu la' tiqabbilu u tanšuku QÂTI AWÎLI ša yimaḫašši* (= Can. *yimḫaṣuha*?) "If ants are smitten, they do not accept (the smiting) quietly, but they bite the hand of the man who smites them" [4]). Judging from this proverb and the two preserved in Proverbs (vi 6; xxx 25), the ant was a popular subject of aphorisms. There is no reason whatever for dating the origin of the two biblical proverbs about the ant any later than this Canaanite one.

I pointed out long ago that chapters viii-ix are full of Canaanite words and expressions, and may go back to Phoenician sources more directly than any other material in Proverbs. The wisdom cosmogony in viii 22 ff. is full of obvious Canaanite reminiscences. Verse 22 begins with four words which transparently reflect a Canaanite *'L QNN R'ŠT DRKTH* "El created me (at) the beginning of his dominion"; *qny* "to create" [5]) and *drkt* "dominion" [6]) are well known from Ugarit and elsewhere in Canaanite areas. In the Baal Epic it is El who is wise above all gods; we read: *tḥmk. 'El. ḥkm. | ḥkmtk* (!)

---

[1]) See his detailed discussion in *Hā-ēlāh ʿAnat* (Jerusalem, 1951).

[2]) This material is still unpublished, but I have gone through it with the author and agree with his approach.

[3]) Amarna Letters (Knudtzon edition) 74 : 17 f.; 75 : 15 f.; 81 : 37 f.; 90 : 42 f.

[4]) *BASOR* 89, p. 29 ff.

[5]) On *QNY* "to create" in general, and on the Canaanite appellation *'El qônê 'ereṣ* "El-Creator-of-Earth", see my forthcoming paper in the *Mowinckel Festschrift*.

[6]) On Canaanite *drkt* "dominion," and Hebrew *DRK* see my remarks in *JBL* 63 (1944), p. 219, n. 82; P. NOBER, *Verbum Domini*, 26 (1948), p. 351-353; M. DAHOOD, *Biblica*, 33 (1952), p. 33, n. 4, and in forthcoming studies elsewhere.

ʿm. ʾlm. | *ḥyt. ḥẓt. tḥmk* = "Thy command, O El, is wise, Thy wisdom lasts for ever, A life of good fortune is thy command" [1]). This tricolon would fit very well into Proverbs, with appropriate changes in vocabulary. In verse 24 we have a direct allusion to the situation repeatedly presupposed in the Baal Epic, where El is said to dwell "at the sources (*mabbikê*) of the Two Rivers, in the midst of the fountains (*ʾapqê*) of the Two Deeps" [2]). The words *THMT* and *MBK* or *NBK* (corrupted in M.T.) occur in both passages. The biblical verse reflects older Canaanite mythological imagery; El brought forth Wisdom even before he had conquered the primordial dragon (Tehom) and established his home. The creation of the mountains (verse 25) was another favourite subject in Canaanite and Hittite mythologies [3]). Among other Canaanite reminiscences we may mention *ʾammôn* (as we must vocalize) "craftsman, master artificer, wizard, etc." (verse 30) [4]).

In chapter ix we have even more Canaanite reminiscences than in viii. The name borne by Wisdom here (as well as in two other verses of Proverbs) is *Ḥokmōt*, which has been correctly recognized as Phoenician by H. L. GINSBERG; it is parallel in form to *Milkōt* (for **milkát*) "Queen" (name of a deity) and comes from the same Canaanite **ḥúkmatu* as Heb. *ḥokmáh*. The seven pillars of her house have nothing to do with the New Year's Festival House (*bīt akīti*) of Sennacherib at Assur, as suggested by B. GEMSER [5]). In the older installation from about 700 B.C. we have two corridors ("Hallen"),

---

1) See my treatment in the *Bertholet Festschrift* (1950), p. 5, and STORY, *JBL* 64 (1945), p. 333 ff., also my remarks in *From the Stone Age to Christianity*, p. 283.

2) *ARI*, p. 72, 194 f. Note that the words for "sources, fountains" are both also dual.

3) For Phoenician mythology, see Philo Byblius, § 9; for Hittite and Horite mythology, see especially the mountain myths studied by GÜTERBOCK in his *Kumarbi* (1946) and *The Song of Ullikummi* (*Journ. of Cuneiform Studies*, 1951-52). In Ugaritic we have scattered indications of the same significance attached to mountains. That Lebanon was considered as a "fossilized" primordial monster even among the Israelites follows from Hab. ii 17, where it is parallel to Behemoth.

4) Cf. my discussion of Phoenician *ʾammun* in *JBL* 60 (1941), p. 210, of *um(m)ânu* "wizard" in the Taanach tablets, *BASOR* 94, p. 18, n. 28 (note that *ummân Aširat* corresponds to *ʿnn ʾAṯrt* in the Ugaritic texts). See also the somewhat parallel, but independent discussion of the word in Accadian, Phoenician, and Hebrew by SIDNEY SMITH, *Bull. of the School of Oriental and African Studies*, 11 (1945), p. 451-464, especially 455-461 and 464 (I am not inclined to accept the combination of this word with the South-Arabian derivatives from the stem *ʾMN* cited by SMITH). The Phoenician and Hebrew words are borrowed from Accadian *ummānu*, older *ummiānu* from Sumerian *ummea*.

5) *Sprüche Salomos* (*Handbuch zum Alten Testament*, ed. O. EISSFELDT), p. 41.

reconstructed by W. ANDRAE as arcades, running along the two sides of the central court, with regular rows of fruit trees [1]). On either side were seven oblong piers of stone, measuring about 2.50 by 1.50 metres in horizontal cross section, and the openings between them were probably vaulted. The only parallel with Proverbs lies in the fact that there were two sets of *seven* piers along two sides of the open court. Closer to the seven *ʿammûdîm* of Proverbs are the seven fallen menhirs which I found in 1924 at Bâb edh-Dhrâʿ, which date from the end of the third millennium [2]). Since the *ʿammûdîm* could be either supporting pillars or free-standing columns, the comparison is possible, and is strengthened by a Greek inscription from A.D. 79-80, discovered by T. B. MITFORD at Amathus in northeastern Cyprus, and published in 1948; it records the dedication of a shrine to Cyprian Aphrodite and calls it: τὸ [ἱε]ρὸν τῶν ἐντὸς [τ]ῶν στηλ[ῶν ἑπ]τά "the shrine of the Seven-inside-the-Stelae" [3]). Verse 3 contains one grammatical peculiarity typical of Ugaritic (agreement of fem. sing. verb with plural antecedent) and three words characteristic of Ugaritic: *ʿal gappê meromê qáret* "on the edge of the acropolis of the town" [4]). It may be remarked that the Canaanite-Phoenician *qart* (for Hebrew *qiryáh*) occurs three times in Prov. viii-ix, once in xi, and once in Job—nowhere else. There are also Canaanitisms in grammar and vocabularly in verses 5, 7 (where the preposition *le* is twice used as "from", though not hitherto recognized), 10 (*qedōšîm*), 13, 14, 18 (*refāʾîm*), etc.

Proverbs teems with isolated Canaanitisms. Since there is no space here even to give a fraction of all cases, even where they are reasonably certain, we shall limit ourselves to half a dozen particularly interesting cases, listed as they occur. An aphorism which appears twice in vi 11 and xxiv 34 runs:

ū-bāʾ kemithallēk rêšékā *ū-maḥsorkā keʾîš MGN* [5])

---

[1]) See W. ANDRAE, *MDOG*, No. 33, p. 24-32; ANDRAE, *Das wiedererstandene Assur*, p. 37 ff., 151 ff.

[2]) *BASOR* 14, p. 10; 53, p. 13 ff.; and N. GLUECK, *AASOR* 14, p. 45 ff.

[3]) *Journal of Hellenic Studies*, 66, p. 40. Philo Byblius calls such stones, which served as abodes of deity, βαιτύλια, λίθους ἐμψύχους. It must never be forgotten that Cyprus and Phoenicia were in most periods closely related in culture, or at least exerted great reciprocal influence on one another. On similar concepts in mortuary stelae see *ARI*, p. 105 f., and the notes.

[4]) *JPOS* 14 (1934), p. 134, n. 175 (the meaning which I then attributed to *gp* was wrong).

[5]) My text draws from both Hebrew recensions but contains nothing not found in one or the other of the verses. Heb. *ʾîš MGN* is syntactically the same as *ʾîš śār*, *ʾîš kôhēn*, *ʾîš nābîʾ*.

M.T. *māgēn* "shield" is meaningless here, and the LXX "runner" looks like a guess from the context; we must follow Ugaritic usage and point *môgēn* or *maggān* "beggar", from *MGN* "to beg, entreat", in parallelism with *mithallēk* "vagabond" (Accadian *muttalliku*):

"And poverty will come upon thee like a vagabond, And want like a beggar!"

In vii 6 we have a description of the adulterous woman which goes directly back to Phoenician practices:

"For I <looked out> from my house window, I gazed through my lattice".

The LXX παρακύπτουσα points to the identification of this pose with the well known 'Αφροδίτη παρακύπτουσα of Cypriote and other Greek cultic terminology, happily combined by HERBIG with the common motif of the Phoenician ivories found at Samaria, Arslan Tash, Khorsabad, and elsewhere, representing the head of a woman (sometimes unmistakably a goddess) looking through a window [1]). Since there is an extensive literature already on this subject, I need not discuss it further here.

Turning to xviii 18, I should like to call attention again to my combination of the text of the eleventh-century spatula of bronze from Byblos with this verse [2]). Our verse may be rendered:

"The lot puts an end to law suits And decides between the mighty."

The word *našbit* in the spatula also appears to mean "let us put an end (to our suit at law" = Heb. *našbēt*); the following words I should render: "If thou dost truly inherit (the property), thy offering(s) shall be incumbent upon thee, while my offering(s) are mine." In other words, the winner in the suit must pay all his vows (presumably vows made to ensure success), while the loser is released from any vows he may have made.

In xxi 9 and xxv 24 we have another doublet which has been clarified by recent Ugaritic and Assyrian discoveries [3]). We now

[1]) See M. DAHOOD, *Biblica* 33, p. 213 ff. In addition to the references given by DAHOOD, note R. D. BARNETT, *Iraq*, 2, p. 182, and J. W. CROWFOOT, *Early Ivories from Samaria*, p. 29 ff.

[2]) See *BASOR* 90, p. 35-37, and *JAOS* 67 (1947), p. 158 f., for the literature as well as for my own treatment of the text.

[3]) See B. MAISLER (MAZAR), *BASOR* 102, p. 10, for references to my own previous work and for additional observations (I first brought the Accadian term *bīt ḫubūri* together with the Ugaritic and Hebrew expressions in *BASOR* 63, p. 28, n. 27). I was wrong in combining Canaanite-Egyptian *ḫubūr*, Heb-Aram. *ḥᵃbûrâh*, etc., with *BT ḪBR*; see below for the recent studies of LANDSBERGER

know that the mysterious *BYT ḤBR*, which even the LXX no longer understood, rendering "community house", meant "brewery", i.e., a building where grain was stored and made into beer. To judge from their pottery, the Philistines were particularly fond of beer [1]), and both philological and archaeological evidence prove that beer was popular in Egypt, Assyria, Babylonia, and Asia Minor [2]). B. LANDSBERGER and A. GOETZE have demonstrated conclusively that Old and Middle Assyrian *bīt ḫubūri* meant "brewery", lit., "house of beer vats", with which storage rooms for grain were connected [3]). In the Keret Epic I, 79-83 (= 171-174), we read:

w-yrd Krt l-ggt	And Keret shall go down from the roof terraces,
ʿdb ʾakl l-qryt	Make ready grain from the granaries [4]),
ḥtt l-bt ḫbr	Wheat from the breweries;
yeʿp lḥm . . .	He shall bake bread . . .

---

and GOETZE, which prove that Accadian *ḫubūru* meant "beer vat," i.e., vat or tub used in fermenting the grain (for Egyptian representations and discussion, cf. H. F. LUTZ, *Viticulture and Brewing in the Ancient Orient* (1922), p. 80).

[1]) Cf. my Pelican *Archaeology of Palestine* (1949), p. 115.

[2]) Cf. the material collected by LUTZ, *op. cit.*, though his treatise needs much revision and expansion to bring it up to date.

[3]) See B. LANDSBERGER, *Belleten* (Türk Tarih Kurumu), 14, No. 54 (1950), p. 239-247; A. GOETZE, *Revue Hittite et Asianique*, 12 (1952), p. 5 f., 12, n. 46. However, GOETZE has decidedly overshot the mark by asserting that Accadian "has nothing to contribute to the explanation of Ug. *bt ḫbr* and Hebrew [*BT ḤBR*]," since quite the contrary is true; the latter words are borrowed from Accadian in the sense of "brewery." GOETZE has also gone too far in stating that Accadian *abussu* (written *a-bu-zi* in early Assyrian times) is not connected with Heb. *ʾēbûs*. He is right in denying the sense "manger" to *abussu* and *abussatu*, but it must be emphasized that Heb. *ʾēbûs* does not mean "manger" at all, but "closed crib for grain, granary." In ancient Israel a manger was a stone (perhaps also wood) trough for feeding, which is most certainly not the meaning of *ʾēbûs* (so undoubtedly in Jes. i 3 and Iob xxxix 9; in Prov. xiv 4 we should read *ʾéfes*, as generally recognized, and in Jer. l 26 we should divide differently and read *pitḥû-m ʾabûséka*, "open up thy granaries," with the enclitic *m(i)* on which HORACE D. HUMMEL has written an excellent dissertation, Johns Hopkins, 1955). We are entirely justified in rendering the Shalimakhum passage (20th century B.C.), *bīt ḫubūri u abūzišu* as "the brewery and its store-rooms"; note that GOETZE himself renders the Accadian term *bīt abuzzi* in Hittite lists from the 13th century B.C. correctly as "store-room" (p. 6, line 2). GOETZE is probably correct in explaining the word *abuzzu* as of Hurrian origin, but since Heb. *ʾēbûs* has the same meaning and no known Semitic etymology, it is obvious that it may perfectly well be a loan from Hurrian (one of a steadily increasing list); note that *z* in cuneiform transcriptions of the earlier second millennium, as well as later in the west, corresponds to the Northwest-Semitic sound which appears as *samekh*.

[4]) This word is Accadian *qārītu* "granary" (especially in the Code of Hammurabi); which may ultimately be identical with Hebrew *qôráh* "plank, boarding" (*qârîṭâ* in Syriac and Jewish Aramaic); both are feminine participles like *ḥômāh* = Ugar. *ḥâmîtu*.

Since the hero of the Keret Epic "scrapes the bottom of the barrel" in searching for man power and for grain with which to feed his huge army, it is not in the least surprising to find granaries and breweries mentioned together as sources for the grain needed by his bakers. The ancient equivalents of English ale and beer were made from different bread grains. Moreover, the Canaanite *bêtu ḫuburi* doubtless catered for customers who wished to drink as well as for those who preferred to carry their drink elsewhere before imbibing. Our verses in Proverbs may now be rendered:

"Dwelling in a roof corner is better Than a quarrelsome woman and a public house."

It is scarcely necessary to explain why the combination of a contentious female and an ale house (or beer parlour) was deemed likely to be disastrous. However, it is not impossible that *ʾŠT MDWNM* meant "flame(s) of contention" in early times, and that the present text is a secondary development [1]).

Our last illustration comes from xxvi 23, where Ginsberg and I have established the meaning "glaze" for *SPSG*, Hittite *zapzaga* and Ugaritic *spsg*; the Hebrew word had been wrongly divided and explained previously [2]). There are additional Hittite occurrences of this word, which Goetze has kindly called to my attention. It may be added that we now have archaeological proof that earthenware was glazed in Syria about the fifteenth century B.C. [3]); it was well known previously that glazed frit of Egyptian type was made throughout the second millennium in most of southwestern Asia. The verse may now be rendered approximately as follows:

---

[1]) Heb. *ʾēš* "fire, flame," has a feminine plural (Ben Sira), just as in Ugaritic; Accadian *išātu* was originally plural. However, there can be no doubt that *ʾŠT* means "woman" in these verses of the Hebrew Bible; cf. especially Prov. xxi 19: "Dwelling in a desert land is better Than a quarrelsome woman and irritation." A source of irritation (*kaʿas*) has the same general effect on an *ʾēšet midwānîm* as a public house; if there were any further doubt about the meaning of Hebrew *bêt ḤBR*, this should remove it.

[2]) H. L. Ginsberg, *BASOR* 98, p. 21, n. 55; Albright, *BASOR* 98, p. 24 f. (A. Goetze subsequently sent me several corrections to my interpretation of the Hittite text, as well as additional Hittite references). *Zapzaga* is presumably of Hurrian origin; in any case it corresponds exactly to a Canaanite-Hebrew *spsg*, since *samekh* was transcribed by cuneiform *z* (see above, on *abuzzu* and *ʾēbûs*).

[3]) See Sir Leonard Woolley, *A Forgotten Kingdom* (Pelican, 1953), p. 93-95, for the discovery of true glazed earthenware at Alalakh in northern Syria, in levels dating from the 16th-14th centuries B.C. The famous recipes for making glaze, handed down from about 1500 B.C. and deciphered by C. J. Gadd, shows that the art was highly prized in Babylonia at that time.

"As glaze coated over earthenware, So are smooth lips and a bad heart."

Read perhaps: *k*ᵉ*-SPSG* (which would presumably have become **sifsāg* in Massoretic Hebrew) *m*ᵉ*ṣuppêh ʿal-ḥâreś* / *ś*ᵉ*fātáyim ḥ*ᵃ*lāqôt* (? — with LXX) *w*ᵉ*-leb-rāʿ*.

In a nutshell my opinion with regard to the provenience and date of Proverbs is that its entire content is probably pre-exilic, but that much of the Book was handed down orally until the fifth century B.C., when we know from Elephantine that Jews were interested in literature of this kind. Since we have seen that the Maxims of Amenemope are probably to be dated in or about the twelfth century B.C., and since many of the Canaanite items in the Book have their closest extra-biblical analogies in the Bronze Age, I should regard a Solomonic nucleus as probable, agreeing in this respect with W. BAUMGARTNER [1]). How much—if any—of our extant Book was actually compiled by Solomon and his scribes, we cannot say. It seems likely that the collections of didactic material credited by tradition to Solomon (I Reg. v 12 f.) [2]), failed to meet later standards of literary taste—or were simply so archaic in content that they were no longer understood. In any case, Solomon's rôle as a patron of didactic literature must have been very considerable or the tradition that Proverbs goes back to him could scarcely have arisen. One thing is certain: while Proverbs may contain a very high proportion of matter originating outside of Israel, it is saturated with Israelite theism and morality.

For lack of space I shall limit myself to only a few comments on Job and Ecclesiastes. My views on the date of Job have been given elsewhere and need not be repeated here [3]). The situation with

---

[1]) See *The Old Testament and Modern Study*, p. 213.

[2]) Note that the wise men whom this tradition compares unfavourably to Solomon, Ethan, Heman, Chalcol and Darda, bear Canaanite names, a fact that can be demonstrated in the case of Ethan and Chalcol; see my concise discussion in *ARI*, 126 f. (which might be greatly extended, since I have collected a great quantity of illustrative data), and the treatment of the alleged Edomite wisdom by VICTOR R. GOLD in his unpublished Johns Hopkins dissertation, *Studies in the History and Culture of Edom* (1951), p. 52 ff. It may be added here that *Kulkul* (= M.T. *Kalkol*) appears as a foreign name (masculine) in Egypt during the 18th Dynasty (RANKE, *AePN*, p. 347, No. 22), as well as at Ascalon as the name of a woman singer in the 19th Dynasty. It thus becomes likely that Chalcol was a Canaanite poet of the latter centuries of the second millennium (though an earlier date is not excluded).

[3]) Cf. *FSAC*, p. 253 f.; *JBL* 61 (1942), p. 123 f. Incidentally, I should now push back the date of the hero himself into the first half of the second millennium.

respect to Job's literary sources is still obscure. CHARLES L. FEINBERG, in his Johns Hopkins dissertation on *Ugaritic Literature and the Book of Job* (1945), has surveyed the material in a necessarily preliminary way. Job has few points of contact with Ugaritic style or syntax; neither the complex varieties of parallelism which are common to Ugaritic and Proverbs, nor the morphological and syntactic peculiarities of pre-exilic Hebrew verse (especially in the earliest times) appear in this Book. On the other hand, there can be no doubt that Ugaritic and Phoenician will ultimately clear up many of its lexicographical difficulties, like the word *'MQ* "strength" (Ugaritic *'mq* and Accadian *emūqu*) in Iob xxxix 21. That Job is dependent on lost Phoenician sources of the Iron Age for much of its imagery is clear; cf. the references to "sons of God", the North (*ṣāfôn*), Death (*máwet* = *Môt*), "sons of Resheph", Dawn (*šáḥar*), the "primordial (?) [1]) serpent" (*nāḥāš bārîᵃḥ* = *bṯn brḥ*), the primordial monsters Leviathan, Sea (*Yam*), *Tannîn*, and *Ráhab* (not yet found in extra-biblical sources). In any case, it remains exceedingly probable that the author of Job lived in the cosmopolitan atmosphere of the sixth or fifth century B.C., and he was certainly conversant with a wide range of lost pagan Northwest-Semitic literature [2]), though Hebrew was still his literary (probably no longer his spoken) language.

My approach to Ecclesiastes is the same as DAHOOD's [3]). I cannot accept the view of H. L. GINSBERG [4]) that it was written in Aramaic and translated into Hebrew, though I gladly accept much of his interpretation (in his forthcoming commentary on Qoheleth). While admitting that some of DAHOOD's arguments are weak by themselves,

---

The name is contracted from original *'Ayya-'abu*, whence *'Ayyâbu*, later Hebrew *'Iyyôb*, and meant originally "Where Is (My) Father?"; on early occurrences from the 20th to the 14th century B.C., see my forthcoming paper "Northwest-Semitic Names in a List of Egyptian Slaves from the Eighteenth Century B.C.," to appear in *JAOS*. [See now *JAOS* 74 (1954), p. 222-233.]

[1]) Cf. *Studies in Old Testament Prophecy* (T. H. Robinson Festschrift), p. 2 f., n. 9 (*bırḥ* is a misprint for *bıḥ* < *brḥ*).

[2]) In this connection we may mention the recently discovered tablets of the Poem of the Righteous Sufferer from a seventh-century temple near Ḥarrân; see the complete edition by W. G. LAMBERT and O. R. GURNEY, *Anatolian Studies*, 4 (1954), p. 65-99. Incidentally, W. VON SODEN now dates this poem by language and poetic style in the last centuries of the second millennium (*Bibliotheca Orientalis*, 10 [1953], p. 8-12).—Since this was written, S. N. KRAMER has announced his discovery of a Sumerian precursor of the genre in question (December, 1954).

[3]) See above for this important study (*Biblica*, 1952).

[4]) *Studies in Koheleth* (New York 1950).

I am convinced that by and large they are much more impressive than the learned, but often tortuous, arguments employed by GINSBERG in order to establish the Aramaic origin of the Book. JAMES MUILENBURG's publication of scraps of Qoheleth from about the late second century B.C., coming from Qumran IV, makes a date for its composition after the third century B.C. very difficult, and provides several minor confirmations of DAHOOD's position [1]). I therefore hold that the author of this Book was an influential [2]) Jew who lived on the Coastal Plain, probably in southern Phoenicia, about 300 B.C., and whose orally transmitted aphorisms were collected after his death and put into writing in Phoenicia. Though intended to be Hebrew, their written form betrays Phoenician influence in spelling, morphology, syntax, vocabulary, and content [3]).

---

[1]) *BASOR* 135, p. 20-28.

[2]) I have for several years been explaining the words "*MLK* in Jerusalem" (Eccles. i 12) as meaning "counsellor in Jerusalem". The word should be pointed either *môlēk* (like Amarna *mâlik* "counsellor") or *mallāk* (Phoen. **mallōk*, whence ultimately Aramaic *mâlôkâ* "counsellor"). This is *a priori* much more likely than GINSBERG's arabicizing *môlēk* "property holder" (*op. cit.*, p. 12-15).

[3]) It must be emphasized that the Qumran finds have proved that normal literary Hebrew in the last two centuries B.C. (including Ben Sira) classicized in conscious opposition to the dominant Aramaic; it was neither like the language of earlier Qoheleth nor like that of the later Mishnah (though nearer the latter than the former, which is definitely aberrant, as far as the evolution of literary Hebrew is concerned).

ZUR LITERARISCHEN ANALYSE DER WEISHEIT DES AMENEMOPE

VON

ALBRECHT ALT

Leipzig

In den dreissig Jahren, die seit der Veröffentlichung des spätägyptischen Weisheitsbuches des Amenemope verflossen sind [1]), ist zur literarischen Analyse dieses eigenartigen Werkes erst sehr wenig geschehen. Nur F. Lexa hat, soviel ich sehe, einen wesentlichen Beitrag dazu geliefert, indem er auf zahlreiche Stellen des Buches hinwies, an denen die logische Verknüpfung der Aussagen von Satz zu Satz zu wünschen übrig lässt oder ganz zu fehlen scheint, und diese Störungen des Zusammenhanges durch die Annahme sekundärer Umstellungen zu beheben suchte [2]). Damit war ohne Zweifel ein wichtiger Gesichtspunkt geltend gemacht; denn man weiss von anderen ägyptischen Weisheitsbüchern mit reicherer Überlieferung, wie weit die erhaltenen Handschriften eines und desselben Werkes dieser Gattung infolge solcher und anderer nachträglicher Änderungen des originalen Textes von einander abweichen können [3]), und hat daher allen Grund, auch bei der Weisheit des Amenemope, für die uns leider bis jetzt fast kein Vergleichsmaterial zur Verfügung steht [4]), mit analogen Schäden zu rechnen. Aber

[1]) Sir E. A. Wallis Budge, *Facsimiles of Egyptian Hieratic Papyri in the British Museum, Second Series* (1923), Pl. 1-14 (Nr. 10474); *The Teaching of Amen-em-apt* (1924); A. Erman, *OLZ* XXVII (1924), p. 241 ff.; H. O. Lange, *Das Weisheitsbuch des Amenemope* (*Kgl. Danske Vidensk. Selskab. Hist.-filol. Meddelelser* XI, 2, 1925); F. Ll. Griffith, *JEA* XII (1926), p. 191 ff.; H. Ranke bei H. Gressmann, *Altorientalische Texte zum Alten Testament* (²1926), p. 38 ff.; J. A. Wilson bei J. B. Pritchard, *Ancient Near Eastern Texts relating to the Old Testament* (1950), p. 421 ff.

[2]) *Archiv Orientální* I (1929), p. 14 ff.

[3]) Vgl. besonders die Texte des noch viel jüngeren demotischen Weisheitsbuches im Papyrus Insinger und in Papyrusbruchstücken der Sammlung Carlsberg bei A. Volten, *Analecta Aegyptiaca* I/II (1940/1).

[4]) Nur für die Kapitel 24-26 des Buches liegt noch eine Schülerabschrift auf einer Palette des Turiner Museums vor; vgl. W. Spiegelberg, *OLZ* XXVII (1924), p. 185; Lange, *a. a. O.*, p. 9 f., 118, 120 f., 124.

selbst wenn mit Hilfe dieser Annahme der ursprüngliche Wortlaut des Werkes, und sei es auch nur hypothetisch, einigermassen sicher ermittelt werden könnte, so wäre in der Hauptsache doch nur ein Stück seiner Überlieferungsgeschichte aufgeklärt und eine bessere Grundlage für seine Interpretation gewonnen, hingegen die entscheidende literarische Frage, die nach seiner Entstehung, noch nicht berührt, geschweige denn beantwortet.

Die letztere Frage ist bisher meines Wissens überhaupt noch nicht ernsthaft erwogen worden, obwohl gerade bei einem Weisheitsbuch die Vermutung naheliegt, dass der Autor neben den von ihm selbst geschaffenen Sprüchen auch solche fremder Herkunft in sein Werk aufgenommen haben könnte. Sogar die Vertreter der Ansicht, dass gewisse Sätze bei Amenemope aus der israelitischen Weisheit entlehnt seien [1]), haben sich durch diese These nicht dazu anregen lassen, auch andere heterogene Elemente, besonders etwa älteres ägyptisches Spruchgut, in dem Buch ausfindig zu machen, sondern pflegen es ebenso wie die anderen ohne weiteres als eine Grösse aus einem Guss zu betrachten [2]). In der Tat hat es in seinem äusseren Aufbau eine Eigentümlichkeit, die nicht zu verstehen wäre, wenn ihm nicht ein einzelner Schriftsteller seinen gestaltenden Willen aufgeprägt hätte, nämlich die Gliederung des Ganzen mit Ausschluss des breit ausgeführten Buchtitels, aber mit Einschluss des Prologs und des Epilogs in 30 durchgezählte Kapitel, zu der es in der älteren ägyptischen Weisheitsliteratur kein Vorbild gibt und die somit wohl geradezu als eine bewusste Neuerung des Autors anzusprechen ist [3]). Dabei ist diese Gliederung durchaus keine rein formale Angelegenheit und nicht etwa schematisch in dem Sinne durchgeführt, dass jedem Kapitel genau oder auch nur annähernd die gleiche Zahl von Versen gegeben wäre; sie ist vielmehr dem wechselnden Umfang der inhaltlich zusammengehörenden Versgruppen angepasst, und es wird sich bald zeigen, wie genau sie wenigstens teilweise Abschnitte verschie-

---

[1]) Vgl. z.B. R. O. Kevin, *JSOR* XIV (1930), p. 115 ff.

[2]) Auch Lexa, *a. a. O.* ist offenbar stillschweigend von dieser Voraussetzung ausgegangen und hat sich daher für berechtigt gehalten, bei seinen Vorschlägen zur Verbesserung der Reihenfolge der Sätze überall denselben Massstab strenger Logik anzulegen, die er damit dem Verfasser des Werkes selbst zuschreibt.

[3]) Vgl. H. Grapow, *Sprachliche und schriftliche Formung ägyptischer Texte* (1936), p. 35 f.; A. M. Blackman, *Orientalia*, N. S. VII (1938), p. 64 ff. Im demotischen Weisheitsbuch ist diese Gliederung nachgebildet und durch die Hinzufügung von Inhaltsangaben zu den Überschriften der einzelnen Kapitel noch vervollkommnet.

dener Art von einander scheidet. Die Ordnung und Einteilung des Stoffes ist also auf jeden Fall das wohlüberlegte Werk eines einzelnen Mannes, und insoweit kann an der Einheitlichkeit des Buches kein Zweifel sein.

Damit ist aber noch keineswegs erwiesen, dass der in ihm verarbeitete Stoff auch seiner Herkunft nach eine Einheit bildet und als das ausschliessliche geistige Eigentum des Verfassers betrachtet werden muss. Verschiedene Anzeichen sprechen vielmehr dafür, dass Amenemope auch schon von anderen gestaltetes Material seinem Buche da und dort einverleibt hat, und ich halte es für eine vordringliche Aufgabe der literarischen Analyse seiner Schrift, die von ihm herangezogenen Vorlagen nach Umfang und Art so weit wie möglich gegen einander und vor allem gegen seinen eigenen Anteil abzugrenzen. Nur so kann ja wohl erkennbar werden, was er mit seinem Werk persönlich gewollt und geleistet hat und welche Stellung ihm daraufhin in der Gesamtgeschichte der ägyptischen Weisheit zukommt. Ich habe vor langen Jahren meinem Vorgänger R. Kittel eine kurze Darlegung dieser Dinge zur Verfügung gestellt, auf die er dann im dritten Band seiner Geschichte des Volkes Israel mit einigen Worten eingegangen ist. [1]) Aber dieser knappe Hinweis hat begreiflicherweise kaum Beachtung gefunden [2]), und auch unabhängig von ihm scheint noch niemand die hier vorliegende Aufgabe in Angriff genommen zu haben. So ist es vielleicht nicht unangebracht, wenn ich meine einschlägigen Beobachtungen hier in skizzenhaftem Umriss der Öffentlichkeit mitteile; ihre Prüfung und weitere Verfolgung, besonders nach der sprachlichen und stilistischen Seite hin, muss ich den Ägyptologen überlassen.

Ein Anzeichen für den Kompositcharakter des Buches kann man schon darin sehen, dass mehrfach genau oder annähernd gleichlautende Sätze zwei- oder dreimal in verschiedenen Kapiteln begegnen. Freilich werden nicht alle diese Fälle in derselben Weise zu beurteilen sein. Wenn sich zum Beispiel dreimal der Vordersatz findet: „Wenn du deine Zeit verbringst, indem dieses in deinem Herzen ist", zweimal mit dem Nachsatz: „so werden deine Kinder es sehen" [3]),

---

[1]) R. Kittel, *Geschichte des Volkes Israel*, III, 2 (1929), p. 723.

[2]) Vgl. J. Hempel, *ZAW*, N. F. XI (1934), p. 311.

[3]) v 18 f. (Kap. 3); xvii 15 f. (Kap. 15). Ich zitiere die Stellen nach den Kolumnen und Zeilen der Handschrift des Britischen Museums und füge in Klammern die Kapitelzahl hinzu.

einmal mit dem Nachsatz: "so wirst du finden, dass es Glück bringt"[1]), so kann es sich sehr wohl um eine generelle Schlussformel handeln, die ein Autor einmal geprägt hat und dann gern wiederholt und variiert [2]). Desgleichen mögen die je zweimal im Anschluss an verschiedene Warnungen auftretenden und sie nur abrundenden Sätze: „damit dich der Schrecken nicht hole" [3]) und: „das ist dem Gott ein Greuel" [4]) Lieblingsausdrücke eines bestimmten Autors und darum mehrfach von ihm verwendet sein [5]). Wenn aber zwei Kapitel hinter einander übereinstimmend die Satzgruppe bringen: „Wahrlich, du kennst nicht die Gedanken Gottes und siehst nicht den morgigen Tag. Setze dich in die Arme des Gottes, so wird dein Schweigen sie zu Fall bringen" [6]), so ist zwar die Herkunft dieser Gruppe aus ein und derselben Quelle nicht zweifelhaft, aber die Wahrscheinlichkeit gross, dass sie von Hause aus nur einmal in dem Buche stand und erst in dessen späterer Überlieferung, vielleicht sogar durch das blosse Versehen eines Abschreibers, wiederholt worden ist [7]). Anders verhält es sich aber mit den Sätzen: „Besser ist die Armut in der Hand des Gottes als Reichtümer im Speicher; besser sind Brote, wenn das Herz vergnügt ist, als Reichtümer mit Kummer" [8]), die weit davon entfernt in einem anderen Kapitel in der Formulierung wiederkehren: „Besser ist es, als Freund der Menschen gelobt zu werden, als Reichtümer im Speicher (zu haben); besser sind Brote, wenn das Herz vergnügt ist, als Reichtümer mit Kummer" [9]). Hier haben wir es nicht mit einer wortgetreuen Wiederholung zu tun, sondern mit zwei teilweise von einander abweichenden Fassungen eines sachlich zusammengehörigen und formal nach demselben Schema gestalteten Spruchpaares, das vermutlich einen gemeinsamen Ursprung hatte und erst im Lauf der Überlieferung der Variation

---

[1]) iii 17 f. (Kap. 1).

[2]) Da die Formel sogleich im Prolog des Buches auftritt, wird man Amenemope für ihren Urheber halten dürfen.

[3]) viii 10 (Kap. 6); xiii 9 (Kap. 9).

[4]) xiii 16 (Kap. 10); xv 21 (Kap. 13).

[5]) Ähnlich wird es sich mit dem zweimal in verschiedenem Zusammenhang vorkommenden unselbständigen Vordersatz: "Wenn du morgen vor ihn trittst" verhalten: xx 16 (Kap. 19); xxvi 4 (Kap. 27).

[6]) xxii 5 ff. (Kap. 21); xxiii 8 ff. (Kap. 22).

[7]) So schon Erman, *a. a. O.*, p. 250 Anm. 1; Lexa, *a. a. O.*, p. 45. Die spezifischen Anschauungen und Ausdrücke der Sätze lassen auch hier auf Amenemope als den Autor schliessen.

[8]) ix 5 ff. (Kap. 6).

[9]) xvi 11 ff. (Kap. 13).

unterzogen wurde, deren Ergebnis uns bei Amenemope vorliegt. Es wäre gut denkbar und ist mir sogar wahrscheinlich, dass eine der beiden Fassungen, nämlich die oben an erster Stelle angeführte, von Amenemope selbst geschaffen ist [1]); auf jeden Fall aber verdankt sie ihre Entstehung einem sekundären Eingriff in einen von der Tradition in geprägter Form dargebotenen Stoff, und da Amenemope an einer anderen Stelle seines Werkes dasselbe Spruchpaar in einer teilweise abweichenden Fassung wiedergibt, so darf man wohl fragen, ob er es nicht dort und hier je einer besonderen Vorlage entnommen und nur von Fall zu Fall verschieden behandelt hat [2]). Dann wäre der Tatbestand bei diesem Spruchpaar im Werk des Amenemope ähnlich dem bei jenen Liedern, die nur deshalb zweimal im biblischen Psalter stehen, weil dieser aus mehreren kleineren Sammlungen zusammengesetzt ist, von denen je zwei die betreffenden Lieder enthielten.

Nun gibt natürlich diese nur aus der Benutzung von Vorlagen erklärliche Dublette in ihrer Vereinzelung noch keine tragfähige Basis für weitgehende Schlussfolgerungen hinsichtlich der Komposition des ganzen Buches ab [3]), auch dann nicht, wenn man die hier gemachten Beobachtungen durch die Erwägung ergänzt, dass Amenemope in anderen Fällen, wo ihm ein einzelner Spruch oder eine Gruppe von solchen in den Werken seiner Vorgänger oder auch in der mündlichen Überlieferung mehrfach begegnete, sich mit einmaliger Wiedergabe—mit oder ohne Umgestaltung im Sinne seiner eigenen Anschauungen—begnügt und uns damit die Feststellung des Ausmasses seiner Abhängigkeit von der Tradition unmöglich gemacht haben mag. Trotzdem glaube ich, dass man in dieser Richtung noch ein gutes Stück weiterkommen kann, wenn man zusieht, in welchem Umfang sein Buch von den Anschauungen beherrscht ist, die in ihm so oft und so stark hervortreten, dass man sie als sein persönliches Eigentum betrachten darf. Dieses individuelle Sondergut des Amenemope gibt sich bei einem Vergleich mit dem normalen Gehalt der älteren ägyptischen Weisheitsliteratur

[1]) Dafür spricht vor allem der nur in dieser Fassung auftretende Ausdruck "in der Hand des Gottes", der für Amenemope charakteristisch ist.

[2]) Auch bei dieser Fassung ist mir nicht sicher, ob sie den ursprünglichen Wortlaut des ersten Satzes bewahrt hat.

[3]) Spiegelberg ging zu weit, wenn er *a. a. O.*, p. 185 aus den wenigen von ihm genannten, aber nicht genauer geprüften Dubletten den Schluss ziehen wollte: "Vielleicht hat Amenemope also seine Weisheit aus anderen Spruchbüchern kompiliert und ist dabei etwas nachlässig verfahren".

leicht zu erkennen und ist denn auch von den ersten Bearbeitern sogleich richtig bestimmt worden [1]); um so eher kann ich hier auf eine eingehende Darstellung verzichten. Amenemope hat es nicht wie die meisten seiner Vorgänger auf die Angehörigen eines einzelnen Standes, nämlich auf die Schreiberbeamten abgesehen, die darüber unterrichtet werden müssten, wie sie sich im Verkehr mit ihren Vorgesetzten, Gleichgestellten und Untergebenen am zweckdienlichsten und für ihr eigenes Fortkommen förderlichsten verhalten. Er fasst vielmehr den Menschen schlechthin ins Auge, wo immer er seinen Platz im Leben haben mag, und verkündet demgemäss keine utilitaristische Standesethik, sondern eine von eigennützigen Motiven freie, allgemeingültige Sittlichkeit. Der Mensch, wie er sein soll, ist für ihn der „Schweigende", der die egoistischen Regungen seiner Gefühle und seines Willens zu unterdrücken und sich auch in üblen Lagen zu bescheiden weiss, im Gegensatz zu dem „Heissen", der seinen Leidenschaften freien Lauf lässt und sich dadurch selbst ins Unglück stürzt. Von diesen beiden Menschentypen war auch in der älteren ägyptischen Weisheit schon manchmal die Rede gewesen; aber bei Amenemope rückt ihre Gegenüberstellung in den Mittelpunkt der Ermahnungen und Warnungen und bekommt vor allem dadurch ein entscheidendes Gewicht, dass er sie mit seinen religiösen Grundanschauungen in unmittelbare Verbindung bringt. Dabei geht es ihm nicht um Mythus und Kultus, nicht um den oder jenen mit Namen zu nennenden Gott, sondern einfach um „Gott" oder „den Gott", der der absolute „Herr des Alls" ist und auch über die Geschicke des einzelnen Menschen allein verfügt. Ihm gegenüber ist die Haltung des „Schweigenden" die einzig richtige; er kann nichts Besseres tun, als sich im Bewusstsein seiner Ohnmacht vertrauensvoll „in die Arme des Gottes zu setzen" und alles der Planung dieses ihm unendlich überlegenen Herrn anheimzustellen, auch wenn er seine Gedanken und Handlungen nicht versteht.

Nun lässt sich aber keineswegs behaupten, dass das Buch des Amenemope in allen Teilen gleichmässig von diesen Anschauungen durchdrungen ist; es fällt vielmehr auf und ist nur bisher nicht genügend beobachtet worden, wie wenig sich von ihnen in vielen

---

[1]) Vgl. ausser den eingangs erwähnten ersten Bearbeitungen besonders R. Anthes, *Lebensregeln und Lebensweisheit der alten Ägypter* (1933), p. 28 ff.; E. Suys, *Miscellanea Biblica*, II (1934), p. 1 ff.; für eine wichtige Einzelheit K. Sethe, *Nachrichten der Gesellschaft der Wissenschaften zu Göttingen, phil.-hist. Kl.* (1925), p. 141 ff.

Abschnitten findet. In der zweiten Hälfte des Buches ist der Sachverhalt insofern besonders klar, als hier die Verschiedenheit des Inhalts regelmässig mit der Abgrenzung der Kapitel zusammentrifft; nur die Kapitel 18, 21-22, 25, 28-29 tragen deutlich das Gepräge der besonderen Gedanken des Amenemope, während die übrigen, also die Mehrzahl, kaum oder überhaupt nicht von ihnen berührt sind, zumeist die alte Standesethik predigen und darum ebenso gut in irgend einem anderen ägyptischen Weisheitsbuch stehen könnten. Die erste Hälfte weist keine so strenge Scheidung der Elemente nach Kapiteln auf, und es erscheint hier schon fast wie eine Ausnahme, dass das Kapitel 4 von Anfang bis zu Ende der Gegenüberstellung der Typen des „Heissen" und des „Schweigenden" gewidmet ist [1]). Sonst, vor allem in den Kapiteln 2-3, 5-10, treten die Ideale des Amenemope nur in einzelnen Sprüchen hervor, die mit solchen anderer Art wechseln, ohne dass sich überall eine scharfe Grenze ziehen lässt. Aber auch da hat mindestens dem äusseren Umfang nach das alte Traditionsgut die Oberhand, und vollends der Buchtitel sowie der Prolog in Kapitel 1 und der Epilog in Kapitel 30 verhalten sich jenen Idealen gegenüber völlig neutral [2]).

Diesem Tatbestand wird man meines Erachtens ohne die Annahme sehr erheblicher Anleihen des Verfassers bei seinen Vorgängern nicht gerecht werden können. Die Zahl und der Umfang der von ihm herangezogenen Vorlagen bleibt freilich im Dunkel; denn nur selten zeigen sich grössere Zusammenhänge über den Rahmen der einzelnen Kapitel hinaus, die auf gemeinsamen Ursprung der betreffenden Stücke schliessen lassen [3]). Solche Zusammenhänge sind aber auch gar nicht mit Sicherheit zu erwarten, wo es sich um Entlehnungen aus einem und demselben Werk eines anderen handeln mag; denn genau wie die Schrift des Amenemope waren auch die älteren ägyptischen Weisheitsbücher schon Kompositionen aus Fremdem und Eigenem und letztlich aus einzelnen Sprüchen, von denen jeder eine Einheit für sich bildete und die daher der Einordnung in ein grösseres Ganzes eher widerstrebten, als dass sie sie mit innerer

[1]) Wie sehr die Durchführung dieser Antithese an den Aufbau des biblischen Psalmes i erinnert, hat schon LANGE, *a. a. O.*, p. 43 mit Recht betont.

[2]) Zur Interpretation des Buchtitels vgl. J. SPIEGEL, *Die Präambel des Amenemope und die Zielsetzung der ägyptischen Weisheitsliteratur* (1935).

[3]) So in dem umfangreichen Kapitel 6, wo dasselbe Thema (Verrückung von Grenzsteinen und -furchen) zweimal behandelt ist; ferner in Kap. 11 und 12 (Begehren der Habe eines Geringen oder eines Grossen) und in Kap. 16 und 17 (Betrug mit Gewicht und Mass).

Notwendigkeit gefordert hätten. Nur wenn einmal durch einen glücklichen Zufall ein anderes ägyptisches Weisheitsbuch gefunden werden sollte, dessen Text mit gewissen Partien bei Amenemope ganz oder annähernd übereinstimmt, könnte man in diesen Fragen zu sicheren Ergebnissen kommen. Aber auch dann bliebe vielleicht ein grosser Teil des Stoffes, der bei Amenemope als Lehngut erscheint, der Feststellung seiner Herkunft entzogen, da gerade in der Geschichte der ägyptischen Weisheit neben der schriftlichen Überlieferung auch die mündliche Weitergabe der einmal formulierten Sprüche eine bedeutende Rolle gespielt haben wird und demgemäss auch Amenemope vieles mit oder ohne Umgestaltung aus dem Gedächtnis reproduziert haben kann. Solche teils literarische teils vorliterarische Wachstumsprozesse ganz aufzuklären wird kaum jemals möglich sein.

Die Analyse des Buches des Amenemope kann und darf sich aber nicht mit dem hier nur in den gröbsten Umrissen skizzierten Nachweis begnügen, dass es eine uns fast seltsam anmutende Komposition aus fremden und eigenen Weisheitssprüchen ist; sie muss auch fragen, warum der Autor seinem Werk diesen disparaten Inhalt gegeben hat. Wäre es für die Wirkung seiner eigenen Sprüche auf die Leser nicht viel besser gewesen, wenn er nur sie ohne Beimischung fremden Gutes in geordneter Folge niedergeschrieben hätte? Wenn er sie aber in einen grösseren Zusammenhang stellen zu sollen glaubte, warum hat er dann nichts getan, um sie aus dieser Umgebung so herauszuheben, dass die Leser an seinen Worten merken konnten, wo für ihn das Schwergewicht des Werkes lag? Besonders der Buchtitel, aber auch der Prolog und der Epilog hätten sich durch entsprechende Formulierung, und sei es auch nur durch Einflechtung der sonst gebrauchten Stichwörter, ohne Mühe diesem pädagogischen Zweck dienstbar machen lassen. Aber gerade diese Stücke, vor allem der Buchtitel, sind so gestaltet, dass der unvoreingenommene ägyptische Leser nach ihnen kaum etwas anderes als die hergebrachte utilitaristische Standesweisheit in dem Buch zu finden erwarten konnte und auf die abweichenden Anschauungen, die dort tatsächlich, wenn auch beinahe versteckt und auf verschiedene Stellen verstreut, zu Worte kommen, in keiner Weise vorbereitet wurde. War Amenemope, der sich im Buchtitel umständlich als Autor vorstellt, in Wirklichkeit vielleicht nur ein Redaktor ohne eigene Gedanken und Anliegen? Und ist sein Werk am Ende nur eine Komposition von allerlei Weisheitssprüchen verschiedener Herkunft, darunter auch denen, die wir als sein persönliches Eigentum in Anspruch nehmen wollten und zu denen der Redaktor dann kein näheres Verhältnis zu haben brauchte als zu den anderen?

Ich glaube aber nicht, dass mit einer solchen Auffassung der literarische Tatbestand besser erklärt wäre, als wenn man wie oben vorgeschlagen in Amenemope den Urheber der Sprüche vom „Schweigenden" und vom „Heissen" und von dem richtigen Verhalten des Menschen „dem Gott" gegenüber sieht und zugleich anerkennt, dass er in seinem Buch diese seine besondere Weisheit mit vielen Sprüchen anderer Herkunft und Art vereinigt hat. Die Dinge liegen hier meines Erachtens ähnlich wie bei dem spätisraelitischen Weisheitsbuch Koheleth, dessen Verfasser ja ebenfalls weithin sehr eigentümliche Anschauungen vorträgt, die der normalen israelitischen Weisheit fremd sind und daher für sein persönliches Eigentum gelten dürfen, und dann doch nicht selten Sprüche einfliessen lässt, die kaum auf dem Boden dieser Anschauungen erwachsen sein können und eher als Lehngut aus älterer Überlieferung zu deuten sind [1]). Mit diesem Vergleich soll gewiss keine nähere Verwandtschaft zwischen den besonderen Gedanken bei Amenemope und denen im Buche Koheleth behauptet sein, obwohl es nicht ganz an Beziehungen der einen zu den anderen fehlt [2]); aber das mit dem Kompositcharakter beider Werke gegebene literarische Hauptproblem ist unbeschadet aller Verschiedenheiten dort und hier dasselbe, und es ist im Grunde genommen gar nicht nur ein literarisches, sondern fast noch mehr ein psychologisches Problem. Vielleicht gerade deswegen, weil diese beiden Autoren sich selbst dessen bewusst waren, dass ihre besonderen Gedanken weiter als üblich von der Linie der hergebrachten, auch ihnen von Jugend auf geläufigen Weisheit abwichen, hat sich in ihnen ein besonders starkes Bedürfnis der Anlehnung an die Tradition entwickelt. Sie schreiben nicht als kühne Revolutionäre, die alle Brücken hinter sich abgebrochen haben, sondern als abgeklärte Weise, die in ihren Büchern auch den Sprüchen ihrer Vorgänger unbedenklich Raum geben, sofern sie sich mit ihren eigenen Anschauungen einigermassen zu vertragen scheinen, und die wohl hoffen, dass ihr Sondergut durch dieses Verfahren sicherer, als wenn sie es den Lesern ganz

---

[1]) Vgl. besonders die Analyse des Buches bei GALLING, *ZAW*, N. F. IX (1932), p. 276 ff., und in seinem *Kommentar* (1940).

[2]) Einiges darüber bei P. HUMBERT, *Recherches sur les sources égyptiennes de la littérature sapientiale d'Israël* (1929), p. 107 ff.; doch liesse sich der Vergleich meines Erachtens noch vertiefen.

für sich darböten, in den Gemeinbesitz der kommenden Geschlechter übergehen wird. Uns mag das Opfer, das sie damit der Macht der Tradition in ihren Völkern gebracht haben, zu gross vorkommen; aber die Erhaltung ihrer Bücher zeigt, dass es sich gelohnt hat.

Für die Schrift des Amenemope ergibt sich aus dem von A. ERMAN erbrachten Nachweis, dass ein bestimmter, wenn auch sehr kleiner Teil des biblischen Spruchbuches von ihr abhängig ist [1]), sogar die bei keinem anderen ägyptischen Weisheitsbuch so sicher feststellbare Tatsache einer literarischen Wirkung bis über die Grenzen Ägyptens hinaus. Und zwar ist es im Sinne der oben skizzierten Analyse das abgeschlossene Werk des Amenemope, dem diese Wirkung beschieden war. Das lehrt nicht nur die ausdrückliche Bezugnahme des biblischen Spruchbuches auf die nur aus der endgültigen Gliederung des ägyptischen Werkes verständliche Zahl der 30 Kapitel [2]), sondern auch der Umstand, dass sich unter den übernommenen, vielfach verkürzten und entstellten Sprüchen ebensowohl solche finden, in denen Amenemope seine eigenen Anschauungen zum Ausdruck bringt [3]), wie solche, von denen anzunehmen ist, dass schon er sie seinen Vorgängern entlehnt hat [4]). Sein Buch muss also fertig komponiert gewesen sein und vielleicht auch schon allerlei Stadien der Überlieferung im ägyptischen Bereich durchgemacht haben, bevor es zu seiner Übertragung ins Hebräische und zu seiner Einverleibung in die israelitische Weisheit kam, von der uns der kümmerliche Überrest im biblischen Spruchbuch, wahrscheinlich als Ergebnis eines längeren Einschrumpfungsprozesses, noch Zeugnis gibt. Die gegenteilige Behauptung einer Abhängigkeit des Amenemope von dem biblischen Spruchbuch wird meines Erachtens den komplizierten literarischen Tatbeständen nicht gerecht, die hier sowohl auf der ägyptischen als auch auf der israelitischen Seite vorliegen und denen noch viel eingehendere Untersuchungen werden gewidmet werden müssen.

---

[1]) A. ERMAN, *Sitzungsberichte der Preuss. Akademie d. Wiss., phil.-hist. Kl.* (1924), p. 86 ff. Der in Betracht kommende Abschnitt des biblischen Spruchbuches ist Prov. xxii 17-xxiv 22, ursprünglich ein literarisches Gebilde für sich.

[2]) Prov. xxii 20; vgl. ERMAN, *a. a. O.*, p. 89 f.

[3]) So besonders Prov. xxii 24 — Amenemope xi 13 f. (Kap. 9).

[4]) Zum Beispiel Prov. xxiii 10 — Amenemope vii 12 ff. (Kap. 6); Prov. xxiii 1 ff. — Amenemope xxiii 13 ff. (Kap. 23). Besonders ist zu beachten, dass auch der Titel, der Prolog und der Epilog des ägyptischen Werkes im biblischen Spruchbuch anklingen: Prov. xxii 17 ff. — Amenemope i 5 f. (Titel). iii 9 ff. (Kap. 1). xxvii 7 (Kap. 30). Hier ist die Abhängigkeit von der endgültigen literarischen Gestaltung der Schrift des Amenemope besonders deutlich.

A PROPOS D'UNE PHRASE DE H. H. ROWLEY

PAR

H. CAZELLES

Paris

Dans *The Growth of the Old Testament* (p. 139) H. H. Rowley remarque que si les débuts de la littérature de Sagesse doivent être reportés dans un passé assez lointain, les livres de Sagesse qui sont venus jusqu'à nous sont tous postexiliques dans leur forme actuelle. De fait ils appartiennent tous à la troisième partie du canon, les Ketubîm, comme on le sait, la plus récente.

Cette remarque prend encore plus de signification si nous écoutons les appréciations que portaient sur la Sagesse les milieux religieux avant l'éxil. On a souvent souligné l'antagonisme des prophètes et des sages [1]), et avec raison, nous y reviendrons. Mais même quand les livres de Samuel ou des Rois parlent de sagesse, s'ils ont une haute estime pour cette faculté que possèdent au plus haut point l'ange de Dieu (2 Sam. xiv 20) ils n'en parlent cependant pas sans une certaine réticence. Il est significatif que dans le texte que nous venons de citer c'est l'expression rare „ange d'Elohîm" qui est employée et non l'expression usuelle, „ange de Yahvé". Cette sagesse (*ḥokmâh*) n'est pas quelque chose de spécifiquement yahviste. Nous connaissons maintenant par les textes de Ras Shamra [2]) les origines ouest-sémitiques de ce terme et nous savons par les inscriptions de Zinjirli [3]) et de Karatépé [4]) que c'était la vertu politique par excellence des princes de la région. Aussi, lorsqu'en ce passage de Samuel, la femme de Tékoa

---

[1]) "That book (of Proverbs) is commonly spoken of as representing a spirit of shrewd worldly-wisdom, and it is certain that we do not find here the religious profundity of either Law or Prophets" (H. H. Rowley, *The Unity of the Bible*, 1953, p. 45).

[2]) Anat, V, 38; II AB (Gordon No. 51), IV, 41; V, 65; II Kér (Gordon No. 126), IV, 3.

[3]) Inscription dite de Panammu l. 11; cf. Cooke, *North Semitic Inscriptions*, No. 62, p. 174.

[4]) Col. I, l. 12s.; cf. O'Callaghan, "The great Phenician Protal Inscription from Karatepe" (*Orientalia*, 1949, p. 176).

loue David d'avoir autant de sagesse qu'un ange de Dieu il ne faut pas croire que sous la plume du rédacteur de la succession de David ce soit là l'expression d'une admiration sans mélange. Cette femme qui vient mentir à David pour le compte de Joab admire l'astuce politique du roi, mais, pour l'auteur, la Sagesse en question est la même que l'insidieuse sagesse de Jonadab [1]) au chapitre précédent (xiii 3) dont les conseils aboutissent en effet à livrer Thamar à Amnon, mais avec les conséquences que l'on sait. La femme de Tékoa est sage (xiv 2) comme est sage la femme d'Abel-Beth-Maakah qui conseille d'exécuter Shéba pour sauver la ville (2 Sam. xx 16). Mais l'auteur se garde d'en faire une héroïne et il préfère ne pas attribuer à David une sagesse aussi cauteleuse [2]).

Mais, dira-t-on, Salomon est le sage par excellence, et ce n'est pas l'auteur du livre des Rois qui lui décerne cette épithète, ce sont les sources même, plus anciennes, qu'il a utilisées. Certes, Salomon est sage et l'octroi que Dieu lui fait de la Sagesse en I Reg. iii 4 ss. est un don que Dieu lui fait car la prière du roi lui a été agréable. Mais ici encore il ne faut pas faire dire au livre des Rois plus qu'il ne dit. La sagesse de Salomon fera de lui un roi sans égal (v. 13), mais elle reste dans l'ordre politique, elle relève de l'art de gouverner un peuple [3]). Que le livre des Rois, d'empreinte si deutéronomique, précise que cet octroi eut lieu au haut-lieu de Gabaon est déjà un indice qu'il n'est pas tellement enthousiaste de la sagesse du roi, d'autant qu'au verset précédant immédiatement le récit il a inséré la phrase rédactionnelle dont il est coutumier sur les sacrifices sur les hauts lieux; et cette phrase, commençant par un *raq* restrictif, marque une réticence dans l'approbation donnée au règne. La sagesse même dont le monarque fait preuve quand il juge entre les deux femmes est plutôt une astuce par laquelle le roi se délivre avec bonheur d'un cas difficile qu'un acte héroïque de fidélité à Yahvé.

Il y a là une ambiguité qui est un trait fondamental du portrait que le livre des Rois nous a laissé de Salomon. C'est le plus grand et le plus fastueux des rois d'Israel, c'est le constructeur du Temple, lieu choisi par Yahvé selon la théologie deutéronomique. Mais

---

[1]) "In this case his wisdom was put to base uses". H. P. Smith, *Samuel*, I. C. C., *in loc.*

[2]) Sur l'ensemble de ces textes, cf. S. R. Driver, *Introduction to the Literature of the Old Testament*, 1909, p. 392 f.

[3]) Montgomery and Gehman, "(The story) reflects one aspect of his administration" (*Kings*, I.C.C., 1951, p. 107).

Salomon est aussi le premier coupable car il a ouvert le pays aux coutumes et aux femmes étrangères [1]). Plus encore il est le premier coupable parce que, a côté du Temple de Yahvé, il a laissé s'établir les cultes étrangers de Moab et d'Ammon, il a même bâti des sanctuaires pour leurs dieux sous l'influence des femmes étrangères qu'il a épousées à la suite de la fille du Pharaon et ce sont elles qui ont „détourné son coeur de Yahvé" [2]). Il y a déjà dans la conduite de Salomon toute l'équivoque que le livre des Rois dénoncera dans la monarchie d'Israel: le peuple de Dieu n'est pas fidèle à la loi de Yahvé, aussi le royaume périra.

Cette polémique latente est reprise par les Prophètes. Elie attaque Achab pour sa politique tyrienne, Amos et Osée interviennent également, mais sans s'en prendre aux „sages". C'est avec Isaïe que les Prophètes condamnent directement ces derniers. Non seulement Isaïe maudit ceux qui sont „sages a leurs propres yeux" (v 21), mais il annonce que la „sagesse des sages périra" (xxix 14) et il considère comme vaine aussi bien la sagesse des ministres égyptophiles d'Ezechias que celle du roi d'Assyrie (x 13) ou celle des conseillers du Pharaon, pourtant dépositaires d'une antique sagesse (xix 11). Le seul sage est Dieu (xxxi 2). Certes si Isaïe prend aussi fortement position c'est qu'il se heurte aux scribes formés depuis Salomon sur le modèle des sages d'Egypte et influencés par eux. Il juge désastreuse une politique d'alliance ayant pour objectif une libération à bref délai du tribut assyrien, et préconise au contraire une lente reconstitution des forces de la nation par le retour aux traditions nationales et une longue patience: „Par la conversion et le repos vous serez sauvés, dans le calme et le confiance sera votre force" (xxx 15). Cette position d'Isaïe est donc fonction des circonstances, mais elle implique une vue théologique qui justifie cette attitude politique. La Foi traditionnelle d'Israel s'oppose aux combinaisons politiques d'une administration non moins traditionnellement orientée vers l'Egypte depuis Salomon.

C'est cependant avec Jérémie que l'opposition atteint son paroxysme. Il est en conflit non seulement avec des prêtres comme Phassur (xx) et des prophètes comme Hanani (xxviii), mais avec les sages. Ces trois catégories se liguent contre lui et l'attaquent l'un avec la Tôrah, l'autre avec le conseil et la troisième avec la „parole"

---

[1]) Sur les réserves faites dans les milieux israélites à la politique de Salomon voir récemment M. Noth, *Geschichte Israels*, 2ème éd. 1954, p. 198.

[2]) 1 Reg. xi 9. Mais voir tout le chapitre.

(Jer. xviii 18). Mais le prophète exerce son ironie non seulement contre les sages d'Israel (viii 9, ix 11), mais contre ceux de Théman (xlix 7) ou de Babel (l 35) et c'est dans ce livre de Jérémie que l'on trouve l'affirmation célèbre selon laquelle les sages ne peuvent dire avoir avec eux la loi de Yahvé parce que le stylet mensonger des scribes en a fait un mensonge (viii 8, 9) [1]. Pour avoir rejeté la parole de Yahvé les sages seront confondus, détruits et saisis. Les sages sont donc encore ici les scribes qui forment l'armature du royaume et le prophète les considère comme en opposition formelle avec la Tôrah.

Telle est la situation à la veille même de l'exil. Or au retour de l'exil nous allons assister au contraire à la canonisation de la littérature de Sagesse qui émane de ces milieux si vigoureusement attaqués par les Prophètes. On a cessé depuis longtemps de voir dans les livres de Sagesse des compositions purement postexiliques [2]. Les différentes collections du livre des Proverbes ont des matériaux qui remontent à l'époque de la monarchie et les maximes royales en particulier ne se comprennent bien qu'en supposant la monarchie encore vivante. Prov. xxv 1 nous avertit que les gens d'Ezechias ont recueilli une série de proverbes; le fond de ces chapitres provient sans doute du Nord à l'époque où à Jérusalem on recueille les restes yahvistes de Samarie tombée en 722. Le fond de la collection salomonienne, plus ample, doit venir des scribes mêmes de Jérusalem. Tout cela n'a pas été intégré dans le patrimoine religieux sans qu'une longue préface, elle certainement postexilique (ch. i-ix), ait rattaché cette littérature à la crainte de Yahvé commencement de la Sagesse, et aux apostrophes prophétiques (i 20 ss.). Mais nous avons dans ces maximes l'écho de l'enseignement par lesquels les scribes étaient formés aux qualités humaines nécessaires au bon gouvernement. C'est le Miroir des gens du roi, pour reprendre l'expression volontairement archaïsante d'H. DUESBERG [3]. C'est donc le travail des

---

[1]) A la différence de W. RUDOLPH, *Jeremia*, 1947, p. 53 le texte ne nous semble pas dirigé contre la Tôrah des prêtres, mais contre l'administration des scribes qui sont seuls ici mentionnés. Cf. *Recherches de Science Rel.*, 1951, p. 20s. Voir aussi la position très nuancée de SKINNER, *Prophecy and Religion*, p. 104.

[2]) Outre la phrase ci dessus citée de H. H. ROWLEY, cf. W. BAUMGARTNER "The Wisdom Literature", in *The Old Testament and Modern Study*, 1951, p. 213: "The existence of a school of wisdom poetry is thus confirmed for the period of the monarchy." Voir aussi A. BENTZEN, *Introduction to the O.T.*, II, p. 173.

[3]) *Les Scribes inspirés, I: Le livre des Proverbes*, 1938, p. 191ss.

écoles de fonctionnaires auxquels se sont heurtés les Prophètes qui a été ainsi canonisé.

Comment les milieux religieux orthodoxes, les plus fidèles à l'héritage de ces Prophètes, d'autant plus fidèles qu'ils feront parler la Sagesse comme un Prophète, comment donc ces milieux ont-ils été amenés a leur être infidèles sur ce point? Il ne suffirait pas d'invoquer le caractère religieux de la Sagesse [1]), En Israel et dans l'ancien Orient religion ne signifie point Yahvisme et c'est ici une question d'orthodoxie yahviste qui est en jeu. Le point d'histoire religieuse à débattre est celui-ci: comment une certaine ligne de pensée en Israel que, pour simplifier, nous appellerons orthodoxe, après avoir rejeté l'enseignement des sages avant l'exil, l'accepte-t-il après l'exil? L'adoption dut se faire en effet assez rapidement car le livre de Job suppose déjà réalisée cette attitude de l' „orthodoxie" qu'il va d'ailleurs critiquer.

La solution, comme on l'a souvent souligné, est certainement a chercher du côté de l'apparition et du développement de l'individualisme religieux, plus exactement de la religion personnelle [2]). Cette part croissante de l'attitude personnelle dans la religion qui avait marqué la religion égyptienne a son déclin se manifeste avec plus de conséquence et d'intensité dans la religion d'Israel [3]). Il était naturel que pour exprimer cette orientation religieuse on ait eu recours aux modes de la littérature sapientiale. Elle était née d'une réflexion sur la vie de l'individu, ses chances de réussite et les dangers qu'elle courait. Le Deutéronome déjà avait marqué la Loi de ce caractère personnel par ses exhortations où il s'adressait à l'Israelite, à son amour et a son coeur. Mais là encore la réponse est-elle tout a fait suffisante? Le grand prophète de l'individualisme et de la rétribution personnelle est Ezechiel, qui au ch. xviii affirme que chacun mourra pour sa faute et que chacun peut se convertir. Or Ezechiel est très loin de la littérature gnomique et ne parle de Sagesse

---

[1]) L. Bouyer, *La Bible et l'Evangile*, 1953, p. 125.

[2]) Que les Prophètes comme Jérémie n'aient pas été de purs individualistes mais aient conçu la religion de l'avenir comme une religion personnelle certes, mais dans une communauté et avec un culte public est une vue de plus en plus répandue. Sur la difficile question du culte, cf. H. H. Rowley, *The Unity of the Bible*, p. 33ss.; M. Schmidt, *Prophet und Tempel*, 1948, p. 98.

[3]) Cf. J. Breasted, *Development of Religion and Thought in Ancient Egypt*, 1912. Voir aussi C. Desroches-Noblecourt, "Les religions égyptiennes", dans l'*Histoire générale des Religions*, 1948, I, p. 281.

que dans son chapitre xxviii sur le roi de Tyr (xxvii et xxviii); la Sagesse est encore pour lui un concept étranger.

Il semble qu'il faille plutôt s'adresser à Jérémie et aux disciples qui ont rédigé le livre de ce dernier [1]). C'est Jérémie qui annonce une nouvelle alliance, alliance où la Loi sera inscrite dans le coeur (xxxi 33) et il proclame en même temps la connaissance directe que chacun pourra avoir de Yahvé aux temps de cette nouvelle alliance (v. 34). Par là même ce prophète qui avait si vigoureusement attaqué les sages de son temps préparait l'assimilation de leur enseignement. Cet enseignement qui cherchait à persuader plus qu'à commander, qui cherchait à atteindre les racines profondes de l'action humaine en lui présentant un idéal de bonheur, cet enseignement devait trouver sa place dans les perspectives d'une nouvelle alliance où ce serait l'adhésion du coeur qui compterait, plus qu'un impératif transmis par des hommes au nom de l'autorité nationale [2]). Au moment où l'Etat d'Israel s'effondre se révèle un nouvel Israel où chacun mourra pour son iniquité (xxxi 29). La communauté de Yahvé n'est plus la communauté où chacun naît en vertu des lois de la nature et du sang, c'est la communauté où chacun vient ou d'où chacun s'en va suivant ses dispositions personnelles. C'est l'adhésion à Dieu qui compte, cette adhésion se fait par la conscience personnelle, les gros problèmes religieux vont devenir des problèmes personnels, orientation de la vie (Proverbes), souffrances, dégoût, immortalité. Il semble donc qu'il faille rattacher aux perspectives de la nouvelle alliance et du nouvel Israel la nouvelle orientation de la pensée juive.

Mais celle-ci reste traditionnelle. Osée, le premier qui ait entrevu un nouveau pacte (ii 20 ss.) avait déjà frayé la voie à la religion personnelle et le scribe qui a apostillé son oeuvre avec une maxime de sagesse (xiv 10) s'en était bien rendu compte. Isaïe avait déjà commencé l'assimilation par l'orthodoxie de la culture de Sagesse, tant dans les attributs qu'il reconnaît au Messie (xi 2 s.) que dans l'apologue par lequel il cherche à faire comprendre la diversité des voies de Yahvé

---

[1]) Il est inutile ici d'entrer dans la discussion de l'authenticité. Mais cette discussion serait nécessaire si l'on voulait apporter plus de précision.

[2]) Sur ces passages voir W. RUDOLPH, *op. cit.*, p. 169ss., et A. D. MACHO, "Cesara la "Tora" en la Edad Mesianica", in *Estudios biblicos*, 1953, p. 126s. Ces textes ouvrent de nouvelles possibilités aux fidèles mais ne suppriment pas les conditions prélables. C'est la même loi qui cesse d'être purement extérieure pour devenir intérieure et Ezechiel montre que cette intériorisation ne supprime pas la Loi pour le fidèle mais en permet l'accomplissement (Ezech. xxxvi 26, 27). Reste à préciser le contenu de la Tôrah pour ces Prophètes.

(xxviii 23-29). Jérémie tout en attaquant les sages proclamait que Yahvé avait affermi le monde par sa Sagesse (x 12). Mais il n'y avait là que des préparations. Pour que l'ensemble de cette brillante culture puisse être assimilée, il fallait que la chute de Jérusalem marque la caducité d'une sagesse trop humaine par la ruine d'une caste qui faisait des projets, mais sans Yahvé, et contractait des pactes, mais sans son esprit (Jes. xxx 1). Leur culture ne serait pas perdue et, désormais rattaché à la crainte de Yahvé, leur héritage allait proliférer dans la magnifique littérature sapientiale d'Israel.

LE MESSIANISME SAPIENTIAL ET LES ORIGINES LITTÉRAIRES DU FILS DE L'HOMME DANIÉLIQUE

PAR

J. COPPENS
Louvain

Les origines de la notion du Fils de l'homme daniélique n'ont pas encore trouvé, semble-t-il, une explication suffisante. Un spécialiste de la littérature iranienne vient d'exprimer ses doutes touchant un emprunt éventuel aux traditions de la Perse [1]). Par ailleurs, on n'a pas réussi à montrer, d'une façon qui emporte l'adhésion, comment la notion se serait développée à partir de conceptions bibliques antérieures au livre de Daniel [2]). Une des plus récentes tentatives pour trouver dans les écrits inspirés mêmes les sources de la figure du Fils de l'homme ne paraît pas non plus donner satisfaction. Faisant appel à une méthode que divers exégètes français récents appellent anthologique et qui consiste à faire des rapprochements problématiques, plus d'une fois artificiels ou dénués de preuves suffisantes, on croit pouvoir rendre compte de la genèse de la figure énigmatique en se référant à une série de textes d'Ézéchiel, puis et surtout, à une influence de la littérature sapientiale. En particulier, le caractère personnel et céleste du Fils de l'homme s'expliquerait dans une mesure appréciable par le recours au thème de la Sagesse, hypostase divine que les livres sapientiaux ont élaborée et proposée à la foi du Judaïsme postexilique [3]). Dans ce recueil de mélanges centrés sur les écrits de la sagesse biblique, c'est la prétendue influence du messianisme sapiential sur le livre de Daniel et sur la figure du Fils de l'homme que nous voudrions examiner.

---

[1]) J. Duchesne-Guillemin, "Ormazd et Ahriman", dans *Mythes et Religions*, Paris 1953.

[2]) Dans son opuscule *Messias. Moses redivivus. Menschensohn*, paru dans les *Abh. Theol. des Alten und Neuen Testaments* 17, Zürich 1948, A. Bentzen essaye de rapprocher les divers courants vétérotestamentaires relatifs au Sauveur. Plusieurs éléments de la synthèse résistent difficilement à la critique.

[3]) A. Feuillet, „Le fils de l'homme de Daniel et la tradition biblique", dans *Rev. Bibl.* LX (1953), p. 170-202, 321-346.

Voici pour sérier les problèmes et jalonner la voie trois affirmations auxquelles il conviendra de prêter attention. La littérature sapientiale, telle est une première prémisse, n'est pas étrangère aux espérances messianiques. Elle a contribué par un messianisme qui possède, il est vrai, ses particularités, à entretenir vivace l'attente d'Israël. La figure de la Sagesse divine participe, elle aussi, au courant messianique. Elle possède même des traits messianiques si manifestes qu'elle apparaît par moments comme le substitut du Messie. Le livre de Daniel, telle est la troisième affirmation, plus spécialement le passage relatif au Fils de l'homme, est fortement imprégné des thèmes et termes sapientiaux. Dès lors on estime pouvoir conclure que la notion de la Sagesse, en tant qu'hypostase divine et substitut du Messie, contribua à donner naissance à la vision daniélique du Fils de l'homme. Personnage mystérieux, céleste et transcendant comme la Sagesse, il est investi comme elle de fonctions qui furent primitivement l'apanage du roi-messie.

Exam nons ces quelques affirmations et demandons-nous dans quelle mesure la voie ainsi frayée conduit à une meilleure intelligence des origines de la figure daniélique.

Et d'abord, dans quelle mesure est-il loisible de parler d'un messianisme sapiential?

Il convient, semble-t-il, de distinguer en la matière entre les Proverbes d'un côté et, de l'autre, l'Ecclésiastique et le Livre de la Sagesse [1]). Les Proverbes renoncent au messianisme classique; du moins, ils en font abstraction. En revanche, on constate que la Sagesse y est parée d'attributs dont les livres prophétiques affublent le monarque idéal de l'avenir [2]). La Sagesse est intronisée par Dieu de la manière que les Prophètes et les Psalmistes réservent au Messie [3]); elle possède les dons et les charismes octroyés par Isaïe au roi futur qui assurera le salut d'Israël [4]); elle exerce le jugement, fonction messianique par excellence [5]); elle dispense les biens eschatologiques, y compris le don de l'esprit [6]); il lui appartient même d'inaugurer le

[1]) L. Couard, *Die religiösen und sittlichen Anschauungen der alttestamentlichen Apokryphen und Pseudepigraphen*, Gütersloh 1907; H. Duesberg, *Les Scribes inspirés. Introduction aux livres sapientiaux de la Bible*, Paris 1939.

[2]) A. Feuillet, *art. cit.* p. 322-327.

[3]) Prov. viii 23. Cf. Ps. ii 6.

[4]) Prov. viii 14. Cf. Jes. xi 2 f.

[5]) Prov. i 24-33.

[6]) Prov. i 23. — On doit toutefois se demander si l'esprit dont il est ici question, est à identifier avec le don eschatologique du même nom.

règne éternel des justes et d'y présider le banquet des élus [1]). Et n'oublions pas qu'à l'occasion la Sagesse revendique une origine et une filiation divines qui sont à comparer à celles dont pouvaient se prévaloir les rois d'Israël, du moins le roi idéal dont on attendait la venue [2]).

Il existe donc, nous n'en disconvenons pas, un certain parallélisme entre les fonctions et les attributs du roi idéal, du roi-messie, et celles de la Sagesse. S'ensuit-il que la littérature sapientiale a servi d'intermédiaire entre la description du Messie prophétique et celle du Fils de l'homme? D'abord, il n'est pas exclu que les traditions sapientiales soient dans leurs origines et leur première expression littéraire contemporaines de l'idéologie prophétique, ou même qu'elles lui soient antérieures et qu'elles aient contribué à enrichir, par exemple dans le livre d'Isaïe, le messianisme royal. Ensuite, même à admettre que la littérature sapientiale s'intercale entre les livres du prophétisme classique et Daniel, est-il vraisemblable qu'elle ait transformé la figure du Messie, la faisant évoluer de celle d'un roi terrestre à celle d'un être transcendant et céleste, „incarnation" pour ainsi dire „de la gloire divine"? Pareille influence, en effet, ne paraît pas pouvoir être attribuée aux Proverbes pour la raison que ce livre ne se situe pas dans une perspective messianique et eschatologique. Les biens que la Sagesse y dispensent, ne surgissent pas sur un horizon lointain, ils ne sont pas promis pour un avenir reculé, pour les derniers temps. Ils sont actualisés. Si le livre des Proverbes dépend en partie des traditions prophético-messianiques, par ailleurs il semble s'en désolidariser. A une vaste espérance dans un avenir meilleur où les bienfaits collectifs et nationaux dominent, les Proverbes substituent une économie de biens dispensés dès à présent, sans distinction et privilèges de races, en vue d'un bonheur avant tout personnel. Certes, dans l'Ecclésiastique et dans le Livre de la Sagesse l'eschatologie reprend vie et vigueur. Elle réoccupe sa place dans la foi et dans l'espérance des hagiographes. Cependant, même ici, surgit une difficulté qui semble exclure la possibilité d'une influence de ces deux livres et des traditions y consignées sur la vision du Fils de l'homme. Il n'y est plus question d'un Messie personnel.

On répliquera peut-être que la Sagesse y obtient un rôle et y exerce une fonction quand bien même dignes d'être appelés messianiques.

---

[1]) Prov. ix 1-5. Cf. Jes. xxv 6, lv 1 f., lxv 13 f.

[2]) Prov. viii 22-31. Cf. Ps. ii 7, cx 3, et, pour le Judaïsme postbiblique, I Hen. 105; 4 Esdr. vii 28 ff., xiii 32, 37, 52, xiv 9. Cf. A. Feuillet, *art. cit.*, p. 345.

Certes, mais précisément elle remplit la fonction messianique trop bien, jusqu'à éliminer le Messie. Et puis, la Sagesse est trop liée à l'être même de Dieu, pour avoir pu servir de prototype à la figure d'un Fils de l'homme, qui en est manifestement distinct. Si en quelques passages la Sagesse possède une subsistance plus indépendante, c'est plutôt en reine qu'elle paraît alors associée à Dieu [1]). Langage sans aucun doute métaphorique. Il n'en reste pas moins qu'une pareille image n'a guère pu favoriser un rapprochement de la Sagesse avec le Messie ou aboutir à la notion du Fils de l'homme.

Récapitulons: quelles que soient les origines des traditions sapientiales, qu'elles soient, du moins en partie, antérieures à l'enseignement prophétique ou qu'elles en dépendent, rien ne nous invite à croire qu'à l'époque de la composition du livre de Daniel, la figure de la Sagesse ait apporté son concours à transformer la physionomie du Messie. Au contraire, elle a sans doute pu contribuer à faire oublier le représentant par excellence de l'espérance prophétique. La vision à laquelle les Sages inclinent, est celle d'une Sagesse entrevue comme la reine des cieux et y trônant à côté de Dieu. Pareille figure ne se prêtait pas à être rapprochée du Messie, même pas d'un Messie céleste.

Si les Sages n'ont guère favorisé ou influencé eux-mêmes la croyance au Messie, ne se pourrait-il pas que d'autres penseurs ou écrivains bibliques se soient inspirés de leurs spéculations pour transformer son aspect traditionnel, pour lui attribuer des traits nouveaux calqués sur ceux de la Sagesse? Cela s'est réalisé, ainsi qu'on le sait, plus tard, notamment à l'époque du Christ, dans la prédication du Sauveur, dans la théologie de la communauté primitive et dans celle de l'Apôtre des gentils. C'est, en effet, d'une combinaison heureuse et admirable du messianisme royal, du messianisme deutéro-isaïen, du messianisme danielique et du messianisme sapiential que s'est progressivement dégagé le portrait du Messie idéal qui s'est vérifié dans le Christ [2]). La question est donc de savoir si le syncrétisme des espérances sotériologiques n'a pas débuté dans le livre de Daniel.

---

[1]) Sap. ix, 4: δός μοι τὴν τῶν θρόνων πάρεδρον σοφίαν. — Cf. A. Feuillet, *art. cit*, p. 334 f.: „La Sagesse . . . . qui a pourtant horreur du paganisme emploie un mot très fort qui fait songer aux divinités parèdres."

[2]) Voir L. Cerfaux-J. Coppens-R. de Langhe-V. de Leeuw-A. Descamps-J. Giblet-B. Rigaux, *L'Attente du Messie*, dans *Recherches bibliques*, Bruges-Paris 1954.

Ne serait-ce pas dans ce livre que les espérances prophétiques et les spéculations sapientiales se rencontrent pour la première fois et donnent ainsi naissance à ce Messie transcendant qu'est le Fils de l'homme?

A l'appui d'une réponse affirmative, on fait valoir que Daniel aime combiner les thèmes littéraires des Prophètes et ceux des Sages [1]). Puis on insiste sur le fait qu'exactement dans le contexte où le Fils de l'homme fait sa première apparition, plusieurs termes de la littérature sapientiale se présentent spontanément sous la plume de l'écrivain sacré [2]). Enfin on fait remarquer que Daniel, tout comme les Scribes inspirés, n'envisage pas la venue d'un Messie de la lignée davidique [3]).

Accordons sans peine que Daniel contient et groupe des expressions et des notions empruntées tantôt aux livres prophétiques de l'Ancien Testament, tantôt aux livres sapientiaux. Ce phénomène ne lui appartient pas en propre. Il caractérise l'ensemble de la littérature apocalyptique à laquelle Daniel ressortit, et il se prolonge jusque dans les écrits du Nouveau Testament [4]). Admettons aussi que la Sagesse et le Fils de l'homme possèdent des traits communs. Le Fils de l'homme est appelé à prendre part au gouvernement du monde [5]), à obtenir une participation au pouvoir divin, participation dont la Sagesse jouit également. En outre, comme il se manifeste sur les nuées [6]),

---

1) Daniel est décrit comme un nouveau Joseph (Dan. i 17), comme un sage ou scribe inspiré (Dan. i 17, 20, ii 21). — Les secrets du livre de Daniel et le bonheur eschatologique entrevu par le visionnaire sont la part réservée aux *maśkîlîm*: Dan. xii 3, 10, xi 33, 35.

2) On insiste en particulier sur la présence de la nuée (Dan. vii 13. Cf. Sap. ix 10; Sir. xxiv 6 f.; Bar. iii 29), sur le règne universel (Dan. vii 14, 18, 22, 27; Sap. iii 8, v 16), sur la connexion avec le peuple élu (Dan. vii 13 coll. avec vii 18, 22, 27; Sir. xxiv 13) et avec le temple (Sir. xxiv 14; Dan. viii 14, ix 24). En revanche, les termes *maśkîl* ou *maśkîlîm* ne se rencontrent pas au ch. vii, mais dans Dan. i 4, 17 ix, 13, 22, 25, xi 33-35, xii 3, 10. De même la splendeur des justes glorifiés apparaît seulement au ch. xii (Dan. xii 3; Sap. iii 7).

3) A. Feuillet, *art. cit.*, p. 330.

4) Cf. pour ce qui concerne les thèmes sapientiaux dans saint Paul, J. Dupont, *Gnosis. La connaissance religieuse dans les épîtres de saint Paul*, Louvain-Paris 1949.

5) Dan. vii 14. Cf. A. Feuillet, *art. cit.*, p. 323: "En viii, 22, (la Sagesse) déclare posséder depuis toujours cette investiture royale."

6) A. Feuillet, *art. cit.*, p. 187 f., accorde une importance capitale à la nuée et y voit l'indice probant du caractère transcendant et divin du Fils de l'Homme. A mon avis, il exagère. Le Fils de l'homme vient „avec une nuée". La nuée n'est peut-être que le moyen auquel le Fils de l'homme doit avoir recours pour monter jusqu'à Dieu qui est au ciel. Remarquons d'ailleurs que le Fils de l'homme n'est pas invité à s'asseoir à côté de Dieu mais à se tenir devant lui: attitude

comme il est l'objet d'un culte [1]), comme il subsiste auprès de Dieu, il dépasse, telle la Sagesse, le souverain idéal, fils de David, entrevu et attendu par le messianisme royal [2]).

N'essayons pas de voiler ces traits communs ou d'en minimiser la portée. Il y a plutôt lieu d'observer que d'autres traits, pourtant non moins caractéristiques, peut-être même plus essentiels, font défaut, tels l'origine prétemporelle et éternelle et le devenir à partir de l'être même de Dieu. D'autre part, au portrait de la Sagesse manquent des traits notables du Fils de l'homme, tels l'aspect humain et, à fortiori, le nom si particulier.

On pourra être tenté de répondre que la figure humaine du Fils de l'homme n'est qu'une apparence [3]). Elle ne serait pas plus à prendre au pied de la lettre en lui que dans les anges ou dans l'Ancien des jours [4]). En réalité, le Fils de l'homme ne serait pas un être humain; il serait plutôt un ange, ou un être supérieur aux anges, et, à ce titre, il mériterait d'être appelé, tout comme les anges [5]), „fils de Dieu". Ainsi nous rejoindrions les spéculations sur la Sagesse, d'autant plus

---

concédée ailleurs au grand prêtre ou au roi. Cf. Ps. lxi 8; I Reg. xvii 1; 2 Reg. xi 14; 2 Chron. xxxiv 31; Jes. vi 2.

[1]) Autre détail sur lequel insiste beaucoup A. Feuillet, *art. cit.*, p. 189, pour conclure au caractère divin de la figure énigmatique. Lui-même toutefois admet qu'un hommage même strictement divin pouvait être rendu à Dieu à travers un intermédiaire créé qui le représente: cf. Dan. vii 27. Ajoutons que dans Jes. lx 7, 10, lxi 6, se présente un usage de *šrt* parallèle, semble-t-il, à celui de *plḥ* dans Daniel.

Dans sa plaquette intéressante sur le livre de Daniel: *Das Buch Daniel und seine Botschaft von den letzten Dingen*, paru dans les *Schriften des Schweizerischen Vereins für freies Christentum*, no. 2 (Bâle 1944), M. W. Baumgartner hésite à se prononcer d'une façon définitive sur le figure du Fils de l'homme. Il se demande un instant si le Fils de l'homme ne cache pas un ange ou un dieu (p. 27), mais il finit par opter pour l'hypothèse qui voit en lui une adaptation israélite de l'*Urmensch* (p. 29). De même à la page 24, il accepte le caractère vraiment humain du Fils de l'homme: „Der einzelne Mensch scheint nur ein Symbol oder ein Repräsentant jenes künftigen Reiches."

[2]) Il faut sans doute faire une exception pour le Ps. cx qui invite le roi à s'asseoir à la droite de Jahvé. Cette invitation ne possède pas de parallèle dans la Bible, du moins si le texte concerne vraiment le roi et la droite de Jahvé, ainsi que la plupart des commentateurs le pensent.

[3]) A. Feuillet, *art. cit.*, p. 187, ne le croit pas, mais ses explications me paraissent confuses.

[4]) Au ch. vii 13 les Septante marquent explicitement qu'ils ne voyaient dans l'appellation qu'une comparaison approximative: cf. A. Feuillet, *art. cit.*, p. 186, n. 8.

[5]) Ps. xxix 1, lxxxix 7; Iob i 6; Dan. iii 25.

qu'elle aussi, au moins dans un seul texte, apparaît non pas comme une reine mais comme le propre fils de Dieu [1]).

Toutes spécieuses que soient ces considérations, elles ne nous convainquent pas. Il est clair que pour l'Ancien des jours l'aspect humain n'est qu'une apparence. Quant aux anges, Daniel leur donne tantôt un aspect de fils de Dieu, tantôt une ressemblance humaine [2]). Les meilleurs commentateurs de Daniel se gardent toutefois d'assimiler le Fils de l'homme à un être angélique [3]) et l'auteur de l'hypothèse étudiée en ces pages ne les contredit pas. En ce qui concerne la Sagesse appelée „fils de Dieu", elle n'est attestée que dans un seul texte, qui est au surplus obscur et difficile à expliquer. Comment ce passage unique et mystérieux aurait-il eu une influence sur la rédaction d'un ouvrage qui laisse précisément tomber le titre „fils de Dieu" pour lui substituer l'énigmatique „fils de l'homme"? Il reste certes qu'à l'époque néotestamentaire diverses conceptions du Messie: celles du Messie royal, du Serviteur de Jahvé, de la Sagesse, du Fils de Dieu et du Fils de l'homme, ont été rapprochées et ombinées [4]). A cette époque où elles existaient toutes et où une synthèse était devenue impérieusement nécessaire, des rapprochements ont pu se faire qui ne se conçoivent pas au moment où ces notions étaient en voie d'élaboration ou même parfois s'opposaient l'une à l'autre.

Dans ces conditions nous ne croyons pas qu'un recours aux traditions littéraires sapientiales, en particulier à la figure de la Sagesse, puisse contribuer beaucoup à expliquer la genèse de la vision du Fils de l'homme. Aussi bien ceux qui y font appel, sont-ils obligés d'alléguer d'autres influences, notamment celle d'Ézéchiel qui nous

---

[1]) Ce serait l'affirmation de Prov. xxx 4. Mais la parole mystérieuse du sage Agour se prête à plusieurs interprétations. Agour a-t-il pris son interrogation au sérieux? Un de nos maîtres, le professeur C. van Crombrugghe, ne croyait pas qu'il s'agissait d'une question ironisante poussée jusqu'à l'absurde. A ses yeux, au contraire, Agour entendait affirmer l'existence d'un vrai fils de Dieu, qui n'était pas à identifier ni avec le peuple d'Israël ni avec les anges. „Il appert, concluait-il, qu'Agour a entrevu la fécondité intellectuelle par laquelle Dieu se donne un fils."

[2]) L'ange, envoyé de Dieu, se présente comme un fils de Dieu dans Dan. iii 25; en revanche, dans Dan. viii 15, x 16, les anges ont l'apparence humaine.

[3]) Cf. J. A. Montgomery, *A Critical and Exegetical Commentary on the Book of Daniel*, (1927), p. 321. Voir aussi A. Feuillet, *art. cit.*, p. 190 n. 1.

[4]) Le rapprochement a déjà commencé dans la littérature apocryphe, par exemple dans Hénoch qui applique au Fils de l'homme les charismes de l'Esprit décrits dans Jes. xi 2, exactement de la même manière que Prov. viii 12, les applique à la Sagesse hypostasiée: cf. A. Feuillet, *art. cit.*, p. 344.

représente la gloire divine sous l'apparence d'un homme [1]). A mon avis, cette documentation supplémentaire ne rémédie guère aux lacunes entrevues. Dans la description relativement confuse du char sur lequel la gloire divine se manifeste, rien n'évoque la présence d'un être, intermédiaire entre Dieu et les hommes, qui ait pu favoriser l'élaboration du Fils de l'homme daniélique. Le titre, il est vrai, se rencontre chez Ézéchiel, mais il n'y désigne ni le Messie, ni la Sagesse, ni quelque médiateur céleste. Il s'applique au contraire au prophète. S'il possède quelque relation avec le terme daniélique comme d'aucuns le croient, il faudrait dire avec M. ENGNELL que la notion s'est démocratisée et a passé du roi au porte-parole de Jahvé [2]).

Mais, nous demandera-t-on, tenez-vous en réserve une nouvelle et meilleure explication de l'origine de la figure daniélique? Hélas, non. Nous croyons jusqu'à meilleure preuve du contraire que la solution la plus obvie consiste à croire que la figure du „fils de l'homme", de „l'homme", a surgi par opposition aux figures des bêtes, symboles des empires terrestres, et que le cadre céleste se comprend par opposition à l'abîme d'où les animaux sont sortis [3]).

---

[1]) Cf. Ezech. i 26 et A. FEUILLET, *art. cit.*, p. 190. Aussi A. FEUILLET n'hésite-t-il pas à appeler le Fils de l'Homme „une sorte de manifestation visible du Dieu invisible" (*art. cit.*, p. 187), „une sorte d'incarnation de la gloire divine" (*ibid.*, p. 189). Nous croyons, au contraire, que la distinction entre le Fils de l'homme et Dieu est nettement marquée: le Fils de l'homme doit être amené en la présence de Dieu. La préposition „comme" qui l'introduit, n'exclut pas que l'écrivain sacré songe à une figure humaine véritable. Elle appartient au style apocalyptique et souligne le caractère visionnaire. Dans Ézéchiel, l'hagiographe marque beaucoup plus clairement en parlant de Dieu qu'il ne s'agit que d'une pure apparence.

Dans le seul endroit de Daniel où l'expression „fils de l'homme" réapparaît (viii 17), elle désigne incontestablement un homme, c'est à savoir le prophète lui-même.

[2]) I. ENGNELL, *Människosonen*, dans *Svenskt Bibliskt Uppslagsverk*, (1952), col. 400.

[3]) A nous tenir strictement au texte, il semble que le Fils de l'homme soit à comprendre comme le représentant, le type des „saints". Ce qui lui est attribué au vers. 14, l'est aux „Saints" dans Dan. vii 22 et 27. Ce qui est vu en vision aux versets 10d-14, se mue en réalité aux versets 26-27. De part et d'autre, il y exactement le même cadre: la cour s'assied pour rendre justice. Mais qui sont les „Saints" dont le Fils de l'homme est le représentant typique? Le livre de Daniel emploie le terme tantôt pour désigner les anges (Dan. iv 13, 17, 23) tantôt pour indiquer le peuple de Dieu (Dan. vii 18, 22, 27, viii 24, xii 7). Dans Dan. viii 13, la signification est moins claire. Habituellement on interprète le passage comme mettant en scène deux anges. Toutefois si Daniel enseigne, — ce que plusieurs auteurs admettent: cf. O. S. RANKIN, *Israel's Wisdom Literature*, (1936) — que les saints morts comme martyrs ont été admis tout de suite auprès de Dieu, il se pourrait que l'Apocalypse de Daniel vise ici quelques-uns de ces bienheureux possédant déjà leur récompense auprès de Dieu, en attendant que

Pour les croyants ce n'est pas à la suite d'une pure coïncidence mais par une disposition providentielle que l'hagiographe a situé le Fils de l'homme dans un cadre céleste, cadre qui pouvait amorcer des vues nouvelles sur le Messie. Il appartenait à des révélations postérieures de remplir ce cadre, de prolonger les visions. Si l'on admet, ne fût-ce qu'à la manière de A. Bentzen et S. Mowinckel, un sens plénier, c'est-à-dire si l'on croit qu'en inspirant la figure énigmatique de Daniel, la pensée divine se portait au delà de la pensée claire de l'hagiographe, il revint à l'Esprit saint d'actualiser dans la suite de l'histoire sainte ce que nous pouvons appeler le potentiel théologique de l'écrivain sacré.

---

sur la terre la domination soit accordée au peuple des saints. Serait-il trop téméraire de se figurer le Fils de l'homme qu'une nuée amène auprès du trône de Dieu, comme faisant partie du groupe de ces bienheureux et comme étant leur représentant? On comprendrait de cette façon d'autant mieux son titre de „Fils d'homme" et la présence de la préposition „comme", bien que par ailleurs celle-ci appartienne au style apocalyptique (W. Baumgartner, *op. cit.*, p. 27).

Ajoutons qu'en attribuant l'empire du monde à ses saints, au Fils de l'homme, le Très Haut réalise une parole angélique (Dan. iv 17): „Le Seigneur accorde le royaume des hommes à qui lui plaît, et il peut élever le plus bas d'entre les mortels."

On peut certes admettre comme l'explication la plus vraisemblable que le Fils de l'homme ne se réfère pas directement à la personne du Messie. Daniel ne semble pas entrevoir l'intervention d'un médiateur dans l'avènement de l'ère eschatologique (Dan. viii 25). Il n'en reste pas moins que la Figure du Fils de l'homme se prêtait admirablement à devenir, moyennant une révélation complémentaire, une figure messianique personnelle. Dès lors il n'est pas interdit de croire que cette signification complémentaire était plus ou moins incluse dès les origines dans le sens collectif et que, dans la mesure même où elle y était impliquée, elle ressortit à ce que nous avons appelé un sens plénier: J. Coppens, *Vom christlichen Verständnis des Alten Testaments*, Bruges et Fribourg-en-Brisgau 1952.

THE COUNSELLOR

BY

P. A. H. de Boer

Leiden

The hypostatization of wisdom in the ancient Near East is a vexed question. After Schencke's [1]) careful treatment of *ḥokma* in the Jewish scriptures, others have collected and criticized texts from Sumer and Akkad, from Egypt, Phoenicia, Iran and from Greece, comparing form and contents with the Biblical material in Proverbs, Job and the non-canonical books [2]). Schencke too did not neglect the mythological data of the non-Biblical texts. In his conclusions he underlined even the possibility of influence from Parseeism in the Jewish conception of divine wisdom. But in his treatment of the Old Testament texts he stressed the probability that there were traces of a Hebrew mythology wherein may be found, in his opinion, the origin of the Jewish personification of wisdom [3]).

A genuinely Jewish character for the Israelite concept of wisdom as a divine figure is supposed by many students. They try, however, to indicate a suppression of mythological ideas, or an intentional alteration of foreign concepts in Israel, in order to present a figure that fits into the supposed purely monotheistic thoughts of Jhwhism. Sometimes one gets the impression that there is a fear of suggesting ideas heterodox to the dogma of the Trinity, a symbol undeniably rooted in the ideas of hypostatization. Remarkable, in this respect,

---

[1]) W. Schencke, *Die Chokma (Sophia) in der jüdischen Hypostasenspekulation*, Kristiania, 1913.

[2]) A thorough investigation of the different theories can be found in H. Ringgren's monograph, *Word and Wisdom: Studies in the Hypostatization of Divine Qualities and Functions in the Ancient Near East*, Lund, 1947. As for Ugaritic influence, attention must be paid also to W. F. Albright, *From the Stone Age to Christianity*, Baltimore, 1940, p. 283 f., and to C. I. K. Story, "The Book of Proverbs and Northwest Semitic Literature", *JBL* lxiv (1945), p. 319-337.

[3]) Schencke, *op. cit.*, p. 91: "Und wenn die jüdische Weisheit Züge aufzeigt, die an irgend eine mythologische Figur als Prototyp hinweisen, braucht man deshalb nicht notwendigerweise an eine fremde Mythologie zu denken; *es wäre wohl denkbar, dass der Ursprung der jüdischen Weisheitsfigur sich innerhalb einer hebräischen Mythologie befände.*"

is the interpretation of the personification of wisdom as a literary, artistic, poetic, device, precisely among those who painstakingly avoid this kind of interpretation for Christian ideas regarding God's pluriformity.

The general statement concerning the suddenness of the personification of wisdom in Judaism seems to me insufficiently explained by the theories—in themselves reasonable to a large degree—of a derivation or of a development from early Hebrew mythological ideas. A derivation from elsewhere supposes some ability to incorporate strange ideas into the life and culture of the nation. And mythological figures have corresponding figures or special qualities of a human kind.

The counsellor has been closely connected with the wise, in Israel as well as in surrounding cultures. A treatment of his function may put a new complexion on the personification of wisdom in Judaism.

(i)

A survey of the passages where "counsel" and "to give, take, counsel" occur gives us the opportunity to fix the meaning of the terms in their context [1]).

Moses' father-in-law said to him: "Hearken now unto my voice, I will give thee counsel, and 'elohim be with thee" (Ex. xviii 19), and his counsel makes Moses able to do his work as judge of the people. Without Jethro's counsel Moses' task was too heavy—"thou wilt surely wear away" (verse 18). Balaam said to Balak (Num. xxiv 14): "And now, behold, I go unto my people; come, I will advertise thee (I will let you know) what this people will do to your people in the future". Balaam's counsel turns out to be his *mašal*, an effective word. That is why Balak is angry. (Cf. below on Mich. vi 5).

A nation "void of counsel", "without understanding" (Deut. xxxii 28) is the reverse of a wise nation which is referred to in verse 29. In Jer. xlix 7 and in Ezech. vii 26 occurs the same expression, **אבד עצה**.

After mentioning the distribution of the parts of the body belonging to the Levite's concubine, the narrator states—"And all who saw it said, 'Such a thing has never happened or been seen from the day

---

[1]) The terms are **עצה** and **מועצה** from the stem **יעץ**; Aramaic **עטא**, **יעט**. Besides the verb **יעץ** we find **מלך** both in Hebrew and in Aramaic. The context brings parallel expressions to the fore, such as **דבר**, **סוד**, etc.

that the children of Israel came up out of the land of Egypt until this day: consider it, take counsel and speak' " (Jud. xix 30). The Levite aimed at a decision. In ch. xx 7 he says—"Behold, ye Israelites, all of you, give here your advice (word — דבר) and counsel". To give counsel means to make a decision.

Ahitophel, David's counsellor, was sent for by Absalom when he was sacrificing in his city Giloh (2 Sam. xv 12). The story of his and Hushai's counsel is full of expressions that elucidate the meaning of our term. David asks his friend Hushai to return to Absalom (2 Sam. xv 34)—"but if you return to the city and say to Absalom, 'I will be your servant, O king; as I have been your father's servant in time past, so will I now be your servant': then shall you defeat for me the counsel of Ahitophel" (פרר עצת א'). Absalom said to Ahitophel (xvi 20)—"Give your counsel as to what we shall do". The counsel of the king's dignitary is an effectual operation, similar to a divine decision. "The counsel of Ahitophel, which he gave in those days, was as if a man inquired at the oracle of God: so was all the counsel of Ahitophel both with David and with Absalom" (xvi 23). In ch. xvii 4-6 the parallel expression is "the saying" — הדבר. When Hushai's counsel is accepted (xvii 14), it is said that the Lord intended to bring evil upon Absalom. "And when Ahitophel saw that his counsel was not followed ('done' — עשׂה; verse 23), he saddled his ass, and arose, and went off home, unto his city, and set his house in order, and hanged himself; and he died, and was buried in the sepulchre of his father." The counsel and the carrying into effect belong together. The counsel is the decision which guarantees life to the nation or to the person who takes counsel. Ahitophel and his counsel form a unity. The ineffective counsel is a dead word, hence the counsellor is a dead man.

Nathan the prophet said to Bathsheba, the mother of Solomon, (1 Reg. i 11 f.), "Have you not heard that Adonijah the son of Haggith has become king and David our lord does not know? Now therefore come, let me, I pray thee, give thee counsel, that thou mayest save thine own life, and the life of thy son Solomon." The counsel guarantees life. King Rehoboam took counsel with the old men, who had stood before Solomon his father (1 Reg. xii 6 ff.). Their counsel is the contents of the royal decision to be made. But the king forsook — עזב — the counsel of the old men and preferred the counsel of his playmates. Their bad counsel brings disaster to his country. It appears to be of decisive importance whether the counsellor is a person with special authority or not. "Counsel and strength (for war)" — עצה וגבורה (למלחמה) — is a standing phrase (2 Reg. xviii 20, Jes. xi 2, xxxvi 5, Iob xii 13). The contrast is "mere, vain words", "a word of lips" — דבר־שפתים (2 Reg. xviii 20).

In the Books of the Prophets we come upon the idea of the divine counsel, favourable and unfavourable, as well as human counsel. In our treatment we follow the order of the books.

The counsellor is parallel with the judge in Jes. i 26. The restoration of the old institutes of judgement and counselling means the re-established life of the city. The Lord's judgment against Jerusalem and Judah consists in the taking away from city and country of stay and staff, summed up in Jes. iii 1-3. The counsellor is one of the dignitaries of the court taken away. He is on a par with the mighty man, the soldier, the judge, the prophet, the elder, the diviner, the captain of fifty, the honourable man, the cunning artificer and the skilful enchanter. The character of effectual action and of indispensability in order to maintain security in state affairs are both evident.

The counsel of the Holy One of Israel is considered an ineffective one by the evil doers, who incur the prophet's anger—"Woe unto them ..." (Jes. v 19). Syria has counselled evil against Ephraim (Jes. vii 5 f.); the contents of the counsel is the decision to go up against it, to vex it and to set up a vassal king in the subdued country.

After deliverance from their enemies the people get a new ruler (Jes. ix 1 ff.) whose names will be "wonderful counsellor" — פלא יועץ — "divine counsellor" (cf. Jes. xxv 1, xxviii 29); "mighty god" — אל גבור; "father of the future" [1]) — אבי־עד; "prince of peace" — שר־שלום. The qualities of the new ruler find expression in the names, and the effect is stated in the following lines, the kingdom is established for ever and ever. Remarkable are the connections with strength, similar to the standing phrase "counsel and strength" and the titles אב and שר. Jhwh himself is holder of the father-title as גאל in Jes. lxiii 16. The new offspring of David will be a prosperous ruler—"the spirit of the Lord shall rest upon him, the spirit of wisdom and understanding, the spirit of counsel and might, the spirit of knowledge and the fear of the Lord" (Jes. xi 2). The planning and the counselling of the Lord shall stand (Jes. xiv 24). "The purpose that is purposed upon the whole earth" (Jes. xiv 26) is an expression similar

[1]) See below, p. 58.

to "the hand that is stretched out upon all the nations". The hand stretched out means intervention (cf. Deut. iv 34). The result is sure— "For the Lord of hosts hath purposed, and who shall annul it?, and his hand is stretched out and who shall turn it back?" (verse 27).

In Jes. xvi 3 our term runs parallel to bring reconciliation and safety to people who need a refuge. "Give counsel — הביא עצה — bring about reconciliation [1]), make thy shadow as the night in the midst of the noonday, hide the outcasts, betray not the wanderer". To give counsel means to restore life, to cause recovery.

The vitality of a nation lies in the strength of its gods. When the Lord comes to Egypt, the idols of that country will tremble at his presence. "The spirit of the Egyptians", records Jes. xix 3, "shall be made void in the midst of it; and I will swallow up its counsel" — ועצתו אבלע. The counsel is their vitality which will be destroyed. Jhwh counselled against Egypt (verse 17), and therefore Judah became a terror unto Egypt. "The counsel of the wisest counsellors of Pharaoh is become brutish: how say ye unto Pharaoh, I am the son of the wise, the son of ancient kings? Where then are thy wise men? and let them tell thee now; and let them know (or, with LXX, O. L., Vulg., "make known") what the Lord of hosts hath purposed concerning Egypt" (verses 11 and 12). The counsellor belongs to the ranks of the wise men, he is a prince of old, belonging to the royal court.

Similarly in Jes. xxiii 8 f. Jhwh's counsel against Tyre is described. Tyre is the crown of the cities and its inhabitants are honourable men, its merchant princes. But Jhwh's counsel brings the town into contempt.

In a thanksgiving hymn (Jes. xxv 1) the Lord is praised, for he has done wonderful things — פלא, counsels of old — עצות מרחוק, faithful and sure. עשׂה פלא means to do things that do not lie in man's power. These divine acts bring salvation to his people (verse 9). The Lord is wonderful in counsel and excellent in effectual action — הפליא עצה הגדיל תושיה (Jes. xxviii 29). After the threshing, the rebuilding of Sion will begin. The parallel term תושיה "effectual working" we find too in Mich. vi 9; Iob xii 16; Prov. ii 7, iii 21, viii 14, etc.

---

[1]) עשה פלילה. Cf. the present writer's monograph, "De voorbede in het Oude Testament", *OTS* iii (1943), p. 125-132. עשׂה פלילה means the act of averting the impending ruin of the exiles. GES.-BUHL, *Handwörterbuch* suggests 'satisfaction', 'aid'.

A striking instance of the identity of counsel and action is found in Jes. xxix 15 — "Woe to those who hide deep from the Lord their counsel, whose deeds are in the dark ..". The same may be true in Jes. xxx 1, where עשׂה עצה "to carry out counsel", and נסך מסכה, probably "to enter into an alliance, to make a league", are parallels.

The fool and the knave will no more be called noble and honourable, for they counsel wicked things, ruining the poor with lying words (Jes. xxxii 7). The opposite is the noble man, who stands by noble things (verse 8).

The expression "counsel and strength for war" (Jes. xxxvi 5) we have mentioned already with the parallel text from 2 Reg. xviii 20.

Verses 12-26 of ch. xl of the Book of Isaiah contain a hymn on El (אל, verse 18), the High God, orderer of heaven and earth. He directed the spirit, "the motive power of the soul" [1]), of Jhwh, the god of Israel. The very strength of El is delegated to Jhwh. Jhwh is the everlasting God, the Orderer of the whole earth; in verse 28,"Have you not known? have you not heard?", the preacher asks his people. Therefore one may expect wonderful deeds. El is the counsellor with whom Jhwh took counsel, who instructed him and taught him the path of judgment, knowledge and the way of understanding (verse 13 f.). The counsel is focused on the action. "The carrying into effect is the manifestation of the very counsel." [2]) Quotations of the ordering powers of El, with whom Jhwh is identified, are regularly an introduction to the creed: our god shall redeem us even from the powers of death, for he is a god of wonderful strength. (Cf. Jes. xliv 24 f.).

Jes. xli 28 f. present the conclusion of a judgement wherein the people, who do not believe in the promises of Jhwh, cannot bring forth a counsellor who is able to give the true decision about coming events. The counsellor must be the wise man who knows the future and who can make a decision which guarantees life and prosperity. "But when I look there is no one" (a similar construction in Jes. lxiii 5), "among these there is no counsellor, who, when I ask, gives an answer. Behold, they are all a delusion; their works are nothing; their molten images are empty wind." The power of making the right decision is connected with the power of the god in whose service the counsellor acts.

---

[1]) Johs. PEDERSEN, *Israel*, I, p. 104.

[2]) *Ibid.*, p. 128. The counsel of the wise man is the effective side of the king whose servant the counsellor is.

Jhwh's power can turn wise men backwards and make their knowledge foolish (Jes. xliv 25). He confirms the word — דבר — of his servant, and performs the counsel of his messengers — ועצת מלאכיו ישלים — (verse 26). The counsel of his servants runs concurrently with the divine promise, the prediction of the rebuilding of Judah's cities. Cyrus is called Jhwh's shepherd (king) (verse 28) and "the man of his counsel" (Jes. xlvi 11). To perform all Jhwh's pleasure is the task of the shepherd, a title also given to Moses (Jes. lxiii 11). A similar expression is found in xlvi 10 — "My counsel shall stand, and I will do all my pleasure". Jhwh's counsellor means here the one who carries out his counsel. And his counsel is his will — חפץ — which produces effect in צדקה "grant, gift" [1]), in תשועה "salvation", and in תפארת "glory" (verse 13).

הגיד and הגיש (Jes. xlv 21) are parallels of "to take counsel together"; cf. Jer. xxxviii 15 — "I declare" used parallel to "I give you counsel" — איעצך.

The aim, and effect, of counsel is possibility of life, salvation. In Jes. xlvii 13 idle counsels are described. "You are wearied in the multitude of thy counsels: let now the dividers of the heaven, the stargazers, the monthly prognosticators stand up, and save you from the things that shall come upon you." From this verse one can gather the function of true counsel. It both predicts and fixes or decides the future. The determination of the calendar, the fixing of *dies fasti et nefasti*, mean a guarantee of life.

The disobedient people walk in the counsels — הלך במעצות — the stubbornness — שרירות — of their evil hearts, instead of observing the way that Jhwh commanded (Jer. vii 24).

Jeremiah has uttered a severe judgment in Jhwh's name "I frame evil against you, and devise a device against you" (Jer. xviii 11). The word of a prophet is a reality. Therefore Jeremiah, uttering such words, is a real danger to the people. "Then they said (verse 18) — "Come, and let us devise devices against Jeremiah — חשב על י׳ מחשבות — for law — תורה — shall not perish from the priest, nor counsel — עצה — from the wise, nor word — דבר — from the prophet. Come, and let us smite him with the tongue, and let us not give heed to any of his words." תורה, עצה, and דבר are realities which effect results. מחשבות is a synonym of עצה (cf. Jeremiah's prayer, "Yet,

---

[1]) צדקה, "right, privilege, grant, gift"; cf. F. Rosenthal, *HUCA* 1950/51, p. 411 ff.

Lord, thou knowest all their counsel against me to slay me", verse 23).

Counsel is a concrete measure, provision for life. "Laying waste counsel" means ruination, death. "And I will lay waste — בקק — the counsel of Judah and Jerusalem in this place; and I will cause them to fall by the sword before their enemies, and by the hand of them that seek their life", etc. (Jer. xix 7).

In the prophet's prayer (Jer. xxxii 17-25) Jhwh is praised as an active god—"great in counsel and mighty in work" (גדל העצה ורב העליליה, verse 19).

Edom becomes a horror (שמה, Jer. xlix 17), powerless, dead, the opposite of the living one, the wise. "Is wisdom no more in Teman?, is counsel perished from the prudent? is their wisdom vanished?" (verse 7). Jhwh has taken his counsel against Edom. Similar to his judgment against Babylon in chapter l 45 runs the prophetic passage Jer. xlix 20 —"Therefore hear ye the counsel of the Lord, that he has taken against Edom; and his purposes — מחשבות — that he has purposed against the inhabitants of Teman: surely they shall drag them away, the little ones of the flock; surely he shall make their habitation desolate with them." The verbs יעץ and חשב are used in parallelism in Jer. xlix 30, as frequently.

Ezekiel presents in ch. vii 26 a vivid description of the destruction of the town. "Disaster comes upon disaster, and rumour follows rumour; they seek a vision of the prophet, but law perishes from the priest and counsel from the ancients." Just like Jer. xviii 18, the functions of priest (prophet) and counsellor are taken as firm conditions of life.

The counsellor belongs to the *śarim*, the princes of the people. Ezech. xi 1 f. reads—"The spirit lifted me up, and brought me to the east gate of the house of the Lord, which looks eastward, and behold, at the door of the gateway there were twenty-five men; and I saw among them Jaazaniah the son of Azzur and Pelatiah the son of Benaiah, princes of the people. And he said to me, Son of man, these are the men that devise iniquity and that give wicked counsel in this city." The men at the door of the gateway are the elders of a town (cf. Iob xxix). The *śarim* are the viceroys [1]), the caste of officials, who uphold the life of the city.

In Hos. x 6 is reported the carrying away into Assyria, as tribute, of the calf-idols. Israel shall be ashamed of his own counsel; the

---

[1]) Cf. Jes. xxxii 1, מלך and שׂרים ruling together.

powers that ensure the safety of the nation, the right decisions, the oracles, are lacking. There is a close relationship between the counsels and the divine decisions. The idleness of counselling in the Israelite manner of life becomes clear now that the idols are carried away. The use of the verb "to be ashamed" seems to me an indication that the contents of the verse, along with the manuscripts and versions, offer no arguments for emendation of the text, as suggested in many commentaries. [1])

King and counsellor are the upholders of normal life without calamities and desolation. "Now, why do you cry out aloud? Is there no king in you, is your counsellor perished, that pangs have taken hold of you as of a woman in travail?" (Mich. iv 9). The thoughts, the counsel of the Lord (Mich. iv 12), bring salvation to the people. The destructive intention of the nations is frustrated; they come as sheaves to the threshing-floor instead of as conquerors of Zion.

In Mich. vi 5 the prophet exclaims—"O my people, remember now what Balak king of Moab consulted — יעץ — and what Balaam the son of Beor answered him!". Balak's wish is to have a safe future. His country is threatened by the Israelites and therefore he let Balaam, an official counsellor, come to bring a decisive judgment against Israel.

Mich. vi 16 contains, besides the parallel "the works", the term "the statutes", parallel to counsel. Keeping of the statutes and the works of the house of Omri is similar to walking in the counsels of the Omrides. LXX reads here—except LXX A — ὁδός.

To purpose evil against the Lord is similar to giving bad counsel (Nah. i 11). Evil gain does not stand, according to Hab. ii 9 f. It is counsel that brings shame, i.e., an idle device.

Counsel of peace — עצת שלום — is the assurance of prosperity for a nation. Joshua ben Jehozadak "shall build the temple of the Lord and he shall bear the glory, and shall sit and rule upon his throne; and there shall be a priest upon his throne (or, by his throne) and the counsel of peace shall be between them both" (Sach. vi 13).

The Book of Psalms begins with the blessing of the wise man, "that walks not in the counsel of the wicked". The parallel expressions "to stand in the way of sinners" and "to sit in the seat of the scornful" show clearly that counsel means the execution of plans,

---

[1]) Cf. Hab. ii 10 and Ps. xiv 6, where we find the same expression, "counsel", connected with shame.

conduct, behaviour (Ps. i 1). The counsels of the evildoers are parallel to their transgressions (Ps. v 11) and may be the cause of their fall. The expression in Ps. xiii 3 — שית עצות בנפשי "to take counsel in my soul"—is unusual, but does not prove the meaning "sorrow" for עצה. Sir. xxx 21 uses the same expression. The meaning of עצה seems to be in this instance "deliberation", a weakened sense.

Ps. xiv 6 mentions the counsel of the poor in a context difficult to understand. [1]) Jhwh himself is the counsellor in Ps. xvi 7, sitting at the right hand of the Psalmist. Therefore he is safe, he will not be moved but will dwell secure (verses 8 and 9). The counsellor is at the right hand, i.e., is the active power of the person who follows his devices. The Lord can fulfil the counsel of man (Ps. xx 5); and he can break the counsel and thoughts of the nations (Ps. xxxiii 10). His counsel and thoughts stand fast for ever (xxxiii 11), and instruct the pious man (xxxii 8) and guide him to victory (lxxiii 24).

Enemies consult to overthrow the believer (Ps. lxii 5), they take counsel together, watching for his life, when his god seems to be far from him (Ps. lxxi 10f.). The term "to walk in their own counsels" is used in Ps. lxxxi 13, as in Jer. vii 24 and xviii 12 (with מחשבות), in parallel construction with "to go after the stubbornness of their heart".

To consult against a person is considered to be a cunning activity. "They take crafty counsel against thy people — על־עמך יערימו סוד — and consult together against those who took shelter with you", reads Ps. lxxxiii 4, proceeding with the remark "they consulted together with one consent" (verse 6).

The identity of counsel and work appears again in Ps. cvi 13— "They soon forgot his works, they did not wait for his counsel", and in verse 43—"they were rebellious in their counsel", parallel to "their iniquity". The words of God are his counsel, according to Ps. cvii 11. The pious man mentions Jhwh's precepts as his delight — שעשעי — his caress—(and) his counsellors (Ps. cxix 24). They are the security of his life.

Iob iii 14 brings kings and counsellors together, using their rank as a symbol of inviolability. El's greatness is illustrated in several instances. Amongst them he is described as a frustrator of the devices of the crafty (Iob v 12), bringing the counsel of the astute men to a quick end (verse 13). In ch. x 3 עצה means "the conduct", "be-

[1]) B. D. Eerdmans, "The Hebrew Book of Psalms", *OTS* iv (1947), p. 134, translates, "The counsel of the poor was: Ye will put to shame, because Jahu was his refuge."

haviour of man" (cf. Ps. i 1 and Iob xxi 16, xxii 18). Job admits that wisdom and might — חכמה וגבורה — are with God (xii 13). He has counsel and understanding — עצה ותבונה ; he has power to lead away counsellors, judges, kings, priests, elders, princes, and the chiefs of the people of the earth (verses 17-25). The strength of the wicked cannot help him, his steps are straitened and his counsel casts him down (Iob xviii 7). The counsel of the wicked (Iob xxi 16, xxii 18) is their conduct, avoided by the pious Job, but in no way a hindrance to their prosperity. Counsel and effectual action — תושיה — are found again together in Iob xxvi 3 — "How you have counselled him who has no wisdom, and plentifully declared effectual action!"

Job is a member of Eloah's court (Iob xxix 4). His seat was in the gateway, he was the first among the princes of the city. His counsel was waited for in silence (verse 21); and his word — דבר — was the decisive word; and nobody spoke after him (verse 22). His wise counsel was as the rain, the condition of life (verses 22 f.). In verse 25 we find a detailed description of the function of counsellor: "I chose their way, and sat as chief, and I dwelt like a king among his troops, like one who comforts, renews the life of mourners." The counsellor indicates the way of life for his people; he is their chief as judge, their general in war, their renovator of life.

Job's rebellious words are, in the ears of the Lord, a darkening of counsel, words without knowledge (xxxviii 2), an utterance repeated in ch. xlii 3.

Refusal of the call and the helping hand of the wise means ignoring his counsel (Prov. i 25, 30). "Therefore they shall eat the fruit of their own way, and be sated with their own counsels" (verse 31). Wisdom says "I have counsel and effectual action" — עצה ותושיה — "I have insight, strength" — בינה, גבורה (Prov. viii 14). Prov. xi 14, xv 22, xx 18, and xxiv 6 have a great similarity. Wise guidance — תחבלות — multitude of counsellors — רב יועץ — bring safety and victory in war. Fabricators of evil lack joy, a share of the counsellors of peace (Prov. xii 20). To take counsel brings wisdom (xiii 10, xii 15, xix 20). Wisdom means security of life in the future. The reciter of the proverbs knows that there is no wisdom nor understanding nor counsel—three equivalents—against the Lord, whose counsel stands (Prov. xxi 30, xix 21).

עצה is compared with deep water, i.e., water that does not run out during the rainless period (Prov. xx 5; and cf. xviii 4, where the words are compared with a fountain of wisdom). Similar to water as a symbol of life are ointment and perfume, parallel to hearty counsel (xxvii 9). The words of the wise (xxii 17) are sayings of counsel and knowledge (verse 20).

Daniel and his friends belong to the wise men of Babel — חכימי בבל (Dan. ii 12)—who are a caste in close contact with the royal court. Daniel returned answer with counsel and prudence — עטא וטעם — to Arioch the captain of the king's guard, who had gone forth to slay the wise men of Babylon (ii 14). Daniel's counsel comes from his god who possesses wisdom and strength (חכמתא וגבורתא, ii 20). Through the spirit of the holy gods he can give the true interpretation of Nebuchadnezzar's dream (iv 5). And his interpretation concludes with counsel — "let my counsel מלכי־ — be acceptable to you, break off your sins", etc. (iv 24). The counsel points to the salvation of the threatened king.

The queen-mother gives wise advice in Belshazzar's difficult situation (Dan. v 10-12). Daniel is called by several names, amongst them משרא קטרין, "he who unties knots, he who solves problems" (verse 12). In Dan. vi 8 we find a summary of the dignitaries of the court—"All the high officials — סרכין — of the kingdom; the governors — סגניא; the satraps — אחשדרפניא; the counsellors — הדבריא (cf. iii 24 f., iv 33) and the governors — פחותא, have consulted together — אתיעטו." The people of the land troubled the Jews while they were building and "hired counsellors against them to frustrate their purpose" (Esr. iv 5). The counsellor is, as in Balak's day, an official belonging to a caste, in possession of uncommon vigour. The Aramaic passage in Esr. vii concerning Ezra — כהנא ספר דתא די־אלהּ שמיא — presents in an official document the connection of the king and his counsellors—"For you are sent by the king and his seven counsellors", etc. (verses 14 f. — מלכא ושבעת יעטהי). The expression recurs in the Hebrew part (vii 28, viii 25)—"the king and his counsellors and all the king's mighty princes". Esr. x 3 offers the term "according to the counsel of my lord", parallel to "according to the law". In verse 8 we find a variant—"according to the counsel of the princes and the elders". Counsel and law are decisive prescriptions.

A weakened meaning of the term "counsel" is found in Neh. iv 9. God brought the counsel, plans, of the enemies to nought. "To meet together in order to plot against enemies" (Neh. vi 2, 10) is also expressed with "to take counsel together" (verse 7). Neh. v 7 is the only text that uses the verb מְלַךְ, which is the usual verb in Aramaic and Accadian.

The rulers of the Philistines sent David away before the battle against Saul upon advisement — בעצה — reports 1 Chron. xii 20. They must have taken counsel with a wise man who could predict coming events. 1 Chron. xiii 1 uses the verb "to take counsel with" in a weakened sense. David consulted with every leader. In 1 Chron. xxvii 32 f. we meet again the official counsellor: Jonathan, David's uncle (or, brother's son) was a counsellor, a man of understanding, and a scribe; and Ahitophel was the king's counsellor. Remarkable is the function of counsellor coupled with that of scribe at the court.

The text of 2 Chron. x 6-13, the story of Rehoboam's taking of counsel, does not present variants from the text in 1 Reg. xii. A weakened sense, to consult with the people, is found in 2 Chron. xx 21 (cf. 1 Chron. xiii 1; 2 Chron. xxx 2, 23). A special caste of counsellors is again mentioned in 2 Chron. xxxii 3, namely the princes and the mighty men; but this category is wider than the circle of wise men in older times. This exclusive group we find in 2 Chron. xxv 16 f.—"And it came to pass, as he talked with him, that he (the king Amaziah) said to him, 'Have we made you a royal counsellor? Stop! why should you be put to death'? Then the prophet stopped, but said, 'I know that God has determined to destroy you, because you have done this and have not listened to my counsel'. Then Amaziah king of Judah took counsel, and sent to Joash, the son of Jehoahaz, son of Jehu, king of Israel, saying, 'Come, let us look one another in the face' ". The prophet of the Lord appears to be a counsellor, bringing the oracle, the decision of the Lord. His conduct is regarded by the king as similar to the conduct of his official counsellors.

According to 2 Chron. xxii 3 the queen-mother is also one of the counsellors at the royal court. We meet her again in this rôle in the next paragraph dealing with the dignitaries.

At the conclusion of this survey of the terms used for "counsel", I draw attention to the rendering of the verb יעץ and its derivatives in the ancient versions.

We find in the LXX in most cases (συμ)βουλεύειν, βούλεσθαι; and βουλή, συμβουλία, διαβουλία, διαβούλιον, σύμβουλος (Jes. xl 13), and βουλευτής (Iob iii 14). "To take counsel", active, and "to determine", "resolve (to do)", passive; "counsel", "senate", and the corresponding words "resolution", βούλευμα; counsellor, βουλευτής, for instance, agrees exactly with the meaning of the expressions dealt with above.

In addition we meet the following renderings. In Jes. xli 28 ἀναγγέλλειν, the rendering of 19 Hebrew verbs, among them frequently הגיד "report" and הודיע "let know", (cf. Jes. xl 13 f., xlv 21, xlvi 10 f.). In 1 Reg. xii 6 we read παραγγέλλειν LXX AB, ἀπαγγέλλειν LXX R, which is a rendering of the Nif., "to take counsel". In Jes. xlv 21 γιγνώσκειν is a free rendering of the Nif. Prov. xiii 10 uses ἐπιγνώμων "arbiter, umpire, judge", which is an exact translation. In Ps. xvi (xv) 7 we find συνετίζειν "cause to understand", which is the rendering of הבין in Pss. cxix (cxviii) 27 and 34, and Neh. viii 7. συμβιβάζων, which is the causal of συμβαίνειν "to bring together", means "to put together, compare, teach", and is found in Jes. xl 13. מועצה is explained as a plot in Prov. i 31, ἀσέβεια "impiety, disloyalty". In Jer. vii 24 and iii 17 we find in the Greek mss. ἐνθύμημα "argument, device", and ἐπιθύμημα "object of desire". In Ps. lxxxi (lxxx) 13 ἐπιτήδευμα "custom, habit of life" is used. Underlining the idea that counsel and action are identical is the rendering in Mich. vi 16 — ὁδός — and in Iob xxi 16 — ἔργον. In Ps. xxxii (xxxi) 8 we find a text different from M.T., which reads ἐπιστηρίζειν "cause to rest on". In the same way Prov. xxvii 9b reads "the soul is torn by trouble" instead of M.T.'s "The sweetness of his friend from hearty counsel".

The usual rendering of יעץ in the Targumim is מְלַךְ, and יעט, יעץ. Once we find עוץ "to encourage, advise" (Num. xxiv 14, Tg Jer.). The usual rendering of עצה, if the same word is not used, is מלכא, once or twice תרעיתא (Prov. i 25, 30, etc.); once עטתא "counsel, order" (1 Chron. xii 20). יועץ is rendered by the participle of מְלַךְ, and of יעט once (Iob iii 14), and by מלוכא (2 Sam. xv 12); the other renderings are paraphrases. For מועצה we find too עצה or מִילַךְ.

Remarkable is the rendering חכימיהון "their wise men" in Jes. xix 3, instead of M.T.'s "Egypt's counsel". A paraphrase is "the plan (consideration) of his great knowledge" (Jes. xxviii 29). In the same way Jes. xl 13 reads—"to the righteous who perform his Memra has he made known the words of his will (pleasure)" — צדיקיא עבדי מימריה פתגמי רעותיה הודענון. The root רעי "to desire, take delight in" we meet too in the Syriac translation. Mich. vi 16 runs as follows —"and you walk in their precepts". איש עצתו (Jes. xlvi 11) has been explained as "the sons of Abraham my chosen one."

The verb יעץ is rendered by the root ܡܠܟ in the Peshiṭta.

A certain number of passages use the root ܪܢܐ (Jes xiv 24, xix 17, xxiii 9, etc.). Once we find ܡܠܟ (Etpe.; 2 Chron. xxx 23).

For עצה we find frequently ܬܪܥܝܬܐ "opinion, device", also ܡܠܟܐ; ܡܣܥܒܬܐ (Jes. xlvii 13; Iob xxi 16); ܡܘܠܟܢܐ "promise, advice" (Iob xxiv 21; Neh. iv 9). יועץ is rendered by ܡܠܟܐ or ܡܠܘܟܐ.

Remarkable are the following passages: Ps. i 1, where עצה is replaced by ܐܘܪܚܐ "the way"; Ps. xiii 3, where "How long shall I take counsel in my soul" is replaced by "How long put you sorrow in my soul?", an alteration influenced by the context; Iob iii 14, where the counsellors of the earth are interpreted as "rulers of the earth", a reading caused by the preceding word "kings". In Esr. vii 15 the sentence "the king and his counsellors" is replaced by a sentence in the "I" style, to conform to the context "(the silver and gold which) I, according to the will of my pleasure, bring". Remarkable too is the reading "and he stood in the midst of the people and said" instead of M.T.'s "he had taken counsel with the people" (2 Chron. xx 21). Moreover there are some free renderings which can be left out here.

(ii)

The preceding survey of the passages wherein "counsel" and "to give, take, counsel" occur enables us to determine some characteristics of the term. In the first place we notice a close connection with wisdom and understanding, a close relationship too between the counsellor and the wise. Secondly, it appears that the action of counselling points to the maintenance or the restoration of life. Security, victory, recovery, salvation are the effects aimed at by counsel. Thirdly, counsel is a decision which determines the future. It may be considered as a synonym for an oracle, the word of the prophet or of the priest. Only in a few late passages does the weakened meaning "device, plan" occur. True counsel, however, is never mere guess-work based on a calculation, nor an idea dependent on sentiments of one or more persons involved. It is a decision in a difficult situation given by an authorized person, and is meant to be followed ("done") on penalty of disaster or death. A fourth characteristic of our term is the identity of counsel and action [1]). In

[1]) This characteristic is excellently described by PEDERSEN, *op. cit.* I, p. 128 ff. The carrying into effect he denominates as the normal expansion of the counsel, an expression of the character of the soul. The counsellor is the strong man, whose counsel "is not only something which he gives to the others; it is his will, determining the unity, to which he himself and the others belong".

the fifth place the passages surveyed lead to the conclusion that the counsellors form a special caste. Besides prophets and priests they are called princes, or persons belonging to the same rank as the prince, scribe, judge, servant, messenger, prognosticator, viceroy, queen-mother. All of them are attached to the king's household or concerned with the government.

Besides the passages mentioned so far, attention must be paid to some other Biblical data in order to amplify our insight into the character of the counsellor, his position and his personality.

Joseph, the interpreter of Pharaoh's dream, is set over all the land of Egypt. Pharaoh said to him (Gen. xli 39 f.) — "Since God let you know all this, there is none so discreet and wise as you are; you shall be over my house, and all my people shall kiss (do homage?) according to your word; only as regards the throne will I be greater than you." [1]) Joseph became viceroy of Egypt. He received Pharaoh's signet ring (verse 42) and as Bearer of the Seal he decided the life and death of the king's subjects. Without his consent no man could lift up a hand or a foot in all the land of Egypt.

In Joseph's words to his brothers (Gen. xlv 8) he describes his position with the following titles—"God has made me a father — אב — to Pharaoh, and lord of all his house and ruler over all the land of Egypt." Joseph, counsellor of Pharaoh in the crucial situation of an unexplained dream, is at the same time the one who carries out his counsel. He saves the country through his wisdom. In his action he is a "father to Pharaoh", i.e., the counsellor of the king. His counsel is a decision that secures Egypt against death.

In Egyptian the title "father of Pharaoh" is hitherto unknown. "Father of god" (*it nṯr*) occurs as a title of the priest. In Hebrew we find אב as a title of the priest in Jud. xvii 10 and xviii 19—"to be unto me (us) a father and a priest". As appears from the context, he is the official who guarantees the life of a family and of a clan by holding the office of sacrificer. The title אב is also used of a prophet. In 2 Reg. vi 21 it is used by the king when addressing Elisha, the man of God, who "tells the king of Israel the words that you (the king of

---

[1]) The reading *ʾagdol min* "greater than", (cf. Arab. *ʾakbar min*, an *ʾafʿalu* form which has the meaning of our comparative and superlative) finds no support in Hebrew except in three adjectives, see W. WRIGHT, *Arab. Gramm.*, 3rd ed., p. 141 A; H. BAUER und P. LEANDER, *Histor. Gramm.*, p. 487. "Only the Throne (= the king himself) is greater than you" would be a fitting translation, and less forced than the reading of M.T. and the ancient versions (accusative of measure).

Syria) speak in your bedchamber" (verse 12). In 2 Reg. xiii 14 when Joash, king of Israel, exclaims at Elisha's death-bed—"My father, my father! The chariots of Israel and its horsemen!" — it is a recognition of Elisha's merits as divine counsellor of Israel, the proper strength of the people. Elisha gives the decisions in the complicated situations of the state, and is honoured by the king as "his father", the strong man who determines the future of the nation. The same expression occurs in the scene of Elijah's disappearance in the thunderstorm (2 Reg. ii 12).

The Targumim use the term "father to the king" — **אבא למלכא** — in Gen. xli 43 as a rendering of the unexplained expression **אברךְ**, with an addition in TgJon." great in wisdom and tender in years" — **(יחי אבוי דמלכא) דרב בחוכמא ורכיךְ בשנייא ; רב בחכמתא ורכיךְ בשנייא** (Jeruš.).

Haman bears the title too (LXX Esth. iii 13) ... ὑπο Αμαν τοῦ τεταγμένου ἐπὶ τῶν πραγμάτων καὶ δευτέρου πατρὸς ἡμῶν .... It is evident that we must interpret the word "father" here as a title without any physical connotation. The same holds for the title in Jes. ix 5. "Father" means in these texts he who makes decisions, the counsellor. In Jes. ix 5 I propose to explain the title **אבי־עד** as "counsellor about the future", who determines coming events, who is master of the future, and therefore wholly sure of his ground and of his fortune. In Jes. xlvii 7 I translate too **גברת עד** "ruler over the future", sure of her position while she possesses the strength to determine coming events. The idea of continuation through domination of the future is, in my opinion, the right sense of **עד**. The usual translation "eternal", "(for) ever", seems to me less exact. The same idea is present in the father-title used for the Lord. The father of Israel is his saviour and redeemer, the god who determines Israel's lot, the work of his hand (Jes. lxiii, lxiv, etc.).

Iob xvii 13 ff. presents the same idea—"If I look for Sheol as my house, if I have spread my couch in the darkness, if I have said to the pit, You are my father, and to the worm, (You are) my mother, or my sister [1]), where then is my trust?" "Father", "mother", and "sister" are here titles of the dispenser of the future. Job's words mean—my confidence is gone if I expect death as my near future.

אם as a title will be treated in the following passage. The name "sister", like the titles "father" and "mother", is no more than an

---

[1]) "My sister" means "my beloved, my bride"; cf. Prov. vii 4.

indication of something familiar. In Prov. vii 4 wisdom is called "sister", i.e., loved one, bride elect (cf. Cant., *passim*, and Sir. xv 2—"She (wisdom) will meet him as a *mother*, and as a *youthful wife* will she receive him."). The loved one determines the life of the young man who is dependent on her.

Deborah is a mother in Israel — אם בישראל (Jud. v 7). There is nothing of a motherly character in the picture of Deborah. In her song she is the strong woman who utters a war-song, and she behaves like a bellicose leader of the united tribes. In Jud. iv 4-10, 14 she is described as a prophetess judging the people—"She used to sit under the palm of Deborah between Ramah and Bethel in the hill country of Ephraim; and the people of Israel came up to her for judgment" (verse 5). She instructed Barak to march against Sisera in Jhwh's name (verse 6). She went with Barak and determined for him the moment to attack the enemy (verses 9, 14).

To call the title "a mother in Israel" a name of honour is, in my opinion, without convincing evidence. The context leads to the interpretation—one who determines the future as a counsellor. In complicated situations one goes to the judge, and she proves to be a strong woman able to give the right decisions. Her presence in decisive moments is a necessity to Barak, the general. He depends on her word, which is a decision having the strength of an oracle, announcing the military operations to be carried out. "Mother in Israel" means counsellor of the people.

I find a similar meaning for אם in the expression אם הדרך in Ezech. xxi 26. The usual translation of this term is "the parting of the way", starting point for roads, cross-road. This rendering is due to the idea "descent", read into the word "mother", and by the phrase following our term—"the head of the two ways" — ראש שני הדרכים. This second term is commonly considered to be a double reading. The ancient versions point to the same sense. LXX reads — διότι στησέται βασιλεὺς βαβυλῶνος ἐπὶ τὴν ἀρχαίαν ὁδόν, ἐπ' ἀρχῆς τῶν δύο ὁδῶν, κ.τ.λ. Tg. reads — ארי קם מלכא דבבל על אם פרשות אורח בריש תרתן אורחן פרשות אורח "cross-road". Pesh. reads—"For the king of Babel arrived at the beginning of the way that is the parting of the ways". The verb עמד אל is exactly rendered in Pesh.

The translation of M.T. runs as follows—"For the king of Babel shall step up to (cf. 1 Sam. xvii 51) the "mother of the way" at the beginning of the two ways to practice divination — קסם קסם; he shall shake the arrows, he shall consult the teraphim, he shall look at the liver." The term "mother of the way" is the continuation of the expression in verse 24—"make a "hand", make it at the beginning of the way to a city". A "hand" — יד — means a signpost, a column. Coming to a cross-road one consults the stone erected at this spot. A cross-road is a place of uncertainty. One takes counsel to get certainty and security as to whether he is taking the right way, the way of success or not. Therefore the "hand", the "mother of the (right) way", advises the traveller. The "mother of the way" is the counsellor who determines the future of the traveller. To go astray means to be lost.

A "hand", a "mother of the way", is by no means the modern signpost of our western roads. Even today marks showing the way in isolated parts of the Near East with their lonely tracks and pistes are things whose use requires experience, knowledge, and often good luck! The Babylonian king, being fully alive to the importance of the right choice, uses divination, he consults the "mother of the way", he takes counsel.

The story of the wise woman of Abel (2 Sam. xx 14-23) supports the proposed meaning of the title "a mother in Israel". She called from the city to Joab and said (verse 18 f.)—"They were wont to say in old time, 'Let them but ask counsel at Abel' — שׁאל ישאלו באבל — and so they settled a matter. I am of them that are peaceable, faithful in Israel; you seek to destroy a city and (which is a) "mother in Israel" — להמית עיר ואם בישׂראל; why will you swallow up the heritage of the Lord?" The verb המית is considered to be unsuitable in reference to a city, hence the suggestion to read השׁחית. The verb המית finds a remarkable explanation in the Midrash. Berešit rabba xciv 9, quoting our passage, understood "the mother in Israel" as a person, viz., the wise woman herself. However, the title is used here for the city. The usual explanation, an important and venerable city with dependent villages, a mother and her daughters, with reference to the expression בנות עיר [1]), does not hit the mark in my opinion. The context shows the probable meaning of the title. Abel is a city of counsel, a famous oracle-place in Israel. Hence its title, "a mother", a counsellor in Israel.

A recollection of the rôle of the queen-mother, (2 Chron. xxii 3) at the court of the kings of Israel—cf. the repeatedly used expression "the name of his mother was so and so"—is in place here. אם המלך,

1) אם occurs too on coins, *metropolis*. See G. A. Cooke, *A Text-book of North-Semitic Inscriptions*, Oxford, 1903, p. 350.

the mother of the king, is treated with honour. She sits on the right hand of the king and her demands are not refused (1 Reg. ii 19 ff.). She is able to be an intermediary, an intercessor who can appeal to the king because she is versed in royal matters as nobody else. In the Midrash, the queen-mother Bathsheba's help is even called in to reprove the king who is neglecting his religious duties (Bemidbar rabba x 4).

The queen too possessed high rank at the court as appears from the title גבירה, mother of the crown-prince (cf. 1 Reg. xv 13; 2 Reg. x 13, etc.). Interesting is the frequent connection of strength and counsel, mentioned above, and the connection of strength and wisdom. The queen — גברת עד — ruler over the future—gives advice in difficult situations and her counsel is acted upon. Queen Jezebel, Ahab's wife, solves the king's crisis in the vineyard affair (1 Reg. xxi 5 ff.). She wrote letters in Ahab's name and sealed them with his seal, and the elders of Naboth's city whom she addressed obeyed her immediately, and sent to Jezebel the news of the performance of her command. They knew therefore that the letters with the royal seal came from the queen. Jezebel was consequently the bearer of the royal seal, just like Joseph at Pharaoh's court.

Queens and princesses at the royal court are often foreigners, being gifts from the kings of neighbouring states. Royal marriages are both diplomatic and economic matters. A foreign princess brings with her a royal household, and it is not a bold guess to look for learned men in these circles, scribes who could maintain relations with foreign countries. A scribe is a counsellor (cf. 1 Chron. xxvii 32). Ps. xlv is a song of such a scribe, glorifying with flattering words the king as bridegroom of the (his?) princess from afar.

The wise and the scribe are identical in Jer. viii 8. The scribe is one of the *śarim*. In Jer. xxxvi 10 ff., he has a chamber at the court where the scrolls are kept. The scribe is the dignitary who reads written messages to the king. He is at the same time the translator of written tidings. It is a legal use of the title when the Targumim use the Aramaic *safrā* to translate *nabī'* "prophet" (1 Sam. xix 20; Jes. iii 2, ix 14, etc.). His explanation brings insight into questions which are obscure without his learned intercession [1]). The wise scribe is the man of good counsel [2]).

---

[1]) Cf. the present writer's "De godsdienst van het Jodendom", in *Het oudste Christendom en de Antieke Cultuur*, Haarlem, 1951, p. 484 ff.

[2]) Thus in the Words of Aḥiqar (see below).

The counsellor, a dignitary of the royal court, or at any rate associated with the leaders of the tribe or the nation, is considered as one who knows commonly hidden, occult matters which are decisive for the future.

(iii)

We met the words **אב** and **אם** in a non-physical sense. In extra-Biblical texts a similar use is found. Making no claim to completeness I refer in the following pages to extra-Biblical material which seems to be of some importance to our subject. Besides the titles "father" and "mother", attention will be paid to the other data concerning counsel and counsellor.

The rendering of the Tg. of Gen. xli 43 — **אברךְ** "father in wisdom though tender in years" — we find too in Berešit rabba xc. All marks of honour ascribed to Joseph are described as suitable because Joseph did not sin. "The plan which is not entertaining impure thoughts comes and is called wisdom" — **מחשבה שלא הירהרה אחר עבירה תבוא ותיקרא חכמה**. **מחשבה** is frequently a synonym for **עצה** "counsel", and is here in reference to Joseph, the "father in wisdom", the "father to Pharaoh", who is "like Pharaoh himself" (Gen. xliv 18). Joseph is called "father", which is explained as "the king's protector", and "lord", i.e., "master", and "ruler", i.e., "governor", according to the same passage in Ber.r.

In Wayikra' rabba i 3 we find the title used for Moses. Starting from 1 Chron. iv 18, Moses is called "father of the prophets who see by means of the Holy Spirit", and "father of those who caused Israel to relinquish idolatry". Moses is "father of wisdom", explained as "main teacher" by Levy [1]), who records as well the titles of Johanan ben Zakkai (j. Ned. v 39b) — **אב לחכמה ואב לדורות** "father of wisdom and father (i.e., teacher, ruler) of the future generation". Moses is in Way. r. i 3 too "the scribe of Israel", a judgment based on 1 Chron. xxiv 6.

The Sages are called the "fathers of the world" in Ber. r. i 15. Moreover, this title is used for scholars, and for the president of the court of justice. In exegetical terminology "father" means a text with authority over other texts, a text with the original meaning which determines the sense of other passages. Besides **אב** we find here **בית אב** and **בנין אב** with the same meaning.

---

[1]) J. Levy, *Wörterbuch über die Talmudim und Midraschim*, 2nd. ed., 1924, *s.v.* **אב**.

Evidently the word "father" means in these passages "he who is master over", "he who brings decisions". I suppose that the Ugaritic titles of 'Il, "father of Šnm" (2 Aqht vi 49, etc.), and "father of man" (Krt i 37, etc.), have the same meaning. The title or epithet "father of Šnm" is used after the title "King".

> "She ('Anat) enters the *abode* of 'Il
> [Comes into the *do*]*micile* of the King, Father of Šnm."
> (2 Aqht vi 48 f. [1]))
>
> "Ye he (Krt) *slumbers*.
> And in his dream 'Il descends,
> In his vision the Father of Man
> And he draws near while asking Krt:
> 'Who is Krt that he should weep,
> The Good One, Lad of 'Il, that he should shed tears?
> Does he wish the kingship of Tôr, his father?
> Or sovereignty, *li*[*ke the Fa*]*ther of M*[*an*]?" (Krt i 35 ff.[1]))

After this follows the counsel given by 'Il, the father of man, concerning Krt's military operations against king Pbl.

The idea in the foreground is not that of progenitor, but rather that of governor, ruler over life and death. The determination of the (near) future is a quality of the deity.

In 1 Macc. ii 65, in Mattathias' last words, Simeon is called "a man of counsel" ἀνὴρ βουλῆς; "give ear to him always, he shall be a "father" to you" αὐτοῦ ἀκούετε πάσας τὰς ἡμέρας, αὐτὸς ὑμῖν ἔσται εἰς πατέρα. After this Judas Maccabaeus is commissioned by Mattathias as the captain who shall fight the battle of the people. Simeon, the counsellor, is the "father", he who determines what shall be done in the near future. The "father" is other than the king or general. The king is the one who carries out the counsel given by the man who is associated with the government.

We meet in 1 Macc. xi 33 a similar use of the word "father". Here, as in Josephus (Ant. XII, iii 4 [2])), the king uses the title "father" for his helper.

The midrash on the wise woman of Abel (Ber. r. xciv 9) I have already discussed when I dealt with the expression "a mother in Israel". In Way. r. i 10 and in Bemidbar r. x 4 אם is explained as *torah*. My mother's house means Sinai, the chamber of my teaching

---

[1]) Translation of C. H. GORDON, *Ugaritic Literature*, Roma, 1949.

[2]) Cf. W. O. E. OESTERLEY in R. H. CHARLES, *Apocrypha*, Oxford, 1913, p. 108, n. 31. Interesting is J. FÜRST's note in A. WÜNSCHE's translation of Ber. r., 1881, p. 551, on Julius Capitolinus.

means the Tent of Meeting, for from there Israel is commanded by the teaching, the Law. "His mother" alludes to the Law which corrected Solomon and which is called the mother of those who study it, as you read, "If you call understanding: mother". (An alteration of the vowel in Prov. ii 3, *'em* instead of *'im*).

A woman is loud in the king's praise when he returns after having gained a victory (Debarim rabba vi 12). She receives the title "mother of the senate".

The exegetical phrase יש אם למקרא (Sanh. 4b, Sukk. 6 b, and frequently) means "there is authority for reading", "there is a traditional ground for reading", etc. Here we find the idea "origin", "descent", combined with the idea "weight", "authority which decides".

The mother of the king is an important lady at the royal court according to several letters from Assyria [1]. *ummi šarri beli-ia* "the mother of the king, my lord" received official letters from servants of the state about the official sacrifices and military operations. She must have occupied an important place among the officials of the court — the crown-prince, the secretary of the land, the gardener, the minister, the general, the palace overseer, the secretary of the palace (all officials to whom letters are addressed).

"And God said, Let us make man" (Gen. i 26). For obvious reasons there is more than one interpretation of the plural in this verse. Ber. r. viii 3 records the sayings of several rabbis. "With whom did he take counsel — נמלך? R. Joshua b. Levi said, He took counsel with the works of heaven and earth, like a king who had two advisers [2] without whose consent — דעת — he did nothing. R. Samuel b. Naḥman said, He took counsel with the works of each day, like a king who had an associate [3] without whose consent he did nothing. R. Ammi said, He took counsel with his own heart, like a king who had a palace built by an architect. He saw it but it did not please him. With whom else is he to be indignant but the architect? As is said, "And it grieved him at his heart" (Gen. vi 6)."When the Lord came to create Adam he took counsel with the ministering angels, said R. Aḥa", according to Ber. r. xvii 4.

A third record of counselling is found in Ber. r. xlix 2, an expla-

---

[1]) The Harper-letters. Cf. L. Waterman, *Royal Correspondence of the Assyrian Empire*, 4 vols.; R. H. Pfeiffer, *State Letters of Assyria*, New Haven, 1935. In this connection the position of Nakiya, Sennacherib's wife and Esarhaddon's mother, may be noted.

[2]) סינקליטין, plur. of סינקליטוס, σύγκλητος 'counsellor'.

[3]) סונקתידרין, plur. of סונקתדרוס, συγκάθεδρος 'associate'.

nation of Gen. xviii 17. After a quotation of Ps. xxv 14—"The secret—סוד "secret" or "counsel"—of the Lord is with them that fear him and he makes them know his covenant", is stated—"The Lord consulted [1]) Abraham as righteous — ישר — and a prophet — נביא — who fears god — ירא אלהים". Abraham is initiated into the plans of the Lord with his people. The rabbis said, "He has already called him their father, as it says, For the father of a multitude of nations have I made you (Gen. xvii 5): 'does one judge the son without the father's consent?'"

In the El-Amarna letters we meet both the title "father" and "mother", and "queen-mother". The letters of Rib-Adda of Byblos to Pharaoh's courtier Amanappa contain the title *a-bi-ia* "my father" for the servant of the king[2]). Amanappa is both courtier, who is asked to intermediate with the Pharaoh (*lines* 7 f., 43), and general who has been in Ṣumura and therefore knows the circumstances (*lines* 39 ff.). The king is called *a-bu u be-lu* "father and lord" (*line* 36).

In a letter to Rib-Adda (EA Nr. 96) he is called the son of the scribe, a high official of Egypt's court (*lines* 1-4). In Aziri's letters to Dudu (Nrs. 158 and 164) we find the titles *bêli-ia a-bi-ia* "my lord, my father" used by the servant Aziri. Dudu is a high Egyptian official. Both the Pharaoh and his official bear the title *bêli-ia* "my lord".

Dudu is described as sitting before the king (EA Nr. 158, *lines* 20 f.). Aziri is submissive to Dudu as if the latter were the king himself [3]). Every wish expressed to his servant will be realized (*lines* 11 ff., 15 ff.). "Behold, you are my father and my lord and I am your son" (*lines* 14 f.). Aziri asks Dudu to intermediate for him if there are accusers. They must be turned away. A similar attitude we find in letter Nr. 164.

The queen-mother Teie, mistress of Egypt—*bêlit* $^{m\hat{a}tu}$*mi-iṣ-ri-i*—ranked first among the courtiers of the Pharaoh. Tušratta, king of Mitanni, writes to her in humbleness (Nr. 26). He knows that she has great influence with the king (*lines* 49 ff.). In Nr. 28 (*lines* 42 f.), Tušratta uses her name and knowledge as an argument in his letter to Amenophis. The same in Nr. 29 (*lines* 7 ff., 45 ff., 66 ff., 123 f., 143 f.)—five times in one letter! [4])

---

[1]) היה סוד ל.

[2]) J. A. Knudtzon, *Die El-Amarna-Tafeln*, Leipzig, 1915, Nr. 73. Cf. Nrs. 77, 82, 86, 87, 93. On the name and identity of this Egyptian official, see W. F. Albright, *JNES* 5 (1946), p. 9 and references there given.

[3]) Cf., e.g., *lines* 15 f. "The countries of Amurri are yours and my house is your house, and all that you desire, write!"

[4]) On the position of Teie see O. Weber in Knudtzon, *op. cit.*, p. 1058 ff.

The scribe of the Pharaoh, addressed in letters from Jerusalem's king Abdiḫiba (Nrs. 287, 288, 289), is treated with humble and flattering words. He could read the letter for the king with beautiful words and herewith influence the king's mood.

Aḥiqar is a wise and ready scribe (*line* 2), an old man, a skilful scribe (*line* 35). At the same time he is called "the wise scribe, counsellor of all Assyria" (*line* 12), "the skilful scribe, giver of good counsel" (*line* 42), "by whose counsel and words — עטתה ומלוהי — all Assyria was (guided)" (*line* 43), the seal bearer of the king (*line* 3). He is called too "a father — אבוה — of all Assyria by whose counsel king Sennacherib and (all) the army of Assyria were (guided)" (*lines* 55 f.). Aḥiqar's person and his position show several characteristic traits of the counsellor which we met in the Biblical and extra-Biblical texts. He is a learned man and wise; his words determine the victory of the Assyrian army; he has an official standing at the court; the king desires and needs his counsel [1]).

A close connection between counsel and wisdom can be observed in the Zadokite fragments too. "God loves knowledge, wisdom and counsel he placed before him, deliberation and knowledge, they minister to him" — (effectual action, counsel) אל אהב דעת חכמה ותושיה הציב לפניו ערמה ודעת הם ישרתוהו (ii 3 f.). "And their children in Egypt walked in the stubbornness of their heart — בשרירות לבם — to take counsel against — להיעץ על — the commandments of God" (iii 5 f.). "For it is a people of no understanding — בינות. They are a nation void of counsel — אבד עצות — because there is no understanding in them" (v 16 f.).

A counsellor possesses insight into things unknown to men in general. His wisdom stems from knowledge of circumstances in foreign countries and from a capacity to have intercourse with a foreign world by reading and writing the language of that world. His counsel is considered as guidance for king and people in matters of life and death. His position is therefore among the high officials,

---

On the independent position of the queen in the Hittite monarchy, cf. too O. R. Gurney, *The Hittites*, 1952, p. 66 f. The votive-stèles, *CIS* 3971, 3946 and 3947, mention votives to the king and his mother. It remains, however, uncertain whether we have here, and in EA Nrs. 26, 28, 29, an example of an official influential position of the queen-mother, or a casual situation, caused by the incapacity of the king.

1) H. L. Ginsberg, in J. B. Pritchard, *ANET*, p. 427, remarks that Aḥiqar may be a reflex of Adadsumuṣur, a priest who officiated in the reigns of Sennacherib and Esarhaddon and exerted a certain amount of influence over them.

and his relation to the prophets and the sacrificers is frequently brought out. It is not to be wondered at that we find a counterpart in the divine world.

The Sumerian title $AD.GI_4.GI_4$ means "counsellor" and is used as a title of a deity. In a text on the absorption of Isin's goddess into Nippur's religious system we read [1])—"Nin-Isina, vornehmste Tochter des reinen An (the high god Anu), geehrteste der Fürstinnen, grosse Schwiegertochter des Herrn Nunamnir, welche die göttliche Ordnung von Ekur vollkommen macht, Ratgeberin der grossen Mutter Ninlil, die *das Wort* ihres Herzens . . ."

In an anthology of Sumerian and Accadian Hymns and Prayers [2]), FALKENSTEIN and VON SODEN have translated texts with many interesting passages about scribes and wisdom. I copy here a single instance [3]):

> "Die grosse Weisheit, die dir die Tafeln der Nisaba gegeben,
> möge im 'Tafelhaus' auf dem Ton nie ein Ende finden,
> möge in diesem 'Tafelhaus' wie ein Heiligtum, das alles erschaft, nie . . . .
> Dem 'Kleinschreiber', der sich (dem Wissen) widmet, es auf die Tafel schreibt,
> möge Nisaba, die strahlende Herrin, Klugheit (verleihen),
> ihm die Hand *führen*,
> ihn an der Stätte der Schreibkunst wie die Sonne strahlen lassen!"

Many gods have an epithet consisting of a sentence with *malâku* "to give counsel"; *maliku*, "counsellor"; *milku*, "counsel"—$AD.GI_4.GI_4$ —or with *dayānu* "judge"—$AD.GI_1.GI_1$ [4]). Thus Enlil and Nusku—*ma-lik mil-ki ša ilani rabūti*, "who decides amongst the great gods"; Adad and Šamaš — *day-yān kibrāti*, "who is judge and dispenser of fortune"; Ištar *mâlikatu*, "counsellor", etc.

(iv)

"Wisdom is from the gods, even to gods she is precious—in heaven she is established, because the lord of the gods (the holy ones)

---

[1]) *Textes religieux sumériens du Louvre II*, Paris, 1950, Nr. 60. Translation of F. R. KRAUS in *Journ. of Cuneif. Stud.*, iii, p. 77 f.

[2]) *Sumerische und Akkadische Hymnen und Gebete*, eingeleitet und übertragen von A. FALKENSTEIN und W. VON SODEN, Zürich/Stuttgart, 1953.

[3]) Hymne auf Iddindagan von Isin, *ibid.*, l. 64 ff., p. 122.

[4]) Cf. K. TALLQVIST, *Akkadische Götterepitheta*, Helsinki, 1938, and J. J. STAMM, *Die akkadische Namengebung*, Leipzig, 1939. AD means "father" and GI_4 probably "answer" (שוב)—"Father of the right answer"?

has exalted her" [1]). Wisdom, knowledge of the future and power to determine coming events, has its origin in the divine world.

The counsellor has an official standing in general life. The wise are men and women with a strong soul, judges in public and private affairs, seal-bearers at the royal court, scribes and diplomats, "father" or "mother" to the people dependent on their words. Their counsel is wisdom, and to take counsel and follow the words of the counsellor is practical wisdom for men whose life and future need protection and guarantee from day to day.

It seems to me worthwhile to read Job's poem on wisdom (ch. xxviii) and the picture of divine wisdom in Proverbs (ch. viii 22-31) in the light of the counsellor's standing in general life.

Job (xxviii).

Silver, gold, iron and copper are precious things in life. Their preciousness is linked with their rarity and with the ingenuity needed to acquire them. But their source is known. Counsel is even more precious. Man cannot make his right choice at the many cross-roads of life without counsel. There are ways to get possession of precious minerals, but from where does counsel come? It is an essential thing in life, and its reality can be put on record gratefully, but no man has control over it. Even the wise man Job, counsellor *par excellence* in his city (xxix), has no possession of counsel in the ill-fated days of his life.

From where does counsel come? The poem in ch. xxviii puts into words in a fine and penetrating way counsel's divinity. Its place and order are fundamentally distinct from man's knowledge, transcending his apprehensive faculty. Only Elohim knows counsel's way and place.

The superhuman character is indicated by *irrealia*. The marks of divine counsel are, humanly speaking, the most invisible act, *giving the wind its weight* — לעשׂות לרוח משקל (verse 25a); the largest immeasurableness, *meting out the waters by measure* — ומים תכן במדה (verse 25b); the most unfixable thing, *making a decree for the rain* — בעשתו למטר חק (verse 26a); the greatest unsearchableness, *making a way for the lightning of the thunder* — דרךְ לחזיז קלות (verse 26b). These impossibilities for man are the very marks of divine counsel. Only Elohim can comprehend them. "He saw it" — ראהּ (verse 27a), "and enumerated it" — ויספרהּ (verse 27b); "he established it" —

[1]) Aḥiqar, *lines* 94 f.

הכינה (verse 27c), "and searched it out too" — וגם־חקרה (verse 27d).

More plainly and clearly counsel's divinity cannot be put into words. Counsel, the action that determines man's future, belongs to the world of God. As the heavens are higher than the earth, so are God's ways higher than man's ways, and his thoughts than man's thoughts (Jes. lv 9). The divine world remains fundamentally unsearchable to man. Man is dependent on the divine counsel whose origin is beyond his control.

The poet becomes a counsellor himself in his conclusion "Man can do nothing else but observe the statutes of his God, of Jhwh" (verse 28). Man's wisdom is to lay his hand on his mouth (Iob xl 4), and to follow counsels given by the wise whose words are similar to oracles.

Proverbs (*viii* 22-31).

"Wisdom is better than jewels" it is said in the preceding passage (Prov. viii 11). She has counsel and effectual action — עצה ותושיה (verse 14), i.e., she is a counsellor. The text continues—"I am understanding" — אני בינה. Just as Job's counsel as a precious thing is considered to be a divine affair, so is wisdom here pictured as a counsellor belonging to the world of God.

Jhwh acquires her at the beginning of his way, in his activities as creator of heaven and earth. "Acquire" — קנה — is preferable to "create", in view of the following verses. They state that her origin lies far back in time before any of Jhwh's acts (verses 23-26). Moreover, קנה is the usual term for "to acquire wisdom, understanding" (Prov. iv 5, etc.). The counsellor exists before Jhwh as the queen-mother at the royal court precedes her son, the king.

When Jhwh established heaven and earth by fixing limits to the waters, she was present שם אני (verse 27). Her presence can be nothing else but giving counsel to Jhwh in his great acts.

Her vitality is described in verses 30 f. She is the object of Jhwh's attention, caress. שעשועים means the object treated with great care in order to get profit from it. Jhwh takes counsel from day to day, and is quite taken up with the carrying out of it. Her counsel is a delight to him, it plays before him. שחק and צחק often denote play or dance with a sexual sense (cf. Gen. xxvi 8; xxxix 14, 17); and apart from this, laughing indicates vitality. Jhwh's counsellor is laughing before him. In other words, the counsel given to him is his delight and life-giving to his acts. She makes a toy of — מְשַׂחֶקֶת בְּ — the earth; her delight is with its inhabitants, the effect of her counsel when carried out. Her vitality, the vital strength of her counsel, manifests itself in mankind. Jhwh's acts are successful, the counsel received appears to be life-giving.

The first part of verse 30 is very troublesome. Jhwh's counsellor beside him is called אמון, a word which has been translated in many different ways [1]). Both the context, shortly rendered above, and the idea of the counsellor at the king's court, lead me to suggest that the term אמון has to do with אם "mother" as a title of the counsellor. The reading אִמּוֹן *'immon*, consists of *'imm* with the suffix *-ân*>*-ôn* [2]), and can mean (*a*) "mother-official", a descriptive term for the function of counsellor, or (*b*) "little mother", a diminutive [3]) like אישון "little man (pupil)", שמעון, a *hypokorisma* of Šemaja, etc. A *hypokorisma* "little mother" fits as well as the descriptive term "the function 'mother' " in our passage.

Human life is dependent on the favour of God's world. Among the leading personalities of human life we meet the counsellor. His words bring a decision in precarious situations. Man's existence is surrounded by visible and invisible dangers. To take counsel is a vital question. Particularly the chief, the king, needs counsellors at his court.

On the supposition that the world of God is a counterpart of human life, the poems of Job (xxviii) and Proverbs (viii) picture divine counsel and a divine counsellor. It may be true that their thoughts are influenced by the mythology of neighbouring peoples. But the main idea of their presentation is the figure of the counsellor and the significance of his and her word. And this idea is known in Israel as well as in its environs.

I wonder whether one can uphold theories on hypostatization and even on personification. Wisdom has been, for the period over which we have information, similar to the word of the prophet,

---

1) "Workmaster", "little child", "nursling", etc. Cf. RINGGREN's treatment of the arguments advanced on behalf of the suggested readings. Cf. too T. H. GASTER's note in *VT* iv (1954), p. 77—"one of those court 'experts' (Bab. *ummanu*) whose function it was at once to advise and to entertain Oriental monarchs."

2) BAUER und LEANDER, *op. cit.*, p. 500.

3) J. BARTH, *Die Nominalbildung in den Semitischen Sprachen*, Leipzig, 1894, p. 348 ff.; BAUER und LEANDER, *op. cit.*, *loc. cit.*

the oracle of the priest. A wise word, counsel, implies a counsellor, just as prophecy implies a prophet. Wisdom in Job (xxviii) is pictured as divine counsel, and hence every true counsellor is a figure with religious authority. Wisdom in Proverbs (viii) is Jhwh's counsellor denominated with her action, counsel, the wise word which is life-giving. There is, as far as I can see, no trace of speculation over unity and distinction in the world of God. A pluriformity is taken for granted. Jhwh's court numbers dignitaries, even older than his kingship. At the same time the world of God can be considered a unit.

PROBLEMS IN THE HEBREW TEXT OF JOB

BY

G. R. DRIVER

Oxford

The following notes have been written with the hope of solving a few of the many difficulties in the book of Job or alternatively, where a proposed solution does not commend itself, of offering something which may ultimately lead others to their correct interpretation [1]).

III 8: 'let them curse it that curse the day,
'who are ready to rouse up Leviathan.'

In the first line the alteration of **יום** 'day' to **ים** 'sea' [2]) is confirmed by an Aramaic incantation which includes **אישפנא לכון באישפא דימא ואישפא דלויתן תנינא** 'I will cast spells upon you with the spell of the 'Sea and the spell of the dragon Leviathan' [3]). In the second line the verb is surely not **עורר** 'roused' (√**עור**), as commonly supposed, but another **עורר** 'reviled' (√**עיר**) from an unknown Hebrew root cognate with the Arab. *ʿâra* (*y*) II 'reviled' VI 'abused one another', Eth. *taʿayyara* 'reviled' [4]); and the LXX's χειρώσασθαι may perhaps reflect this verb [5]).

---

[1]) The translation of each passage discussed is taken from the English Revised Version of the Old Testament.

[2]) Schmidt *ap.* Gunkel, *Sch. u. Ch.* (1895), p. 59[1].

[3]) Montgomery, *Aramaic Incantation-Bowls* 121-2, 2 3-4.

[4]) Hence also Heb. **עיר** 'reviling' (Hos. xi 9; see Michaelis *Jer. Vat.*, p. 129 and Guillaume in *JRAS* LXIX [1942], p. 122). There is another Heb. **עיר** 'raid, invasion' (Am. vii 17; Jer. xv 8) from the same root as the Arab. *ǵâra* (*w*) III 'raided' (Freytag).

[5]) A distinct Heb. **עיר** 'to be indignant' = Arab. *ǵâra* (*y*) 'was invidious, jealous' = Syr. *ʾeṯtʿîr* 'was excited, roused' may be recognized in **ונקי על־חנף יתערר** 'and the innocent is roused, indignant at (the success of) the godless' (Iob xvii 8).

IV 14: 'fear came upon me and trembling,
'which made all my bones to shake.'

Here 'all my bones' is a hardly legitimate paraphrase of the Heb. רֹב עצמותי 'the multitude of my bones', and this in turn seems a barely credible figure of speech; the bones of the body are in no sense a multitude! Consequently רֹב 'multitude' may perhaps be taken as an error of vocalization for a Heb. רִ(י)ב 'trembling', with which the Acc. *rîbu* 'quaking' will be cognate [1]); the line then means 'and quaking shook my bones'.

VI 4: 'the terrors of God do set themselves
in array against me.'

The use of the accusatival suffix in יערכוני 'they draw up (their line of battle) against me' can perhaps be justified at any rate by Assyrian usage [2]), but it is surely harsh according to Hebrew idiom. The awkwardness however is easily avoided by postulating another Heb. ערך = Arab. *'araka* 'wore out' [3]), especially as it appears in *'arakathumu-'lḥarbu* 'the war wore them down' (Lane), which is a strikingly analogous expression. A preferable translation therefore is 'the sudden assaults [4]) of God wear me down' [5]).

VII 5: 'my flesh is clothed with worms and clods of dust,
'my skin closeth up and breaketh out afresh.'

In the first line 'clods of dust' is nonsense and in the second the unjustified addition of 'afresh' alone produces sense. Further, the rhythmical balance of the verse shows that גיש עפר עורי must be taken together and that רגע וימאס are superfluous. The usual assumption is that the Jud.-Aram. גּוּשָׁא 'clod of soil, hard crust of earth' here has a figurative medical connotation [6]) and means 'pustules' or the like; and the semantic development is not altogether impossible, since the Arab. *jas'u(n)* 'rough skin' means also 'frozen water' and 'hard pebbly

---

[1]) Cf. Iob xxxiii 19, where the same word has been found again (Dhorme, *Job*, p. 453 f.).

[2]) Cf. Ass. *duluḫḫū amât limuttim suddurūni* 'confusion (and) evil words are ranged against me' (Streck, *Assurb*. I, p. 252-3 R. 7).

[3]) Cognate Syr. *'rak* 'kneaded'.

[4]) Cf. Arab. *bagata* 'came suddenly upon, overtook.' The idea of suddenness is always present in this root.

[5]) LXX κεντοῦσί με 'they sting me.'

[6]) LXX βώλακες, Vulg. *glaebae*, and so on.

ground' 1). If then עָפָר is vocalized עָפַר (not as a noun but as a verb), a Heb. עָפַר may be compared with the Arab. *ǵafara* 'covered' and *ǵafira* '(cloth) became rough, (a wound) cracked and re-opened'. The sense will then be

'my flesh is clothed with worms 2) and scab covers my skin,'

on which רגע וימאס 'it is cracked and gapes open' will be an obvious gloss.

The exact sense or senses of the √ *RG*ʿ must now be traced. A glance through the Arabic dictionary reveals a number of words with the same opening phoneme: such are *rajja* 'moved, agitated; trembled', *rajaba* 'was terrified', *rajaḥa* VIII 'oscillated', *rajuda* 'quivered', *rajafa* 'was in commotion'. These suggest that slight repeated movements are the underlying idea, and indeed *rajaʿa* 'came back, brought back' as well as *rajaẓa* 'recited' and *rajasa* 'growled, roared' and also *rajama* 'attacked with calumnies, threw stones at (a person)' as describing essentially repetitive acts all reflect the same basic sense 3). The Heb רגע shows a similar semantic development along two different lines. First, coming back home is coming to rest; hence רָגַע in several themes denotes resting or coming to rest (Deut. xxviii 5, xxxiv 14; Jer. xxxi 2, xlvii 6, l 34; Sir. xxxvi 26, 31) 4). Then, since resting is a form of stagnation, the Eth. *ragʿa* 'coagulated, congealed, grew dense or solid' may safely be connected with it; hence the Heb. רֶגַע is misrendered ἀθροισμός (Ps. lx 6, Aq.) and ἀθρόα (Ps. xxxv 20, Aq.) 5).

Second, a moment is but a *vibramen* or *movimentum* in time, whence רֶגַע 'moment' is easily derived from the same root 6); and an obvious denominative verb is הִרְגִּיעַ 'made instantaneously to appear, to flash forth' 7)

---

1) Also Arab. *majsûʾatu(n)* 'rough (ground)'; see Freytag, *Lex. Arab.-Lat.* I, p. 277 and Köhler, *Lexicon*, p. 177.

2) The figure of speech is the same as that in the Bab. (*il*) *Sin . . iššubbā kî lubāri lîlabbisu* 'may (the god) Sin . . . clothe him in leprosy (as) a garment' (Peiser *Ki.B.* IV, 80-1, iii, 18-9).

3) Cf. Heb. רגז 'was agitated, quivered', רגן 'murmured' רגשׁ 'was in commotion'.

4) This sense is further confirmed by the LXX's incorrect κατέπαυσεν where the required sense is 'stirred up, shook apart' (Iob xxvi 12).

5) Reider in *JQR* NS. IV, p. 596, 611.

6) Orelli, *Zeit und Ewigkeit*, p. 26-8.

7) Rhythmically ארגיע must go not with what follows (Kittel w. LXX) but with what precedes (Vulg.); but the sense is not 'I will make to repose' (B.-D.-B. and Vulg's *requiescet*) in view of the parallel תצא 'it shall go forth', since this verb here as often connotes shining forth (see *Bibl.* XXXII 190).

(Jes. li 4)[1]). Hence the noun as denoting *movimentum* comes easily to connote 'emotion' (Jes. liv 7) and 'disquietude' (Ps. xxx 6)[2]). The verb then comes to have a similar sense, as when the Lord is described as רִגַּע (<רֹגַע) הים ויהמו גליו '(who) stirs up[3]) the sea and its waves roar' (Jes. li 15, where it is translated ταράσσων by LXX; Jer. xxxi 35). The root then *vires acquirit eundo* and its sense is perceptibly strengthened in בכחו רִגַּע (<רָגַע) הים 'by his strength he shook the sea apart' (Iob xxxvi 12; Tg. גזר), which is shown to be the sense of the verb here by the parallel מחץ 'smote'; the reference is to the primeval struggle with the mythical sea-dragon which was then split or cleft in twain[4]). This same sense appears in another passage where it has been hitherto recognized only by the LXX; this is פתאם שדדו אהלי רֻגַּע (or רֻגְּעוּ) (<רֶגַע) יריעתי 'suddenly my tents are destroyed, my curtains are shaken apart' or 'rent' (Jer. iv 20; LXX διεσπάσθησαν); the parallelism of the thought supports the LXX's translation, which makes excellent sense and is philologically justifiable. This last passage will explain a number of curious translations in the LXX: for example, why הִרְגִּיעַ is rendered ὀλλύναι (Jer. xxxi 2) and רֶגַע is rendered ἀπώλεια (Iob. xx 5; Ezech. xxvi 16), πτῶρις (Ezech. xxxii 10) and πληγή (Ex. xxxiii 5). These renderings, though incorrect in the passages cited, show that the root must have acquired the sense of '(sudden) destruction' at some time or other; for, if it had not, so persistent a mistranslation would have been impossible.

The explanation of רגע וימאס 'it hardens and (then) runs (again)' (B.-D.-B. and R.V.) may now be attempted. This translation is in any case impossible, since sense is obtained only by inserting 'then' and 'again'; and this is not justified by the language. Clearly רָגַע must be altered to רֻגַּע 'is cracked', which yields good sense, though not supported by the Vss[5]). Then יִמָּאֵס may be taken as a by-form of יִמַּס 'melts' in the sense of 'suppurates'[6]); or preferably, if read יְמָאֵס,

---

1) Driver in *JTS*. XXXVI, p. 401. But ארגיעה is probably a noun (B.-D.-B.).

2) Driver in *JTS*. XXXVI, p. 299.

3) Since the Piʿel is required as the causative form, the verb must be put in the 3rd person of the perfect tense, which is permissible in the relative clause (see Driver in *Nötscher* p. 58).

4) Langdon, *Creation* 140-1, iv, 101-2.

5) Vulg. *aruit*, Pesh. *qpûd* 'is contracted' and Tg. רְטַט 'pulsates'; Saʿad. אולם 'is pained.'

6) So Pesh. *ʾeṯmsî* and Tg. אִתְמְסִי 'melts'; but Vulg. *contracta est*, Saʿad. תמאסי 'gaped open'.

the Heb. מאס may here be equated with the Arab. *ma'asa*, *ma'isa* '(a wound) gaped' [1]). Both translations have ancient authority, and the choice must be subjective; on the first interpretation מאס describes the result of רגע, in the second it is a synonym explaining it.

IX 27: 'if I say [2]) I will forget my complaint;
'I will put off my (sad) countenance and be of good cheer'.

The insertion of 'sad', which is a key-word, before 'countenance', is indefensible, while the translation of 'forsook' as 'put off' is dubious; the verb therefore must be otherwise explained. It must be another Heb. עָזַב = Arab. *'aḏaba* IV 'made agreeable', whence *musta'biḏu(n)* 'pleasant fellow' (Dozy) is derived [3]); then אֶעֶזְבָה פני (or rather אַעֲזִיבָה) will mean 'I will make pleasant my countenance', *i.e.*, 'put on a cheerful look'.

X 22: 'a land of thick darkness [4]), as darkness itself,
'a land of the shadow of death without any order
'and where light is as darkness.'

This verse is overloaded and the R.V's 'without any order' introduces an alien thought. Clearly כמו אפל צלמות, as the *pāsēq* indicates, is a gloss based on the preceding line and intended to explain ולא סדרים. The Acc. *sadāru* 'to arrange in order, to align', is the root of the Heb. סֵדֶר 'order'; but here this word must have the sense of a 'line, beam of light', as suggested by the Arab. *sadira* 'was dazzled by the glare' [5]), and the LXX's φέγγος supports this interpretation of the word. Then תֹּפַע comes not from הופיע 'shone' but from

[1]) So Neubauer, *Ibn Janâḥ*, p. 360.
[2]) Namely אִם־אָמַר (cf. I Sam. xx 21 f.).

[3]) Five homonyms must now be distinguished: (i) עזב 'left' = Arab. *'azaba* 'was remote'; (ii) עזב 'helped' = Eth. *'azaba* 'helped' (Sir. xi 21; see Driver in *JQR* N.S. XXVIII, p. 125-6); (iii) עזב 'repaired' = Ugar. *'db* 'made' and S.-Arab. *'ḏb* 'repaired'; (iv) עזב 'grieved' = Arab. *'aḏaba* I 'hindered' II 'punished, tormented' (Iob xx 19 and Sir. iii 12; see Driver in *JBL* LIII, p. 237 and Yellin *HwM*. I, p. 49); (v) 'was pleasant', as above. Which, if any, of these roots may be identified?

[4]) Or perhaps rather 'dark mist, fog'; cf. Am. iv 13, where עיפה is rendered ὀμίχλη by the LXX.

[5]) The idea underlying the root is that of lines, beams or rays, of light streaming down from the sun.

another Heb. הופיע 'showed dark clouds', with which the Arab. *yaf'u(n)* 'cloud foreboding rain' will be cognate [1]). Hence

'a land of darkness without ray of light,
gloomy as deep darkness'

will be the meaning of the verse.

XIV 12: 'so man lieth down and riseth not up,
'till the heavens be no more, they shall not awake
'nor be roused out of their sleep.'

This translation is barely intelligible, and the majority of the ancient Versions imply 'till the heavens be no more [2]), he shall not wake up' (reading יקיץ for יקיצו.) [3]), which makes good sense but leaves the rest of the clause unexplained. The sense of עד־בלתי שמים לא יקיצו is without doubt 'while [4]) = so long as the heavens do not burst' [5]), *i.e.* 'for ever and ever'; for the expression can be interpreted without altering the text in the light of the Arab *fa'iḏa kâna kaḏālika qâḍat hā ḏă-'lsamă-'ldunyâ 'an 'ahlihâ* 'so, if it happens thus, this lowest heaven shall burst from its (*sc.* the earth's) inhabitants' (LANE under *qâḍa* 'burst'). There must therefore have been a Heb. קיץ 'to burst' and ולא יערו משנתם will be an incorrect gloss, due to misunderstanding the double negation [6]).

XV 4: 'yea, thou doest away with fear.'

The dictionaires take תָּפֵר from פָּרַר 'broke' in the sense of 'annulled' (B.-D.-B.); but does it not rather come from another Heb. פָּרַר = Syr. *par(r)* 'departed' = Arab. *farra* 'fled', so that the clause will mean 'thou puttest fear to flight' [7])? Surely banishing fear is a more likely figure of speech than breaking it. Ultimately the two roots are probably identical, as the Engl. 'to break away' suggests: and the same idea underlies the Heb. פטר 'loosed; departed'.

[1]) YELLIN, *HwM.* I, p. 25; cf. LXX's ἐσκοτώθη for יָעַף at Jud. iv 21. There the reference is clearly to σκότῳ θανεῖν (Euripides); for a *hysteron proteron* arises if והוא נרדם וַיָּעַף וימת 'for he was fast asleep and exhausted; so he died' (BURNEY) is read.

[2]) GEIGER with several Vss. (Aq., Theod., Symm., Vulg., Pesh.).

[3]) Corresponding to the Vulg.'s *evigilavit.*

[4]) See YELLIN in ABRAHAMS, p. 451 and DRIVER in *WO*, I, p. 412.

[5]) The LXX's οὐ μὴ συρραφῇ expresses this sense of the verb in negative form (see ORLINSKY in *JQR* N.S. XXVIII, p. 57-68).

[6]) Cp. Ex. xiv 11 (see BROCKELMANN, *GVGSS* II §§ 59b, 107b²).

[7]) Cf. Ps. lxxxv 5 and lxxxix 34 (cf. Pesh.'s *'a'bar* (BUHL)).

XV 22 'and he is waited for of the sword.'

Here צפו(י) is the passive form corresponding to the active צופה in צופה רשע לצדיק 'the wicked marks down the righteous' (Ps. xxxvii 32), so that the clause ought to be rendered 'he is marked down [1]) for the sword'. The cognate Acc. *ṣipû* 'to surround, enclose, delimit, mark off, survey, scan' shows the semantic development of the root [2]).

XVI 12: 'I was at ease and he brake me asunder;
yea, he hath taken me by the neck and dashed me in pieces.'

The picture here intended seems to be that of a beast of prey catching small game; in this, as indeed in almost any other, connection, 'he brake me asunder' and 'he dashed me in pieces' are unlikely figures. The Heb. פרפר is then best explained after the Arab. *farfara* 'shook (out), tore, mangled (*e.g.* sheep, goats)' (Lane); this agrees to some extent with the LXX's διεσκέδασεν 'dismembered'. Again, the Heb. פצפץ may be explained in the light of the Arab. *faṣfaṣa-'l'iḏâma* 'separated the bones, dismembered' (Dozy), which in its turn agrees with the LXX's διέτιλέ 'he plucked me' rather than with the Vulg.'s *confregit me* and the Tg.'s פצפץ, which reflect the Arab. *faḍḍa* 'broke in pieces'. The verse may now be rendered

'I was at ease, and he worried me;
'he took me by the neck and mauled me.'

God treats Job as a wild beast worrying its prey and tearing the flesh from its bones.

XVII 2: 'and my eye abideth in their provocation.'

That this clause, as so translated, is absurd goes without saying. I therefore prefer to take הַמְּרוֹתָם [3]) from a lost Heb. *הַמָּרָה [4]) which the Arab. *hamratu(n)* 'angry words' and *hammâru(n)* 'garrulous old man' from *hamara* 'poured out (water, tears, words)' will easily explain. This entails altering תָּלַן עֵינִי into תִּלְאֶין (=תִּלֶן) עֵינַי 'mine eyes are (= I myself am) wearied'. Thus Job says 'I am tired of your stream of peevish complaints', which well suits the parallel התולים 'mockeries'.

---

[1]) Hence LXX's ἐντέταλται and Tg.'s אטימוס (= ἑτοῖμος).
[2]) Driver in *Anal. Or.* XII, p. 50-53.
[3]) Cp. שְׁבִתוֹתַי for form with suffix.
[4]) Formed like בַּלָּהָה and חַטָּאָה (see Barth, *Nominalbildung*, p. 145 f. § 93).

XVIII 2: 'how long will ye lay snares for words?'

The meaning of קִנְצֵי למלין has long been discussed without any satisfactory solution of the problem being found [1]). May not צִינֹק למלין 'a bridle for words, a gag for speech' be read? The Heb. צִינֹק occurs again in the sense only of 'collar, pillory', but the Syr. *ṣanqâ* 'band, bridle' suggests a wider reference; and the cognate Acc. *zanāqu, sanāqu, šanāqu* 'to bind' and the Arab. *zanaqa* 'bound' support this suggestion.

XVIII 15: 'there shall dwell in his tent that which is none of his;
'brimstone shall be scattered upon his habitation.'

Neither the Hebrew text nor the English translation of the first line can be defended. Obviously מִבְּלִי־לוֹ must conceal something parallel to גפרית 'brimstone' and therefore some substance used in an apotropaic rite [2]); is מַבְלוֹל, מַבְלֵ(י)ל or מַבְלוּל 'mixed brew' [3]) possible? Assyrian exorcists used herbs mingled with sulphur or various mixed herbs for such purposes [4]), and the Ass. *riqqū ballūtu* 'mixed spices' [5]) shows exactly how the $\sqrt{}$ *BLL* can be usedin this connection. Thus

'mixed herbs shall lie in his tent
'and brimstone be strewn on his dwelling place'

describes the owner as one accursed and requiring purification.

---

1) The Acc. *qinṣu* 'bridle', usually cited to explain the Heb. קֶנֶץ (ZIMMERN, *ap.* G.-B.) does not exist, being misread; the word is *kurṣu* 'bond', which is glossed *appātu* 'reins' in a native text (BOISSIER in *R.A.* XVI, p. 161-4 R. 23, where it is written *ku-ur-ṣi-šu-nu* 'their bonds'; s. LANDSBERGER *ana ittišu*, 137 on 28_{10}).

2) Cf. *veniat quae lustret anus lectumque locumque praeferat et tremula sulphur et ova manu* (Ovid *A.Am.* ii 329-30).

3) Formed like מַעְשֵׂר 'tithe' and מַקְהֵל 'assembly', מִטְמוֹן 'hidden treasure' or מַסְלוּל 'heaped up causeway'. The final *-ô* must be detached and prefixed as 'and' to the following word.

4) MEIER, *Maqlû*, 35 v 30-38 (mixed herbs) and 61 ix 100-7 (chicory mingled with sulphur).

5) EBELING, *KARI*, **139** (= *Quellen* II 47-9) O. 7-8.

XIX 20: 'my bone cleaveth to my skin and to my flesh
'and I am escaped with the skin of my teeth'.

In the first line בעורי is hypermetrical and can be deleted as a faulty anticipation of בעור in the following clause [1]); and the second line as translated offers a figure of speech which, although it has passed into the English language as a proverbial expression for a narrow escape, if examined closely is seen to convey no real sense. In any case, escaping does not suit the context, which requires rather some idiom indicative of worried anxiety. I suggest therefore that the Heb. מלט is here used like the Acc. *marāṭu* 'to rub (*e.g.* eyes, cheeks, lips)", Arab. *maraṭa* 'plucked out (*e.g.* hair), gnawed', Syr. *mraṭ* 'plucked out', and the Eth. *malaṭa* 'depilated'; in fact, all these verbs may be safely identified, since *l* and *r* are frequently interchanged [2]). This interpretation of the verb agrees with that which Symmachus offers, namely καὶ ἐξέτιλλον τὸ δέρμα μου ὀδοῦσί μου, which seems at first sight to reflect not so much the M.T. as it stands as ואתמלטה עוֹרִי בְּשִׁנָּי [3]); but the alteration of the text is not necessary. It can be rendered literally 'I gnawed myself on (the) skin (with) my teeth'; for the pronoun may be omitted with the term denoting the part affected [4]), which may be introduced by a preposition [5]) or be put in the accus. case [6]), and the organ of the body with which the action is performed may stand also in the accus. case [7]). Syntactically therefore the proposed translation is unexceptionable, as it is also philologically. An alternative possibility, however, that the Heb. עור is not here the well-known word for 'skin' but the same word as the Arab. *ġâru(n)* 'bottom of palate, pit of chin', calls for consideration; but this second עור is otherwise unknown. In either case the sense will approximate to Tennyson's 'gnawed now his under, now his

---

1) Or perhaps rather as a gloss showing that בשׂר 'flesh' has here the same sense as the arab. *baššaru(n)* 'skin' (cf. Ps. cii 6; cxix 120).

2) So Heb. התעלם = התערם 'was heaped up' (Iob vi 16); cf. Heb. חלצים = Aram. חרצין 'hips' and the Heb. רחת 'fan' = Syr. *laḥtâ* 'palm (of hand)'. The interchange takes place in every position.

3) Cf. Mich. iii 5 (הנשכים בשניהם).

4) Cf. Ezech. xvi 43 (דרכך נתתי בראשׁ), Jes. xxxvii 22 (ראשׁ הניעה) and Ps. xxii 8 (יניעו ראשׁ).

5) Cf. 2 Chron. xvi 12 (s. König, *Syntax*, § 328 e-f).

6) Kautzsch-Cowley 'H.G.', § 117 11 and Joüon, *Gramm. de l'Hébr. Bibl.*, § 126 g.

7) Not the nomin. case (Kautzsch-Cowley 'H.G.', § 144 l-m); cf. Langdon *Etana*, 17_{30} w. 18_{14} (Ass. example) and Qur'ân cii 7 (Arab. example for the acc. case).

upper lip', so that the expression will indicate, as the context requires, acute or harassed perturbation.

XX 23-25: 'when he is about to fill his belly
'God shall cast the fierceness of His wrath upon him
'and shall rain it upon him while he is eating.
'He shall flee from the iron weapon
'and the bow of brass shall strike him through;
'he draweth it forth and it cometh out of his body;
'yea, the glittering point cometh out of his gall.'

The Hebrew text is clearly in disorder and the English translation perhaps makes the best of a bad job, apart from admitting the ridiculous figure of a brazen bow piercing the victim and being drawn out of the wound.

In verse 23 יהי למלא בטנו is omitted by the LXX [1] and is marked by a *pāsēq* in the M.T.; it is suspect because it overloads the line, because the jussive form of the verb is inexplicable, and indeed because the whole clause makes no sense in the context. It is a marginal note inserted by a reader indignantly exclaiming 'let him have his belly-full of God's wrath!' If he were such a sinner as Eliphaz describes, he would deserve no mercy, is the reader's reaction; and the gloss probably takes its form from the misunderstanding of בלחומו 'in his body' [2]. This word, however, cannot here mean 'in his belly' but, as the parallel חרון אפו shows, must describe God's wrath or the instrument with which it is executed; there must therefore be admitted to the vocabulary of the O.T. Heb. I לְחוּם = Arab. *luḥûmu* 'fleshy parts of the intestines' [3], and Heb. II לְחוּם = Arab. *liḥâmu(n)* 'buffeting' from *laḥama* I 'struck' III 'buffeted' (cf. LXX's ὀδύνας). In verse 24 again 'he shall flee' is not parallel to 'it shall strike him through' and cannot be right; the context suggests that יִבְרַח 'he shall flee' ought to be vocalized יִבָּרַח 'he shall be wounded' on the assumption of a Heb. בָּרַח 'wounded' = Arab. *baraḫa* 'bruised', whence *barḫu(n)* 'blow of a sword' is derived [4]. Next, a 'bow of

---

[1]) Marked by an asterisk (Rahlfs; see Field, *Hexapla* II, p. 38).
[2]) Cf. Tg.'s בשלדיו 'on his corpse'.
[3]) Only in Zeph. i 17 (s. Driver in *JTS*. XXXIX, p. 398).
[4]) So Ehrlich *Rg. A.T.* VI, p. 263 (cf. LXX's τρώσῃ for M.T.'s יבריח at Iob xli 20). This verb may also be restored, against the ancient Vss., in מידו (יִבְרָח >) בְּרוּחַ יִבָּרַח 'he shall be sorely bruised by its force' (Iob xxvii 22, where 'escape' is premature and out of place).

brass' [1]) is absurd, being inconceivable and inapposite; here then קשת 'bow' must stand for 'arrow', as it perhaps does elsewhere. In verse 25 the LXX's βέλος for שָׁלַף reflects not a noun but a verb, namely a Heb. *שלף corresponding to the Syr. *šlāpâ*, *šelpâ*, *šûlpâ* 'blade of a knife' [2]) and this may be accepted, whether the order of the words is retained on the assumption of a postponed *wāw* (as often in the Ugaritic poems) [3]) or that the first and second words are interchanged to ensure the usual order. Further, the LXX's διὰ σώματος αὐτοῦ shows that מְגֵוָה ought to be pointed מִגֵּוֹה 'from his back' [4]). At the end of the verse עליו אמים 'terrors upon him', which ruins its rhythmical balance and is *extra constructionem*, is a sympathetic scribe's or reader's exclamation meaning 'how awful for him!' and can be relegated to the margin.

The passage may now be translated

> 'He shall send the fury of this wrath upon him
> 'and rain down blows upon him
> '(may he have a belly-full!).
> 'He shall be pierced by a weapon of iron;
> 'a bronze-tipped arrow shall transfix him,
> 'the blade shall come out by his back
> 'and the flashing point issue from his gall
> (how awful for him!),'

whereby sense is wrested from the passage at no excessive cost of emendation.

I have here rendered קשת 'bow' by 'arrow' for the obvious reason that a bow of brass is an impossible weapon; for brass is neither flexible nor resilient. Only a god's bow might be *auratus* 'gilded' or *aureus* 'golden' [5]), while bows of bronze were but votive offerings or weapons in the hands of statues [6]); these were no ordinary weapons. The magic bow in the Ugaritic legend of Aqhat was made of *ʿqbm* 'yews(?)' from Lebanon, *gdm brʾumm* 'sinews from wild oxen', *qrnt byʿlm* 'horns from mountain-goats', *mtnm bʿqbt ṯr* 'tendons from the hocks of a bull' and *bǵl il qnm* 'rushes from El's reed-beds' [7]). Bows from the tomb of Tut-ankh-amun

---

1) So again in 2 Sam. xxii 35 = Ps. xviii 35.
2) So Beer in *B.H.*[2] II, p. 1086.
3) For example *hwt w-aʾtnyk* 'a word, and I will repeat (it) to thee' (Gordon, *Ugar. Handb.* p. 188, iii 19).
4) Hoffmann *ap.* Buhl, *Handwörterb. ü. d. A.T.*[17], p. 133.
5) Ennius, *Trag.* 30 (*Alcum.*) ii 7-8, Ovid, *Metamorph.* i 697.
6) Galling, *Bibl. Reallex.*, p. 114.
7) Gordon, *Ugar. Handb.*, p. 183 (A II vi 20-23).

are made of several strips of horn and wood (possibly yew) glued together and covered with bark (possibly of birch or cherry) [1]. The usual bow in the earliest times was *corneus* 'made of horn' [2], but it might also be *ligneus* 'wooden' [3]. A common type of bow, found already in the Homeric age, was made of wood and horn combined; and the tips over which the bow-string was passed were plated with metal which might in an exceptional case be gold or gilt [4]. The medieval cross-bow was made of steel, whence the A.V. speaks of a 'bow of steel' [5] by an anachronism which has found its way also into English poetry [6]. Arrows were made of wood, tipped in the earliest ages with stone but usually in historical times with metal [7]. Consequently, when קשׁת is qualified by a metal, the reference must be either to a metal-plated bow or to an arrow with a similar tip; since however the bow *per se* cannot pierce anyone, as the קשׁת does in the passage under discussion, nor 'dash young men in pieces' (Jes. xiii 18), and since it cannot, in the strict sense, be aimed (2 Sam. xxii 35 = Ps. xviii 35) [8], in such connections קשׁת must stand *per synecdochen*, as τόξον also does [9], for 'arrow'. Once this usage is admitted, several ridiculous translations disappear from the English Bible [10].

XXI 21: 'when the number of his months is cut off.'

This phrase may perhaps be translated 'few days are allotted to him' if the Heb. חצץ is equated with the Arab. *ḫaṣṣa* I 'was allotted' IV 'allotted' [11], or 'the number of his days is fixed' if it is equated with the Arab. *ḫaṣṣa* II 'fixed' [12]; but it is perhaps rather the Acc. *ḫaṣāṣu* 'to break off', Eth. *ḫaṣaṣa* 'was curtailed, diminished' (B.-D.-B.) which gives most point to the expression [13].

---

1) Albright & Mendenhall in *JNES* I, p. 227-9.
2) Ovid, *Amor.* I viii 47-8, *Metamorph.* i 697.
3) Vegetius, *Milit.* i 15.
4) Hence κέρας 'horn' may stand for 'bow' (Hom., *Od.* xxi 393-5) and the bow-maker was called τέκτων κεραοξόος 'horn-polishing carpenter' (Homer, *Il.* iv 110).
5) At 2 Sam. xxii 35 = Ps. xviii 34 and Iob xx 24. This translation, though wrong, at any rate has the merit of making sense.
6) *E.g.* Milton, 'Paradise Lost' iii 305.
7) Nowack, *Lehrb. d. hebr. Arch.* I, p. 363.
8) Here the verb is not נחת Pi. 'caused to descend, pressed down' (B.-D.-B.), but נחה Q. 'led, guided', Pi. 'directed, aimed' (see Driver in *WO* I, p. 410, II p. 26).
9) Sophocles, *Philoctetes* 652-3; Euripides, *Ion* 256, 524.
10) The bow would be equally unbendable if brass meant a mixture of copper and tin (Barnes in Hastings' *D.B.* I p. 312 b)!
11) Eitan, *Contribution*, p. 47[85].
12) Yellin *HwM.* I, p. 54.
13) The ancient translators seem to have taken חצץ as a by-form of חצה 'halved' (Aq., Vulg., Tg.).

XXII 26: 'for then thou shalt delight thyself in the Almighty
'and shalt lift up thy face unto God.'

The corresponding phrase suggests that the Heb. ענג here corresponds not to the Arab. *ǵanaja* I 'coquetted' II 'fondled', but to the Arab. *'anaja* I 'drew, pulled, tied, bent' IV 'arranged with a rope; supported', whence *'inâju(n)* 'rope; basis of an affair' comes. Hence ענג is elsewhere translated by the LXX πεποιθέναι (Jes. lviii 4), by the Pesh. *tkal* 'trusted' (Jes. lviii 4; Iob xxvii 10) and *sab(b)ar* 'hoped' (Ps. xxxvii 10). Here then the clause in question will mean 'thou basest thyself on' or 'dost depend on the Almighty' [1]). The same root yields also תַּעֲנוּג 'control' (Prov. xix 10, where the parallel מְשֹׁל 'ruling' determines its sense).

XXVI 9: 'he closeth the face of (his) throne,
'he spreadeth his cloud upon it.'

The Acc. *aḫāzu* 'to encase', as applied to encasing a substance [2]), and the Arab. *'uḫiḏa* '(a wall) was encased (in marble)' [3]) makes the sense of מאחז perfectly clear [4]). The same cannot be said of פַּרְשֵׁז, which is a unique word and indeed in form a solecism; the only possible explanation of it is to assume that it is a *forma mixta* offering a choice of פָּרַשׂ 'he has spread out' and פֵּרַז 'he has extended' [5]). The ancient Vss. are not precise enough to help in such a case as this, and the Hebrew mss. offer no variant readings; but another instance of such a solecism will illustrate the procedure of the scribes. The form of זרזיף in כרביבים זרזיף ארץ 'like showers that water the earth' (Ps. lxxii 6, R.V.) is as peculiar [6]) as the syntax which requires a verb governing ארץ 'earth'; it is evidently a *forma mixta* made up from alternative verbs, namely *זרף 'flowed' [7]) and *רזף

---

[1]) Cf. YELLIN in *Abrahams*, p. 453.

[2]) As in *paṭār parzilli šibbi šâ iḫzušu ḫurāsu* 'a dagger of iron on a belt which gold encased' (STRECK, *Assurbanipal* II, p. 14-15, ii 12).

[3]) SHAFÍ' in *A Volume of Oriental Studies presented to E.G. Browne*, p. 435.

[4]) This same usage is recognized by the ancient Vss. in two other doubtful passages (I Reg. vi 10 and 2 Chr. ix 18; s. PERLES in *AOf.* IV, p. 218).

[5]) So BEER; cf. M.-Heb. הִפְרִיז *ampliavit, superaddidit* (BUXTORF) and Arab. *faraza discrevit, segregavit* (FREYTAG).

[6]) This verb, like פרשז, is supported by no analogous forms in the cognate languages; for the Rabb. זַרְזִיף 'shower' and the derived זִרְזֵף 'watered' are based on this passage.

[7]) Cf. Arab. *ḏarafa* '(tears) flowed; streamed (with tears)', of which the root appears also in Syr. *zāripṯâ* 'violent rain'.

'dripped' [1]). Consequently something like מְרַזֵּף ארץ or כִּרְבִיב מְזָרֵף 'like a shower' [2]) streaming down on' or 'besprinkling the earth' must be read [3]). That both verbs do not occur elsewhere in the O.T. has aided the confusion.

XXIX 17-20: 'and I brake the jaws of the unrighteous
'and plucked the prey out of his mouth.
'Then I said: I shall die in my nest
'and I shall multiply my days as the sand;
. . . .
'my glory is fresh in me
'and my bow is renewed in my hand.'

In verse 17 there is no need to alter אַשְׁלִיךְ into אֶשְׁלֹף 'I drew forth' (Köhler); for the verb may be identified with the Phoen. שלך as found in such names as βααλσιλληχ meaning 'Baal has rescued', as the Arab. *salaka* I 'saved himself' II 'drew (a sword)' from the scabbard and also 'rescued (a person)' from misfortune shows. The Graeco-Phoenician vocalization suggests however that יְשַׁלֵּךְ is perhaps the correct Hebrew form in this sense [4]). In verse 18 קן 'nest' can hardly be the word intended by the author; the figure of speech is peculiar and scarcely suitable to the parallel clause. Another Heb. קן = Eg. *qn* 'strong' and *qn.t* 'strength' [5]) ought therefore in all probability to be postulated (Herz), and philology supports the suggestion. The Acc. *qannu* 'rope, cord' = Arab. *qannatu(n)* 'strand, rope' are cognate with the Eg. *qn* = Heb. קן 'strength', just as the Acc. *qû* = Heb. קו 'cord' are cognate with the Arab. *qawiya* 'was strong'; the underlying idea is that what is twisted becomes taut or tight and what is taut or tight becomes firm and strong [6]). In verse 20 'glory' is totally out of place over against 'bow', especially as the two predicates are closely parallel; I suggest therefore that כְּבוֹדִי 'my glory' ought to be vocalized as כְּבֵדִי 'my bow-handle'. Amongst

---

[1]) Syr. *rzap* 'dripped; sprinkled.'

[2]) Sing. רְבִיב w. Syroh. Vers. (Haupt in *ZAtW* XXIX, p. 286), like Ugar. *rbb* 'shower' and Arab. *rabâbu(n)* 'white cloud'.

[3]) Contrariwise, the initial ר in רטפש (Iob xxxiii 25) is a dittograph of the final ר of the preceding word.

[4]) Driver in *AJSL.* LII, p. 163; cf. משלך as a Jewish proper name (Cowley, '*A.P.*', **10** 2, 23; **22** 73, 68).

[5]) Erman & Grapow, *Wb. Ä.S.* V, p. 44-5.

[6]) Cf. *Eph. Theol. Lovan.* XXVI 343-4, where other instances of this semantic development are cited.

the Arabs the various parts of the bow have each their own proper name, and the central part where it is grasped is called *kabidu(n)* 'heavy part, central piece' [1]). May not the centre-piece or handle have been similarly named in the Hebrew language and, if so, may not its name have been used in poetry *pars pro toto* for the entire weapon? Only one apparently serious objection can be raised against this suggestion, that כָּבֵד 'liver' and, as suggested, 'handle of bow' is feminine [2]), whereas the predicate is here masculine; but the objection may be dismissed as groundless, since congruence of genders may be disregarded when any word, even a pronominal suffix or a proclitic particle, intervenes between subject and predicate [3]).

The proper translation of these verses then is

'and I brake the tusks of the wrong-doer
'and rescued the prey from his mouth.
'Then I said: I shall die in [4]) my full strength
'and I shall multiply my days like the sand;
. . . .
'(while) my bow-handle is fresh with me
'and my bow is ever-new in my hand.'

Thus the strange figure of the bird's nest disappears and the phoenix, the subject of much speculation, may disappear with it.

XXIX 21-24: 'unto me men gave ear and waited
'and kept silence for my counsel;
'after my words they spake not again,
'and my speech dropped upon them.
. . . .
'If I laughed upon them they believed it not
'and the light of my countenance they cast not down.'

In verse 21 the only correction necessary is to interchange יחלו and ידמו, which have perhaps been accidentally transposed; and יִדְּמוּ (√דמם) 'they moaned' must obviously be vocalized as יִדְמוּ (√דמה) 'they kept silence', as indeed the Revisers have tacitly ad-

---

[1]) Lane, *Arabic-English Lexicon*, I, vii 2584.

[2]) Like Syr. *kabdâ* and Arab. *kabidu(n)* 'liver'; cf. Gen. xlix 6, where the M.T.'s כְּבוֹדִי 'my glory' is shown to be an error for כְּבֵדִי 'my liver' not only by the LXX's τὰ ἥπατα μου but also by the fem. תחד 'she shall be united'. Where it is apparently masculine, the predicate precedes it and therefore does not necessarily agree with it.

[3]) Cf. Ps. xxii 16 and Iob xxx 17 (see Driver in *JRAS* LXXV [1948], p. 167-9).

[4]) Cf. Ps. lxxxix 14 for this use of the preposition.

mitted [1]). In verse 22 דְּבָרִי 'my word' ought probably to be vocalized דַּבְּרִי 'my speaking' [2]). In verse 24 the R.V. yields no conceivable sense, although the Hebrew text is practically in good order. In the first clause the negative לא must be understood in an interrogative sense and therefore as in effect having an affirmative force [3]), as occasionally in Hebrew and also in Arabic literature [4]); and האמין 'showed firmness' here means not 'believed' but 'felt assurance, was re-assured'. In the second clause the whole structure of the sentence has been misunderstood. Here אור פני balances אשחק עליהם, so that אור is not a noun but a verb [5]); and the clause is the protasis of a condition of which the apodosis is set out without an introductory particle [6]). Lastly, an ellipse of the object, namely פניהם, must be assumed after יפילון, quite naturally since פני stands as the subject of אור in the preceding clause. The whole passage accordingly means

'men gave ear unto me and kept silence
'and they waited for my counsel;
'after my speaking they had nothing to say
'and my speech flowed over them.
. . . .
'If I laughed, were they not re-assured?
'if my face lighted up, they showed no downcast looks.'

The translation of this last clause rests on the assumption that יפלון

---

1) Three, if not four, verbs are hopelessly confused in the M.T.: (i) דמה 'failed; came to an end', Ni. 'was ruined, brought to an end, perished'; (ii) דמם Ni. 'was struck down; was petrified', cognate with M.-Heb. הדמים 'struck down', Arab. *damma* 'broke; exterminated' and Eth. *tadamma* 'was struck with astonishment, stupefied'; (iii) דמם Q. 'muttered; groaned' with which Acc. *damāmu* 'to moan' and Arab. *damdama* 'hummed; mumbled; snarled' are cognate; (iv) דום Q. 'to stand still, stay; continue' (not recognized in the vocalization of the M.T.) cognate with Arab. *dâma* (*w*) 'stood still; continued, lasted'. All the occurrences of these verbs call for investigation, since they have not yet been properly disentangled (see MICHAELIS, *Supplementa*, p. 417; HAUPT in *AJSL*. XXVI, p. 4-5 and SCHICK in *JBL* XXII, p. 219-43).

2) So BEER; cf. Iob xxi 3.

3) The commonest form of this idiom has ולא rather than the simple לא, as the Pesh. and the Tg. indeed have here.

4) HAUPT in *OLz*. X, p. 305-6; SMITH in *JBL* XXIV, p. 30; EITAN in *RÉJ* LXXIV, p. 7-11; DRIVER in *Bibl.* XXXV, p. 152; NÖTSCHER in *VT*, III p. 374-5; cf. BROCKELMANN, *G.V.G.S.S.* II, § 105 c and WRIGHT, *Arab. Gr.*[3] II, p. 305 f.

5) Singular predicate preceding plural subject (see KAUTZSCH-COWLEY *H.Gr.*, § 145 k).

6) Cf. Iob xxiii 10 (בחנני כזהב אצא); see S. R. DRIVER, *Hebrew Tenses*[3], p. 193 § 154.

(פניהם) is the causative form of נפלו פנים 'the countenance fell' (Gen. iv 5 f.). The full form of the idiom occurs in

שבה משבה ישראל ··· לוא־אַפִּיל פני בכם

'turn again, thou turn-coat Israel [1]) . . .
'(that) I make not my face to fall upon you' (Jer. iii 12).

Both passages, however, raise the question: why does the intransitive נפלו פנים require a transitive הפיל פנים? That a man's countenance falls is an intelligible concept, but how can he make it fall? Contrariwise, one of the best-known expressions for anger in the Semitic languages is the blackening of the face, *e.g.* the Heb. השחיר מראה איש 'blackened a man's visage' and הקדיר פניו 'darkened his visage', both meaning 'annoyed him' (Sir. xxv 16), and the Arab. *wujûduhum muswaddata(n)* 'their faces were black' = 'they were angered' (Qur. xxxix 61; cf. xliii 16); is it then not possible that יַפִּילוּן and אַפִּיל stand for respectively יַאֲפִילוּן and אַאֲפִיל and that the two expressions mean 'they darkened not their faces', *i.e.*, 'showed no angry looks' and '(that) I may not darken my face', *i.e.*, 'show myself angry with them' [2]). That אָפֵל 'was dark, black' does not occur again [3]) may be the reason why the Massoretes have vocalized both forms as from נָפַל 'fell [4]), whose use with פנים will have easily come to mind. Whichever view is taken of the verb, however, the general sense of the passage is not affected, while the construction here proposed yields a sense preferable to that expressed in the R.V.

XXXI 12: 'for it is a fire that consumeth unto destruction
and would root out all mine increase'.

Whether עד־אבדון means 'unto destruction', as here translated, or 'for ever' [5]) may be an open question; but the idea of rooting out, although accepted by all the ancient translators, is surely alien to fire.

---

[1]) As the parallel בוגדה or בגדה 'traitors' shows, the abstract משבה 'apostasy' is used as a kind of title for Israel as apostasy personified; it does not agree with but stands in apposition to the proper name.

[2]) Cf. Iob xxx 26, where אור and אפל are again contrasted.

[3]) The Heb. אָפֵל 'dark' and אֹפֶל 'darkness', as well as Arab. *ʾafila* '(the sun) set', justify the assumption of such a verb.

[4]) Possibly then יָפִילוּן and אָפִיל ought to be read; cf. אָזִין for אַאֲזִין (Jer. v 8) and perhaps מַשְׂכִּים for מַאֲשִׂכִּים (Iob xxxii 11).

[5]) TORCZYNER; see YELLIN in *Abrahams* p. 443.

Is then a suggestion to read תְּרַשֵּׁשׁ 'shall scorch up' too bold? The Acc. *rašāšu* 'to be red-hot' is evidence justifying the assumption of a Heb. *רָשַׁשׁ Q. 'was burning hot', Pi. 'made burning hot, scorched up' [1]); and this sense, which is suitable, can be obtained by a mere transposition of letters.

XXXV 14: 'the cause is before him and thou waitest for him.'

Elihu is here arguing that men cry in vain to God because they do so only when they want something from him. This verse, then, as thus translated is singularly insipid and indeed has no point. Further, all the ancient Vss [2]). and parallelism of thought suggest that דִּין conceals a verb. May it not be referred to an otherwise unknown Heb. *דּוּן 'to be abased' = Arab. *dâna* (*w*) 'was base, mean weak'? If so, the verse can be translated 'be lowly in his presence and wait anxiously upon him' [3]), or perhaps rather 'be circumspect in regard to him' [4]); this, says Elihu, is preferable to pouring out a stream of empty charges against God.

XXXVI 31-33: 'for by these He judgeth the peoples;
'He giveth meat in abundance.
'He covereth His hands with the lightning
'and giveth it a charge that it strike the mark;
'the noise thereof telleth concerning him,
'the cattle also concerning the storm that
cometh up.'

No one has yet made much sense of these verses, and the R.V.'s rendering offers only a dubious sense; indeed, much of the text must be corrupt.

In verse 31 יָדִין Q. 'he judgeth' from דִּין 'to judge' makes no sense either in the general context or in parallelism with יתן אכל 'he giveth meat' or rather 'food'; and the only possibility seems to be the

---

1) Cognate Acc. *rašāb/pu* 'to glow', whence Heb. רֶשֶׁף 'fiery flash' and so on come, and Eth. *rasana* 'was burning hot'; cf. Syr. *ḥam(m)* Pe. 'scorched; was dry; withered', Pa. 'heated; made dried, dry' for the development of the sense. A corruption of the obvious שרף (BEER) into the senseless שרש is improbable; contrariwise a false emendation of the quite unknown רשש into the well-known שרש lies ready to hand.

2) Whether 'be thou judged' (LXX, Vulg., Tg.) or 'judge thou' (Pesh.).

3) DRIVER in *WO.* I, p. 408.

4) Cf. LXX's εὐλαβηθήσετε for M.T.'s תחילו (Jer. v. 22) after Arab. *ḥâla* ʿ*alā* 'took care of' (HAVA).

assumption of a Heb. *דון = Arab. *dâna* (*w*) V 'enjoyed absolute abundance' [1]), from which יָדִין (Hi.) 'he provides abundance' can be derived. Such a verb makes some sort of sense of the verse [2]). In verse 32 both clauses are oddly expressed. In the first 'he conceals light upon (his) hands' must mean that he grasps it in his hands, so covering it; as thus explained it may be compared with בצל ידו החביאני 'in the shadow of His hand He hides me', *i.e.*, He grasps me in his hand 'like a polished sword' (xlix 3). In the second בְּמַפְגִּיעַ appears to be an error for בַּמִּפְגָּע 'at the mark', as read elsewhere [3]); for the form of the noun is unique. Then ויצו עליה 'and He gave command about it' is certainly corrupt; I therefore propose reading וַיַּצְלִיעָהּ (= וַיַּצְלִיעוֹ) 'and He caused to come forth', postulating a Heb. *הִצְלִיעַ 'caused to emerge' = Arab. *ṣallaʿa* '(the sun) emerged (from the clouds).' In verse 33 the *m*- of מִקְנֶה 'cattle', which is barely appropriate, belongs to רֵעוֹ 'its noise', which may then be read רַעְמוֹ 'its thunder'. Is then עָלָיו 'concerning it' an error of punctuation for *עֲלִיוֹ or *עֱלְיוֹ 'its coming up'? For an otherwise unknown *עֲלִי 'coming up' is a noun legitimately formed on the analogy of עֲדִי 'onset', a *nomen actionis* which occurs or may be restored in several passages [4]). At the same time the unwanted אף 'also' and the impossible על־עולה may be emended to אפּה עַלְעוֹל (= אַפּוֹ) [5]); the resultant קָנָה אַפּוֹ עַלְעוֹל 'in His anger he creates the storm' makes excellent sense in itself and suits the context, even though the two

---

1) Freytag, *Lex. Arab.-Lat.* II, p. 73-4.

2) Four verbs must be distinguished, namely דּוֹן Q. 'to abide' (Gen. vi 3, LXX) and דון 'to be lowly' and דון Hi. 'to enrich, confer benefits on' and דון as well as דִּין 'to judge'. There are also two nouns which must be kept distinct, namely דִּין 'judgement' from this last verb and דִּין 'religion' (Esth. i 13), which is a loan-word from Pers. *daena* = Elam. *dên* 'religion' (s. Brockelmann, *Lex Syr.*[2], p. 151 b).

3) So Ehrlich; cf. Iob. vii 20.

4) So in Ps. xxxiii 9 and Sir. xxxi (xxxiv) 28 as well as Iob x 17, where תְּחַדֵּשׁ עֱדְיָךְ נֶגְדִּי 'thou renewest Thine onset against me' must be read (see Ehrlich, *Psalmen*, p. 69 and *Rg.A.T.* VI, p. 223; Yellin in *Abrahams*, p. 451 f. and Driver in *JTS* XLIII, p. 153).

5) So Graetz and Beer; cf. Aram. *ʿalʿûlâ* and Syr. *ʿûlʿālâ* 'storm'.

halves of this verse must be interchanged. The whole passage now runs [1]).

'for with these [2]) He enriches peoples,
'giving food in abundance.
'He grasps the light(ning) in (His) hands
'and discharges it to reach the mark;
'in His anger [3]) He creates the storm
'and by His thunder [4]) announces its coming,'

which continues the thought of verses 27-30, which tell how God has created the clouds and dispenses the rain.

XXXVIII 24: 'by what way is the light parted
'or the east-wind scattered upon the earth.'

Objection has been taken to this verse on the two grounds that the creation of light has already been mentioned in verse 19 and that נחלק 'was distributed' can only by stretching its meaning be translated 'was parted', *i.e.*, diffused over the universe. Both objections are valid. First, surely **אוֹר** 'light' is an error of vocalization for **אוּר** 'heat', which nicely balances the east-wind; for that is hot and stifling in Palestine. This Heb. **אוּר**, which the Arab. *'uwâru(n)* 'heat (of sun or fire)' explains, occurs in several other passages of the O.T. (Jes. xxxi 9, xliv 16, xlvii 14, l 11; Ezech. v 2) and must be restored in one other place (Sach. xiv 6) [5]); and the cognate Arab. *'ûru(n)* 'east-wind' (Freytag) is instructive as illustrating the connection between heat and the east-wind in Semitic lands. Secondly, the verb will not be חלק 'divided' but another Heb. חלק = Arab. *ḫalaqa* 'created' [6]) which, though not found in the O.T. [7]), is common enough in the Wisdom of Ben Sira; there the author's grandson uses the Gr. κτίζειν to render it [8]). The verse may now be translated

---

1) Reading עָלָיו רַעֲמוֹ or קָנָה אַפּוֹ עַלְעוֹל וְיַגִּיד עָלָיו in verse 33, with inversion of the two clauses.

2) Namely, the rain and the showers of heaven.

3) Cf. Jes. xlii 25 and Iob xvi 9 for the acc. case.

4) Cf. Jes. x 30 for the acc. case (see Brockelmann, *GVGSS* II, p. 306-7).

5) Chajes in *GSAI* XIX, p. 176.

6) Whether these two verbs are ultimately derived from the same root is a difficult question.

7) Except perhaps חֵלֶק 'creatures' (Am. vii 4), if this translation is accepted (Montgomery in *JBL* XXII, p. 95-6).

8) In xxxviii 1, xliv 2 (ἔκτισεν), xxxi 13, 27, xxxix 25, xl 1 (ἔκτισται), xxxiii 13 (*nil*).

'by what way is the heat created
or the east-wind spread over the earth?'

which restores the parallelism of thought in its two clauses.

XXXVIII 37: 'who can number the clouds by wisdom
or who can pour out the bottles of heaven?'

This translation can hardly be right, since numbering the clouds is not only a weak conception in itself as compared with giving rain but also is not analogous to tilting up, *i.e.*, emptying out, the containers in which the rain is stored. I suggest therefore 'who can clear away the rainclouds by wisdom?', taking the Heb. סִפֵּר here as equivalent to the Arab. *safara* '(wind) chased away (clouds from sky); (woman) uncover her face; (dawn) broke'. The meaning then is 'who can send the clouds scudding by his wisdom?'. This root perhaps appears elsewhere in the Heb. *šāp̄ar* 'was fair, pleasing' (Prov. xvi 6; cf. Iob xxxvi 13, where it is applied to the sky) = Syr. *šp̄ar* 'was beautiful', whence *šap̄râ* 'dawn' is derived. If this explanation is admitted, either יספר is an error for ישפר (in spite of the ancient Vss. which all imply ספר Q. 'counted' or Pi. 'recounted') or יְסַפֵּר is an Arabizing by-form of יְשַׁפֵּר 'clears away'; this is not entirely impossible, since the same mutation occurs in יִסַּר = אִשֵּׁר 'strengthened, supported' (Hos. vii 17; Iob iv 3) [1]).

XXXIX 3: 'they bow themselves, they bring forth
their young, they cast out their sorrows.'

Such a translation can hardly be considered satisfactory, if only because 'sorrows' is a strange use of an abstract for a concrete term; and Ovid's *nate, dolor matris* cannot be said to support such a figure of speech in a Semitic language. Fortunately, however, there is nothing wrong with any of the words in the verse. The use of פלח 'clave', to which commentators object, is simply an Aramaism in the sense in which it is here used; for the M.T.'s פטר רחם 'what opens the womb' is translated פתח וולדא 'opening the womb' in Tg. O. and פלחי וולדא 'breaching the womb' in Tg. Jer. II (Ex. xxxiv 19); this shows that פלח is a synonym of פתח and פטר in Hebrew and Aramaic usage in reference to birth. The Vulg.'s *pariunt* approximately represents

[1]) DRIVER in *JTS* XXVI, p. 295 f.; cf. Heb. כבס '(trod), washed' = כבשׁ '(trod down), subdued' and Heb. כנס 'gathered in' = Arab. *kanasa* 'swept together' = Aram. כנשׁ 'assembled' (see NÖLDEKE, *NBSS.*, p. 37[3]).

this sense. Then the Heb. חֶבֶל or perhaps *חָבָל [1]) is here none other than the Acc. *ḫablu* as found in *ḫabliša itêzib* 'she deposits her unborn child' [2]) and the Arab. *ḥabalu(n)* 'embryo of a camel' [3]); and the Pesh.'s *bnaihôn* 'their young ones' comes close enough to this sense. The verse can now be translated

'they crouch, they open (their wombs),
'they bring forth their young',

where the only doubt is whether פלח is used with ellipse of the natural object, *sc.* the womb, or whether some word denoting this has accidentally fallen out [4]). Otherwise, neither emendation nor transposition of words is necessary.

I am happy to have the opportunity of making this small contribution to the complimentary volume being offered to Professor H. H. Rowley as a token of appreciation both of his friendship and of his scholarship. He has ever shown himself a true friend, ready unstintingly to pour out full measure of his stores of learning, pressed down and overflowing, for the benefit of colleagues and of pupils alike; and he has proved himself a scholar זריז בכ״ד ספרים, who by his wide knowledge and clear insight has rendered eminent service in furthering a right understanding of the Scriptures of the Old Testament.

המכבד את התורה גופו מכובד על הבריות

1) So Beer in *Bibl. Heb.*³, p. 1150.
2) Ebeling, *T.u.L.* I, p. 175; **37** R. 15.
3) Cf. Meissner, *K.A.G.*, § 8 b (Acc. *ḫ* = Arab. *ḥ*)
4) Cf. Saʿad.'s *tafsaḫu ʾaulâdahâ* 'they deposit their young ones'; but the object required with פלח is a term for the womb rather than for the offspring.

RELIGIONSHISTORIE UND RELIGIONSPOLEMIK IM ALTEN TESTAMENT

von

OTTO EISSFELDT

Halle

Dass die alttestamentliche "Weisheit" sich von dem, was wir Heutigen als "Wissenschaft" bezeichnen, unterscheidet, nämlich vorab Regeln zu rechtem Verhalten Gott und Mensch gegenüber zum Inhalt hat, also praktisch und nicht wie unsere Wissenschaft theoretisch ausgerichtet ist, gilt ganz allgemein als ausgemacht und trifft in der Tat auch weithin zu. Aber ganz fehlt es dem Alten Testament an Regungen wahrhaft wissenschaftlichen Geistes doch nicht. In dem das erste Menschenpaar zur Übertretung des göttlichen Gebotes, vom Baum der Erkenntnis zu essen, führenden Drange [1]) ist doch gewiss wenigstens etwas von dem faustischen Triebe, zu wissen, was die Welt im Innersten zusammenhält, zu spüren, und dasselbe wäre von dem uns im Zusammenhang des Hiob-Buches erhaltenen Gedicht auf die Unerreichbarkeit der Weisheit [2]) zu sagen. So steht denn auch fest, dass—wie die ihm in Ost und West benachbarten Babylonier und Ägypter—auch Alt-Israel eine als listenförmige Aufreihung zusammengehöriger Grössen aus der Tier- und Pflanzenwelt gestaltete Naturwissenschaft gekannt hat [3]), die nicht nur und wohl nicht einmal in erster Linie praktischen Zwecken gedient hat, sondern aus der „Neugierde", dem Quell aller Wissenschaft, entsprungen ist. Darüber hinaus enthält das Alte Testament auch

---

[1]) Gen. iii 6-7.

[2]) Iob xxviii.

[3]) Vgl. EISSFELDT, *Einleitung in das Alte Testament* (1934), p. 93; A. ALT, „Die Weisheit Salomos", *ThLZ* LXXVI (1951), p. 139-143. Die von ALT genannte Literatur zur „Listen-Wissenschaft" der Ägypter ist jetzt zu ergänzen durch H. GRAPOW, „Wörterbücher, Repertorien, Schülerhandschriften", *Handbuch der Orientalistik*, hrsg. von B. SPULER, I. Band: Ägyptologie, 2. Abschnitt: Literatur, 1952, p. 187-193. Von den Anfängen wissenschaftlicher Erforschung der Natur und systematischer Ordnung ihrer Phänomene zeugen etwa auch manche Abschnitte der Gottesreden im Hiob-Buch (c. xxxix-xli) und der Schöpfungsbericht der Priesterschrift Gen. i-ii 4a.

beachtenswerte Zeugnisse geisteswissenschaftlicher Betätigung. Dass die im 10. oder im 9. Jahrhundert v. Chr. verfasste „Geschichte von der Thronnachfolge Davids" 2 Sam ix-xx + 1 Reg. i-ii keine praktische Abzweckung hat, sondern darstellen will, „was gewesen ist", und insofern geradezu ein Vorbild wissenschaftlicher Geschichtsschreibung bedeutet, ist anerkannt, und mancherlei spricht für die Annahme, dass damals schon der Wurf einer an den Anfang der Welt oder die Entstehung der Menschheit anknüpfenden Geschichte Israels gewagt worden ist und dass die „Thronnachfolge-Erzählung" einen Teil dieser Gesamtdarstellung bildet.

Mit der Geschichtsschreibung hängen Chronologie und Geographie aufs engste zusammen, und so weist das Alte Testament bereits in verhältnismässig früher Zeit Ansätze zu dieser Wissenschaft auf. Ist die mit einer absoluten Ära, nämlich der der Weltschöpfung, rechnende Datierung von Geschehnissen auch erst ziemlich spät, nämlich zur Zeit des Priesterkodex, also um 500 v. Chr., aufgekommen, so finden sich Datierungen nach Regierungsjahren von Königen [1]) oder nach Aufsehen erregenden Naturereignissen [2]) doch schon Jahrhunderte früher, und das ebenfalls ziemlich alte synchronistische System, das unseren Königsbüchern zugrunde liegt [3]), stellt sogar eine — gewiss von aussen, nämlich von Babylonien, beeinflusste — bewundernswerte chronologische Leistung dar. Was die Geographie, genauer: die historische Geographie — denn die physikalische Geographie wird im Zusammenhang mit der listenartigen Naturwissenschaft, von der die Rede war, gepflegt worden sein — angeht, so verdanken gewiss viele der im Alten Testament erhaltenen Ortslisten [4]), etwa die von Jos. xiii-xxi oder Num. xxxiii, praktischen Bedürfnissen ihre Entstehung. Aber erhalten sind sie uns doch nur dadurch, dass sie historischen Anliegen dienstbar gemacht worden

---

[1]) 2 Sam. v 4-5.

[2]) Am. i 1.

[3]) Vgl. A. Jepsen, *Die Quellen des Königsbuches* (1953), p. 30-54.

[4]) Vgl. die hierher gehörigen Arbeiten Alt's, wie sie in der von K. Heinrich Mann zusammengestellten *Bibliographie Albrecht Alt* (*Geschichte und Altes Testament* (1953), p. 211-223) aufgezählt sind, und — neben manchen hier verarbeiteten Aufsätzen aus seiner Feder — M. Noth, *Kommentar zum Buche Josua*, 2. Aufl. 1953 sowie seinen Aufsatz "Der Wallfahrtsweg zum Sinai: 4. Mose 33", *PJB* XXXVI (1940), S. 28. In Auseinandersetzung mit Alt's und Noth's hierhergehörigen Arbeiten tritt Yehezkel Kaufmann, *The Biblical Account of the Conquest of Palestine*, Jerusalem 1953, jetzt dafür ein, dass die Ortslisten von Jos. xiii-xxi und Jud. i nicht praktischen Bedürfnissen entstammende Dokumente, sondern Erzeugnisse der Geschichtsschreibung darstellen.

sind, und von dem „negativen Eroberungsverzeichnis" Jud. i wird man ja wohl sagen müssen, dass es von vornherein als ein historisches Dokument abgefasst ist.

Um von anderen Spuren wissenschaftlichen Geistes, die das Alte Testament aufweist, abzusehen, mögen hier nur noch die Anfänge archäologisch-prähistorischer Forschung, von denen es zeugt, genannt sein. Die Deut. ii 10-12, 20-23 stehenden Angaben, dass den Moabitern die Emiter, den Edomitern die Choriter, den Ammonitern die Samsumiter, den Kaphtoritern die Awwiter im Besitz ihrer Länder vorangegangen seien, und die Mitteilung von dem noch in der Ammoniterstadt Rabba stehenden riesigen Basaltsarg Ogs, des Königs von Basan, des letzten von den Überresten der Rephaiter, stellen solche Anfänge dar.

So mangelt es dem Alten Testament nicht an Spuren eines von praktischen Zwecken, von Nutz oder Schaden ganz absehenden theoretisch-wissenschaftlichen Sinnes. Aber auf einem Gebiet wird man nach dergleichen vergeblich suchen, auf dem der Religion. „Ich bin der Herr, dein Gott, der ich dich aus Ägypten aus der Sklaverei geführt habe. [3] Du sollst keine anderen Götter haben neben mir. [4] Du sollst dir kein Schnitzbild machen und keinerlei Abbild von dem, was im Himmel droben, und dem, was auf Erden unten, und dem, was im Wasser unter der Erde ist. [5] Du sollst das nicht anbeten und dich nicht zu seinem Dienst verführen lassen. Denn ich, Jahwe, bin ein eifernder Gott, der die Schuld der Väter an den Söhnen heimsucht bis ins dritte Glied und bis ins vierte bei meinen Feinden, [6] aber Huld erweist auf Tausende bei meinen Freunden, die meinen Bund bewahren" [1]) — ein Volk, dessen Gott in dieser Weise für sich den Ausschliesslichkeitsanspruch erhebt, kann nur von dem Geist unerbittlichen Kampfes gegen alles, was diesen Ausschliesslichkeitsanspruch seines Gottes gefährdet, erfüllt sein und ist damit unfähig zu objektiver Würdigung nicht nur anderer Religionen und ihrer Götter, sondern auch der geschichtlichen Entwicklung seiner eigenen Religion. Nicht religionshistorische Objektivität ist seine Losung, sondern dogmatische Intoleranz und polemische Aggressivität.

So sind denn Jahwes Diener mit leidenschaftlichem Eifer darauf bedacht, dass jedenfalls innerhalb Israels ihr Gott allein und nur in der ihm genehmen Art verehrt werde. Empört über den Abfall des

---

[1]) Ex. xx 2-6.

Volkes, das, während er zur Entgegennahme der von Gottes eigener Hand geschriebenen und so zu feierlicher Bestätigung der vom Volke bereits angenommenen zehn Bundesworte dienenden Steintafeln auf den Horeb gestiegen ist, sich durch Verehrung des Jungstierbildes gleich gegen das erste Wort vergangen hat, zerschmettert Mose die Steintafeln und nimmt an den Schuldigen furchtbare Rache [1]). Mit derselben Leidenschaftlichkeit schlachtet Elia, nachdem sich sein Gott auf dem Karmel als wahrer und einziger Gott erwiesen hat, am Bache Kison die Baals-Propheten, die das Volk zum Hinken auf beiden Seiten verführt haben, ab [2]). Es sind aber keineswegs nur diese Recken unter Jahwes Dienern, die so für ihren Gott eifern, vielmehr ist das ganze Alte Testament von solchem Geist erfüllt. Wo immer da von anderen Göttern die Rede ist, wird ihrer nicht in objektiv-historischer Art Erwähnung getan, vielmehr werden sie, etwa von Deuterojesaja, in aggressiver Polemik als Machwerke menschlichen Irrtums gebrandmarkt [3]). Das macht dann dem Religionshistoriker, der die Geschichte des alttestamentlichen Gottesglaubens sowie das Wesen der im Alten Testament erwähnten anderen Götter, der in Israels kanaanäischer Umwelt verehrten ebenso wie der bei seinen Nachbarvölkern, Moabitern und Ammonitern, Babyloniern und Ägyptern und anderen, geglaubten, erkennen möchte, den Gebrauch des Alten Testaments als Quelle für seine Forschungen so schwer. Die Baale und Astarten etwa, von denen im Alten Testament immer wieder erzählt wird, dass die Israeliten zu ihnen abgefallen seien [4]), machen, aufs ganze gesehen, einen blassen und schemenhaften Eindruck und lassen sich, obwohl es, etwa bei der Erzählung von dem durch Elia herbeigeführten Sieg Jahwes über den Baal, an schärferer Profilierung einzelner von ihnen nicht ganz fehlt, vom Alten Testament allein aus kaum mit Leben und Farbe füllen. Da müssen ausseralttestamentliche Dokumente und Monumente zu Hilfe genommen werden, und diese stehen ja seit einem Vierteljahrhundert in den dem Boden von Ras Schamra abgewonnenen Schätzen gerade für die Baale und Astarten glücklicherweise auch reichlich zur Verfügung.

Aufzählungen von Göttern anderer Völker, die sich den vorhin

---

[1]) Ex. xxxii.
[2]) 1 Reg. xviii 16-40.
[3]) Jes. xliv 9-20.
[4]) Insbesondere geschieht das in den deuteronomistischen Rahmenstücken des Richterbuches: ii 11-19, iii 7, viii 33, x 6-16 sowie in 1 Sam. vii 4.

erwähnten prähistorisch-archäologischen Notizen über die Vorbewohner der von Israels Nachbarvölkern besetzten Gebiete an die Seite stellen liessen und wie sie von dem Geist objektiver tendenzfreier Forschung beseelt wären, wird es also in Israel schwerlich gegeben haben. Wohl aber finden sich im Alten Testament nicht wenig Fälle, in denen das auf Wahrung des Ausschliesslichkeitsanspruches Jahwes gerichtete Streben und die objektive Mitteilung religionshistorischer Fakten offenbar als sich gegenseitig nicht ausschliessend empfunden wurden und jenes, wie man meinte, durch diese gar noch unterstützt wurde oder doch jedenfalls von ihr nichts zu fürchten hatte, und zwar gehen die hierher gehörigen Angaben den Werdegang der israelitischen Religion selbst ebenso an wie die von anderen Völkern geübten Kulte.

Was das erste betrifft, so darf es zu den erstaunlichsten und erfreulichsten Beweisen von der sich schliesslich doch als stärker denn alle Tendenz erweisenden Wucht geschichtlicher Tatsachen gerechnet werden, dass die im übrigen von der Überzeugung der seit der Urzeit bestehenden Einzigkeit des später unter seinem Namen Jahwe offenbar gewordenen *einen* Gottes beherrschte Überlieferung dennoch deutliche Spuren von einer oder gar von mehreren tief einschneidenden Umwälzungen in der Geschichte der israelitischen Gottesverehrung erhalten hat. Soll es sich nach Meinung der von jener Überzeugung erfüllten Verfasser der hier in Betracht kommenden Erzählungen Ex. iii und Ex. vi, also des Elohisten und des Autors der Priesterschrift, auch nur um einen Wechsel im Namen — statt des bisherigen Elohim oder El Schaddaj fortan Jahwe — des seinem Wesen nach von Uranfang gleichen *einen* Gottes handeln, so darf es doch als ausgemacht gelten, dass es damals in Wahrheit um mehr ging als um die Ersetzung eines alten Gottesnamens durch einen neuen, nämlich um die Einführung des Kultes eines anderen, dazu noch von auswärts übernommenen Gottes.

Diese den genannten Erzählungen abgewonnene Erkenntnis findet darin ihre Bestätigung, dass — wiederum im Widerspruch mit dem Dogma von der immer in Israel geübten Verehrung des *einen* wahren Gottes — das Alte Testament noch deutliche Spuren davon erhalten hat, dass Israels Vorfahren dereinst andere legitime Götter gekannt haben, nämlich einerseits „Götter der Väter", anderseits El. Dabei gilt die von Abraham, Isaak und Jakob geübte Verehrung Els als eine in jeder Hinsicht legitime Vorstufe der Jahwe-Religion, wie denn El der Gott Abrahams, der Gott Isaaks und der Gott Jakobs ist, mit dem sich Jahwe Ex. iii 6, 15, 16 und vi 2 für identisch erklärt [1]). Der Kultus von Göttern wie der „Gott Abrahams" [2]), der „Gott Nahors" [3]) und der „Verwandte Isaaks" [4]) aber ist nach dem Zeugnis von Gen. xxxv 1-5 und Jos. xxiv 2, 14-16, 23 in der Folgezeit als ein überwundenes Stadium betrachtet worden [5]) und die Erhaltung solcher Spuren wohl nur der Tatsache zu danken, dass die historische Tragweite dieser Angaben gar nicht erkannt [6]), die hier erwähnten Götter vielmehr in naiver Selbstverständlichkeit dem *einen* wahren Gott gleichgesetzt worden sind. Jedenfalls beginnt, wenn man von der hier nicht in Betracht kommenden Urgeschichte Gen. i 1-xi 9

---

1) Alt hat in seinem Buche *Der Gott der Väter*, 1929 (wieder abgedruckt in Alt, *Kleine Schriften zur Geschichte des Volkes Israel*, I (1953), p. 1-78) den Nachweis geführt, dass Israels Vorfahren in vormosaischer Zeit Götter, die nach den Empfängern ihrer ersten Offenbarung und Stiftern ihrer Kulte als "Gott des NN" bezeichnet wurden, verehrt haben, und damit die Anfänge der israelitischen Religionsgeschichte in neue Beleuchtung gerückt. Seine These, unter dem Gotte Abrahams, Isaaks und Jakobs, mit dem sich Jahwe in Ex. iii identifiziert, seien diese in eins zusammengeflossenen Väter-Götter zu verstehen, bedarf jedoch der Nachprüfung. Vieles spricht, wie an anderer Stelle ausführlicher darzulegen ist, dafür, dass mit dem Gott Abrahams, Isaaks und Jakobs in Ex. iii vielmehr El gemeint ist.

2) Gen. xxxi 42. 53.

3) Gen. xxxi 53.

4) Wie W. F. Albright, *From the Stone Age to Christianity* (1946), p. 189, 327 = *Von der Steinzeit zum Christentum* (1949), p. 248 f., 434 wahrscheinlich gemacht hat, ist das gewöhnlich als "Schreck" übersetzte פַּחַד (*paḥad*) in der Genetiv-Verbindung פַּחַד יִצְחָק (*paḥad yiṣḥāq*) Gen. xxxi 42. 53 vielmehr als "Verwandter" oder dergleichen zu verstehen. Jedenfalls passt die so verstandene Bezeichnung viel besser zum Typus des Väter-Gottes als "Schreck Isaaks". Müsste es doch bei dieser Auffassung sein Bewenden haben, so wäre jedenfalls aus "Schreck" eher das Moment der Ehrfurcht als das der Angst herauszuhören. Ob auch אֲבִיר יַעֲקֹב (*ᵃbîr yaᶜᵃqōb*), wie Alt (*Kleine Schriften* I, S. 24 f.) will, als Bezeichnung eines von Israels Vorfahren verehrten Gottes vom Typus des Gottes der Väter aufzufassen ist, muss dahingestellt bleiben. In der Sagen-Überlieferung kommt diese Gottesbezeichnung nicht vor, sondern — von späteren Stellen (Jes. xlix 26, lx 16; Ps. cxxxii 2-5) abgesehen — nur im Segen Jakobs Gen. xlix 24, und hier muss sie wohl auf El bezogen werden, wie denn gleich darauf, Vers 25, wo das sinnlose וְאֵת *wᵉʾēt* in וְאֵל *wᵉʾēl* zu korrigieren ist, El Schaddaj erwähnt wird.

5) Vgl. einstweilen C. Steuernagel, "Jahwe und die Vätergötter" (*Beer-Festschrift* (1935), p. 62-71), p. 62 f.

6) Wo das doch geschehen ist, hat man durch Textänderung den Anstoss zu beseitigen gesucht, vgl. die Kommentare zur Genesis, etwa A. Dillmann, 6. Aufl. 1892, p. 357 oder H. Gunkel, 3. Aufl., 1910, p. 353, sowie Stanley A. Cook, "The Theophanies of Gideon and Manoah", *JThSt* XXVIII (1927), p. 368-383; p. 377 und Alt, *Kl. Schr. I*, p. 16 f.

und auch von dem Stück Gen. xii 1-3, das nach allgemein anerkannter und auch zutreffender Auffassung nicht zum alten Sagenbestand gehört [1]), sondern vom Jahwisten herrührt, absieht, die Offenbarung des wahren Gottes an die Väter erst an den El-Kultstätten des Landes Kanaan, in Beerseba [2]) und in Beerlachajroi [3]), in Sichem [4]) und in Bethel [5]). Es ist also El — gewiss in verschiedenen Hypostasen: El Olam [2]), El Roi [3]), El Israel [4]) und El Bethel [5]), aber doch derselbe El — und El allein, der in der vormosaischen Zeit zu Israels Vätern gesprochen hat und insofern wirklich als Vorläufer Jahwes oder gar mit ihm der Person nach identisch gelten kann. Dem wird die geschichtliche Tatsache entsprechen, dass die Jahwe-Religion von der El-Religion viel übernommen hat, während die Kulte der „Götter der Väter" eher als abgöttisch und einer überwundenen Entwicklungsstufe angehörend betrachtet wurden.

Von den Fällen, in denen das Alte Testament über Götter anderer Völker statt der sonst üblichen leidenschaftlichen Polemik gegen sie objektiv berichtet, können hier nur zwei genannt werden, der von 2 Reg. iii und der von 2 Reg. xvii 29-31. In dem ersten geht es um den Erfolg der in der Erzählung von dem Feldzug des israelitischen Königs Joram gegen den Moabiterkönig Mesa von diesem auf der Mauer seiner belagerten Hauptstadt vollzogenen Opferung seines erstgeborenen und zur Thronfolge bestimmten Sohnes: „Als der König von Moab sah, dass der Kampf zu seinen Ungunsten auszugehen drohte, nahm er 700 schwerterprobte Männer, um sich zum König von Edom durchzuschlagen, aber sie hatten keinen

---

[1]) Vgl. ALT, *Kl. Schr.* I, p. 66 f. Dass der Auszug Abrahams aus seiner Heimat mit einer Offenbarung des wahren Gottes an ihn verbunden gewesen sei, hat in der alten Sagen-Überlieferung schwerlich gestanden. Der Elohist sagt vielmehr, dass Gott ihn zum Verlassen der Heimat verführt habe. Mag diese Darstellung des Geschehens auch in ähnlicher Weise dem Elohisten zuzuschreiben sein, wie die andersartige von Gen. xii 1-3 dem Jahwisten, so hätte doch E schwerlich jene Wendung gebrauchen können, wenn die alte Sagen-Überlieferung den Auszug Abrahams aus seiner Heimat auf eine Offenbarung des wahren Gottes an ihn zurückgeführt hätte.

[2]) Gen. xxi 33.

[3]) Gen. xvi 13.

[4]) Gen. (xii 6-7) xxxiii 20.

[5]) Gen. (xii 8) xxviii 10-22, xxxv 6-15. — Eine genauere Darlegung der hier nur angedeuteten Gedanken muss an anderer Stelle gegeben werden. Da wird denn auch der historische Hintergrund der Gen. xiv 14-24 erzählten Begegnung Abrahams mit Malkiṣedek von Salem, dem Priester des El ʿEljon, zu würdigen und hinsichtlich des El Schaddaj darzulegen sein, dass dieser Gott oder vielmehr diese Hypostase des El wahrscheinlich an Hebron haftet.

Erfolg. [27] Nun nahm er seinen erstgeborenen Sohn, der nach ihm König werden sollte, und brachte ihn auf der Mauer als Brandopfer dar. Da kam ein gewaltiger Zorn über die Israeliten, und sie zogen von ihm ab und kehrten in ihr Land zurück" [1]). Hier wird also von einem israelitischen Erzähler zugegeben, dass ein fremder Gott, der moabitische Gott Kamos, unter dem Eindruck des ihm dargebrachten kostbaren Opfers Mesas Gebet um Hilfe erhört, Israel mit seinem Zorn heimgesucht und es zum Abzug in seine Heimat genötigt hat. Dass eine israelitische Erzählung in dieser Weise von der — freilich auf moabitischem Gebiet, nicht etwa auf Israels Boden — durch einen fremden Gott über Israel verhängten Katastrophe berichten und somit die Existenz und die Macht dieses Gottes anerkennen konnte, ist höchst auffällig. Indes fehlt es auch sonst nicht an Zeugnissen dafür, dass die Zeit, der unsere Erzählung zuzuschreiben sein wird, das 9. Jahrhundert v. Chr., in Israels eigenem Gebiet freilich ausschliesslich Jahwes Macht anerkannt wissen wollte, die Beherrschung anderer Länder durch andere Götter aber nicht bestritt und dass erst eine jüngere Zeit für die ganze Welt die Ausschliesslichkeit der Macht Jahwes in Anspruch genommen hat. Die ebenso auffällige Tatsache aber, dass die spätere Zeit trotz der veränderten Einstellung zu den Dingen unsere Erzählung, insbesondere ihren von der Macht des Gottes Kamos zeugenden Schluss, weiter gegeben hat, wird darin ihre Erklärung finden, dass man — wie das in ähnlicher Weise manche Kommentatoren auch noch in neuerer Zeit tun [2]) — den anstössigen Erzählungszug um- und weggedeutet hat. Hinzukommen mag noch die Erwägung, dass es ja ein König des später als abgöttisch betrachteten Nordstaates Israel war, der — jedenfalls in erster Linie — von der Katastrophe betroffen wurde und dass man sie ihm schon gönnte.

Eine gegen den Nordstaat oder richtiger: gegen die Nachfolgerin des Nordstaates, die Gemeinschaft der Samaritaner, gerichtete Tendenz ist jedenfalls für die Erhaltung der 2 Reg. xvii 29-31 stehenden Angaben verantwortlich zu machen. Denn wenn es hier von den nach xvii 24 vom assyrischen König in dem durch Deportation grosser Teile der alteingesessenen Bewohner entvölkerten Samarien angesiedelten Leuten aus Babel, Kutha, Awwa, Hamath und Sepharwajim heisst, dass sie — neben dem in ihren neuen Sitzen heimischen Jahwe — ihre angestammten Götter in Kult-

---

[1]) 2 Reg. iii 26-27.

[2]) Vgl. etwa J. A. MONTGOMERY, *The Book of Kings* (1951), p. 364.

bildern verehrt hätten, die aus Babel die Ṣarpanitu [1]), die aus Kutha den Nergal, die aus Hamath den oder die Aschima, die aus Awwa den Nibchas und die Atargate, die aus Sepharwajim Adrammelech und Anammelech, d.h. Hadad, den König, und ʿAnat, die Gemahlin dieses Götterkönigs, so will diese Mitteilung deutlich den Kultus der Samaritaner als üblen Synkretismus brandmarken, steht also offensichtlich im Dienst der gegen sie gerichteten Polemik. Aber diese Polemik hat uns eben doch historisch zuverlässiges Material erhalten. Denn wenn die Namen der von den einzelnen aus Babylonien und aus Syrien nach Samarien verpflanzten Gruppen verehrten Gottheiten leider auch weithin entstellt sind, so ist doch im einen oder anderen Falle die Wiederherstellung des Ursprünglichen, wie es scheint, bereits gelungen, und man darf hoffen, dass neu zu Tage kommendes Material auch wenigstens einen Teil der noch undurchsichtigen Namen verständlich machen wird.

Es ist also in der Tat an dem, dass das im übrigen von dem Geist religionspolemischer Aggressivität beseelte und zu objektiv-religionshistorischer Würdigung der Phänomene unfähige Alte Testament allerlei Angaben enthält, die als zuverlässiges religionshistorisches Material in Betracht kommen und der vollen Auswertung harren. Wenn diese bisher nur unvollkommen vorgenommen worden ist, so liegt das daran, dass die das Alte Testament beherrschende religionspolemische Tendenz viele der hier in Betracht kommenden Stellen mit Beschlag belegt und den Blick für ihren Wert als religionsgeschichtliches Quellen-Material getrübt hat. Es mussten, wie im Vorangegangenen wiederholt angedeutet worden ist, durch neu erschlossene ausseralttestamentliche Quellen der Forschung erst die Augen dafür geöffnet werden, ehe sie die religionsgeschichtliche Bedeutung der betreffenden Angaben des Alten Testaments erkennen konnte. Die sonst — insbesondere auch bei der Bemühung um besseres Verständnis der alttestamentlichen Weisheitsliteratur — mit grossem Erfolg geübte Methode, Phänomene des Alten Testaments in das Licht neu zu Tage gekommener ausseralttestamentlicher Dokumente und Monumente zu rücken und sie so besser zu verstehen, erweist sich also auch hier als fruchtbar.

[1]) Zu den teilweise entstellten Namen der hier genannten Gottheiten darf auf den soeben angeführten Kommentar von MONTGOMERY verwiesen werden. Dass סֻכּוֹת בְּנוֹת (*sukkôt bᵉnôt*) aus Ṣarpanitu und תַּרְתָּק (*tartaq*) aus Atargate entstellt ist, scheint mir sicher zu sein. So sind in der obigen Übersetzung diese beiden Korrekturen vorausgesetzt. Zu Adrammelech und Anammelech aber darf ich verweisen auf EISSFELDT, "Adrammelek und Demarus", *La Nouvelle Clio* VII (1955), p. 153-159.

"KNOWLEDGE" AND "LIFE" IN THE CREATION STORY

BY

I. ENGNELL
Uppsala

When the enormous literature on the Creation story and the Paradise myth in Gen. i ff., including all detailed problems, is taken into consideration, every attempt to throw light upon the problem must seem both presumptuous and doomed to failure. This paper is, however, presented with very modest pretentions. It owes its existence, first and foremost, to the fact that the present writer wishes very much to pay homage to Professor Rowley, and to thank him for his contribution towards making Swedish scholarship internationally known, as well as, and not least, for his personal kindness and friendship. No one regrets more than the present writer that the references to literature cannot, for reasons of space, be as thorough and comprehensive as they ought to be in a paper of this kind, dedicated as it is to such a well-known specialist in the literature as Professor Rowley. The writer can only assure him that he has read more on the subject than would seem; in fact, he is even bold enough to believe that he has read most of what has been written on the problem, during more than twenty-five years' occupation with the relevant texts and their problems.

In addition to the rather remote connexion with the "Wisdom Literature", a strong contributory cause to the choice of the subject has been the fact that it seems to the writer as if a great deal of modern exegesis of Gen. i ff. has been precisely too "modern", has too strong a flavour of an *interpretatio europeica moderna*, indeed an *interpretatio christiana*, the latter, of course, being justified from the point of view of faith and as being in the service of homiletics, but not at home in a strictly scientific treatment. Many exegetes, who no doubt believe themselves to be giving a presentation of the latter type, in reality seem inclined to read too much of a modern, "philosophical", profoundness of thought both into the creation story and the Paradise myth, a judgment that does certainly not mean that profoundness should be wanting. It may, however, be worth while to seek, and try to capture, the forms of expression which the traditions in question use, their ideological categories, and the view of life, the dialectics ultimately lying behind them.

At the outset of such an undertaking we do perhaps best to deal with the problem expressed in the term *Sitz im Leben* and the question of the so-called "form-literary" type of the texts, properly including the adducing of the relevant comparative material, an aspect of the matter which must, however, here be presupposed rather than carried through. In the second place comes the quite as important examination of the common literary-critical view, and the question whether this view has anything positive to give, or even if it is at all necessary, and if not, from what aspect the matter ought instead to be considered. (The present writer's answer and alternative will, of course, be a *plaidoyer* for the traditio-historical view.) Then we may be prepared to seek the ideological contents of the traditions, their categories of thought and representation, trying in that connexion to answer the question in the rubric of the paper from the point of view of the contents.

Concerning the problem of the setting of the traditions in Gen. i ff. and their "form-literary" type, the alternative next to hand is cult text or "narrative" text, and in the latter case whether of the "wisdom" or "doctrine" text type, or of the mythic-historical type. It is inescapable that the comparative material should here play a not unessential rôle, and it is apparent that the Creation story in Gen. i (the "P" of literary criticism) has its nearest parallel in *Enūma eliš*, the Akkadian creation epic, on which it is also no doubt ultimately dependent, though merely indirectly, by intermediation westwards in very ancient times, being taken over by Israel *via* Canaanite literature and, possibly, cult. However, in the same way as the *Sitz im Leben* of the *Enumā eliš* is lively discussed, whether cultic or not [1]), this applies also, and to a greater degree, to Gen. i. Thus, as is well known, a cultic setting of this text has been argued by GRAHAM-MAY[2]), and carried through above all by HUMBERT [3]). HOOKE adopts a similar position. "P" in Gen. i "has not the form of a narrative", but "rather the appearance of a strophical arrangement with a repeated refrain",

[1]) Cf. e.g. my *Studies in Divine Kingship* (1943), p. 23, 34 ff., etc.
[2]) *Culture and Conscience* (1936), p. 136.
[3]) *Revue d'Histoire et de Philosophie Religieuses*, XV (1935), p. 1-27.

its form suggests a liturgical purpose, and "P" in i 1-ii 4a is in reality the creation liturgy at the Israelite Annual Festival. [1]) With this may be contrasted the opinion of, for example, CASSUTO and VON RAD — so different in matters of literary criticism, but alike in what concerns the problem of the setting of the texts: the Creation story in Gen. i emanates according to CASSUTO from "wisdom circles" [2]), and is, according to VON RAD, *Priesterlehre* in its most pure form, speculative and anti-mythological with "saubere Ausschmelzung alles Mythologischen", all that is left being that God has "das Prädikat des Schöpfers" [3]). The present writer's opinion is well reflected in a paper (in Swedish) by RINGGREN, who answers "no" to the question put in the title, whether the Creation story is a cult text, and, concerning its presupposed "wisdom" character, reaches the conclusion that "any intimate relationship between the Creation story of Genesis and the wisdom literature does not seem to be at hand", a judgment which I also share [4]). To me the state of things seems to be that it is clearly possible, it is true, to see from, for example, the form-literary type, the seven days' creation, the Chaos-Cosmos motive, etc., that the story in Gen. i has had from the beginning a cultic association — in a form about which we know nothing — but that, in its present form, as included in the "P-work" (to which we shall revert), in the "history" representation" of the "P-circle", it is "de-culticized" and transformed, having now the character of a "historical narrative". The *Priesterlehre* character, read into the text, for example, by VON RAD, I am not able to accept, since in my view the "P-circle" is not, as a matter of fact, a very typical priestly circle, but rather — to use a *very* anachronistic metaphor — of the type of the Israelite "Academy of Literature, History, and Antiquities", though, of course, with its root and keen interest in the cult [5]).

Concerning the Paradise myth in ii 4 ff., its parallels outside the Bible and its indirect sources of inspiration are evidently to be found in such Sumero-Akkadian texts as the Dilmun-text, the Epic of

---

1) *In the Beginning* (1947), p. 36.

2) *Annuario di Studi Ebraici*, 1 (1934), p. 22 ff.

3) *Das erste Buch Mose, Kap. 1-12, 9* (1949), p. 36 f.; cf. p. 50 f. This *Entmythologisierung* thesis is very exaggerated and leads, e.g., the author wholly astray in his opinion of the seven days' creation, p. 51.

4) "Är den bibliska skapelseberättelsen en kulttext?" *Svensk Exegetisk Årsbok*, XIII (1948), p. 9-21 (p. 14).

5) I have to refer my reader to ENGNELL-FRIDRICHSEN, *Svenskt Bibliskt Uppslagsverk*, I-II (1948-1952), especially the article *Moseböckerna*, II, col. 324 ff.

Gilgamesh and, above all, the Adapa myth. Here we may join VON RAD in his opinion that what we have before us is not a "doctrine" but a "narrative" — and that already before it was taken over by the P-traditionists — as well as that the story is presented in "etwas wie eine herkömmliche Stilform", although he says nothing about this *Stilform*, but gives merely a reference to the Gilgamesh epic [1]). In fact VON RAD elsewhere states in contradiction that we have to do with a *unicum* [2]). We shall revert to the question in connexion with the problem of the thought and representation categories in this ancient tradition. We may note in passing that for HOOKE what he, as well as almost all others, calls the "J" story belongs to the Annual Festival, too, where it was recited by the priests, though without forming the creation liturgy (which is the "P"story) [3]).

With this we have, though in an all too brief and unsatisfactory way, at least touched upon the "form-literary" problem and the question of the *Sitz im Leben* of our text. We can only underline how necessary such a consideration always is, since a treatment of texts of this kind as pure literature, with disregard of their possible ritual and cultic setting, may lead to the most fearful misinterpretations concerning O.T. texts, as well as, for example, Sumero-Akkadian texts [4]). And now we have to proceed to the literary-critical and the traditio-historical view of our material.

It may be unnecessary to repeat here what seems to be almost an axiomatic *commune bonum* among literary-critical exegetes. They might perhaps be divided into a radical, a more cautious, and an undecided or mixed group. Among scholars who have in a special way occupied themselves with our problem are in the first group, for example, MOWINCKEL [5]), HUMBERT [6]), ZIMMERLI [7]), J. CHAINE [8]), and VON

---

1) *Op. cit.*, p. 60.

2) P. 79 f.

3) *Op. cit.*, p. 36.

4) As an instance of the latter may serve A. HEIDEL's judgment on the Gilgamesh epic in his *The Babylonian Genesis* (1942), p. 71 ff.

5) First and foremost in his *The Two Sources of the Predeuteronomic Primeval History (JE) in Gen. 1-11* (*Avhandl. utg. av Det Norske Videnskaps-Akademi i Oslo*, II. Hist.-Filos. Klasse, 1937:2). MOWINCKEL's view probably finds few scholars today to support it.

6) *Études sur le Récit du Paradis et de la Chute dans la Genèse* (1940).

7) *1. Mose 1-11, Die Urgeschichte, I Teil* (1943). ZIMMERLI works in a purely literary-critical manner, dividing the Paradise myth into a "two-trees version" and a "one-tree version", even if he for certain reasons avoids the term "Quellenschrift", and speaks instead of "Zeugen", "Zeugenstimmen" etc.

8) *Le livre de la Genèse* (1949). Also CHAINE fully accepts "P" and "J" as

RAD [1]). To the middle group of more cautious or sceptical critics might be assigned, among others, HOOKE [2]), HEINISCH [3]), and LEFÈVRE [4]). To this group we do best to assign ROWLEY [5]), and possibly also the scholar who has lately devoted himself in a thorough and interesting, at the same time also very typical, way to the study of the problem, H. J. STOEBE [6]). The result of his introductory investigation into the literary-critical problem in his paper, which is called *Gut und Böse*, is that the addition *in der Jahwistischen Quelle des Pentateuch* is not covered in the author's subsequent treatment and is, apparently, only an expression for his confining himself to a traditional *a priori* thesis. Not least from STOEBE's examination emerges the fact that a literary-critical, source-analytical "solution" falls short. It does not render any positive contribution to the interpretation of the contents.

Having given credit to BUDDE for his attempt at a synthetical interpretation [7]), as also to DE BOER for his work concerning the unity of Gen. ii-iii [8]), we turn to the reliable anti-literary critics, reminding our readers first of CASSUTO's treatment of the problem [9]). This prominent scholar speaks of the story "A" in i 1-ii 4 and "B" in ii 5 ff., which,

---

independent sources; cf. a statement like this: "Chacun des deux récits se suffit à lui-même. Le second ne suppose pas du tout le premier ...", p. 41.

1) *Das erste Buch Mose, Kap. 1-12, 9* (1949). VON RAD, known for his division of "P" into "P¹" and "P²", states that the "Hexateuch", as proved by two hundred years' research work, consists of three sources running parallel, J, E, and P, to be dated *ca.* 950, 850-750, and 538-450 respectively (p. 16), and that it is, in its present form, the result of the work of editors (p. 19). But it is worth noting that VON RAD opposes a mere literary-critical analysis of the J-story, demanding also what he calls "Stoffkritik" (p. 59 f.). Cf. however, on the other hand, the extreme source analysis in iii 17 ff., which is divided into a "bedouin recension" and a "fellah recension" (p. 76 ff.).

2) *In the Beginning* (1947). In spite of his formal adherence to the results of literary criticism, the main point in HOOKE lies on another plane which gives his brief commentary its enduring worth.

3) *Probleme der biblischen Urgeschichte* (1947). HEINISCH stresses, however, how much "P" and "J" have in common in their ideological view. But he is also bold enough to maintain that we owe the Paradise story to Moses (p. 57, 61 f., 103).

4) In *Recherches de Science Religieuse* (1949), p. 455-480, with which cf. the criticism by COPPENS in *Analecta Lovaniensia Biblica et Orientalia*, II: 21 (1951), p. 91 ff.

5) Cf. *The Unity of the Bible* (1953), where ROWLEY calls attention to the fact that the differences between the "P" and "J" stories are often pointed out, while "some important elements which the two have in common are less frequently emphasized" (p. 73 f.). Among these common traces ROWLEY reckons the conception of man, a question to which we shall have to revert.

6) *ZAW*, 65 (1953), p. 188-204.

7) *Die biblische Paradiesesgeschichte*, *Beih. ZAW*, 60 (1932).

8) *Genesis II en III, Het verhaal van den hof in Eden* (1941).

9) *La Questione della Genesi* (1934), p. 257 ff.

however, together "formino un'unità inscindibile" [1]). This judgment is formed primarily from the point of view of content, and with a right emphasis on the fact that "A" and "B" *together* furnish us with the answer to the question how evil got into God's created, good world. However, as is well known, CASSUTO's unitary conception of Genesis is at the same time very "bookish", conditioned by his thinking in writing categories. And thus the first chapters of Genesis also form "l'opera organica di uno *scrittore* (ital. here) originale di altissimo genio", even if based on various traditions current among the people [2]).

A prominent position among the anti-literary critics is also held by COPPENS. In the above-mentioned paper called "L'unité littéraire de Genèse II-III", which is a criticism of LEFÈVRE, COPPENS has admittedly come very near the truth when he declares that the best solution of the literary problem of Gen. i ff., or at least a solution "to which he would not object", is to reckon with "l'existence de deux traditions orales antérieures à la rédaction de notre texte", traditions which "l'auteur du récit, par scrupule de fidélité n'a pas entièrement harmonisées" [3]).

We have now reached the traditio-historical alternative. Among its earlier adherents STAERK is especially worthy of mention in this connexion. In his view of Gen. i ff. he grants that remodelling and redactory work may be traced, but that does not mean that we are able to discern different sources or recensions, much less to reconstruct a "primary text". Thus it is also wrong to detach two "tree recensions", in which connexion we may quote the following sentence: "Les éléments d'une tradition transmise par la bouche du peuple ne peuvent pas être ressuscités par le scalpel disséquant de la critique littéraire" [4]). A synthetical view is the only way towards the right understanding of the traditions, a point of view which will be further stressed below.

And now it may be appropriate to sketch briefly the present writer's view of the "literary problem" of Genesis, hinted at before, as far at least as it is relevant in this connexion. According to this view the Creation story and the Paradise myth form part of the first great tradition work of a narrative character, Genesis to Numbers — called

---

1) P. 275.
2) P. 276.
3) P. 98, 99 n.
4) *Revue d'Histoire et de Philosophie Religieuses*, VIII (1928), p. 67 f.

by me the "P work" or the "Tetrateuch" — handed down to us by a traditionist circle, which may in the same way be called the "P circle". This circle is responsible for a great deal of tradition material of a distinctive character, transmitted within the circle itself from ancient times [1]). With this ("P") material has been brought together a lot of other material, transmitted both in written form and, above all, orally. But in "sources", in the sense of written, parallel, works running through what is usually called the "Pentateuch", the present writer does not believe at all; and he even thinks it impossible to separate "J" and "E" as layers of tradition, owing to the intimate fusion of the tradition material as early as at the stage of transmission by word of mouth. Following a hypothesis of PEDERSEN, I consider Ex. i-xv, the so-called "Exodus legend", the central complex of the "Tetrateuch". Before this, as a kind of introduction, is placed Genesis with its very distinctive tradition material, the central complex of which are the Patriarchal narratives in chs. xii-l, introduced in their turn by the "Primeval history" in chs. i-xi. And here the first larger complex is formed by i 1-vi 4 [2]). It is true, of course, that already this complex is very composite, being made up of tradition material issuing from various directions and with various primary *Sitz im Leben*. It is also true that, within this complex, what is called by literary criticism the "P" creation story in Gen. i really consists of the "P circle's" own tradition material. But to distinguish in ii 4 b ff. the "source J" is to the present writer an impossible view. It is evident that tradition material *other than* the "P circle's" own comes in here. But as elsewhere it is futile to call it "J material" or "JE material", and as so often it is so well worked into the narrative of the "P circle" as to form in this case an integral part of the coherent, topically uniform and well disposed "P" story, in which the "P traditionists" with their own creation story in ch. i have, as we say in Swedish, "placed the church in the midst of the village", giving their own fundamental view of the matter. But, as I have already tried to say, the "variant" in Gen. ii — though it ought not even to be called so — is not placed thereafter haphazard. It forms an organic transition to the story of the Fall in ch. iii. And thus we can do no better than take the whole for

---

[1]) And that is why I have used the designation "P", though it is from my special point of view rather "dangerous" since it may be associated too much with the source "P" of literary criticism. It has also been pointed out above that the circle is in reality not very "priestly", at least, less priestly than the "D circle".

[2]) Thus also DE VAUX, *La Genèse* (1951), p. 29.

what it really is, a single unitary story. And as to the specially relevant problem in this connexion, that of the two trees, the tree of "knowledge" and the tree of "life", it may be stated here that it is in the present writer's view wholly evident that *both* trees are from the very beginning organically at home in the narrative.

A consequence of what has been said hitherto is that the investigation can, and ought to, be made internally and ideologically, though, of course, with due regard to the relevant comparative material [1]). However, it is accordingly not least important to make clear to oneself in what category *Adam*, "the first man", is thought of and depicted, since this may contribute a great deal to our understanding also of the nature of the "knowledge" and "life" that plays so central a rôle in the dialectics of the whole story.

The different categories to be considered here are "Man" as such, as humanity, "Man" as ancestor, *Urvater*, "Man" as Primeval man, *Urmensch*, and "Man" as primeval king, *Urkönig*. The boundary-lines between these categories are, of course, not very clearly marked, but it may be useful to try to keep them apart.

It must be granted, I believe, that the first alternative has been too easily applied, not least since modern scholarship learnt the significance of the collective view in old Israel, and devoted its interest to the "participation thought" and the idea of "corporate personality" [2]). There is no doubt that this aspect is inherent in the narrative from the very first and plays a great part, and it is only natural that this very aspect consistently grew more and more important in the interpretation of the story — already in ancient Israel — till it became wholly dominant. Yet there can be no doubt that the *original* thought category was different, and therewith also the deepest intention of the story, and that the mere mankind view does not do justice to the matter. We need hardly dwell upon the ancestor category interpretation. It lies close to the former, but is certainly less appro-

---

[1]) Thus PIDOUX, who has most recently dealt with the problem, is right so far in his statement that "le moins qu'on puisse faire, c'est d'interpréter ces chapitres [i.e. Gen. ii-iii] à la lumière de la Bible elle-même" — even if I would prefer "de l'Ancien Testament" to "la Bible". Cf. *Encore les deux arbres de Genèse 3!*, *ZAW*, 66 (1954), p. 37 ff. (p. 38).

[2]) PEDERSEN, WHEELER ROBINSON, A. R. JOHNSON *et al.* Many of those who hold that the human, that mankind as such, is primary in the notion *'ādām*, then draw the — most misleading — line from here *via* Ezechiel to the "Son of Man" in the N.T., with the same stress here too, thus, e.g. PROCKSCH, *Theologie des A.T.'s* (1950), p. 312 f.

priate, especially since it has undoubtedly its roots in, and associations with, a pre-Canaanite period and milieu which obviously plays no great part in this story with its special origin and setting.

Concerning the "primeval Man" category which is the one by far most frequently resorted to, we would properly require a full investigation into this subject here. But for reasons of space, and since the present writer hopes to publish such an investigation elsewhere [1]), we must restrict ourselves to the following remarks. The notion of "primeval Man" in its mythic-cosmic form has played a very modest part among both Eastern and Western Semites [2]). This holds true also of ancient Israel. It is in later times that the notion in question begins to play a greater part, especially in gnostic systems like Mandaeism and Manichaeism, as well as in Philo and in Jewish-Rabbinical and Christian apocalyptic speculation [3]). But within the O.T. itself an analysis of the texts that are usually referred to as relevant in this connexion shows that we have in reality to do with another thought and representation category, to wit, the sacral king — thus, apart from the Adam tradition in Genesis, Ezech. xxviii, Ps. viii, Iob xv 8, etc. [4]). Paying due regard to such phenomena as "disintegration" and "democratization", and to the problem of the various *Sitz im Leben*, etc., of these texts, I believe we are justified in stating that nowhere are we concerned here with the "primeval Man" category, but with the sacral king category [5]).

These brief remarks concerning the relevant material within the

---

[1]) In *Svensk Exegetisk Årsbok* for 1955. There the texts mentioned here, Ezech. xxviii, Ps. viii, etc. will be dealt with in detail.

[2]) So far MOWINCKEL is right in his exposition in *Han som kommer* (1951), (esp. p. 274), so far, but no further!

[3]) Cf. B. MURMELSTEIN, *Adam, ein Beitrag zur Messiaslehre, Wiener Zeitschr. f. d. Kunde des Morgenlandes*, 35-36 (1928-1929).

[4]) As to Ps. viii, cf. my preliminary remark in *SEÅ*, XVIII-XIX (1953-1954), p. 185.

[5]) It may be worth noting here that BENTZEN has seen that in Ezech. xxviii and Iob xv we have in reality to do precisely with "disintegrated royal texts", cf. his. *Messias-Moses Redivivus-Menschensohn* (1948), p. 39. But his assertion that the "primeval Man" category must be prior and superior to the sacral king category ("der übergeordnete sein m u s s" — ital. here) is nothing but an *a priori* judgment based on an evolutionary idea of prehistoric conditions about which we know nothing. The same *a priori* argumentation recurs concerning the ʿEbed Yahweh figure whose origin from the religio-phenomenological point of view (as *Urphänomen*) "m u s s breiter, allgemeiner bestimmt werden", i.e., as *Urmensch* (p. 62, ital. here). It is, however, preferable to keep to the representation category used by the sources themselves.

O.T. must suffice as a necessary *memento* when we are facing the problem of the right understanding also of "Adam" in the *Urgeschichte* in Genesis. It was not for nothing that Israel lived on the soil of Canaan for hundreds of years, with the experience of a sacral kingship during these very hundreds of years that has left its traces not least upon the narration categories, whether it concerns the patriarchs, Moses, the judges, and, sometimes even great prophets like Isaiah and Ezechiel or, of course to a still higher degree, the saviour figures that have in different ways arisen from the figure of the sacral king: the Davidic Messiah, 'Ebed Yahweh, and the "Son of Man".

It is certainly no new discovery that Adam in the Creation story is described in royal categories, but it may nevertheless be useful to remind ourselves of the following royal features in this representation, though without any claims to completeness.

First and foremost Adam is "divine", even if there is, as we shall see soon, a very important exception. He is created *bᵉṣalmēnū*, *kidmūtēnū*, "in our image, after our likeness", i 26, an expression the second half of which I confess I am absolutely unable to consider as a limitation of the former, but as an equivalent and strengthening of it [1]). The conception is "naively" anthropomorphic [2]). Adam is a divine being among other such beings [3]). In ch. ii Adam's share in the "divine" is expressed by his having the breath of God blown into his nostrils, ii 7, which should not be taken as contrary to the former, but as meaning much the same.

As a second feature may be mentioned the "enthroning" of Adam as the ruler of Cosmos, i 28 [4]).

As a third feature we have the placing of Adam as "gardener" in the paradise of Eden, ii 15. CHAINE says of this: "Quant à la garde du jardin, on ne voit pas à quel besoin elle répond, puisque l'homme est seul et va dominer sur tous les animaux" [5]). But the pattern of sacral

[1]) *Vs.* KÖHLER, *Theol.Zeitschr.*, 4 (1948), p. 16 ff., *et al.*

[2]) Thus I cannot share the view of HEMPEL, HEINISCH, VRIEZEN, G. E. WRIGHT and ROWLEY that the expression refers merely to the spiritual plane. A reference to the spiritual standard of the "P" source which would not allow such a naive anthropomorphism is no proof; it is a vicious circle type of reasoning.

[3]) Cf. the parallelism with the king of Tyre in Ezech. xxviii. Cf. also Gen. iii 5 and iii 22, as well as later on vi 1 ff., passages which undeniably refer to what is usually called a "polytheistic stage". Yahweh is the high god and creator, enthroned in the *puḫur ilāni*, his *ṣᵉbāʾōt*, "hosts".

[4]) Cf. especially Ps. viii 7 ff., and see BENTZEN, *Det sakrale Kongedømme*, p. 76 f.; RINGGREN, *SEÅ*, XIII, p. 18. The original motive is here "democratized" to a high degree, and more so in Gen. than in Ps. viii.

[5]) *Le livre de la Genèse*, p. 38.

kingship gives a clear answer to this question. For it is an almost primeval feature in this mythic-ritual pattern that the king is "gardener", to wit, of the "tree of life" in the mythical garden — symbolized cultically in the temple grove — with the "water of life", at the *narāte killanē*, ii 10 ff.; that the world rivers are four in our case makes no essential difference [1]). It is thus to be observed that the expression in ii 15 "to dress it and to keep it" (*ʿābad, šāmar*) has not in view work on the land, of an easy kind, in comparison with the hard work following Yaweh's cursing of the soil [2]). It is not improbable that we have here a conscious play upon the double meaning of *ʿābad* as "serve (in the cult)" and "work" [3]). The theme of the gold and the precious stones, recurring in Ezech. xxviii, is also worthy of emphasis. Behind it lies, at least partially, the royal robe. In the same connexion belongs probably also Yahweh's giving of the coats, iii 21, a detail which may originally be inspired by Anu's giving of the heavenly robe to Adapa in the Adapa myth.

More important is another feature in the royal ideology, namely, Adam's share in the creation of the animals — for this is the deepest meaning of the "giving of names" in ii 19 ff. — and the creation of Eve, "the mother of all living", directly out of Adam, ii 21 ff., iii 20 (though the etymology of the name given in the latter passage is no doubt secondary).

Finally, there is the *hieros gamos* motive which from of old belongs to the royal pattern, and with which we meet also here, though in a very characteristic and distinct form. At the same time this motive plays a very prominent, we might even say, the central, rôle in our story, as will be pointed out in the following in connexion with the

---

[1]) Cf. with this theme my *Studies* (1943), Topical Index, s.v. „Tree (plant) of life", my articles in *Svenskt Bibliskt Uppslagsverk*, II (1952), "Livets träd" and "Telning", and my paper on Ps. i, " 'Planted by the Streams of Water' " in *Studia Orientalia Ioanni Pedersen dicata* (1953), p. 85 ff., and for a detailed study WIDENGREN, *The King and the Tree of Life in Ancient Near Eastern Religion*, *Uppsala Universitets Årsskrift*, 1951: 4. The motive has also been dealt with by BÖHL in *Mededeelingen der Koninklijke Akademie van Wetenschappen*, Afd. Lett., N.R. 12 : 8 (1949), p. 41 ff. The right connexion in our case has been observed by PIDOUX, *ZAW*, 66 (1954), p. 38 f.

[2]) As held, e.g. by ZIMMERLI, *op.cit.* (1943), p. 223; VON RAD, *op.cit.* (1949), p. 64, *et al.*

[3]) The above explanation would be further supported if DE BOER's suggestion could be accepted that the fem. suffix in לעבדה ולשמרה does not refer to גן which is masc., but to עץ taken as a collective, *op. cit.*, p. 4. However, this conception seems far-fetched and, in fact, impossible. But the case is quite clear in spite of that.

special problem of the "tree of 'knowledge' ". We also have a clear reminiscence of the old royal dragon killing motive, and that too in a unique form, the fight between the "seed of the woman" and the serpent, iii 15, though we have no right to read a so-called "proto-evangelion" into the text here [1]).

And now at last we come to the question of the "tree of the knowledge of good and evil", though it is, of course, impossible to treat this very intricate and still unsolved problem as comprehensively as it deserves. May I be permitted first to declare briefly what kind of "knowledge" we are *not* concerned with? Thus we are not concerned with the "ethical sensorium", or whatever it may be called; nor with "what is useful and harmful", or anything like that, even if one has recourse to the personal experience category, as, e.g., LAGRANGE [2]) and lately ZIMMERLI [3]). Neither do I believe in the now so popular *antonym* interpretation, according to which "good and evil" as a word pair should mean "everything", a knowledge which includes all aspects [4]). There is no doubt that the expression several times has such an antonymic import, but such is not the case here in the Creation story. Nor is it a general cultural development that is intended. And the "anti-conception" theory of COPPENS is no more acceptable[5]).

HOOKE's opinion is indeed interesting. With a reference to comparative material like the Adapa myth and the Gilgamesh epic, where the story deals with a magic knowledge of "powerful incantations and rituals" by which the forces of life and death may be controlled, and since these sources must have had something to say to our narrator in Genesis—else he would not have used them—HOOKE concludes that the eating of the fruit of the "tree of knowledge" reveals the nature of the "tree of life" and its locality, which were from the

---

[1]) Thus rightly, e.g., HOOKE, *op.cit.*, p. 33, who also gives a good exposition of the rôle of the serpent and its background.

[2]) *Revue Biblique* (1897), p. 344: "La connaissance expérimentale qui fait éprouver par une pénible constatation personelle quelle différence il y a entre le bien et le mal".

[3]) *Op.cit.*, p. 201: "dass der Mensch jetzt selber weiss, was er zu tun hat", i.e., man's acting of his own accord, and with the stress laid not so much on the "knowledge" itself but "dass es um Raub geht, das ist entscheidend" (p. 195). In much the same category fall also the interpretations by ROBERTSON, *JMEOS*, 22 (1938), p. 35; EICHRODT, *Theologie des A.T.'s*, II (1935), p. 62 f., and DE BOER, *op.cit.*, p. 5 ff., who, however, is opposed to the *imago dei* thesis.

[4]) Thus, e.g., HUMBERT, VON RAD *et al.*; cf. G. LAMBERT in *Vivre et Penser*, 3 (1945), p. 91 ff., and A. M. HONEYMAN, *JBL*, 71 (1952), p. 11 ff.

[5]) *De Kenning van Goed en Kwaad in het Paradijsverhaal*, *Mededeel. van de Koninklijke Vlaamsche Academie voor Wetenschappen*, Afd. Lett., VI: 4 (1944).

beginning secret, hidden from Man [1]). This may sound attractive, and from the ideological point of view HOOKE is not wholly on the wrong track. Yet we must say that he has allowed himself to be misled by the comparative material.

The decision has, however, to be made from internal considerations, having regard to contents, continuity of thought, and the meaning of *daʿat ṭōb wārāʿ* in other relevant passages in the O.T. Unfortunately, it is impossible to give here a thorough exposition so far as the latter is concerned. I have to content myself with what I have pointed out earlier in another connexion, that in several cases in the O.T. the expression undoubtedly refers to the sexual sphere, thus e.g. in Deut. i 39; 2. Sam. xix 36, and Jes. vii 15; cf. also the use of *ṭōb* in Gen. vi 2 [2]). In the former respect everything points in the same direction: Man is cut off from the "tree of 'knowledge' ", that is what distinguishes him from the rest of the "gods" [3]). When Adam and Eve cease to observe the prohibition, they secure the divine "knowledge" which they did not have before: their eyes are opened, they "know" (*waįįēdᵉʿū*, iii 7) that they are naked, they are mutually ashamed of their nakedness and cover themselves. That the nakedness and the shame form a central motive is to be seen also from Yahweh's words in iii 11. Of the utmost importance, moreover, is the connexion of the curse upon the woman with the sexual: she shall bring forth sons, though in pain, and, although her husband is to be her ruler, her desire shall be to him, iii 16. Central too is the context in iv 1 ff. Adam "knows" Eve, she conceives and bears a son of whom she says: *qānītī ʾīš ʾæt-Jahwǣ*. However these words be interpreted, as referring to Cain or, which is far more probable or even certain, to Adam, their ultimate meaning is that Adam is now like the "gods" in that respect, too, that he is now capable of begetting [4]).

What has been said implies, however, an essential modification. It is not a question of sexual life in itself. It is meaningless to put the question if our text intends to say that Adam and Eve had sexual in-

---

[1]) *In the Beginning*, p. 28 ff.

[2]) Cf. my (Swedish) paper *Kain och Abel. En rituell interpretation* in *Svenska Jerusalemsföreningens Tidskrift*, 46 (1947), p. 93.

[3]) In the Sumero-Akkadian parallels Man is instead locked out from the "tree of life", he has no share in "eternal" life—thus Gilgamesh and Adapa; the only exception is Ūmnapishtim, "the Akkadian Noah".

[4]) Cf. BUDDE in *ZAW*, 31 (1911), p. 147 ff., and my above-mentioned paper on Gen. iv, p. 93 f. A short philological survey is given by RINGGREN in his *Word and Wisdom* (1947), p. 101.

tercourse before their eating from the "tree of knowledge". The whole stress is laid on the ability to procreate. This is the decisive fact: Adam and Eve in Eden have not been allowed earlier to reproduce offspring. It is to be taken for granted that they had access to the "tree of life". By eating thereof they obtained "life", "eternal" life — on the individual level we might perhaps say in a doubtless too modern mode of speech. But that they should *both* have eternal life *and* ability to multiply themselves, that was out of the question, from the point of view of Yahweh himself and the other "gods". On this point iii 22 f. is most instructive: "But God Yahweh said: 'Behold, when the man is now become as one of us, to know good and evil, lest he (further) put forth his hand, and take *also* of the tree of life and eat and live forever' therefore God Yahweh sent him forth from the garden of Eden . . ." [1]). This means that the collective aspect is indeed the dominant one, and there cannot be any doubt that the reason for this is the inclusion of the Paradise myth in the narrative context and the ultimate aim with the primeval history as an introduction to the stories of the Patriarchs and the history of Israel. For this very aim is, from ch. iv onwards, to relate how mankind grows and spreads, at the same time as the "development" inexorably represents a consistently increasing decay, involving such things as the eating of flesh, polygamy (Lemek, the "sons of god"), violence, manslaughter, etc., a "development" that cannot be stopped either by the "flood", or the "confounding of language" and the "scattering" in the story of the tower of Babylon in ch. xi. The result is a world of peoples in dissolution, out of which Yahweh, by the sharpest contrast, chooses Abraham, and in him Israel, to let his blessing come to the chosen people through the fathers, the patriarchs.

The dialectics dictating the Creation story and the Paradise myth is thus the antithesis between life and death, the permanent fight for life against death, the same central problem that dominates also the Sumero-Akkadian parallels, though the Israelite shaping of the motive is all through original and superior; there can be no doubt about that. This dialectics reaches in a natural way its tragic climax in the cursing of the man, iii 17 ff., with its culmination in the "returning unto the ground". As it ought to be, the divine threat is thereby fulfilled which

---

[1]) Naturally OBBINK is right on this point; it is by no means the narrator's intention to say that Adam had never had access to the "tree of life"; cf. his excellent paper in *ZAW*, 46 (1928), p. 105 ff. STAERK, in *RHPhR*, 8 (1928), joins him

was from the beginning bound up with the "tree of 'knowledge' " [1]). Thus we may state in passing that Yahweh has not told a lie, while the serpent has told the smartest, most seductive half-truth [2]). And for this very reason, consideration for the unity of the narrative, Adam, the "primeval king", is thus cut off from that "knowledge" in which the king in Ezech. xxviii shares fully. This "wisdom", which is the same as vitality, "life", here through procreation, is intended also by the term *lᵉhaśkīl* in iii 6. And it is certainly not a mere coincidence that the same word stem recurs in Jes. lii 13 with reference to the ʿEbed Yahweh figure, depicted all through in royal categories, and in a psalm like xlv (in the rubric under the form *maśkīl*) on the one hand, as well as in "ʿEbed Yahweh psalms" such as lxxxviii and lxxxix, down to Dan. xii 3 on the other [3]). For, however different these texts may be with regard to their types and setting, one thing they have in common: they deal with the victory of life, the conquering of death. Typically enough this is also a central theme in the so-called "wisdom literature", Eccles. iii 19, etc.

It still remains for us, however, to indicate at the same time as we thereby revert to the royal category representation and the problem of the royal pattern, how the narrators in Gen. i ff. have used the ancient royal *hieros gamos* motive. This rite, belonging to the drama of the Annual Festival, was no doubt the one that in the most central manner aimed at the renewal and sustenance of fertility, the most vigorous and earth-bound form of the victory of life over death, of Cosmos over Chaos. But here this is turned wholly into the opposite.

---

[1]) For the unitary interpretation shows that those scholars are wrong who maintain that the curse upon the man should not involve death, thus, e.g., ZIMMERLI, *op.cit.*, p. 220 f., and VON RAD, p. 45, 77. With typical modern western demands for logic and accuracy in the modes of expression, the latter raises the objection that the text does not say (in verse 17) "wirst du sterblich werden" but "musst du sterben" (p. 65, cf. p. 77). For the same reason the conception of DE BOER (who joins in his turn VRIEZEN) is impossible. According to him nothing is said in ii 17 or iii 22 of a state of death that succeeds an earlier immortality. The text merely states the penalty of death for the transgression of a command. (*Genesis II en III*, p. 7 f., 15 f.) The core of the narrative is to give an explanation of how the heavy existence of the simple farmer has replaced the life without work in Paradise. The present writer has earlier issued a warning against reading too much profoundness of thought into our texts, but he has a definite feeling that this is too simple a solution, as shown precisely by the synthetical interpretation, the same kind of interpretation for which DE BOER himself rightly pleads (p. 16).

[2]) Cf. e.g., ZIMMERLI, p. 224.

[3]) Cf. with this my paper on the ʿEbed Yahweh songs in *BJRL*, 31 (1948), p. 24 ff.

The result of the new "knowledge" is "life", it is true, "life" in the sense of a numerous progeny. But the earth and its vegetation are cursed, the lot of the offspring is hard work, pain, destruction and death. This is verily an *interpretatio israelitica* of Canaanite tradition material almost without equal. And in this respect Gen. iv offers an ideological parallel — there is certainly more than one reason why this tradition is chosen for its present place. Ultimately we are here dealing with another royal Annual Festival ritual of the so-called "Tammuz type", namely *as an inspiring motive*, whereas the theme, here too, is turned into its opposite, into reaction and polemics against the Canaanite ideology round the "king sacrifice motive". And again the result is the same as in Gen. i-iii, a curse upon the earth (iv 12) and an unsteady nomadic life as a hunted wolf for Cain, the son of Adam [1]). We must refrain now from entering upon a discussion of other characteristic Israelite features, which does not mean that they do not exist. They certainly do, for example, with regard to the idea of god, the form of the disobedience motive as sin, etc.

Let me instead in conclusion point out anew that I do not by any means claim to have solved all the problems of Gen. i ff. There are, of course, many other aspects of the text which have not even been touched upon, aetiological motives, etc. Neither can the interpretation given above of "knowledge" and "life" be called exhaustive. But I do myself believe, of course, that I have hit upon the most central theme, the deepest motive in the story. I am fully aware of the fact that many objections may be raised, especially if one starts from certain inconsistent details and then enlarges them. Such an objection may refer, for example, to Gen. i 28, where Adam is ordered from the very beginning to "be fruitful, and multiply, and replenish the earth". A banal refutation would be a reference to the somewhat misused quotation *quandoque dormitat bonus Homerus*. As a traditio-historian I prefer to point to the first command of the traditionist: faithfulness to the traditions taken over, liberty in selecting them and in arranging them in their places in the work as a whole. And seldom, if ever, has greater methodical skill in this respect been shown than by the "P circle" in its great narrative work. Thus I think I can do no better

---

[1]) Cf. my above-mentioned paper in *Svenska Jerusalemsföreningens Tidskrift*, 46 (1947), p. 92 ff. May I be allowed to point out that JOHNSON's criticism of this paper in *Exp. Times*, lxii (1950), p. 41, n. 1, shows that he has missed the most essential point, the reactionary re-interpretation of the motive, apparently through difficulty with the language.

than conclude with the following quotations from W. STAERK, to whom I have referred earlier: "Les exégètes qui cherchent à expliquer les traditions bibliques ne devront pas oublier que la seule méthode vraiment féconde est celle qui consiste à interpréter les détails par l'ensemble et à considérer d'abord le sens naturel et l'essence des récits." And: "Les contradictions, comme aussi les doubles traditions qui paraissaient d'abord s'exclure réciproquement, se révéleront alors plus d'une fois comme partie intégrante de l'idée totale. Et c'est ainsi que l'on échappera aux résultats décevants d'une critique qui opère toujours avec le scalpel de l'analyse et qui considère seulement les apparences extérieures et non les réalités" [1]). These words might indeed serve both a traditio-historian and a true "patternist" as a manifesto.

---

1) *RHPhR.*, 8 (1928), p. 69.

THE *RÎB*-* OR CONTROVERSY-PATTERN IN HEBREW MENTALITY

BY

B. GEMSER

Pretoria

1. THE FREQUENCY OF DISPUTES IN ISRAELITE LIFE

The frequency of quarrelling in the life of the ancient Hebrews is reflected on many pages of the Old Testament. Materials for comparison as between the Hebrews and other ancient peoples in this respect will be difficult to obtain. The occurrence of so many cases of strife in the Old Testament is perhaps more proof of the honesty of the narrators than of the quarrelsomeness of their people. Cain and Lamech are certainly not represented as ideal Hebrews or model people in Gen. iv. The strife between the herdsmen of Abram and Lot is attributed to the circumstances in which these family chiefs had to live, to lack of "Lebensraum" (Gen. xiii). Quarrels about wells are bound to arise in arid regions. The names of three wells are connected with such controversies in Genesis: Beer-Sheba (Gen. xxi 26-32, ending in a "covenant"), Esek "Contention" and Sitnah "Enmity" (Gen. xxvi 18-20, 21), and a fourth with a happy absence of animosity, Rehoboth "Room" (Gen. xxvi 22). An illustrative example of a *rîb* is offered in the narrative of Laban's overtaking of Jacob on his flight with Laban's daughters (Gen. xxxi 25-55), with its diversity of accusations, threatenings, pleadings of innocence and ignorance, contra-accusations, appeal to ancient herdsman rights, and finally to God. In the *rîb* between Jacob and Laban (verse 36) God *hôkîaḥ* 'decided' (verse 42, not "rebuked 'you' "), according to Jacob, beforehand by his warning of Laban in a dream (verses 24, 29); the outcome of the contention is also here a "covenant", with an everlasting witness (a *maṣṣēbâ* according to one tradition, a heap of stones according to the other, verses 44 ff.).

---

*) In transcribing Hebrew words no distinction has been made between consonants with and without *dāgēsh*.

The quarrelling (*niṣṣâ*) of the two Hebrews in Egypt (Ex. ii 13 f.) was like the *rîb* supposed in the Book of the Covenant (Ex. xxi 18 f.), not with words only, but with fist or stick or stone [1]).

In the late narrative on the altar built by the Transjordan tribes in Jordan's borderland (Jos. xxii), we find a dispute between two halves of the Israelite *'ēdâ*, or national-cultic community, on an eventual threat to their national and cultic unity; although not called a *rîb*, integral elements of it are represented in the accusations of a *ma'al* or "encroachment upon the rights" of the one God and his cult and the unity of his people (verses 16 ff.), the assurance to the contrary in the form of an oath of purgation (verses 21 ff.), and the settling of the dispute by providing a guarantee and witness (by giving a name to the altar, which unfortunately has fallen out, verse 34).

A genuine tribal dispute threatened to arise between Gideon, head of the Abiezer-clan of the tribe of Manasseh, and the tribe of Ephraim, but their "violent upbraiding" was dexterously and quickly appeased by the "Judge" (Jud. viii 1-3). A similar case arose between the Ephraimites and Jephthah the Gileadite, this time with much more serious consequences (Jud. xii 1-6); it is interesting here, in the reproach of Jephthah against the Ephraimites, that he calls himself and his "people" (*'am*) a *'îš rîb* "a person with a case, a feud" against the Ammonites, in which he had not been "helped" (his right had not been vindicated, *hôšîa'*) by the Ephraimites.

The haughty and ungrateful treatment experienced by David and his "young men" from the wealthy farmer Nabal constituted a case; Nabal's sudden death was considered by David as a divine vindication of his right: *bārûk yahwê 'ašer rāb 'et-rîb ḥerpātî miyyad nābāl* lit. "Blessed be the Lord who has given judgement in the law-suit of the disgrace suffered by me from the side of Nabal" (I Sam. xxv 39). The continuous persecutions by king Saul form another instance of litigation in which David feels himself involved and in which he hopes for divine judgement: *wehâyâ yahwê ledayyān wešāphaṭ bênî ûbênèkâ wejērè' wejārēb 'et-rîbî wejišpeṭēnî miyyādèkâ* (I Sam. xxiv 15). These and similar experiences, like the rebellion of his son Absalom (2 Sam. xv ff.) and the rivalry between the men of Judah and of Israel (2 Sam. xix 41 ff.,

[1]) Deut. xxxiii 7 also speaks of a *rîb* with the hands; cf. the same verb with *bêt instrumenti*, Am. vii 4 (uncertain text); Jes. xxvii 8; and *nišpaṭ be*, Ezech. xxxviii 22, indicating the means of punishment.

xx) form the *rîbê ʿām* from which the author of Ps. xviii knows that he has escaped (*pallēṭ*), delivered by Yahweh (verse 44).

Striking examples of disputes arising out of the fulfilment of their prophetic mission are the encounters between Samuel and Saul (I Sam. xv 10 ff.), and between Elijah and Ahab after the king's taking possession of the vineyard of Naboth, especially the last with its questioning and counter-question, its accusations and threatenings and finally the mitigation of the sentence (I Reg. xxi 17-29). Several times Nehemiah, the governor, started a *rîb* with the nobles and officials of Judah (Neh. v 7, xiii 11, 17), and with groups of his people (Neh. xiii 25), in his struggle against all kinds of evil; here again *rîb* means much more than a quarrel, as the A.V. "I rebuked, contended with", and, for example, the American Revised Standard Version "I brought charges against, I remonstrated with (*bis*), I contended with", rightly express.

Israel's "wise men" found it necessary to warn their pupils and people earnestly and incessantly against quarrelling, as more than twenty proverbs prove [1]). The proverbs iii 30, xx 3, xxvi 17, and especially xxv 7c-10 testify (not only by the use of the expression *rîb*) that in these admonitions dehortation from litigation is certainly included.

2. SEMANTICS

The juridical contents or at least connotation of *rîb* (the substantive as well as the verb) is proved by its use in the legal clauses of the Book of the Covenant, Ex. xxiii 2, 3, 6, in Deut. xvii 8, xxv 1, and, for example, in the prophetic admonition *šiphṭû yātôm rîbû ʾalmānâ* "Defend (help to justice) the fatherless, plead the cause of the widow" (Jes. i 17, cf. 23; the *ʾiš rîb*, Iob xxxi 35, is the adversary before the court). L. KÖHLER, in his exemplary study of the style-forms of Deutero-Isaiah [2]), has proved how fruitful the study of the metaphorical use of the *rîb*-pattern is for our knowledge of the legal terminology and of the proceedings of a lawsuit in ancient Israel, the more so since the legal texts of the Old Testament do not

---

[1]) Against *mādôn*, Prov. vi 14b, 19b, x 12a, xv 18, xvi 28, xvii 1, 14, 19, xviii 6, 10, xxii 10, xxiii 19, xxviii 25, xxix 22, xxvi 20, 21, xxx 33; against the contentious woman, xxi 9, 19, xxv 24; against *maṣṣâ*, xiii 10, xvii 19; in accordance with their Babylonian and Egyptian colleagues, cf. the texts referred to in my *Sprüche Salomos*, 1937, at iii 30 and xxii 24 f.

[2]) LUDWIG KÖHLER, *Deuterojesaja stilkritisch untersucht*, (*Beih. z. ZAW*. 37, 1923, p. 110-120).

give a clear picture of the course of the judicial proceedings [1]), and many questions remain unanswered. Some additions may be made here to the picture so ingeniously derived by KÖHLER from Deutero-Isaiah. The expression for the first act in a lawsuit, the bringing of the matter "into court" seems to have been *yāṣā'* or *hôṣî' lārîb* (Prov. xxv 8). The expression for summoning is *hô'îd* (Jer. xlix 19; Iob ix 19). To lay the case before the assembly of judges, witnesses and adversaries is *'ārak mišpāṭ* (Iob xiii 18, xxiii 4; Ps. l 21). The adversary is the *'îš rîb* or *'îš maṣṣût* (Iob xxxi 35; cf. Jes. xli 11 f.), *mērîb* (I Sam. ii 10), *jārîb* (Jer. xviii 19; Jes. xlix 25; Ps. xxxv 1) and *ba'al mišpāṭ* (Jes. l 8). During the proceedings the judge sits (I Reg. vii 7; Jes. xvi 5; Dan. vii 9) on his *kissē'* "chair, seat", which in Iob xxiii 3 (cf. xxix 7) also seems to be called *tᵉkûnâ*; only when he proclaims his judgement does he seem to have stood (Jes. iii 13, *niṣṣāb lārîb*, *'ômēd lādîn*; cf. the expression *'āmād lišpoṭ* for "to act as judge", Ezech. xliv 24, *qûm lammišpâṭ*, Ps. lxxvi 9 f., and *qûm* in the appeal of the psalmists to the Divine Judge, Ps. iii 8, vii 7 f., xxxv 1 f.). The contending parties stood (cf. *'āmad liphnê* "to appear before", Deut. xix 17, *na'amdâ yāḥad* "Let us stand up together", Jes. l 8) the plaintiff (Mich. vi i *qûm rîb*; cf. Ps. lxxiv 22, and Jes. liv 17 *kol-lāšôn tāqûm-'ittāk lammišpāṭ*) as well as the accused (Ps. i 5, lxxvi 8b, cxxx 3; Jer. xlix 19; Esr. ix 15; I Sam. vi 20), and also the witnesses (Deut. xix 15 f.; Ps. iii 2, xxvii 12b, xxxv 11; cf. Sanh., fol. 19 a/b, Ch. II 2).

As has long been observed, the accuser takes his stand at the right hand of the accused (Sach. iii 1; Ps. cix 6, *wᵉsāṭān ya'ᵃmōd 'al-yᵉmînô*, lit. "and let an accuser stand up at his right hand", which the American Rev. Stand. Vers. translates "and let an accuser bring him to trial"), as does also the defender (Ps. cix 31; cf. cxlii 5, xvi 8; in battle too the helper takes his stand at the right hand, the left side being protected by the shield; cf. Ps. cx 5, cxxi 5).

The accusation (*śiṭnâ*, Esr. iv 6), certainly mostly brought orally before the court, could also be handed in in writing (Iob xxxi 35, *mî yitten-lî .... sēpher kātab 'îš rîbî* "O that I had the indictment written by my adversary!"; cf. the reference to record-books of deeds or misdeeds lying before the court, Jes. lxv 6a; Dan. vii 10 *dînâ yᵉtab wᵉsiphrîn pᵉtîḥû* "The court sat in judgement and the books were opened"; perhaps also Ps. cxlix 9a). Also the defence could be presented in writing (Iob xxxi 35, *hen-tāwî* "Here is my signature!").

---

[1]) Cf. JOHS. PEDERSEN, *Israel I-II*, 1926, p. 400, 410.

Among the witnesses (*ʿēdîm*) eye- and ear-witnesses could be distinguished from other kinds by the expression *yôdēaʿ* (Jer. xxix 23, "I am the one who knows, and I am witness, says the Lord"; cf. Lev. v 1 and the Babylonian term *mûdû*) [1]).

The hearing (*šāmaʿ*, Iob xxxi 35) of the case and the interrogation of the parties is expressed by several terms, like *dāraš*, Deut. xix 18; *ḥāqar*, Iob xxix 16b (cf. xiii 10); *bāḥan*, Iob vii 18; Jer. xvii 10; Ps. xxvi 2, (parallel *pâqad* and *niššâ*, as in Ps. xvii 3 parallel *pāqad* and *ṣāraph*; cf. *pāqad*, Iob xxxi 14). As there is no sharp distinction between judges and witnesses [2]), it is often not clear in which capacity the members of the tribunal are summoned to act (Jes. i 2 f., v 3; Mich. vi 1). The decision given by the judges is more of the nature of a settlement through mediation, arbitration, than a verdict based on law-clauses [3]). This explains the use of the verb *pillēl* "to arbitrate" (I Sam. ii 25) and its derivatives for judicial activity in general (Ps. cvi 30; Ezech. xvi 52; Deut. xxxii 31; Jes. xvi 3; Iob xxxi 11, 28) and the extensive use of the verb *hôkîaḥ* and derivatives (I have counted 26 occurrences in Proverbs and 19 in Job) for all kinds of action by the different actors in a dispute [4]).

---

1) Cf. ARNOLD WALTHER, *Das altbabylonische Gerichtsverfahren*, *Leipz. Semit. Stud.*, VI, Hft. 4-6, 1917, p. 249 ff., and G. R. DRIVER and JOHN C. MILES, *The Babylonian Laws*, i, 1952, p. 95.

2) Cf. L. KÖHLER, *op. cit.*, p. 110: "Wer der Rechtsgemeinde einen Rechtsfall zur Entscheidung .... vorlegen will, ruft zunächst ins Gericht, und zwar zwei Gruppen: erstens die Rechtsgenossen, welche Zeugen und Richter in Einem sind oder doch sein können, und zweitens den oder die Rechtsgegner". In Babylonia the *puḫrum* or "assembly", before which lawsuits were brought, consisted of the *šibûtum*, or "elders", and the *awîlû* "patricians", the "free burghers", over whom the judges presided in virtue of their technical qualifications; cf. DRIVER and MILES, *op. cit.*, p. 78 ff., and ARNOLD WALTER, *op. cit.*, p. 45 ff.; the term *šibûtum* "elders" is, according to WALTHER, only another plural form alongside *šibûm* "witnesses".

3) Cf. L. KÖHLER, *op. cit.*, p. 110: "billige Vermittlung ...., nicht die Feststellung der Strafe, heisst genau *šāphaṭ*; der *šôphēṭ* ist in erster Linie der Helfer zum Recht, nicht der (strafende) Richter"; and p. 115 "*mišpāṭ*, das Urteil, die Rechtsentscheidung. Sachlich stets = Schiedsspruch, nie = Strafurteil im modernen Sinne der Feststellung, dass ein verklagtes Verhalten unter den Tatbestand und die Straffolgen eines Gesetz fallen". The same applies even to the more advanced judicial conditions in Babylonia; cf. A. WALTHER, *op. cit.*, p. 227 ff.; the Babylonian judicature is more sensitive and more adapted to life than is often the Roman. The judges often do not decide according to the verbal articles of the law, but even contrary to these when justice required it. The professional judges, as well as the lay-judges, the "elders", often dealt in a friendly way with the people, brought them to compromise or let themselves come to an arrangement.

4) From starting a (legal) dispute (Hitp. Mich. vi 2, Hi. Iob xxii 4), complaining

The *'îš môkîaḥ* is the man whose office and duty it is to warn and to reprove (Ezech. iii 26), but also one who vindicates justice in "the gate", the judicial assembly of the free burghers (Am. v 10; Prov. xxiv 24 f.), the mediator, arbiter, "umpire" (Iob ix 33: "There is no (Would that there were an) umpire between us who might lay his hands upon us both!" (LXX μεσίτης καὶ ἐλέγχων); other expressions for the one who intervenes are *maphgîa'* (Jes. lix 16; cf. liii 12) and *maṣṣîl* (2 Sam. xiv 6). Acquittal can be expressed by the verb *plṭ* (Iob xxiii 7) or by the substantive *ṣ^edāqâ* (Ps. lxix 28).

3. THE *RÎB* IN TRADITIONAL RELIGIOUS PHRASEOLOGY

The religious sentiments expressed in personal names are usually among the most traditional. The name Jehoiarib (I Chron. ix 10; Neh. xi 10, xii 6, 19, chief of a priestly generation or division in the time of or before Nehemiah), in its contracted form Joiarib (Neh. xi 5, chief of a Judaean family in the fifth generation before Nehemiah; Esr. viii 16 a *mēbîn*, "man of insight, teacher" in the time of Ezra) means "May Yahweh (as judge) contend the cause (for the bearer of the name)". The dating back of this name into the time of king

(Gen. xxi 25; Hab. ii 1; Iob xl 2), arguing (Iob xiii 3, 6, xv 3, xix 5, *tôkāḥôt* "arguments", Iob xxiii 4), reasoning (Ni., Iob xxiii 7; Jes. i 18; Hi. Lev. xix 17), reproving and rebuking (Iob vi 25 f., and very often in Proverbs), defending (his cause, Iob xiii 15), confuting (the adversary, Iob xxxii 12), to the actual doing of justice (Iob. xvi 21), the deciding of the case (Jes. xi 3 f.; cf. ii 4, Gen. xxxi 42, and in a wider sense "to decide, to assign, to appoint", Gen. xxiv 14, 44) and punishing (Hos. v 9; Jes. xxxvii 3; Ezech. v 15, xxv 17; Ps. xxxix 12, cxlix 7; also chastening or chastising, cf. 2 Sam. vii 14; 1 Chron. xii 18; Jer. ii 19; Hab. i 12; Ps. vi 2, xxxviii 2, lxxiii 14, xciv 10; Prov. iii 11f., xix 25, xxix 15; Iob v 17, xxxiii 19). The Ni. *niwwāk^eḥâ* in Jes. i 18, occurring at the end of the *rîb* of verses 2-20, may mean "let us come to an arrangement, a decision". The verb and substantive *dîn*, so well known from Accadian, and also occurring in Ugaritic texts, is less frequent than *rîb* in Hebrew, but shares its wide and fluctuating sense; it means to act as judge, to do justice, mostly in favour of the wronged and oppressed (about 18 times; Gen. xxx 6; Deut. xxxii 36 = Ps. cxxxv 14; Jes. x 2; Jes. v 28 f., xxi 2, xxii 16, xxx 13; Ps. liv 3, lxxii 2—probably also Ps. ix 9, xcvi 10, and Prov. xxix 7, xxxi 5, 8, 9; cf. *'āsā dîn*, Ps. ix 5, cxl 13, and the personal names Daniel, Dan, Dina and Abidan, and the substantive *dajjān* "judge", I Sam. xxiv 16; Ps. lxviii 6), but also against evildoers (Gen. xv 14; I Sam. ii 10; Jes. iii 13; Ps. l 4 ff., Iob xix 29, xxxvi 17), when it gets the sense of "to execute justice, to condemn, to bring judgement on" (even by battle, Ps. cx 6); it can have the general meaning of "to rule" and *m^edînā* "district of jurisdiction, administration" (Sach. iii 7; cf. Gen. xlix 16), but can also be used for "to strive, to contend, to dispute" (Eccles. vi 10; Prov. xxii 10; 2 Sam. xix 10; cf. the substantive *mādôn*, always 'strife, contention", e.g., Jer. xv 10; Hab. i 3; Ps. lxxx 7 and 19 times in Prov.). It cannot be said that *rîb* would mean "to conduct the cause", and *dîn* "to decide the cause" (cf. I Sam. xxiv 16).

David (I Chron. xxiv 7; apart from the organisation of clergy) is justified in view of the shortened forms Jeribai (I Chron. xi 46, one of David's "mighty men") and Ribai (2 Sam. xxiii 29; I Chron. xi 31, the father of one of David's heroes). Although the surname Jerubbaal of the "judge" Gideon etymologically probably does not fall under the root *rîb* "to contend", the humorous passage Jud. vi 28-32 proves that the occurrence of this root in a personal name is not considered strange in this period by the narrator. Hebrew (like Babylonian and Sumerian) personal names are often shortened lines from hymns and prayers [1]). Well known is the prayer from the Psalms "Plead my cause!" (Contend for me in my controversy) *rîbâ rîbî* (Ps. xliii 1, parallel *šophṭēnî* "judge me"; cxix 154, parallel *geʾālēnî* "redeem me"—the same parallelism occurs again in the individual lamentation Thren. iii 59; Ps. xxxv 1 *rîbâ yahwè ʾet-yerîbai leḥam ʾet-lōḥemāi*, lit. "contend, Yahweh, with my contenders, fight with my fighters!"). In the beautiful psalm passage added to the Book of Micah (Mich. vii 8-10) it is quite clear from verse 9 that it is the Divine Judge whose help is invoked in this prayer. In the prophecies of weal this help and vindication of rights is promised to Israel (Jes. xlix 25 f., parallel *hôšîaʿ* and *gāʾal*; Jes. li 22; Jer. l 33 f., parallel *gāʾal*; Jer. li 36, parallel *niqqam*, "to avenge"; cf. Jes. xxxiv 9 where a *yôm nāqām* "a day of vengeance" and a *šenat šillumîm* "a year of recompense" is promised *lerîb ṣiyyôn* "for the cause of Zion").

The psalmists' supplication so strongly reminds us of the appeal in the Babylonian prayer hymns *dînî dîn*(*a*) *purussāiā purus*(*a*), lit. "Judge my judgement, decide my decision!" that a distinctive characteristic of Hebrew mentality or religiousness can hardly be seen in this expression, rather a typical Semitic religious notion, although already in Sumerian wisdom the prayer occurs as a quotation "O, Sungod, thou art judge, judge my cause, thou takest decisions, decide for me!" [2]) Especially at home in the cult of

---

[1]) Cf. my *Babylonisch-Assyrische Persoonsnamen*, 1924, p. 22, 26 (for Sumerian nomenclature), 53 n. 13, 60 n. 8, 61, 73, 147 n. 18, 176 (for Accadian names). The remarkable list of the last ten names of I Chron. xxv 4 forms part of a hymn, or contrarily part of a hymn could be taken as a list of personal names.

[2]) S. N. KRAMER, "*Sumerian Literary Texts from Nippur*", *AASOR*, xxiii, text 149 rev. II 8 ff., cited in J. J. A. VAN DIJK, *La sagesse suméro-accadienne*, 1953, p. 9: ^{d}utu di-ku$_{5}$-me-en di-mu ku$_{5}$-dè, ka-a$_{5}$ bar-bar-re-me-en ka-aš-mu bar-re. The Accadian *dînam dânum* and *purussâm parāsum* are juridical terms, meaning "to act as judge (in a certain cause) " and "to come to a decision (after finding the facts of the case)" cf. DRIVER and MILES, *op. cit.*, p. 72-74.

Šamaš as god of justice, this confession and prayer is used in connection with several kinds of gods, even with the star Sibzianna[1]). Although expressed in legal phraseology, the case in which the help of the god is invoked is sickness and all kinds of evil brought about by sorcery and demons. Also of soothsaying and the interpretation of omens, legal terms like *warkātam parāsu* "to give a decision about the facts underlying the case", *dîna dânu* and *purussê parāsu* are used[2]).

These analogies and background of the *rîb*-terminology in the

---

[1]) Cf. the Šamaš-hymn in a ritual against illness caused by demons and magically harmful materials, E. EBELING, *KARI*, Nr. 184 R, l. 19 ff., especially l. 27 ff.: *dîn ḫablim u ḫabilti tadân, purussâšina tuštēšir*, "The cause of the afflicted man and woman judgest thou, the decision for them directest thou", ... *dînu amēlu marṣi ša iṣbatanni ana dîni kansāku, dîni dîn purussāia purus*, "In the (legal) cause of the illness which has caught me, I am lying on (my) knees for judgement. Judge my cause, give a decision for me!" A. FALKENSTEIN and W. VON SODEN, *Sumerische und akkadische Hymnen und Gebete*, 1953, p. 323 ff., rightly observe that Šamaš is asked here for a revision of a previous judgement which resulted in sickness. The gods of Hades, the Annunnaki, are praised in a ritual against spirits of the dead and other demons as *pārisu purussī ana nišê šaplāti, dāinu dîni ša kala tenišēti* "Who decide the cause of the deep-dwelling men, judge the judgement of all mankind". The subordinate fire-god Girra is praised like Šamaš in the incantation text of the Maqlû-series (*KARI*, Nr. 235, R., l. 1-5): *tustēšir ilāni u malki, tadâni dîn ḫabli u ḫabilti*, "Thou directest gods and princes, thou judgest, etc.", and the supplicant prays for delivery from witches in the words: *ina dînia izzizama kima Šamaš quradu, dîni dîni purussâi purus*, "Stand up (Act) in my case like Šamaš, the warrior (hero), judge my judgement, etc.", cf. in the Girra hymn, *KARI*, Nr. 235, R., l. 6-12 *ina ûmi anni* ("in this day") *ina dinia izzizamma*. Especially in the Prayers of the Lifting of the Hand (L. W. KING, *Babylonian Magic and Sorcery*, 1896; latest translations and commentary by B. A. VAN PROOSDIJ, 1952, and by E. EBELING, *Die akkadische Gebetsserie „Handerhebung"*, Deutsche Akad. d. Wiss., Akademie-Verlag, Berlin, 1953) the praise of and prayer to several gods as judge and decider occur, for example, to Ninurta, KING 2, l. 19, to Gula, KING 4, l. 28-30: *ana dîni dâni purussê parāsi ḫibiltu šullumi, asḫurki aše'ki ulinnuki aṣbat kima ulinni iliya u istariya .... dîni dîni purussâia pursi alakti limdi* "That my judgement be given, my decision be made, my damage be compensated, I have turned to thee, I have sought thee, I have grasped the fringe of thy garment like the fringe of my (protective) god and goddess, give my judgement, make my decision, learn my behaviour!"; also to Gula, KING 6, l. 47-49, to Belit-ili KING 7, l. 47-49, to Šà-zu (Marduk), KING 13, l. 27 f., with the variation *šuršî dîni purussaia purus* "Let me obtain (Grant) my right, etc.", to Ištar, KING 30 l. 8 f., to the star Sibzianna, KING 50 l. 10 f., with the request of an assembly of the gods: *šisima ittika ilani rabuti lizizu, dîni dîn purussaia purus* "Summon and let the great gods stand with thee, etc.!", to Enlil, *KARI* 68, l. 15 *gamir dîni* "who brings my case to an end", to Nusku, *KARI* II 58, R., l. 4-6, *aššum dînia uznêia putî, aššum dînia dîni šuršî, aššum dînim šanimma zukur amata amiš* "On account of my case open my ears (give me understanding), on account of my case grant me my right, on account of the other case (the case of the adversary) announce the word: I disregard it!"

[2]) See A. WALTHER, *Altbabyl. Gerichtswesen*, p. 222, n. 2; cf. 219, n. 2.

Hebrew Psalms, and its occurrence even where the distress of the psalmist clearly arises out of sickness (Ps. xxxi 10-13, xxxv 13-15, lxix 2 f., 15 f., 21, 27, 30), prove that the *rîb*-pattern is often, if not mostly, used metaphorically, although not as a purely literary style-motif, but rather as a form of thinking and feeling, a category, a frame of mind. There are at least twenty-five Psalms in which parts and expressions of this pattern occur [1]). To interpret this class of Psalms as representing a real lawsuit and trial before a temple tribunal with decision by ordeal looks like a hermeneutic "trans-substantiation" or substantializing of metaphor into reality. Undoubtedly the phraseology is often thoroughly judicial [2]), but with this metaphor other comparisons vary [3]). The "scarcity of motifs" to which H. Schmidt has drawn attention finds its explanation in the use of the controversy-imagery for all kinds of distress, and this results from a distinct frame of mind which will be analysed at the end of this article.

4. In the preaching of the prophets

In Israel's prophetism as it arises in the stern and strong personalities of the eighth and following centuries, the *rîb*-metaphor receives a thoroughly new content and application. These prophets do not proclaim a *rîb* between Israel and the nations in which the Divine Judge is expected to decide in favour of his people, but a controversy

---

[1]) Ps. iii, iv, v, vii, xi, xvii, xxvi, xxvii, xxxi, xxxv, xlii f., liv, lv, lvi, lvii, lix, lxii, (lxiv), lxix, lxx, lxxxvi, cix, cxl, cxlii, cxliii. Cf. H. Schmidt, *Das Gebet der Angeklagten im A.T.*, *Beih. z. ZAW* 49, 1928, and *Die Psalmen*, 1934, p. VI f.

[2]) Cf. Ps. vii, the oath of purgation, verses 4-6, the summoning of the tribunal, verses 7 f., the appeal to the judge, verses 9-12, the announcement of punishment, verses 13 ff.; Ps. xvii, the declaration of a "just cause", verse 2, the declaration of innocence, verses 3 f., the appeal to the judge, verses 6-9, the complaint, verses 10-12, the request for sentence and punishment, verses 13 f., and for his own justification, verse 15; Ps. xxvi, the supplication for a hearing and investigation, verses 1-3, the declaration of innocence, verse 4 f. negatively, verses 6-8 positively; Ps. xxxv, the request for a trial, verses 1 ff., the invoking of punishment, verses 4 ff., the complaint, verse 7 ff.; renewed complaint and accusation, verses 11-16, for the third time complaint and accusation, verses 19-21, appeal to the judge, verses 22-24, invocation of punishment, verses 25 f. and of justification, verses 27 f.; Ps. cix, the complaint of the defendant, verses 2-5, quotation of the accusation (the curse invoked against him), verses 6-19, invocation of God's verdict, verse 20, and of his doing justice to the needy innocent, verses 21-31.

[3]) Cf., e.g., Ps. xxxv, the images of a battle, verses 2 f., wild animals, verses 17, 25, hunting, verses 7 f.; Ps. lvi, expressions derived from wild life, and siege, verses 2 f., and spying, verse 7; Ps. lix, the imagery of wild dogs, verses 7 f., 15 f.

in which Israel's God summons and accuses, threatens and decides against his chosen people. Though Amos does not yet use the expression and phraseology of *rîb* in this connection, the strophes of his great oration against the neighbouring nations (i 3-ii 3), culminating in the sternest charges and accusations against Israel (ii 6-8), and followed by divine self-defence, renewed charges and threats of punishments (ii 9-16), form what K. CRAMER rightly calls "Die Anklageschrift", or better still compares with the monotonous summoning by the officer of the court of a panel of accused and sentenced persons [1]). Hosea, perhaps the least "legal-minded" of the prophets, is the first to proclaim emphatically a *rîb* between Yahweh and his people and its leaders, religious as well as political (iv f., cf. iv 1, 4 *rîb*, v 1 *mišpāṭ*; the accusations beginning with *kî*, iv 1b, 6b, 10b, 12b, v 1b, 3b, 4b, etc., an attenuating circumstance being admitted only once, iv 14; witness against being cited v 5, vii 10, *ʿānâ be*). Also xii 3-15 is represented as a *rîb* between Yahweh and his people on the theme: Ephraim still shows the genuine cunning nature of his ancestor Jacob, the four accusations, verses 4-7, 8-11, 12, 13-15, interspersed with appeals and threatenings, as a proof that Yahweh still, as always in history, tries to correct his wayward people. A remarkable variation in the *rîb*-pattern is seen in ii 4 ff.: the individual members of the people ("the sons and daughters") are called by Yahweh and his prophet to start a *rîb* with their people ("their mother"), and a whole series of accusations is enumerated the threatenings being mostly introduced by *lākēn* (verses 5, 8 f., 11-15, 16 ff.), aggravating circumstances are adduced (verses 7, 10), but suddenly in verse 16 threats become promises of a change of heart and life, and a striking picture of the future relation of the accused, Israel, and her divine husband, prosecutor and judge is displayed (verses 17-25).

Isaiah in a picturesque introductory sentence represents the Lord as a judge of nations (var.: judge of his people), opening the case against the elders and princes of his people (iii 13-17). In the remarkable passage, beginning like the song of a minstrel, and developing into a controversy (v 1 f., 3-7), the "inhabitants of Jerusalem and men of Judah" are, like two groups of witnesses [2]), summoned to judge

[1]) K. CRAMER, *Amos*, *BWANT*, III 15, 1930, p. 156 ff., 194: "Die lapidaren Sätze wirken in ihrer monotonen Gleichmässigkeit wie das Ausrufen des Gerichtsdieners, der immer neue Sträflinge zur Exekution führt."

[2]) Cf. L. KÖHLER's "Zweizeugenruf", *op. cit.*, p. 112 f.

between Yahweh and his vineyard (verse 3), i.e., against themselves! (verse 7). The whole of the introductory chapter is composed as the protocol of the proceedings of a *rîb*, although the word itself is not used here: the summoning of the witnesses or jury ("heavens" and "earth") (i 2a), the complaint (verses 2b, 3), the addressing of the accused with accusations, interrogations and threats (verses 4-9, 10-15), the appeal for betterment (verses 16 f.) and the offer of an agreement (verses 18-20), with final complaint (verses 21-23), and lastly the announcement of different treatment of the obstinate offenders and the repentant (verses 24-31).

In Mich. i 2-9 the prophet acts as the court-official of Heaven, summoning "all peoples" and "the earth and all that is in it" to attend to the epiphany of Yahweh on earth as a "witness" [1]) against Judah and Israel; here again explanations, accusations, questions, and menaces, with the prophet's lament at the end of the passage (verses 8 f.). The announcement of the punishment in the "geographical" taunt-dirge (verses 10-16) could be included in this *rîb*, and it is continued in chs. ii and iii in the form of a dispute between the prophet and the leaders of the people, political as well as spiritual (cf., e.g., the refutations by Micah's adversaries, ii 6 f., iii 11, and the prophet's contra-argumentation, ii 8 ff., iii 12). A striking and very impressive variation of the *rîb*-pattern is presented in Mich. vi (similarly, but not quite the same, Hos. ii 16 ff.; cf. above). Again the prophet acts as summoner at divine command to the *rîb Yahweh* (verse 1). Now the mountains and the foundations of the earth are cited as witnesses, and again Yahweh's people as accused (verse 2). But the heavenly prosecutor speaks as if He and not his people are the accused; his charge is worded as the complaint of one disappointed in the reaction to his well-doing (verses 3-5, *ṣidqôt* verse 5). The reply put on the lips of the people is not a counter-accusation, not even a complaint, but an accumulation of questions out of embarrassment and anguish of soul (verses 6 f.). The *rîb* closes with the answer of God's commissioner indicating the solution of the people's perplexity, the clearest and finest formulation of God's demands in the Old Testament (verse 8). Masterly and royally the

[1]) Heb. *ʿēd* can mean plaintiff, accuser, as well as witness and even judge; cf. A. WEISER, *Die Propheten Hosea-Micha*, 1949, p. 207; also T. H. ROBINSON, *Die zwölf kleinen Propheten*, 1954, 2te Aufl., p. 130, and H. J. STOEBE, *Das achte Gebot* (*Ex*. 20 v. 16) in *Wort und Dienst, Jahrbuch der Theolog. Schule Bethel*, Bethel bei Bielefeld, 1952, p. 108-126, and already L. KÖHLER, *op. cit.*, p. 110.

prophet disposes here of the *rîb*-pattern in the service of his calling and kerygma. Although the phraseology of the lawsuit resounds in the following passage too (cf. the summons, verse 9b, the questions, verses 10 f., the verdict, verses 13 ff.), the heights of the previous poem are not attained.

Jeremiah, whom we shall meet below as the *'îš rîb par excellence*, uses this metaphor in its traditional sense, if the prophecy of weal for Israel (l 33-40; cf. li 34-40), and of woe for the nations (xxv 30-38) can be retained for this prophet, but the distinctively prophetic line is continued in the great composition ii-iv 4 (excluding the insertion iii 6-18), the indictment against God's unfaithful bride, Israel; the whole situation or relation between Yahweh and his people in generations past, present and to come, is characterized as a *rîb* (ii 9), and several elements of this conception can be discerned [1]).

In Ezech. xvii the very lively series of questions, already present at the end of the allegory of the two eagles and the vine (verses 9 f.), but especially in its application (verses 11 ff.), and the expression *nišpaṭ* "to go into judgement" (verse 20), show the use of the *rîb*-metaphor as directed against the king of Israel and his people. A different turn takes its application in xx 33-44, where the divine *hiššāphēṭ* with Israel gets the meaning of an action for sifting, refining, purging the people (verses 35-38), reminding us, but in a less delicate, tender form, of the unexpected turn in Hosea's *rîb*-poem (ii 16 ff.).

Deutero-Isaiah, the "Evangelist of the Old Covenant", applies the *rîb*-category in a most developed, perfected form, undoubtedly resulting from the way in which he fulfilled his prophetic mission (in discussion and dispute), from his literary skill, and certainly also from the two clearly distinguishable subjects of his kerygma: the superiority, yea, incomparableness of Yahweh, the Creator, the Ruler and Director of world-history, as against all other gods, and the fair and just and righteous way in which He has treated his wayward people, Israel, in punishment, forbearance and redemptive loyalty [2]).

[1]) E.g., the question ii 5 f., the address to the witnesses (the heavens, and perhaps the earth, verse 12 f.), the accusation (verse 13), the series of questions (verses 14 ff.), the supposed complaining of the people (verse 29), the denying of guilt (verse 35), the dialogue of the heavenly Judge-Father and the penitent people (iii 21-iv 4), reminiscent of Mich. vi 6-8.

[2]) As L. KÖHLER has worked this out in a most lucid way (cf. p. 122, n. 2 above), I feel justified in confining myself to this summary of Deutero-Isaiah's use of the *rîb*-conception. Cf. also J. BEGRICH, *Studien zu Deuterojesaja*, *BWANT*, N.F. 25, 1938; and B. J. VAN DER MERWE, *Onverdiende genade* ("Undeserved Grace"; An exegetical study of Is. xliii 22-28), *Herv. Teol. Studies*, X 4, Pretoria, 1954.

In "Trito-Isaiah" the first of the two main subjects of Jes. xl-lv is dropped, the "monotheistic argument", but not the *rîb*-phraseology. The parties here are Yahweh and his people, or part of the people, the matter in dispute is the cause of Israel's misery and of the delay of salvation. Ch. lvi 1-8, the *tôrâ* concerning the foreigners and eunuchs who want to join, supposes disputes about this question (cf. verse 3). In chs. lvi 9-lvii 13, the great penitential sermon against the leaders of the people and its own idolatry, lvii 3-13 represents a formal *rîb* with its summoning (verse 3), interrogation (verse 4), accusations (verses 5-10), re-interrogation (verse 11), and threats (verses 12 f.). A strange contrast is formed by the passage which follows (lvii 14-21), the prophecy of the new way of salvation, in which Yahweh says "I will not contend for ever" (verse 16). Ch. lviii 1-12, 13 f., denouncing Israel's guilt, especially with regard to their fasting and observance of the sabbath, again shows the controversy-pattern in the accusation (verse 1), the counter-question (verse 3a), the answering of it in a statement (verse 3b) and in the form of counter-questions (verses 4 f.) and an appeal (verses 6 f.) and promise (verses 8 ff.). Ch. lix 1-8 on the cause of Israel's misery and the delay of salvation is an answer to implied contentions (verse 1); the people's confession of guilt (verses 9-15a), and the promise of Yahweh's intervention (verses 16b-21), though not necessarily the continuation of the previous passages, abound in judicial phraseology.

In the "booklet of consolation" of "Trito-Isaiah" (lx-lxii), with its strong reminiscences of Deutero-Isaiah, the prophecies of the arising of the glory of Yahweh and Zion (lx), the triumph of Yahweh's redemptive justice (lxi), and Zion's vindication (lxii), the strict *rîb*-form is absent, but not expressions derived from legal phraseology. In lxiii 1-6, the magnificent picture of the divine Vindicator, the images of the treader in the wine-press, the warrior, and the executioner mingle. In the penitential liturgy (lxiii 7-liv 12), the confession of guilt and the pleading prayer are directed to Israel's *môšîaʿ* and *gôʾēl* (verses 8, 16, both designations of juridical content). Yahweh's answer (lxv) contains his self-defence (verses 1, 2a), accusations (verses 2b-5), and verdict (verses 6 f.), the announcement of a sifting judgement (verses 8-16), and the promise of a new heaven and earth (verses 17-25). In lxvi 1 f. a controversy on the building of a temple is supposed, cultic practices are condemned (verses 3 f.); the eschatological promises and threats of the concluding passage (verses 5-24) contain the mighty picture of Yahweh's epiphany as universal judge, giving judgement and carrying it out (verses 15 f.).

The last prophet in the canonical series, Malachi, does not use the *rîb*-metaphor in such a powerful way. His *rîbôt* were real disputes with his comtemporaries, and his preachings represent the answers which the prophet gave as inspired by his God. Even so it is remarkable that Yahweh is pictured and announced as the one who will "approach them for judgement", and will be "a swift witness" against the sinners among them (iii 5-13) [1]).

Thus from Amos to Malachi this typically prophetic, and genuinely Israelite-prophetic, mighty theme of a controversy between God and his people gives expression to the conviction of Israel's spiritual leaders that there is something basically wrong in the religious and ethical relation and conduct of their nation.

5. MAN'S CONTROVERSY WITH GOD

M. A. BEEK, in his informative inaugural lecture, *Het twistgesprek van de mens met zijn God* [2]), has remarked (p. 7) that in the initial stages, in connection with the collectivism of Israel's mentality, the controversy with God is a matter of the people. The local names of Massa and Meriba represent for the Biblical narrators and the national tradition the remembrance of this faultfinding by the people with God's treatment of them in the wilderness [3]). Moses, in his twofold position as representative of God as well as of the people, can be described as the object of the people's contending (Ex. xvii 2; Num. xx 2 ff.), but also as co-responsible with them, and bearing the punishment for their behaviour (Deut. i 37, iii 26; Ps. cvi 32). But already in the narrative usually ascribed to JE (Num. xi 4 ff.), we encounter a personal *rîb* between Moses and God about the too heavy burden which his office has laid upon his shoulders (cf. Deut. i 9-12), quite in a "Jeremian" way. Bold as this conception of man

---

1) The picture of the judgement with all the nations in the valley of Jehoshaphat (Jo. iii) falls in line with the traditional eschatology as encountered above in passages of Jeremiah.

2) Subtitle: *Een paragraaf uit de godsdienst van Israël*, 1946.

3) Ex. xvii 1-7; Num. xx 1-13; cf. Num. xxvii 12-14; Deut. i 37, iii 26, vi 16, ix 22, xxxii 48-52; Ps. xcv 8, cvi 32; a different tradition takes God as subject of the contending and testing (Deut. xxxiii 8; Ps. lxxxi 8). How old this tradition of the people's quarrelling with God is, is difficult to fix; the pericope of Ex. xvii is usually attributed to JE, that of Num. xx to J and P; in any case Jeremiah knows his people as quarrelling with God (ii 29), also Deutero-Isaiah (xlv 9-13).

contending with Almighty God may be, perhaps still more remarkable is the conviction that such contending, although not without chastisement, is tolerated by Yahwe, and that He continues to bear with such a people and individual [1]).

"In Jeremiah a contender of flesh and blood stands before us" [2]). Although soft and sensitive and peace-loving, not at all quarrelsome by nature, he characterizes himself as "a man of strife and contention to the whole world" (xv 10). This world comprises his own family, fellow-villagers, familiar friends (xii 6, xi 21, xx 10), as well as his whole people and its political and spiritual leaders (i 18). The subject-matter of his controversy with them is their self-reliance and assuredness of being "safe" as a most religious people (vii 8-10). But Jeremiah stands out foremost among the prophets as being involved in yet another controversy, namely with his God and Sender, of which his "confessions" are the bold and frank expression (xi 18-20, xii 1-6, xv 10-12, 15-21, xx 7-13, 14-18). Here the subject-matter is the unbearable burden of his office as prophet of doom for his beloved people and the alienation and enmity which results from this, finally even his bare existence as a man who has become the laughing-stock of everyone (xx 14-18,7). His dialogues with God, with their accusations, questions, declarations of innocence, divine answers, rebukes and vindications, are full of judicial praseology, and are characterized by the prophet himself as *rîb* and *mišpāṭîm*, a case presented for judgement (xii 1). The fact that Jeremiah himself has allowed, or even caused, these most intimate and intrepid disputes with God to be put in writing and preserved for posterity, reveals the prophet's deep sense of individual personality, as well as his innermost conviction that God finally does not reject but tolerates and vindicates even his "revolting prophets" [3]), a conviction which also finds expression in Habakkuk's *tôkàḥat* "complaint, rebuke" against Yahweh (Hab. i 2-ii 5, especially ii 1).

In the book of Job this audacious religious individualism is carried still further, where it is not a prophet who revolts against the burden of his office, but an individual as such, albeit a distinguished ,"blameless", "servant of God" (i 1, 8), who enters into judgement with his God on account of his personal experiences and sufferings. The

---

1) Cf. Beek, *op. cit.*, p. 8.
2) *Ibid.*, p. 16.
3) *Ibid.*, p. 20.

book not only abounds in judicial phraseology [1]), but formally it cannot be better understood than as the record of the proceedings of a *rîb* between Job and God Almighty in which Job is the plaintiff and prosecutor, the friends of Job are witnesses as well as co-defendants and judges, while God is the accused and defendant, but in the background and finally the ultimate judge of both Job and his friends [2]). Since several ancient Sumerian texts, individual lamentations directed to a god, whose subject is the sufferings of an innocent person, have come to light [3]), it can no longer be maintained that in Babylonia the gods are not directly addressed and approached in the matter of the problem of suffering [4]). That in Israel this problem received a quite different aspect and extent and acuteness and urgency in connection with its belief in the one and thoroughly righteous God is certain. It is remarkable that, where the composition of the Book of Job as a whole strongly reminds us of the Sumerian a d a m a n - d u - g a "duels with words", a kind of "tensons" [5]), its subject-matter is quite different. Playful texts of this kind are totally absent in Old Testament literature [6]), and anything comparable to the conception of the Book of Job is equally absent from this Sumerian-Babylonian literary text-form, as far as can be judged from what has been preserved of it. The book of Job still can be considered as the apex and consummation of genuine Israelite individual religious consciousness, and of a mentality and phraseology deeply stamped with the *rîb*-pattern so inherent in the Hebrew mind.

---

[1]) Especially the chapters ix f., xiii, xvi, xix, xxiii, xxxi (Job's oath of purgation), xl (where Job is characterized as the *râb ʿim šadday*, the *môkiaḥ ʾᵉlôhim*, "the contender with the Almighty, the arguer with God").

[2]) L. KÖHLER, *Die hebräische Rechtsgemeinde*, 1931 (reprinted as supplement in his *Der hebräische Mensch*, 1953, p. 143 ff.), has rightly stressed the importance of the Book of Job for our knowledge of the proceedings of a trial in ancient Israel (152-158). Cf. also the remark of J. J. STAMM, "Die Theodizee in Babylon und Israel", *Jaarbericht Ex Oriente Lux*, No. 9, 1944, p. 104: "Dieses Buch ist kein Gespräch von Weisen, sondern eine "Rede vor Gericht", hebräisch ein *rîb*"; his presentation of the cast as "Hiob ist der Kläger, Gott der Angeklagte, und die Freunde sind die Richter" is not quite relevant.

[3]) Cf. J. J. A. VAN DIJK, *op. cit.*, p. 119-134 "Les justes souffrants"; cf. p. 13-17 "Les lettres aux dieux".

[4]) Thus BEEK, *op. cit.*, p. 12.

[5]) VAN DIJK, *op. cit.*, p. 29-85; cf. his remark p. 40, n. 48, and Thesis xv.

[6]) The fables of Jotham (Jud. ix 8-15) and of Jehoash of Israel (2 Reg. xiv 9 f.), as well as Ezekiel's comparison of the wood of the vine (xv 1-8, to which Prof. VAN SELMS has drawn my attention) can only serve as remote references to the possibility of the existence of such literary forms in ancient Israel. On the play-element in human culture, cf. the masterly study of J. HUIZINGA, *Homo ludens*, 1928, especially p. 111 ff. "Spel en rechtspraak".

6. CONCLUSIONS

The frequency and diversity of the application of the *rîb*-phraseology in the Old Testament reveals a frame of mind, and not only a way and means of expression. Partly perhaps due to an innate disposition of Semitic mentality, Israel's own genius, as acquired and developed in its history, and especially in its spiritual experiences (revelations as seen from the religious point of view), is to be considered as the main cause and source of this remarkable phenomenon. It reveals an unusual vivacity of mind, a definite personal approach to fate and circumstances. There is nothing naturalistic or mechanical in their view of, and reaction to, the entourage in which they live and work and suffer and die. They always stand in an I-Thou-relation.

This applies especially to the religious sphere. Israel's experience of, and attitude to, the Divine are of a lively, active, personalistic character. BEEK rightly observes that the first supposition of the controversy of individual man with God is a radical monotheism (*op. cit.*, 6). In polytheism the objections to one's fate could easily be motioned away by referring to another god as the cause of misfortune.

Secondly, the *rîb*-phraseology reveals the decidedly ethical, normative conception of God and the religious relation. The controversy is exponent of the feeling that there is something wrong in the relations of the entities concerned, that there is a hitch somewhere, that something is out of joint. This presupposes that there is an order of things which cannot be disturbed with impunity. This is the *ṣᵉdāḳâ*, the "justice", the God-maintained moral order in world- and national- and individual affairs. It is not a mechanical, automatic order of nature and natural "laws", but of thetic, genuine, God-given laws and regulations. "Justice" is the dominant conception in Israel's religious and ethical way of thinking [1]).

Both the personalistic and the judicial conception of the relations in life and the universe bring about the dramatic view of the history of the world as well of the nation and the individual. A drama is enacted with all its tension, its depths and heights of action and emotion, its possibilities of failure or victory, its final unravelling and resolution. Nothing is neutral, indifferent, nothing undecided at the end. One is wrong or is right, comes out justified or doomed.

---

[1]) Cf. the eminent article of GOTTFRIED QUELL, "Der Rechtsgedanke im Alten Testament", in *Theol. Wörterbuch z. N.T.*, hrsg. v. G. KITTEL, Bd. 2, 1935, p. 176-180; also L. KÖHLER, *Der hebr. Mensch*, p. 135-135, 170.

Lastly, the *rîb*-pattern reveals the undogmatic, unsystematic way of thinking, in religious matters, of the Old Testament. All is ultimately left to, lies in the hands of, the Supreme Judge and Ruler, whose judgement is righteous, but unpredictable, and inscrutable for human understanding, whose ways are not ours. He is a person, not a system or an order. But this implies that there is an appeal to Him, even an irrational, undeserved, unjustifiable appeal to his heart, his compassion, his grace. "God has consigned all men to disobedience, that He may have mercy upon all. O the depth of the riches and wisdom and knowledge of God!" (Rom. xi 32 f.).

THE STRUCTURE AND CONTENTS OF THE BOOK OF KOHELETH [1])

BY

H. L. GINSBERG

New York

In *SSK*, after demonstrating that, apart from the superscription and the epilogue(s), the Book of Koheleth contains at the most six main divisions and maybe only four, I was so optimistic as to add (p. 58): 'Further study may lead to a more clearcut decision.' This hope has been realized, and I now have no hesitation in declaring that there are exactly four main divisions in the book. The first three are as delimited in *SSK*, and the fourth extends from the end of the third right through xii 8. The details follow.

I. ANALYSIS

1. Superscription, i 1.
2. Body, i 2-xii 8.
3. Epilogue, xii 9-14.

2. Body of the Book

A. All is zero (*hebel*, vanity; *reʿut* (*raʿyon*) *ruaḥ*, cultivation of wind).

The only plus (*yitron*, profit; *ṭob*, good; *ḥeleq*, portion) there is for man is the utilization of his goods (*ʿamal*, *maʿseh*), i 2-ii 26.

B. All happenings (*ḥefeṣ*, *maʿseh*) are foreordained, but never fully forseeable.

Therefore the only plus there is for man is the utilization of his goods, iii 1 - iv 3.

A′. A pendant to A, iv 4-vi 9.

B′. A pendant to B, vi 10-xii 8.

---

[1]) Note my two relevant earlier publications: *Studies in Koheleth* (= *Texts and Studies of the Jewish Theological Seminary of America*, XVII), New York 1950 (siglum *SK*); "Supplementary Studies in Koheleth", in *Proceedings of the American Academy for Jewish Research* 21 (1952), p. 35-62 (siglum *SSK*). Justifications for views expressed below are often omitted if they have already been pleaded in one of the foregoing and have not since been modified.

A i 2-ii 26.

1. The Problem, i 2-11.

(a) The question, i 2-3.

Since everything is zero ("vanity") what plus ("profit") is there in the *goods* one acquires?

(b) Proof that all *is* zero, i 4-11.

It just keeps happening (*hāyā, na'sah*, verses 9-10) over and over, achieving nothing.

2. Koheleth's Discovery of the Solution i 12-ii 26.

(a) The fact of vanity, i 12-ii 2.

i. I know from observation that all is vanity, i 12-15.

ii. Including the advantage of wisdom over folly, i 16-18.

iii. Including revelry, ii 1-2.

(b) How I discovered what is the only plus, ii 3-26.

(i) I acquired a large fortune (*ma'seh*), (verses 4, 11), and had the good sense to apply it to the gratification of my desires, 3-10. *And that was all I ever did get out of it.*

(ii) Nevertheless, wisdom is ultimately no better than folly, because fool and sage alike die and are forgotten, 12a, 13-17.

(iii) And wealth, in itself, is also vanity; because you leave it to another, and he may be a fool, 11, 12b, 18-23.

(iv) So the only good, or positive something, is the using of the wealth. That, however, is a gift of God. Only to the lucky does He give the good sense to do it, 24-26.

Intermezzo: On the Terminology of Koheleth

a

It will be seen from the foregoing that:

1. *Ṭob lifne ha-Elohim* (*lefanaw*) and *ḥoṭe* mean respectively (as is today generally recognized) 'pleasing to God' and 'displeasing', or 'lucky' and 'unlucky'—*not* 'righteous' and 'wicked'. This applies not only in ii 26, but also e.g. in vii 26.

2. *'Anah*, literally 'to respond', means 'to occupy one's mind', and the substantive *'inyan*, 'occupation of the mind', in i 13, ii 26, iii 10, v 19. [1])

[1]) There is no point in including *midbarot*, *'inyanot*, *piqdonot*, and *ma'akalot* among illustrations of a growing tendency to *-ot* plurals in mishnic Hebrew (*JBL* 71 [1952], p. 100) unless the biblical plurals of these words are formed with *-im*. Presumably, therefore, the author can prove by examples that they are; but he unfortunately neglects to do so.

3. The verb *'āmal* and the substantive *'āmāl* mean nearly always 'to earn or acquire' and 'earning or acquisition' respectively. The same is sometimes true of the verb *'asah* and the substantive *ma'seh* (ii 4, 11, iii 9, 22).

4. *Na'sah* (nifal) nearly always, and *hayah* not infrequently, means 'to happen'; and the substantive *ma'seh* often means 'happening' (See i 9, 13, 14).

b

In studying Grand Division B of the Book of Koheleth, we shall discover further that:

1. A corollary of a 4 is that *'asah* when said of God means 'to cause to happen'; and 'the *ma'seh* of God', or 'the *ma'seh* which God *'asah*', means the things that happen on earth.

2. A synonym of *ma'seh* 'happening' is *ḥefeṣ* 'phenomenon' (iii 1, 17, v 7, viii 6). (*Ḥefeṣ* also means 'pleasure' — v 3, xii 1, 10 — but never, in Koheleth, 'purpose'.)

3. *Mishpaṭ* when effected—or thwarted—by man means 'justice' (iii 16, v 7), but when effected by God it means 'doom (death)'. (In the sense of 'judgment' it is employed only by the last epilogist, who wrote xi 9b as well as xii 13-14.) So, too, the verb *shafaṭ* is used by Koheleth only of God and only in the sense of 'to doom (cause to die)'.

We are now prepared to tackle Grand Division B.

B. iii 1-iv 3

1. The Lesson of Predestination, iii 1-13.

(a) The fact of predestination, iii 1-8.

Every happening or phenomenon occurs at its predestined hour.

(b) The bearing of this fact on the problem of A.

(i) The question: What *is* its bearing upon it? iii 9.

(ii) The answer, iii 10-13.

I, Koheleth, observed that the God who made everything happen at its appointed hour put into the hearts of men that striving (read *'amal*; cf. the verb *ya'mol* in the identical context, viii 17) to anticipate his timetable, but without their ever guessing everything correctly.

Is it not, therefore, obvious that the only plus which some men—the lucky ones—*can* get out of life is the enjoyment of their goods? [N.B. 'To do good' in iii 12 means 'to do that which we concluded it was good to do' in ii 24; cf. p. 142 below on vii 20.]

2. Another Way of Learning the Lesson of Predestination, iii 14-22.

(a) What God causes to happen will happen forever (14a), and the same things always have happened and always will (15a).

(b) That some people are pious is likewise something which God causes to happen (14b), and so is the fact that some are oppressors (read *harodef* for *nirdaf* 15b). And, as a matter of fact, I have always found righteousness and wickedness side by side (16).

(c) And for wicked and righteous alike there is a predestined hour of death (17; read *sam* 'he has appointed' for *sham* 'there').

(d) And death is an absolute cessation, for man and beast alike (18-21).

(e) So again the only plus one can get is enjoying one's acquisitions while one may (22).

3. A Further Reflection on Predestination, iv 1-3.

Because oppression too is one of the things God causes to happen (above, paragraphs 2a-b), there is no relief for the oppressed and no check on the oppressors (iv 1), so that death is preferable to life (iv 2-3). Cf. v 7.

A′, a Pendant to A

Main Line of Reasoning, iv 4-8; v 9-vi 9[1]).

1. If the only positive value is the utilization of one's means for the gratification of one's desires (A), then the following phenomena obviously make no sense:

(a) People acquiring means out of sheer competitiveness, not stopping to enjoy them, iv 4-6.

(b) A person without dependents who goes on acquiring insatiably —for whom? iv 7-8.

(c) A person who loves mere money and does not realize that he is acquiring more wealth only for others to consume (tax-collectors, employees, relatives, etc.), whereas for himself there will only be more to look at and to lose sleep worrying about, v 9-11. [*Saba*ʿ in verse 11 means not 'fullness'—which would be vocalized *soba*ʿ— but 'plenty', as in Gen. xli 29-31, 34, 47, 53. Cf. further Prov. iii 10,

---

[1]) iv 9-v 8 constitutes a block of associative digressions. For the contents and logic of this block, see *SSK*, p. 43. It may be added that the sense of iv 16 can only be this: There were countless people in the world before the present 'living who walk under the sun'; who naturally knew nothing of the wild enthusiasm of the latter for the poor but clever lad who has become king. And neither will those who come after our generation enthuse over him; cf. i 11, ii 16, ix 5 end.

where *saba'*, *we-tirosh* . . . means 'corn, and . . . wine', as *šbʿ wtrš* does repeatedly in the longest of the Karatepe inscriptions.]

(d) A person who saves his wealth and loses it, without him or his son having got anything out of it, v 12-16.

2. Moral: The only 'portion' one can hope for is eating and drinking and enjoying oneself for one's money. Both to have money and to utilize it in this way—that is God's gift. Those upon whom he bestows it are too happy to have time for introspection, v 17-19. [*Zakar* means 'to take thought of', exactly as in ix 15 (xi 8, xii 1); to say nothing of Jes. xlvii 7; Thren. i 9.]

3. But what a tragedy is the man to whom God does give wealth but not the good sense to utilize it (vi 1-6) [1])! All of a man's earning is for his mouth, yet (in this case) the gullet is not filled [2]). Then what advantage has the clever man over the fool, he who knows how to walk in the direction of (Dan. vi 11) life over the pauper? (Rd. *mehe'ani layyodea'*). Is, then, the beholding of the eyes better than the fullness of the gullet? (Read *mmlw'* for *mhlk*, the latter being due to the intrusion of *hlk* from *lhlk* in the preceding verse.) So that too is vanity and striving for naught (vi 7-9).

B′, a Pendant to B

Main Line of Reasoning, vi 10-ix 16, x 14b, 20-xii 8 [3]).

1. General reflections and advice in the light of the inscrutability of the future, vi 10-vii 29 —Note that vii 11-12, 19 (reading *'osher hash-shalliṭim*) come between verses 6a and 6b, and verse 20 between verses 16 and 17, and see *SSK*, pp. 48-51. [In vii 20, 'who does good etc.' means 'who does the advantageous thing and does not err', which is the problem of this section as defined in vi 12. Cf. p. 141 above on the same expression in iii 12.]

(a) 'Whatsoever happens was designated and destined long ago to happen (*'asher hu'* being a mistranslation of *dy (y)hw'* 'that it would happen'), and no man can (read *we-lo yukal 'adam*) contend with what is stronger than he. So the more words the more vanity. What is to a man's advantage? Why, who can *know* what is advantageous (*ṭob* 'good') for a man in life—the few days of his fleeting life—to do? [Positively no other translation of this question is possible in the light of ii 3b.] Because (*kaṣṣel 'asher* renders Aramaic *ktl dy* misread—under

[1]) For details of exegesis, see *SSK*, p. 44-45. [2]) With 7, cf. Prov. xvi 26.

[3]) ix 17-x 14a, 15-19 is a block of associative digressions with some internal dislocations; cf. p. 144-145 n.

the influence of the preceding 'days'—for *mṭl dy* 'because'; exactly as in viii 13) who can tell a man what is going to happen next under the sun?' (vi 10-12.)

(b) In the way of general rules, one can name seven things that are 'good' (*tob*), vii 1-6a, 11-12, 19, 6b-8.

(c) And a couple of don'ts (*'al*), vii 9-10, 13-16, 20, 17-18, 21-22.

(d) But foolproof wisdom is unattainable, because the schedule of events cannot be discovered, vii 23-24.

(e) I, Koheleth, tried to find it, but only discovered that, for example, a woman of wiles is more bitter than death [1]), but not how to avoid her. That depends entirely upon God's favour. Man cannot discover the system (*ḥeshbon*) of events, but he will insist on trying to master all sorts of systems that are beyond his grasp, vii 25-29.

2. The special problem of authority in the light of the inscrutability of the future, viii 1-4. (See *SSK*, p. 52 ff.)

(a) Who here is wise (read *kh ḥkm—ko ḥakam*), and who knows the meaning of the saying 'A man's gladness (read *ḥedwat*) lights up his face, fierceness darkens (read *yeshanne*) his face'? (It means) Watch the king's face (read *'anpe*), and in the matter of an oath by God be not overhasty. Tarry not in a king's presence (read *lifne melek*) when there is something evil (in his mien), for he can do whatsoever he lists. Inasmuch as a king's word is authoritative, and who can say unto him 'What doest thou?' He who obeys the (king's) command

1) That the Aramaic for the strongly alliterative **ומצא אני מר ממות** is the less alliterative **ושכח אנא מריר ממותא** (*sic!—JBL* 71 [1952], p. 108) is on the same high linguistic level as—I cite only by way of example—the argument that although the plural of **פרדס** is in tannaitic Hebrew always **פרדסות** except in the phrase **גנות ופרדסים**, the fact that the regular **פרדסות** often asserts itself even in the said phrase proves (*sic!—ibid.*, p. 100 n. 19) that its failure to do so always is *not* due to influence of the phrase **גנות ופרדסים** in ii 5 (contrast *SK*, p. 24 f.): and on the same lofty scientific plane as the confusion of the two masculine plural endings *-īm* and *-ē* (< *-ai*) despite their distinct origins and the very numerous cases where the latter in the construct state or suffixed forms does not correspond to an absolute in *-īm* (*JBL* 71 [1952] 100): and of the same exalted standard as the assertion that the word **דיברות** in the phrase **עשרת הדיברות** is from a singular *dabar* and is to be vocalized **debarot*; notwithstanding the unanimous tradition of all Jewish communities, which vocalizes it *dibberot*, as from *dibber* (Jer. v 13), is confirmed by any number of occurrences of *scriptiones plenae* (and even Genizah vocalizations) of this word both in Hebrew and in Aramaic (see, e.g. P. Kahle, *Masoreten des Westens* II, p. 26: **דִּבֶּירַיָּה, דְּבֶרוֹי**; *ibid.* 58: **דבירייה, דבֵּירה**): and it is of the same impressive calibre as the egregious linguistic rulings which I have discussed in *SSK*, p. 56-57.

will not (personally) experience the evil something; yet the heart of the wise man will bear in mind the hour of doom. Because for every phenomenon there is an hour of doom; for a man's calamity rushes upon him. (For he knows not what will happen. For who can tell him when it will happen?) No man (not even a king, whose word is authoritative, verse 4) has authority over the spirit, to hold the spirit back (from returning to him who infused it, xii 7), and there is no authority over the day of death. Nor is there any release from the grave (Aramaic *qbr'*, which the Hebrew translator misread as *qrb'*), nor can wealth (read *'osher*) rescue him that has it (viii 1-8).

(b) All this have I seen, as I observed all the happening that happens under the sun, what time man has authority over man for his harm. So too I have seen wicked men approach to serve (as priests; read *qerebim*) and profane (read *yeḥallelu*) Holy Place, whereas those who acted uprightly were forgotten in the city (viii 9).

(c) Koheleth tries to comfort himself with the ultimate discomfiture of the wicked and triumph of the righteous, but reflects that experience contradicts that doctrine (viii 10b-14).

3. Moral: It all goes to show that the only plus in life is extracting the pleasure that money (*'amal*) can buy (viii 15).

4. Only death is certain, viii 16-ix 6.

(a) You can't figure out the schedule of future events, viii 16-17.

(b) Even the actions and emotions of the wise and the good are predestined, ix 1-2.

(c) And every life ends in death, which is even worse than life, ix 3-6.

5. Again the moral: Enjoy your worldly goods, ix 7-10.

6. The successes of talent are rendered illusory by death, which comes suddenly, ix 11-12.

7. And such success cannot even be assured in life, as when the talent of wisdom is possessed by a poor man, ix 13-16. [*Umillaṭ hw'* (= *hwā*) can only mean 'and he might have saved'. For, of course, the city was *not* saved when nobody bethought him of the poor man, whose wisdom was despised and whose words were not listened to.] [1])

[1]) x 14b cannot be made to fit into the context in which it now stands without forensic legerdemain. The objective investigator will agree that it can only be the introduction to a paragraph consisting (at least approximately) of x 14b, 20—xi 6. The true continuation of x 12-14a can only be x 3b; see Prov. xvii 28 (and cf. Prov. xii 23). As for the continuation of verse 3a, it obviously is not verse 3b, and it obviously can be verse 15. In the latter, incidentally, עמל misrenders an Aramaic עטלות- 'stupidity, sloth' (for the kinship of the two

8. Further advice dictated by the inscrutability of the future, x 14b, 20, xi 1-6.

9. And a final great exhortation, xi 7-xii 8,

(a) to enjoy every year of life because of the finality of death, xi 7-8.

(b) or rather, to enjoy life in the years of youth because of the impracticability of enjoyment in old age, xi 9-xii 8. [N.B. (a) In the context of Koheleth, xi 9b is utter nonsense [1]), and can only stem from the epilogist of xii 13-14. Cf. above (B 2 c) on iii 17, and (Intermezzo b 3) on the root *špṭ* in Koheleth.]

(b) In the context of Koheleth in general and of the present exhortation in particular, xii 1 can *only* mean: Remember your *vigour* in the days of your prime, before you enter upon days and years of a very different sort. Cf. Aramaic and post-biblical Hebrew *bori* (= *beri'ut*).—Koheleth is here deliberately varying a probably familiar saying of the wise which we find in Sir. xxvi 19: 'My son, guard the prime of thy life in health'; i.e., Take care of your health while you are young. Koheleth says 'remember' instead of 'guard' because, in the context, he unmistakably means 'Remember you will only have your vigour while you are young.'

II. SYNTHESIS

1. *Summary of Koheleth's Teaching*

Every happening is predestined by God and takes place at the moment which he has appointed for it. This is true of every action and feeling of even the best and the wisest (ix 1 ff.), and it is likewise

ideas, cf. iv 5; Prov. xxiv 30), or some other formation from the root עטל with the same meaning, as if it were עמלות־, or some other formation of the root עמל with the same meaning. But it is safe to anticipate that some trial lawyer masquerading as an objective investigator will argue that *ʿṭl* cannot have become corrupted to or mistaken for *ʿml* here, since *ex hypothesi* the same translator did the right thing with it in verse 18. [For our suggestion, cf. the gender of the verb in 15a.]

[1]) For Koheleth, the enjoyment of one's earthly goods is not something which God has commanded, but something for which he gives the good sense as a gift. It is as much God's will that those to whom he has denied the impulse to enjoy shall not enjoy as that those whom he has favoured with it shall enjoy. Whoever argues to the contrary has been studying some screed that exists only in his own imagination, not the Book of Koheleth. (And how much faith has Koheleth in retribution anyway—see especially viii 14—apart from the feeling that direct affronts to the Deity, but not ordinary nonfeasance or even malfeasance or misfeasance, must surely bring down his wrath upon the culprit? And would not, in Koheleth's view, non-enjoyment itself be sufficient punishment?)

true of piety and oppression (iii 14b, 15b, v 7). And although the same things always have happened and always will (iii 14a, 15a, i 4-11), yet no man has ever been able to guess all future events correctly (iii 11, vi 12, viii 17, x 14b, 20, xi 1-6). The only thing one can foretell with certainty is death, but even of that one cannot foretell the hour (iii 1-2a, 17, viii 5-8, ix 3, 12, xi 8, xii 7). Moreover, death means extinction for man as well as beast (iii 18-21).

The fact of death renders nugatory the advantages and successes of wisdom (ii 13-16) and other talents (ix 11 f.). Even the memory of the wise and the successful is eventually lost (ii 16, iv 13-16), just like everybody else's (ix 5). (It is the oblivion of past events that makes present ones seem novel, i 10-11.) As a matter of fact, talent does not necessarily achieve even this nugatory success. Thus, wisdom may never be given a chance to prove itself because it happens to be lodged in the person of a poor man (ix 13-16); but above all, it is because of the predestined yet unpredictable character of events and careers that no human calculations are dependable (vi 10-12, viii 16-ix 2).

It does not follow, for Koheleth, that no attempt should be made to exercise foresight and energy. On the contrary, the uncertainty of the future is employed by him as an argument for endeavouring to provide for every eventuality (x 14b, 20, xi 1-6).

And although contemplation of the fact of oppression wrings from him the exclamation that the dead are happier than the living and the unborn even more so (iv 1-3), and although he considers the stillborn better off than him who has lived without experiencing the good that life has to offer (vi 1-6), yet he declares elsewhere that 'the dog alive is better off than the lion dead' (ix 4) and 'sweet is the light, and goodly it is to behold the sun' (xi 6) because of the profit or plus (*yitron*), the good (*ṭob*), or the portion (*ḥeleq*) that life holds for those whom God favours. What that is, Koheleth makes clear not only immediately after those two affirmations of life (namely, in ix 7-10, xi 7), but repeatedly throughout the book. For he begins the book with the question 'What profit (*yitron*) is there for man in all the earning (*ʿamal*) which he may earn (*yaʿmol*) under the sun?' And that there is no plus for him at all other than eating and drinking and gratifying his desires with his earnings is not merely the conclusion of that first Main Division (A)—as stated in ii 24-26—but the practical lesson of every one of the four Main Divisions of the book, as we have seen.

If, however, Koheleth were merely a shallow pleasure-seeker, he could never have written a book which has so charmed the ages (even when it was only half understood) by its melancholy beauty. We have noted his sensitive reaction to social wrongs as also his advice to work hard and exercise a maximum of prudence and foresight. And, as a matter of fact, there is no mistaking his horror of empty merry-making. 'It is madness!—What is it for?' he exclaims in ii 2; without feeling called upon to give any reason, as he does when he declares wisdom (for example) to be an illusory value in practice (e.g. i 17-18). Compare further his uncomplimentary remarks on banquets and parties in vii 2-4. It has rightly been argued that Koheleth's advice to enjoy one's material goods has good rabbinic analogies, and that his advice to 'follow the imaginings of thine heart and the sights of thine eyes' does not contradict Num. xv 39b, since Koheleth only means 'Don't be an ascetic,' *not* 'Pay no attention to right and wrong.'

At the same time, there is no denying that Koheleth is not altogether orthoprax and certainly by no means orthodox. He has little use for the temple cult, advising the reader to avoid the necessity for sacrifice by avoiding vows. Though he warns against the appalling folly of failing to fulfil any vows (v 3-5), he calls sacrifice itself 'the gift of fools' (iv 17), and vowing the utterance of a fool (v 2). His coolness towards the cult was at least in part due to the spectacle of unworthy men functioning as priests (viii 10).—His real heterodoxy appears in his views on God and the world order. His only admonitions on conduct vis-à-vis God are the foregoing one, not to be quick to vow, another not to be quick to swear ('and in the matter of an oath by God be not overhasty', viii 2-3), and a third not to indulge in futile rage over hard times, since they are God's decree, and are moreover balanced by the good times which he decrees (vii 10, 13-14). For Koheleth regards God as the absolute *and arbitrary* master of destiny; who bestows the gift of extracting the potential plus out of life upon those he likes (regardless of merit), and denies it to those he does not like (again regardless of merit)—ii 24-26, iii 13, v 18—who does not reward righteousness and punish wickedness (viii 14), and in fact wills the existence of oppression and injustice (iii 14a, 15, v 7), and who can only be expected with high probability to punish such slights to his person as the breaking of vows and oaths (v 3-5, viii 3 plus the first two words of viii 4).

In practising and championing righteousness (though not perfection) while doubting that God discriminates between the righteous and the wicked, Koheleth is strongly reminiscent of Job; however much we may regret that in the recollection of his prosperity he only remembers the self-indulgence he practised with it (ch. ii), with never a syllable about any good deeds to which he may have applied it (contrast Iob xxix-xxxi). The very language of vii 14 brings to mind Iob ii 10, i 22b, even as that of v 14 recalls i 21, and at least the thought of v 7 is very much the same as that of Iob ix 22-24. Both these works have lost the easy optimism of the Book of Proverbs; but whereas the author of Job tries to save some faith in a just world order, Koheleth does not try.

2. *Date*

The language of Koheleth points to a late date. So does the urging to enjoy one's money since one can't take it with one; which is a commonplace of Hellenistic popular philosophy, and is due to the phenomenon of the self-made man whom the wider communications and expanding economy of the Hellenistic period made possible. Moreover, the misogyny of vii 26, 28 (shared by Ben Sira) and the high esteem of youth in xi 9, xii 1 are due to Greek influence. The early Greek period (third century) rather than the late is indicated by points of contact with Ben Sira (*ca.* 190-180 B.C.), in which Ben Sira usually *seems* to be the borrower, and by the difficulty of conceiving of such a book being both written and accepted as Scripture in the atmosphere of the awakened national and religious consciousness of the Maccabean age.

3. *Authorship*

If Koheleth dates from the third century, he is, of course, not Solomon. The fact is that he does not even pretend to be. The words 'son of David' are found only in the superscription (i 1), and 'over Israel' only in i 12. Since the latter phrase is added in the Septuagint to i 1 in order to avoid the strange description 'king in Jerusalem', one may ask whether *mlk* here really means king, seeing that the author never reports any kingly activities (war, administration of justice, incognito observation of subjects), and says that he surpassed other or former kings (i 16; ii 7-9). As a matter of fact, *mlk* quite certainly means not 'to be king' but 'to own' in ii 12b ('for of what sort will be the man who will come after me, who will own all that I have already acquired'—reading *'aḥarai* ... *hammolek* ... *'asiti*), whose proper position is immediately after ii 11; cf. the identical use of *šlṭ* in ii 18-19, which expresses the identical thought. We therefore conclude that all Koheleth asserted in the original form of i 12 was 'I, Koheleth, was a property owner in Jerusalem'.[1]) He says 'was' because the fact is only of importance for explaining how Koheleth was in a position to study life; that he still is a man of means is irrelevant. The only other information about his person is given in the epilogue; he was a sage who collected many beautiful dicta.

He was a man of some education. He is apparently influenced by the Book of Job (above, para. 1). v 20-21, xii 7 are clearly influenced by Gen. ii-iii. iv 17 *ab* is a sort of parody on 1 Sam. xv 22; iii 14a on Deut. iv 2; xiii 1; ix 11a on Deut. i 13. There may also be an allusion to Proverbs, and there are echoes of the old Aramaic Book of Ahiqar and other non-Jewish Oriental wisdom literature. We have seen that he also has something in common with the popular Greek moralists of his day, but nothing which indicates an actual acquaintance with Greek literature. The resemblances are due to the fact that, like his pagan counterparts, he was a child of his age.

The verb *qhl* 'to collect, convoke' was originally current in all Aramaic dialects, and it was there used in the qal, as may be inferred from the situation which still obtains in Syriac. In the Aramaic original the author styled himself *qāhlā*, which is a participle qal *masculine emphatic*, meaning 'the Convoker' (in Hebrew, literally, *haq-qōhēl*). The form, however, is homonymous with the participle qal *feminine absolute* (in Hebrew, literally *qōhelet*), and unfortunately that is how the translator took it. Correct parsing and idiomatic rendering would have yielded *ham-Maqhīl*. Whether he convoked his hearers in a school or in little groups in public places we do not know.

---

[1]) I cannot feel that any other view does justice to the further circumstance that where Koheleth boasts that he surpassed "all that were before me in Jerusalem" he does not speak of kings (i 16; ii 7, 9), and when he does relate that he amassed "treasures (as) of kings" (ii 8) he does not say "*other* kings" or "*the other* kings" nor claim that he outdid kings.

LE MODERNISME DE JOB

PAR

PAUL HUMBERT
Neuchâtel

Dans les innombrables publications du dernier quart de siècle sur le livre de Job, une des analyses les plus pénétrantes et les plus intelligentes est, sans contredit, celle de M. JOH. PEDERSEN [1]). Sans ressasser les lieux communs, cet orientaliste a expliqué de façon laconique mais frappante ce qui fait le centre de gravité et l'unité profonde du livre de Job et de l'ancienne conception israëlite de la vie, à savoir le concept de justice concrète, et l'harmonie organique, la solidité intrinsèque qui existent entre ces deux pôles: justice divine et justice de l'homme. Quand bien même notre manière de voir va au-delà de cette interprétation, nous tenons à attirer d'emblée l'attention sur elle et à reconnaître notre dette envers son auteur.

Précisons ensuite que, longtemps fidèle aux positions critiques habituellement adoptées quant au livre de Job, à la réflexion nous sommes devenus sceptiques à cet égard: en effet, quelle que soit la provenance orale et traditionnelle du récit en prose, il a manifestement été adopté par l'auteur du poème et fait désormais partie intégrante de son oeuvre qu'il introduit, qu'il encadre et à laquelle il s'incorpore. Quant aux discours d'Elihou, comme M. PEDERSEN [2]), nous ne voyons pas de raison solide et contraignante pour en refuser la paternité à l'auteur du poème, car ils traitent le même thème que lui et selon des lignes de pensée très cohérentes avec les siennes. Si Elihou n'a pas été cité auparavant, c'est qu'il est volontairement soustrait par là au blâme qu'encourront les trois amis et, surtout, grâce à Elihou qui fait transition, l'homme peut préluder à la solution que Dieu seul énoncera avec pleine autorité, et Elihou sape, en pénétrant jusqu'à l'orgueil subconscient inhérent au coeur humain, une des données maîtresses de la solution traditionnelle, la croyance en la possibilité d'une justice de l'homme. Enfin les peintures de

[1]) *Israel, its life and culture*, I-II, Copenhague 1926, p. 363-374.
[2]) *Ibid.*, p. 531.

l'origine de la Sagesse (xxviii), de l'autruche (xxxix 13-18), de l'hippopotame et du crocodile (xl 15-xli 26) ne sont pas plus des hors d'oeuvre que ces nombreuses tirades où le poète se laisse entraîner par la rhétorique. Il faut se garder de désarticuler ce livre si original au nom d'un canon formel classique, mais le prendre tel qu'il est, avec ses disparates, avec sa grande et étrange allure, et ne pas fermer les yeux sur son architecture concertée [1]).

L'auteur de Job, et c'est là un premier trait de son modernisme, a voyagé par le vaste monde: s'il connaît la vie des villes palestiniennes (p. ex. xxix 7-11), il a vu aussi ces wadys désolés où des misérables vivent dans des grottes, parmi les rochers, n'ayant pour se nourrir que des pousses épineuses et des racines (p. ex. xxx 4 suiv.); il a certainement traversé le désert (p. ex. xxxviii 26) et connaît les rezzou des pillards arabes et araméens (i 15, 17); il semble familier avec les parages de l'Idumée (i 1 suiv.) et avec les oasis et les immensités désertiques que sillonnent les caravanes (p. ex. vi 19). Si bien que, devant ce caractère d'autopsie, Renan a pu parler de ce livre „rempli d'un parfum aussi fort de la vie nomade" [2]). Il en concluait, trop précipitamment croyons-nous, „que le fonds d'idées qu'on y trouve est celui qui appartient en commun à la branche nomade de la race sémitique" [3]). Mais, à y regarder de près, un milieu urbain transparaît à maintes reprises (cf. xix 13 suiv.; xxiv 10, 12, 16, xxix 7 suiv., xxx 28) à travers la fiction patriarcale; la vie „nomade" et patriarcale n'est qu'un décor, une atmosphère poétique et impressionniste, mirage d'un poète qui garde en son imagination les formes et les couleurs des paysages parcourus en ses voyages: la gazelle qui met bas dans les sables (xxxix 1 suiv.), la silhouette de l'onagre des steppes (xxxix 5 suiv.), les moeurs de l'autruche (xxx 29, xxxix 13 suiv.), les chacals (xxx 29).

Mais il est allé plus loin, il a visité les mines (xxviii 1 suiv.), de la presqu'île du Sinaï sans doute, et les esclaves fouillant les entrailles de la terre pour en extraire métaux et pierres précieuses.

---

[1]) A propos de la revue par C. Kuhl de la „Neuere Literarkritik des Buches Hiob" (*Theol. Rundschau*, 1953), Hempel a exprimé son impression de piétinement quant à ce problème (*ZAW*, 1954, p. 307). Nous partageons entièrement ce sentiment et c'est pourquoi nous tentons ici une voie nouvelle, essayant de montrer que les tensions, qui semblent manifester la non-unité du livre, révèlent au contraire une sorte de progression existentielle de l'oeuvre conçue comme une unité.

[2]) Renan, *Job*, p. XXXI.

[3]) *Ibid.*, p. XVI.

Surtout il a des souvenirs très précis de l'Egypte [1]: les pyramides (iii 14), les nécropoles (iii 18, 21), les palais regorgeant d'un luxe pharaonique (iii 15), les esclaves tremblant à la voix du garde- chiourme armé de sa courbache (iii 18, vii 1, 2), les vastes étendues marécageuses, fourrés de roseaux et de papyrus (viii 11), le Nil et ses canaux où filent les barques légères en brassées de joncs (ix 26), la décrue du fleuve et l'assèchement des campagnes (xiv 11), l'hippopotame couché sous les buissons épineux de la rive et le monstrueux crocodile (xl 25 suiv.) dépeints avec complaisance dans deux morceaux de bravoure [2].

Tous ces souvenirs de voyage détonnent dans cette littérature hébraïque confinée dans l'horizon de la Terre-Sainte, ils y mettent une note d'exotisme pittoresque et de cosmopolitisme.

Même modernisme dans la forme littéraire de Job. Ce n'est pas un drame, a prononcé PEDERSEN, parce qu'il n'y a pas de progrès dans l'action, ni un discours philosophique, car la pensée ne progresse pas non plus [3]. Ce jugement semble trop restrictif: d'abord les mots de drame et de discours philosophique viennent presque instinctivement sous la plume du critique, mais surtout et en réalité la pensée s'affirme, se précise et se développe bel et bien tout au long de l'oeuvre. Il y a bel et bien là un drame, intérieur et extérieur aussi, un sentiment toujours plus dramatique de la vie s'exprime en ces pages, leur conférant un accent presque unique dans l'Ancien Testament. Il y a bel et bien là un dialogue, avec interlocuteurs variés et qui incarnent des points de vue différents, dialogue où une véritable discussion se noue puis se dénoue, où les idées s'affrontent, se précisent. Il y a surtout toute une problématique dans ce livre, c'est-à-dire une démonstration progressive, alors que l'Ancien Testament est tout entier affirmation, hormis ce seul Ecclésiaste, tardif lui aussi et si étranger à la tradition yahviste. Tout le poème est poussé en avant, conduit, soulevé, animé par la plainte grandissante du juste

---

[1]) Cf. nos *Recherches sur les sources égyptiennes de la littérature sapientiale d'Israël*, 1929, p. 75 suiv., où nous avons signalé aussi les idées égyptiennes auxquelles l'auteur de Job fait écho.

[2]) Il résulte des fouilles archéologiques que l'hippopotame a vécu en Palestine sur la plaine côtière, jusqu'au IVe s. av. J. C. (Cf. G. HAAS, *BASOR* 132, p. 30 suiv.). Toutefois sa mention dans Job accompagne tant d'allusions, non seulement aux sites, mais aussi aux croyances de l'Egypte (p. ex. balance de la justice divine xxxi 6; pesée des coeurs vi 2; confession négative xxxi 1-40; confession positive xxix 12-17 etc.), que la description de l'hippopotame doit sans doute nous transporter aussi sur les bords du Nil.

[3]) *Op. cit.*, p. 363.

souffrant qu'exaspèrent les contradictions — facteurs d'un progrès du drame —, plainte qui éveille des échos divers où s'expriment les faces diverses aussi du problème. Angoisse tendue vers l'intervention divine qui, seule, apportera la réponse décisive, le dénouement. Dans tout cela il y a bien un mouvement et une lutte d'idées, une action, nous dirions presque des „actes", marchant à une „péripétie" proprement dite, quoique, naturellement, sans la logique serrée, sans l'ordre et l'harmonie d'un art classique.

Cette forme dialoguée si insolite ne s'inspire-t-elle pas de modèles étrangers comme on en a cités en Egypte [1]) et à Babylone, comme la Grèce en fournissait, des modèles peut-être plus prochains encore? Cet encadrement en prose, ces cycles de discours poétiques, cette orientation vers une parousie et une réponse de Dieu mais si différente de ce que l'on attendait, ce vrai „deus ex machina" et cette péripétie que sont la théophanie et les questions finales de Dieu (xxxviii 1-xlii 6), cette architecture, tout cela dépasse ce qu'on trouve en général sous la plume des Sages d'Israël. La part de la composition et de la rhétorique y est beaucoup plus grande qu'ailleurs dans l'Ancien Testament, et ici RENAN sentait juste: „C'est une composition artificielle, où les épreuves du vieux patriarche sont prises pour thème de discussions philosophiques" [2]). On songe involontairement, à propos de cette forme dialoguée, au dialogue cynique ou stoïcien où, selon la comparaison de Chrysippe, l'interlocuteur ressemble au mur sur lequel rebondit la balle au jeu de paume [3]), à ce dialogue à tendance protreptique.

A lire entre les lignes on a maintes fois l'impression que le poète décrit moins ses expériences toujours personnelles qu'une de ces grandes infortunes comme, dans notre adolescence, nous en lisions dans une littérature classique, types du destin de l'Homme éternel. Certes il y a unc part évidente d'expérience vécue dans ce poème de Job, mais la fiction y est non moins sensible et ressortit souvent à la leçon plus qu'à la biographie. Or cette préoccupation rhétorique, ce quelque chose de factice, cette recherche de l'expression, c'est aussi un indice de modernisme. Job est sans doute un individu, mais il est aussi un type, un type de l'Homme.

Et le style? Quelles concessions il fait au verbalisme! Certes, en

---

[1]) Cf. nos *Recherches* . . ., p. 77 suiv.

[2]) *Op. cit.*, p. XXXII.

[3]) Cf. Sénèque *De Ben.*, II, 17, 3, cité par P. GRIMAL, dans son *Commentaire du* "De constantia sapientis" *de Sénèque*, Paris 1953, p. 11.

bien des passages, originalité et beauté de la forme, force de l'expression, souffle passionné, fulgurantes lueurs. Poète inégal, grand poète pourtant et qui touche en nous la haute corde de la lyre. Art d'assembler mots, sonorités, rythmes, accords, et d'exprimer la misère et la souffrance humaines en poignantes images. Un style, quoique pas très pur.

Mais aussi accumulation de mots, répétitions, variations sur un thème. Disons-le: souvent remplissage ou emphase. Que d'effets purement sonores et verbaux, que de tirades que la pensée ne remplit plus, où la forme est plus ample que l'idée, que de recherche parfois, et, dès le chapitre III déjà, quel amour de l'amplification et du décor, d'où ces digressions descriptives que certains puristes croient devoir sacrifier mais qui sont, au contraire, conformes à ce style baroque et à effets si éloigné du classicisme hautain d'Esaïe et de sa netteté incisive. Il y a là un étalage de virtuosité et une complaisance en les prestiges du verbe fort étrangers à la littérature classique d'Israël mais qui suggèrent un rapprochement avec la rhétorique et la sophistique grecques, avec le goût hellénistique, qui trahissent en tout cas le modernisme d'un scribe qui a bu à d'autres sources que celles du Jourdain. Ce n'est pas à celui auquel sont dédiées ces pages que nous apprendrons qu'un de ces lettrés anglais nourris également de la Bible et de la Grèce, MACAULAY, relevait en 1825 déjà, dans son Essai sur Milton, „la grande ressemblance" entre Job et Eschyle pour la conduite du drame et l'art du dire.

Comme HÖLSCHER aussi l'a bien aperçu [1]), l'expression passablement ampoulée, le recours constant à l'image et le pathos font songer à la poésie hellénistique et, lorsque DUHM comparait l'exécration de Job contre son jour de naissance avec celle de Jérémie (xx 14-18), cet exégète d'un goût si sensible notait déjà ce qu'il y a de surchargé dans l'imprécation de Job: „Périssent le jour où je suis né et la nuit qui dit: un mâle a été conçu . . . [2]).

Et la richesse, voire la prodigalité du vocabulaire dont tous les trésors sont exploités, y compris les nombreux emprunts à l'araméen! On s'écarte de la sobriété un peu sèche de la langue antique puis classique d'Israël en sacrifiant à un goût décadent pour une forme plus brillante et diaprée que solide et nette. Ce n'est plus le chant si pur du chœur d'Israël.

---

[1]) HÖLSCHER, *Das Buch Hiob*, 2e ed., 1952, p. 7.
[2]) DUHM, *Hiob*, ad loc.

Mais c'est dans le domaine de l'idée que s'affirme principalement le modernisme de Job. Et d'abord dans cette opposition tranchée de la thèse et de l'antithèse en un dialogue que résoudra enfin la synthèse. L'Ancien Testament procède généralement par affirmations et révélations excluant toute discussion. L'auteur de Job, lui, pose un problème, des questions, qu'il discute terme à terme, dégageant par une lente maïeutique la pensée finale. Semblable problématique étonne et détonne dans la littérature hébraïque: n'est-ce pas l'écho d'un monde où la tradition a été déjà ébranlée, où le rôle de la dialectique devient dès lors nécessaire. Aussi bien et quoi qu'on dise, les idées progressent au travers de ce „dialogue en monologues", la révolte de Job se fait toujours plus consciente et brutale, l'affirmation de sa justice (p. ex. xxvii 2-5), maintenue et postulée jusque par delà la mort (cf. xix 23 suiv.), triomphe de la casuistique toujours plus spécieuse des amis, la conscience du mal radical en l'homme s'approfondit progressivement (cp. iv 17 suiv., ix 2, xiv 4, xv 14 suiv., xxv 4 suiv., xxxiii 17 suiv., xxxvi 9), la thèse de la puissance et de la sagesse transcendantes de Dieu est formulée avec toujours plus de netteté. C'est même le thème dominant de l'œuvre, le thème de la puissance et de la sagesse suréminentes de Dieu et, par conséquent, de sa justice inadéquate à notre humaine capacité de comprendre. Thème de la grande fugue des chap. xxxviii-xlii, mais motif qui s'esquisse déjà, se répète, se formule tout au cours du poème jusqu'à ce qu'il s'épanouisse dans le finale de la symphonie (cf. iv 17 suiv., viii 9, ix 1 suiv., 32 suiv., xi 6 suiv., xii 13, xv 7, 8, 14, 15, xxi 22, xxii 12 suiv., xxiii 13, xxv 2 suiv., xxvi 5 suiv., xxviii 20 suiv., xxxiv 12 suiv., xxxv 5 suiv., xxxvi 22 suiv., xxxvii 23, xxxviii suiv.).

Cette discussion d'un problème d'idées n'est pas dans le droit fil de la révélation d'Israël, serait-ce un rayon du génie de Pallas?

Serait-ce point aussi le cas de l'ironie dans le livre de Job? Lourde ironie des amis (p. ex. xi 1 suiv., xv 7 suiv.), ironie mordante dont Job lui-même accable ses pairs (p. ex. vi 25 suiv., xii 2 suiv., xvi 1 suiv., xxvi 2 suiv., xxx 1 suiv.) ou la divinité elle-même (p. ex. vii 17 suiv., xiii 25 suiv., xxi 19 suiv., etc.), ironie pateline d'Elihou (xxxii 6 suiv., xxxvii 14 suiv.), et surtout ironie altière de Dieu. Ironie qui remet en question les vérités d'habitude. „Aporie" de l'homme acculé, au terme du débat, à l'aveu de son impuissance (cf. xxxviii 4, 12, 21 etc.).

Un pressant γνῶθι σεαυτόν traverse tout le livre de Job: interrogations obstinées des amis qui conjurent Job de mieux se connaître soi-même en prenant conscience de ses péchés; interrogation tragique de Job qui descend en soi et y trouve sa justice, aussi inébranlable que le roc; interrogations nuancées d'Elihou qui tendent à faire découvrir à l'homme le secret fatal de son orgueil; interrogation ironique de Dieu qui réduit à néant la superficielle prétention de l'homme et l'oblige à constater et confesser sa radicale inintelligence. De toutes parts l'indiscutée cohérence de la vieille psyché israëlite est ainsi mise en doute, elle se dissocie et se désagrège.

C'est, naturellement, dans la discussion de la thèse maîtresse que se marque le plus ce caractère de modernisme. On va répétant que Job traite le problème de la théodicée; la formule est trop générale et M. Pedersen a admirablement analysé la situation: le fond du débat c'est un problème de relation, un problème à deux termes, c'est-à-dire la relation, la solidarité entre justice humaine et justice divine, ces deux pôles de la vie selon Israel; il y a donc une bipolarité essentielle qui est en jeu [1]. Or voilà le point où le penseur de Job se révèle le plus révolutionnaire.

Le prologue, par manière de précaution, a servi à démontrer que Job n'est point un hypocrite, que sa justice est authentique, sa piété désintéressée, son islâm parfait: „Dieu a donné, Dieu a repris, béni soit le nom de Dieu!". Les deux termes du problème sont donc établis, ce n'est pas un pseudo-problème: la justice de Job prouvée par l'exorde, et la justice de Dieu implicitement et traditionnellement indiscutée. Désormais le pour et le contre vont s'affronter et s'ébranler mutuellement dans la controverse des divers interlocuteurs: les amis ne cesseront jamais de contester la justice de Job, sur la base de la vieille conception orthodoxe qui lie nécessairement et organiquement justice divine, et partant rétribution, à justice humaine; mais, ce faisant, ils commencent cependant à rendre fluide la situation et tendent à insinuer dans l'esprit du lecteur le doute sur la réalité de la justice humaine. En effet, en s'engageant sur le terrain d'une discussion, les amis de Job enlèvent quelque chose à l'autorité de la tradition; en argumentant, ils se prennent dans l'engrenage d'une dialectique. Le problème est désormais en mouvement.

De son côté Job, avec une obstination farouche, se cramponne au bon droit de sa justice et doit, sans craindre le blasphème, accuser Dieu de tyrannie et invoquer Dieu contre Dieu lui-même (p. ex. xiv 13 suiv., xviii 19 suiv.). Le second des termes corrélatifs, la

---

[1]) *Op. cit., p.* 368-370.

justice divine, est nié à son tour. Les deux partis maintiennent, en principe, la bipolarité du problème, ils poussent même à l'extrême soit la justice divine, soit la justice humaine, pour en tirer, à vrai dire, des conclusions pratiques diamétralement opposées. En dépit des apparences, tout est cependant mis en question et, nouveau Samson, l'auteur de Job a ébranlé les deux colonnes du temple.

Passagèrement il évoque alors au chapitre xxviii l'idée de l'inintelligence foncière de l'homme incapable d'atteindre la sagesse dont Dieu seul détient le secret (cf. déjà xi 7, 8, xv 7 suiv.). Une brèche s'entrouvre dans l'édifice orthodoxe et laisse entrevoir cette idée peu hébraïque d'une sagesse supérieure, mystérieuse et cachée.

Sur ce intervient Elihou qui s'en prend immédiatement et corps à corps (xxxiii 8 suiv.) à l'affirmation par Job de son innocence. Rôle des songes qui doivent, sur son lit de douleur, instruire l'homme des semences de mal qui sont en lui, de son subtil orgueil (xxxiii 17, xxxvi 9), et allusion à un ange qui intercèderait pour le malade auprès de Dieu. Or, s'il y a intercession, c'est donc que la justice humaine est précaire. La souffrance prend ainsi un aspect pédagogique (xxxiii 19, xxxvi 15) en réduisant l'homme à l'humilité: „Dieu ne regarde même pas les prétendus sages" (xxxvii 24). Rejoignant une intuition passagère d'Eliphaz (v 17 suiv.), Elihou desserre donc l'étreinte de la logique (justice humaine — justice divine) pour passer sur le plan psychologique: à la souffrance rétributive qui maintient l'équilibre des deux justices est substituée une souffrance salvatrice, à une nécessité naturelle et logique une initiative providentielle. La voie est ainsi ouverte à cette liberté d'un Dieu que la doctrine orthodoxe solidarisait presque organiquement avec l'homme et ses actions.

Enfin, d'un coup le noeud gordien est résolument tranché par Dieu. Si, fidèle à l'antique doctrine solidariste, les amis et Job luimême admettaient au fond implicitement que l'homme et sa justice sont la mesure de la justice divine, les discours de Dieu annihilent au contraire l'homme devant la puissance cosmique d'un Dieu qui transcende toutes nos notions. „Dieu, objecte cependant M. Pedersen, ne dit pas que l'homme doive abandonner sa justice" [1]. Certes, il ne le dit pas explicitement, mais avec une implicite ironie; aussi bien toute la sagesse et la justice de Job viennent-elles se briser comme verre contre le granit de la mise à la question divine, et l'homme, ce soi-disant juste, ne trouvera plus un mot à répliquer, il

[1] *Op. cit.*, p. 373.

avouera avoir déraisonné sur des matières impénétrables au sens humain et se repentira sur la poussière et sur la cendre (xlii 6). Toute justice humaine est donc pulvérisée, le penseur a catégoriquement rompu avec la conception traditionnelle, il ouvre un monde nouveau. La justice divine n'est pas à notre humaine mesure, elle n'est pas un dû que l'homme puisse calculer et revendiquer, la justice humaine est comme volatilisée, l'homme ne peut plus s'arroger la capacité de juger Dieu, il ne peut que s'en remettre au Dieu souverain par delà notre horizon humain. Notre sagesse, notre justice, vaines ombres, ombres décevantes au regard de l'éblouissante sagesse, gage de la justice infinie de Dieu.

On aperçoit la conséquence: de la bipolarité si justement reconnue par M. Pedersen au point de départ de la discussion, nous sommes finalement passés à l'unipolarité: Dieu et l'homme ne sont plus solidaires, il n'y a plus qu'un seul pôle, Dieu.

La liberté divine, affranchie de l'arithmétique morale humaine, est désormais absolue et souveraine. L'exaltation de la puissance de Dieu considéré surtout sous l'angle de son empire dans la Nature et dans le Cosmos abolit le rapport entre justice de l'homme et justice de Dieu, soustrait cette dernière à nos chétives notions de rétribution et projette l'être humain dans un univers totalement nouveau où il n'a rien à faire valoir que son ignorance et son néant devant Dieu et ne peut s'attendre qu'à une justice dont Dieu seul est la norme, toutes coordonnées humaines étant abolies. Ne voilà-t-il donc pas Job au seuil, mais au seuil seulement de la foi? en tout cas hors de la pensée séculaire d'Israël?

Mais, dira-t-on, l'épilogue n'y contredit-il pas et ne marque-t-il pas un retour à la mentalité solidariste et rétributive?

Sans doute, tandis que l'épilogue reproche aux trois amis de n'avoir pas parlé correctement de Job, il félicite Job pour sa façon de répondre à Dieu. Mais cela se réfère de toute évidence aux protestations de soumission et d'humilité de Job (xl 2-5, xlii 1-5) et non à sa révolte passionnée: „Quel est celui qui obscurcit le dessein de Dieu par des discours hors de sens?" (xxxviii 2), ou „Quel est celui qui obscurcit le plan divin, faute de savoir? J'ai parlé sans intelligence de merveilles qui me dépassent et que j'ignore" (xlii 3). L'épilogue tient certainement pour acquis le résultat des discours de Dieu; la bénédiction finale apparaît au fond comme une grâce accordée à celui qui s'est tu et a fait acte de contrition.

Bien plus, la bénédiction finale de Job, qui n'est point selon la stricte justice puisqu'elle se fait „au double", renoue manifestement et fait symétrie avec ce que PEDERSEN a justement appelé le motto du livre de Job [1]): „Yahvé a donné, Yavhé a repris, béni soit le nom de Yahvé!". Cette bénédiction finale, après le blâme deux fois répété de xxxviii 2 et xlii 3, ressemble, répétons-le, moins à un dû qu'à une grâce, sinon dans la légende originelle, du moins dans la perspective où l'auteur du livre l'a volontairement inscrite aujourd'hui. Et s'il reste quelque discordance entre ces bénédictions dont Job est finalement comblé et la conclusion des discours de Dieu à laquelle lui-même avait souscrit (xlii 3), elle est à imputer à la source prosaïque assez mécaniquement adoptée et imparfaitement assimilée par le grand poète. Job ne l'a-t-il pas confessé de sa propre bouche: l'expérience personnelle prime le savoir traditionnel: „Je ne te connaissais que par ouï-dire, mais maintenant je t'ai vu de mes propres yeux".

La vieille conception israëlite de la vie fait place à une conception totalement différente: l'anthropocentrisme doit céder la place au théocentrisme. La discussion poursuivie à travers affirmations traditionnelles, raisonnements, révoltes et blasphèmes, songes révélateurs, souffrances éducatives, élans désespérés de la foi, s'achève en illumination théophanique: „Je t'ai vu de mes propres yeux". De passagères intuitions avaient bien pu suggérer à Job qu'il faut dépasser le niveau de la justice humaine (p. ex. iv 17-20, xv 14-16, xxii 2,3, xxv 5), le dernier mot, celui qui fait table rase et porte la conviction, appartient à Dieu seul et c'est Lui-même qui éblouit de sa sagesse suprême l'homme qui se prosterne alors dans le silence, l'humilité et l'acceptation. Le poème didactique s'achève ainsi par une profession de σωφροσύνη qui est le comble de la Ḥokmâ. Dirons-nous que la „Sagesse" un peu terre-à-terre d'Israël s'approfondit ici et s'élargit en une Sophia teintée d'hellénisme?

Une omission est caractéristique dans le livre de Job: l'effacement de la révélation de Dieu dans l'histoire d'Israël et par la Loi [2]), le culte et ses rites: il y aurait pourtant eu là matière à arguments en faveur de la confiance en la justice rétributive et la Providence de Dieu. Or jamais l'auteur ne recourt à cet ordre de considérations proprement israëlites et juives: il y a là une contre-épreuve significative.

---

[1]) *Op. cit.*, p. 374.

[2]) L'unique mention du mot *tōrah* (xxii 22) entend ce terme d'une didascalie par Dieu directement à Job, donc au sens actuel et non historique.

En revanche, au cours des discours de Job et de ses amis aussi (p. ex. v 9,10, ix 5 suiv., xxii 12, xxvi 5 suiv., xxviii 20 suiv.), puis dans les monologues d'Elihou (xxxiv 13 suiv., xxxvi 27 suiv., xxxvii 1 suiv.), mais surtout dans les apostrophes de Dieu (xxxviii suiv., *passim*), c'est la révélation de Dieu dans la Nature qui est célébrée, la révélation de sa puissance cosmique. Rien de moins spécifiquement hébraïque que cette insistance sur la théologie naturelle, que cette intégration de la terre dans un univers désormais sidéral (cf. ix 7-9, xxii 12, xxxviii), que cet accent mis exclusivement sur l'argument cosmologique. Car, aussi bien, n'est-ce point devant le Dieu trois fois saint et dans le sentiment de son péché que l'homme profane doit ici s'abîmer, mais devant la souveraine, mystérieuse et insondable puissance de Celui qui gouverne les mondes et manifeste son empire dans la Nature entière. C'est à l'échelle de ce plan cosmique qu'est la justice divine, et non point à celle de l'intellect borné de l'homme (xxxviii 2,21, xlii 3). Désolidarisée des heurs et malheurs et des calculs du Lilliput humain, la justice suprême ne peut qu'être l'objet d'un acte d'adhésion à cette incommensurable sagesse divine qui éclate de toutes parts dans un univers incommensurable comme elle. Allâh akbar!

On le voit, le livre de Job se clôt par une méditation plus philosophique que religieuse, et cette curiosité pour des questions de sciences naturelles et pour des problèmes cosmogoniques (ch. xxxviii-xl *passim*) dépasse l'horizon moyen de l'Ancien Testament: le Ps. civ, par exemple, qui évoque des mystères semblables, est cependant animé d'un souffle bien différent puisqu'il commence et finit sur des accents hymniques (vers 31-35), bénissant Dieu (vers 1,35) et exultant en Lui, tandis que Job s'achève dans le mutisme et sur un aveu d'impotence, de soumission résignée, de contrition et d'*islâm* (xlii 1-5); et puis le Psalmiste parcourt la Nature sur les ailes du lyrisme religieux, mais Job xxxviii suiv. la considère avec une attention plus analytique, plus scientifique, et sous un angle plus littéraire que religieux.

La note finale donnée par Job a donc une résonance inédite dans la littérature d'Israël, ce n'est plus la séculaire harmonie entre la justice humaine et la justice divine, avec la logique rétributive qu'elle implique, ce lien a été coupé et l'auteur s'engage hardiment dans une voie toute nouvelle: „l'apothéose de la justice" dit M. PEDERSEN, mais nous précisons: l'apothéose de la seule justice divine, incommensurable et impénétrable à l'intelligence de l'homme. Et, d'autre part, la justice humaine progressivement réduite à zéro (iv 17 suiv., vii 20, ix 2,3, xiv 4 auth.?, xv 14-16, xxii 3, xxv 4-6, xxxiii 8 suiv., xxxv 5, xxxvi 9, xl 4,5, xlii 6), même celle des anges (iv 18, v 1, xv 15).

Des deux termes du rapport harmonique, l'un est donc annulé (la justice de l'homme), l'autre exalté à l'infini (la justice de Dieu); un seul pôle demeure: le Dieu infiniment puissant et dont la sagesse, la justice par conséquent aussi, sont insondables mais indubitables. Le problème est donc résolu de façon tout à fait originale et dans une perspective absolument nouvelle.

En effet, nous ne pensons pas, répétons-le, comme M. PEDERSEN, que la vieille conception israëlite de la vie n'ait point été ébranlée dans le livre de Job qui ne traiterait que d'exceptions à la loi ordinaire de la vie [1]). C'est l'Homme en général, l'Homme comme tel qui est constamment pris en considération dans ce poème, et non point un cas d'exception. Il n'est que de relever à cet égard l'emploi dans Job du mot *ènōš* qui y désigne le type et non un être d'exception (cf. p. ex. iv 17, vii 1,17, ix 2, x 4,5, xiv 19, xv 14, xxv 4, xxxiii 12 etc.). D'ailleurs la réponse donnée à un juste tel que Job vaut *a fortiori* pour ceux qui n'auraient pas la même vertu à produire: à plus forte raison leur conduite ne limite-t-elle pas la liberté divine; leurs heurs et malheurs, leur manque même de rétribution adéquate, ne ressortissent pas à la logique humaine bornée mais à l'incommensurable, à l'insondable justice de Dieu (cf. p. ex. chap. xxi et spécialement les v 22 suiv., xxxvii 23,24).

Exagérons-nous donc en avançant, pour les raisons de forme et de fond que nous avons dites, la thèse du modernisme de Job? Bien entendu, ce livre pourrait être envisagé sous d'autres points de vue encore et apprécié selon d'autres normes. Notre étude aura du moins fait ressortir une fois de plus l'allure internationale et oecuménique de la littérature sapientiale d'Israël si perméable aux influences étrangères qu'elle tentait de combiner aux pensées traditionnelles du yahvisme. Le livre de Job est un exemple de cette prise de contact d'Israël avec l'étranger, de ce péril peut-être, de cet effort en tout cas vers une culture universelle.

Israël, où est, pour parler le langage de Pascal, le „Dieu d'Abraham, Dieu d'Isaac, Dieu de Jacob"?

---

[1]) *Op. cit.*, p. 373.

מָשָׁל

BY

A. R. JOHNSON
Cardiff

The repeated examination of this term during recent years may seem to require an apology for treating it afresh [1]; and the writer's plea must be a long-standing interest in the subject [2] and a growing conviction that this term is of more importance for the understanding of Scripture than is commonly recognized. What is offered in this short article is no more than a preliminary investigation of the problem, and, as such, it is restricted to the use of this term in the Hebrew Bible.

It is, of course, hardly necessary to point out that in a semantic investigation of this kind it is important to give due consideration, so far as possible, to both etymology and actual usage. In this case there is no reason to doubt that basically the term implies "likeness", and the recognition of this fact is of the first importance for understanding the different shades of meaning which it seems to have acquired [3].

Apart from the evidence offered by the cognate languages [4], the fact that the term is derived from the thought of "likeness" is indicated quite clearly by certain forms of the Hebrew verb. Thus the

---

[1]) See especially O. Eissfeldt, "Der Maschal im Alten Testament", *BZAW* XXIV (1913); A. H. Godbey, "The Hebrew *Mašal*", *AJSL* XXXIX (1922-3), p. 89-108; G. Boström, "Paronomasi i den äldre hebreiska maschallitteraturen", *Lunds Universitets Årsskrift*, NF 1 23 8 (1928) ; M. Hermaniuk, *La Parabole Evangélique* (Louvain, 1947), p. 62-189; J. Pirot, "Le 'Mâšâl' dans l'Ancien Testament", *Recherches de Science Rel.*, XXXVII (1950), p. 565-80; F. Hauck, *ThWNT* V (1954), p. 744-8; A. S. Herbert, "The 'Parable' (*Māšāl*) in the Old Testament", *Scottish Journ. of Theol.*, 7 (1954), p. 180-96.

[2]) Cf. A. R. Johnson, *The Cultic Prophet in Ancient Israel* (Cardiff, 1944), p. 37, n. 4.

[3]) Cf., in addition to the examples cited later, the Accadian *mišlu* "half" (i.e., of like portions) and the Arabic مِثْل "likeness" as used to convey the thought of "retaliation".

[4]) Cf., e.g., the preceding note and p. 164, n. 5.

Niph. of the root משל is used on five occasions with the meaning "to become like" or "to be comparable with", e.g. [1]),

> "Hide not Thy face from me,
> Lest I become like those who go down into the Pit."

The Hithp., again, is used with much the same force, when Job despairingly says [2]):

> "I think of myself as dust and ashes."

Similarly the Hiph. occurs once with reference to the matching of objects which are alike, i.e., with the obvious meaning "to compare" [3]).

> "To whom will ye liken Me and make Me equal,
> And compare Me that we may be alike?"

Finally there is one occurrence of a nominal form מֹשֶׁל (or, it may be, the form מָשָׁל under discussion), where the basic meaning is again unmistakable; i.e., when, in the book of Job, it is said of the crocodile [4]):

> "Upon earth there is not his like." [5])

In actual use the term מָשָׁל sometimes corresponds quite clearly to the English term "proverb" as denoting "a short pithy saying in common use" [6]). The language is picturesque and forceful, and the type of saying in question is one which may be used, because of its recognized associations, to convey in summary fashion the speaker's judgement on what appears to him to be an analogous situation with somewhat similar implications, e.g. [7]):

> "Is Saul also among the prophets?"

On the other hand, it may represent a conclusion which has been reached through widespread recognition of a corresponding expe-

---

[1]) Ps. cxliii 7. Cf. Ps. xxviii 1, xlix 13, 21 (EVV. 12, 20); Jes. xiv 10.
[2]) xxx 19.
[3]) Jes. xlvi 5.
[4]) xli 25 (EVV. 33).
[5]) מָשְׁלוֹ (or מְשָׁלוֹ ?) = Arabic مِثْلُهُ.
[6]) *The Shorter Oxford English Dictionary*, 3rd. ed. rev. (Oxford, 1944), s.v.
[7]) 1 Sam. x 12 (repeated in xix 24).

rience, and in that case it serves to convey what appears to be a truth of general application, e.g. [1]):

> "Out of the wicked there cometh forth wickedness",

and [2])

> "Fathers eat sour grapes,
> And the children's teeth are set on edge."

The use of such sayings was developed as a means of instruction in the professional circles of "the wise", whose teaching was important enough to be classed along with that of the priest and the prophet [3]). Thus, in the first place, we have to note the development of such lore in the form of similar pithy sayings which could be used to communicate moral and spiritual truths in an arresting and memorable way. This is the type of saying which bulks so largely in the book of Proverbs [4]). In fact it is almost wholly characteristic of the two collections which are introduced by Prov. x 1 and xxv 1. Such sayings were composed from the first with a didactic purpose, i.e., that they might be effective in creating men of sound moral character by setting before them the lines of action which lay open to their choice—the unhappy example to be avoided and the happy model to be copied [5]). They represent an attempt to inculcate principles of action or modes of behaviour by means of colourful word-pictures or object-lessons, drawn from the many and varied experiences of everyday life, which will bring about the desired end by moving the hearer to consent to a particular line of action. That is to say, the conclusion to be drawn may also be an issue to be shunned or an end to be achieved; and the real effectiveness of these sayings lies in the degree to which they can be used intelligently [6]) to influence the hearer in terms of moral persuasion.

However, the term מָשָׁל could also be used of more elaborate compositions, in fact complete poems, of the type which is especially

---

[1]) 1 Sam. xxiv 14 (EVV. 13); cf. Ezech. xvi 44, "Like mother, like daughter".

[2]) Ezech. xviii 2 f. (corresponding to Jer. xxxi 29); cf. xii 22 f.

[3]) Cf. Jer. xviii 18. See also such passages as Prov. i 6, xxii 17, xxiv 23; Eccles. xii 9.

[4]) Cf. i 1.

[5]) Cf., e.g., the Accadian *tamšîlu* "image, picture" and the Arabic مَثَّلَ, II "to depict, copy, make an example of", V "to imitate", تِمْثَال, "image, statue", مِثَال, "example, pattern, model".

[6]) Cf. Prov. xxvi 7, 9; also Iob xiii 12.

characteristic of Prov. i-ix [1]). As is well known, these chapters form a collection of addresses or exhortations of varying length, which reveal a didactic purpose similar to that already described; and throughout one may recognize a technique of graphic portrayal which makes them a valuable mirror of the social life of ancient Israel. Outstanding examples are the warning against participation in highway robbery [2]), Wisdom's personal appeal to those who neglect her [3]), the warning against the lurking seductiveness of the adulterous woman [4]), and, in studied contrast, the frank and open appeal of Wisdom herself as Yahweh's intimate companion from before the Creation and, therefore, the surest guide to true happiness [5]). Thus the term מָשָׁל, besides denoting the simple proverb, was also used to describe something of the same literary *genre*, although more technical and much more elaborate, which could likewise be employed as a recognized medium of instruction by those who claimed to know something of the mystery of living and the secret of a happy life [6]).

The book of Proverbs, however, is not alone in offering examples of the more elaborate type of composition just described. Thus Ps. xlix, which is referred to quite specifically as embodying a מָשָׁל [7]), is clearly a didactic poem of much the same kind, which has as its object-lesson the fact that the rich, for all their vaunted power, "are like the beasts that perish" [8]), and its aim is obviously that of securing contentment with one's lot. Similarly Ps. lxxviii, which is also described as embodying a מָשָׁל [9]), turns out to be a sketch of Israel's history which is presented in such a way as to make it an object-lesson in obedience to Yahweh. It is, perhaps, less surprising to find that the term under discussion is also used to describe Job's final words in self-defence [10]); and it is to be observed that in this case we have a summary account of his personal history to date, the

[1]) Cf. i 1-6.
[2]) i 10-19.
[3]) i 20-33.
[4]) vii 1-27.
[5]) viii 1-36.
[6]) Cf. Prov. i 5 f.
[7]) Cf. verse 5 (EVV. 4).
[8]) Verses 13 and 21 (EVV. 12 and 20), i.e., נִמְשַׁל כַּבְּהֵמוֹת נִדְמוּ, as referred to above, p. 163, n. 1.
[9]) Verse 2.
[10]) xxix-xxxi: cf. xxvii 1 ff.

conclusion to be drawn being that he has not merited his present suffering and the end to be achieved being, of course, his vindication.

More closely allied to these didactic utterances than is commonly recognized is the type of composition, likewise described as a מָשָׁל, which is to be found in Jes. xiv 1 ff., Mich. ii 4 and Hab. ii 6. Each of these has a dirge-like quality, and each anticipates some form of retribution which will make the person or persons concerned an object-lesson in the abuse of power. Indeed it is this aspect of the poems in question which gives them that suggestion of mockery or derision which has led to the view, now commonly accepted, that here מָשָׁל may best be regarded as denoting a "taunt-song" (*Spottlied*). The suggestion of derision, however, in so far as it is present, is really quite secondary; and such a rendering tends to obscure what seems to have been the primary purpose of the poem, i.e., that of forecasting the plight of an individual or a group of people in terms which imply the creation of a public example [1]).

We are now in a position to understand the corresponding use of the term מָשָׁל which is sometimes indicated in English by the rendering "byword", i.e., its use with reference to the type of disaster which overtakes an individual or a group of people and assumes such proportions that it becomes proverbial. Thus, on some occasion of national disaster about which we can only conjecture, a psalmist cries on behalf of his people [2]):

"Thou makest us a reproach to our neighbours,
A figure of scorn and derision to those around us.
Thou makest us a proverb (מָשָׁל) [3]) among the nations,
A shaking of the head among the peoples."

Similarly we find an individual sufferer saying of those who find in him an object of scorn [4]),

"I have made sackcloth my clothing,
And I am become a proverb (מָשָׁל) for them.

I am the theme of those who sit in the gate
And the song of men at their drink."

---

[1]) Cf. the use of the stocks as instruments of punishment; for these served to make the culprit a public example and, as such, an object of ridicule. See also p. 164, n. 5.

[2]) Ps. xliv 14 f. (EVV. 13 f.).

[3]) EVV. "byword".

[4]) Ps. lxix 12 f. (EVV. 11 f.).

Here again, however, in this particular use of the term מָשָׁל, we also find the accompanying thought of an object-lesson or public example, as when Ezekiel, speaking in the name of Yahweh, thus denounces the type of man who combines a faith in idols with his profession of faith in Yahweh [1]).

"I will set My face against that man,
And make him [2]) a sign (אוֹת) and a proverb (מָשָׁל).
I will cut him off from My people,
And thus ye shall know that I am Yahweh."

In the circumstances it is not surprising that an object-lesson or example of this kind could also be thought of as furnishing occasion for a curse or even, perhaps, providing the pattern for one. This is evident from the way in which Jeremiah, speaking like Ezekiel in the name of Yahweh, thus describes the impending doom of Zedekiah and those of his subjects still left in the southern kingdom [3]).

"I will make them a grievous cause of trembling for all the kingdoms of the earth, a figure of scorn and a proverb (מָשָׁל), a taunt and a curse (קְלָלָה) in all the places to which I shall scatter them."

This brings us to the use of the term under discussion as it occurs in the Balaam stories [4]), where it denotes, not a parallel which already exists and thus serves as an example whereby its like may be avoided or brought into being, but one which is first pictured in the mind, possibly under so-called "ecstatic" conditions [5]), and then given colourful expression in words with a view to its corresponding appearance in actual life, i.e., the pattern or shape of things to come as envisaged by the speaker in terms of Yahweh's purposeful action. In the passages in question it clearly forms the pattern of a blessing or curse, expressed here and there in somewhat allegorical language, and, as such, it serves as an instrument of magical or, better perhaps,

[1]) Ezech. xiv 8; cf. Iob xvii 6 (LXX., Vulg., Tg., etc.). See also, for the same idea on a national scale, Deut. xxviii 37; 1 Reg. ix 7; 2 Chron. vii 20. Cf., too, Num. xxi 27 (JE); Jo. ii 17 (?).

[2]) Reading וְשַׂמְתִּיהוּ with LXX., Vulg., Tg., etc. Cf. A.V. At the same time there is something to be said for the view that the consonantal text should be vocalized so as to read וַהֲשִׁמֹּתִיהוּ, "And I will make him a figure of horror to serve as a sign", etc. Cf. R.V.; and, for the language, see Deut. xxviii 37, as cited in the previous note.

[3]) xxiv 9.

[4]) Num. xxiii 7, 18, xxiv 3, 15, 20, 21, 23 (all JE).

[5]) Cf. Num. xxiv 4, 15, 16.

magico-religious action—in short a spell which can be effective in and of itself.

Somewhat similar is the use of the term in the book of Ezekiel to denote a composition which offers in equally colourful and even more elaborate allegorical language a forecast of some impending event which is likewise envisaged by the speaker in terms of Yahweh's purposeful action—in each case, as it happens, a warning of imminent doom for Ezekiel's contemporaries in the southern kingdom. The examples in question are the account of the two eagles, the cedar and the vine [1]), that of the forest fire in the south [2]), and that of the cauldron which, on being put to use, is revealed as so rusted that it is fit only for destruction [3]). Elsewhere in the book of Ezekiel, as already noted [4]), the term מָשָׁל is employed to denote much the same as the English term proverb as used to sum up a lesson based on common experience. In the passages under discussion, as one ought surely to expect, its purpose is basically the same, for here again it refers to something which serves to convey a lesson, although in this case the composition takes on the character of what we should call a parable rather than a proverb.

This is not all, however, for these three lone examples of a מָשָׁל as used by Ezekiel hardly justify the summary reference to his work as a prophet which forms the sequel to the second instance, i.e., when Ezekiel complains that his contemporaries are saying of him הֲלֹא מְמַשֵּׁל מְשָׁלִים הוּא [5]). These obviously contemptuous words suggest that, so far as Ezekiel's work is concerned, the presence of a מָשָׁל should probably be recognized even where the term itself is not actually used. This again is important, because the third example given above, i.e., that of the rusty cauldron, is so dramatic in quality as to make it likely that the prophet's words were accompanied by some form of symbolic action of the type which, beginning perhaps as a pure spell [6]), had come to be a recognized means of making one's message more effective [7]), and was, in fact, an outstanding feature of

[1]) xvii 1 ff.
[2]) xxi 1-5 (EVV. xx 45-9).
[3]) xxiv 3 ff.
[4]) See above, p. 164.
[5]) xxi 5 (EVV. xx 49).
[6]) Cf. 1 Reg. xxii 11 (= 2 Chron. xviii 10); 2 Reg. xiii 14-19.
[7]) E.g., 1 Reg. xi 29 ff., xx 35-43; Jes. xx; Jer. xiii 1-11, xix 1 ff., xxvii-xxviii, li 59-64.

Ezekiel's own ministry [1]). Accordingly there is reason to believe that the term מָשָׁל could also be used to denote a parable and originally, maybe, a spell [2]) which was expressed not merely in words but also in mime.

In conclusion it is to be observed that the verb Qal, which is nowhere found with the basic meaning "to be like", seems to have been employed in a secondary sense to denote the utterance or recitation of any composition, simple or complex, which might be covered by the term מָשָׁל [3]). What is more, we are now in a position to grasp more fully the thought in Ezekiel's mind, when he complained that his contemporaries were saying of him הֲלֹא מְמַשֵּׁל מְשָׁלִים הוּא. In the standard English versions this is rendered by "Doth he not speak in parables?" (A.V.) and "Is he not a speaker of parables?" (R.V.); but, if we are to do justice to this solitary example of the verb Pi. as well as the noun, we must think first of some such rendering as "He is always concocting parables", and then, if we wish to think in terms of contemporary idiom, "He's always preaching"!

---

[1]) Cf. iv 1 ff., v 1 ff., vi 11 f., xii 1-16, 17-20, xxi 11 f., 23 ff. (EVV. 6 f., 18 ff.), xxxvii 15 ff., and, for the recognition of some form of symbolic action in the case under discussion, see H. Schmidt, *Die Schriften d. A.T. in Auswahl*, ii 2, 2nd. ed. rev. (1923); J. Herrmann, *KAT* (1924), and G. A. Cooke, *ICC* (1936), *in loc.*

[2]) Cf. Godbey, *op. cit.*, *passim*. This is a work which merits attention, even though the author appears to overstate his case.

[3]) Num. xxi 27 (JE); Ezech. xii 23, xvi 44, xvii 2, xviii 2 f., xxiv 3; Jo. ii 17 (?). Godbey, *op. cit.*, goes on to suggest that the verb מָשַׁל "rule", which has no parallel outside the Canaanite area, may have acquired this meaning from its being used to denote the activity of one who knew how to fix the pattern of life which his subjects were to follow.

"MAN AND HIS GOD"

A SUMERIAN VARIATION ON THE "JOB" MOTIF

BY

SAMUEL NOAH KRAMER

University Museum, University of Penna.

INTRODUCTION [1])

The text of the Sumerian poetic essay presented in this study under the title "Man and His God" [2]) has been pieced together from five tablets and fragments, three of which are located in the University Museum in Philadelphia, and two in the Museum of the Ancient Orient in Istanbul. All five pieces were excavated at Nippur more than fifty years ago by an expedition of the University of Pennsylvania, but only two have as yet been published [3]). To judge from their script and from other criteria, all the pieces were inscribed, to put it very roughly, about 1700 B.C.; the date of the original composition of the poem may, of course, have been considerably earlier, perhaps as early as the Third Dynasty of Ur, about 2000 B.C. The pious contents of this essay should be of no little interest to students of comparative religion, and it is a privilege to publish it in a volume honouring a distinguished Biblical scholar.

The problem of human suffering [4]), particularly relative to its rather enigmatic causes, and potential remedies, has troubled thinking men throughout the ages, and the Sumerians were no exceptions. Their teachers and sages believed and taught the doctrine that man's misfortunes were the result of his sins and misdeeds. They were

---

[1]) In the final preparation of the manuscript I was assisted by EDMUND I. GORDON, and quite a number of his valuable suggestions have been incorporated into this study.

[2]) The Sumerian title of this work is *lú-lu₇ nam-maḫ-dingir-re-e*, cf. *BASOR* 88, p. 18 ("Louvre Catalogue", line 46).

[3]) The contents of these two pieces were treated most competently by J. J. A. VAN DIJK, *La Sagesse Suméro-Accadienne*, p. 122-127.

[4]) For an Akkadian text from approximately the same date dealing with the problem of human suffering, cf. J. NOUGAYROL's recently published "Une Version Ancienne du Juste Souffrant," *RB* 59, p. 239-250.

convinced, moreover, that no man is without guilt; as our Sumerian poet-theologian puts it: "Never was a sinless child born to its mother" [1]). In spite of surface appearances to the contrary, therefore, there are no cases of unjust and undeserved human suffering; it is always man who is to blame, not the gods. But the truth of such theological premises and conclusions is by no means readily apparent, and in moments of adversity, more than one sufferer must have been tempted to challenge the fairness and justice of the gods, and to blaspheme against them. It may well be that it was in an effort to forestall such resentment against the gods and to ward off potential disillusionment with the divine order, that one of the sages of the Sumerian academy, or *É-dub-ba* [2]), composed the edifying essay presented in this study.

The main thesis of our poet is that in cases of suffering and adversity, no matter how seemingly unjustified, the victim has but one valid and effective recourse, and that is to continually glorify his god and keep wailing and lamenting before him until he turns a favourable ear to his prayers. The god concerned is the sufferer's "personal" god, that is, the deity who, in accordance with the accepted Sumerian credo, acted as the man's representative and intercessor in the assembly of the gods [3]). To prove his point our author does not resort to philosophical speculation and theological argumentation. Instead, with characteristic Sumerian practicality, he cites a case: Here is a man, unnamed to be sure, who had been wealthy, wise and righteous, or at least seemingly so, and blest with both friends and kin. One day sickness and suffering overwhelmed him. Did he defy the divine order and blaspheme? Not at all! He came humbly before his god

---

[1]) This dogma was in line with the accepted world-view of the Sumerian theologian, according to which the gods in control of the cosmos planned and instituted evil, falsehood and violence as part and parcel of the fabric of civilization; cf., for the present, *IEJ* 3, p. 219 and n. 3.

[2]) For a discussion of the Sumerian *é-dub-ba*, its faculty, student body and curriculum, cf. *Studies Presented to David Moore Robinson*, I, p. 238-245.

[3]) The notion of a personal god was evolved by the Sumerian theologians in response to the feeling that the leading deities of the pantheon were too distant and aloof from the individual man, and that the latter should therefore have an intermediary, a kind of "good angel" to intercede on his behalf when the gods assembled (probably every New Year's Day) to judge all men and decide their fates; cf. especially H. and H. A. FRANKFORT, *et al.*, *Intellectual Adventure of Ancient Man*, p. 203-204. Just how these personal gods were selected by the individual or head of a family is uncertain, but we actually have the names of the "personal" deities of a number of Sumerian rulers from the second half of the third millenium B. C.

with tears and lamentation, and poured out his heart in prayer and supplication. As a result his god was highly pleased and moved to compassion; he gave heed to his prayer, delivered him from his misfortunes, and turned his suffering to joy.

Structurally speaking, the poem may be tentatively divided into four sections [1]. First comes a brief introductory exhortation that man should praise and exalt his god and soothe him with lamentations (lines 1-9). The poet then introduces the unnamed individual who, upon being smitten with sickness and misfortune, addresses his god with tears and prayers (lines 10-20 plus). There follows the sufferer's petition which constitutes the major part of the poem (lines 26 minus -116). It begins with a description of the ill-treatment accorded him by his fellow men—friend and foe alike (lines 26-55); continues with a lament against his bitter fate, including a rhetorical request to his kin and to the professional singers to do likewise (lines 56-95); and concludes with a confession of guilt and a direct plea for relief and deliverance (lines 96-116). Finally comes the "happy ending," in which the poet informs us that the man's prayer did not go unheeded, and that his god accepted the entreaties and delivered him from his afflictions. All of this leads, of course, to a further glorification of his god.

The pieces used in the reconstruction of the text are:

A = CBS 13394 (*STVC* no. 1) (plate I);
B = CBS 8321 (*STVC* no. 2) + Ni 4137 (plates II and III);
C = Ni 4587 (plate III);
D = CBS 15205 (plate IV).

Line by line, the text is reconstructed as follows:

1-20	= A obv. i	82-104	= A rev. iv (NOTE: lines 82-102, which are very poorly preserved, were not copied by CHIERA).
26-47	= A obv. ii	95-116	= D rev. i (rev. ii contains another composition).
26-37	= B obv. i	113-118	= B rev. iv
49-54	= C obv. [2]	118-131	= C rev.
52-73	= A obv. iii	130	= A rev. v
62-79	= D obv.		
62-75	= B obv. ii		

[1]) Because of the numerous lacunae in the text and the obscurity of a number of crucial passages, the suggested section division is not quite certain.

[2]) C obv. has been placed in the composition at this point since it is assumed (a) that C rev. follows immediately upon D rev. (the two pieces may even be a "join"), and C obv. therefore immediately precedes D obv.; (b) that the *giš*(?)-*gim* of C obv. 5 corresponds to *giš-gim* in A iii 2 (= line 53).

TRANSLITERATION [1])

1. lú-lu$_7$ nam-maḫ-dingir-ra-na zi-đè-eš-šè ḫé-im-me
2. guruš-e inim-dingir-ra-na kug-ge-eš ḫé-im-i-i
3. kalam-si-sá-a ukù-dúr-ru-na-bi gu-gim ḫa-ba-si-il-e
4. é-ba[la]g-di(?)-[ka] usar-ku-li-ni(!)-ir(!) . . [ḫu]-mu-un-na-búr-e
5. šà-[ga-ni ḫé-i]b-ḫun-e
6. . . . . [ḫé-ni]-in-è . . . . ḫé-ni-ib-bé
7. . . . . ḫé(?)-ág-e
8. ka-i-si-iš-gál-la-ni šà-dingir-ra-na ḫé-im-ḫun-e
9. lú-lu$_7$ dingir-da-nu-me-a kú la-ba-ag-e
10. guruš-e á-ni ki-lul-la ḫul la-ba-e-gá-gá
11. . . . á-sìg du-lum-gig-ga . . im-ma-ni-i[n]-. .
12. . . . -ra nam-tar-? -SU(?)-KA^x ?-e . . mu-un-ni-ib-te
13. . . . -gig-ga . . -bi mu-sùḫ . . . -na mu-un-dul
14. . . . . šu-ḫul mu-ni-ib-dug$_4$ . . . . -šè im-ag
15. . . . . [di]ngir-ra-na
16. . . . . [ḫu]l(?)-gar-ra-na . . . . ì-še$_8$(?)-še$_8$(?)
17. . . . [š]u-kin si bí-in-sá
18. . . . . [du]-lum-ma-ni [mu-na]-ni-ib-bé
19. . . . . šà-súr ? -a-na
20. . . . . [mu-na]-ni-in-. .
21-25. . . . . (Approximately 5 lines destroyed)
26. guruš-me-en zu-me-en [á(?)]-zu-mu si nu-mu-da-sá-e
27. zi-dug$_4$-ga-mu lul-šè ì-tu
28. lú-lul-la-ke$_4$ ul$_{12}$ [2]) -lu mu-un-dul šu-kin mu-un-na-díb
29. á-nu-zu [3]) -mu ma-ra-pe-lá-en
30. du-lum-ma [4]) ki-gibil-gibil [5]) -la-bi [6]) sag-e-eš mu-e-rig$_7$
31. é-a ù-mu-un-tu-re-en ḪUR mu-BAD
32. guruš-me-en sila-šè um-è-en [7]) šà mu-un-sìg

---

[1]) Two dots stand for one missing sign; three dots for two missing signs; and four dots for three or more broken signs. In the case of A and B, the reader should consult the photographs on plate I whenever the transliteration seems to differ from the copies; note, too, that in lines 2-5 of A, several of the signs copied by CHIERA are no longer on the tablet.

[2]) ul$_{12}$ = GÀL.

[3]) So A; B: *-zu-a-*.

[4]) So A; B: *-e* for *-ma*.

[5]) So A; B: *-gibil$_4$-gibil$_4$-*.

[6]) So A; B omits *-bi*.

[7]) So A; B seems to have *um-ta*(?)*-è*(!?)*-en*.

33. šul-me-en sipad-zi-mu mu-da-íb [1]) igi-erím mu-un-du$_{8}$ [2])
34. na-gada-mu lú-erím-nu-me-en-na [3]) á-ḫul ma-kin-kin
35. du$_{10}$ -sa-mu inim-gi-na na [4]) -ma-ab-bé [5])
36. ku-li-mu inim-zi-dug$_{4}$-ga-mu-šè(?) [6]) lul [7]) ma-ši-gá-gá
37. lú-lul-la-ke$_{4}$ [8]) KA-téš mu-un-dug$_{4}$
38. dingir-mu nu-mu-na-ni-ib-gi$_{4}$-gi$_{4}$-in
39. KU-mu ba-an-ta-túm-un
40. ḫul-gál-e KA-téš mu-DU
41. mu-un-íb-en u$_{4}$-gim mu-un-dù šà-ḫul mu-un-dím
42. gal-an-zu-me-en šul-nu-zu-ra a-na-aš mu-un-na-lá-en
43. zu-me-en múrub-lú-nu-zu-ka a-na-aš mu-ni-šed-dè-en
44. ninda ì-gál-gál su-kú ninda-mu-um
45. u$_{4}$ ukù-šár-re-ḫa-la-ba-ba du-lum ḫa-la-ba-mu-um
46. šeš ... in mu-un-dúb [šà-ḫ]ul mu-un-dím
47. .... -ga-mu ....
48. ....
49. .... mu(?)-un(?)-z[i(?)-z]i(?)
50. .... -da-túm-mu
51. ....? igi-gál- ? -e imi mu-sar-sar-re
52. ḫar-ra-an DI sag-bi ? -kin-kin
53. kaskal-la ... -la-b[i(?)] giš-gim mu-un-tar-re
54. ugula-a a ga(?)-....
55. nu-bànda mu(?) .... mà(?)-....
56. dingir-mu .... igi-z[u(?)]-š[è(?)] ....
57. ga-mu-ra-ab-dug$_{4}$ .. nu(?) -mu(?)-...
    inim-mu šà-ne-ša$_{4}$
58. ga-ra-ni-ib-dug$_{4}$ a-rá-mà níg-g[ig(?)-ga(?)-bi(?)]
    gu-gim ga-mu-ra-si-il
59. níg-...-en sùḫ-a-bi ....
60. giš-ḫur(?)-mà gal-an-zu ḫu-mu-u[n]-...
    níg-ír nu-gul-lu-dam
61. ku-li-mu-úr mu-na(?)-an-lá-en
62. du$_{10}$-sa-mu-úr a-ga(?)-šè(?) mu-un-ši-gi$_{4}$ -in

---

1) So B; A omits *šul-me-en sipad-zi-mu mu-da-íb.*
2) So A; B seems to have *mu-dè-du*$_{8}$.
3) So A; B: *-nam* for *-na.*
4) So B; A omits *na-.*
5) So A; B probably has *-bé*(!) also.
6) So A; B omits *-šè.*
7) So A; B seems to have an inexplicable -KAM following *lul-.*
8) So B; A: *lú-lul-e.*

lower edge

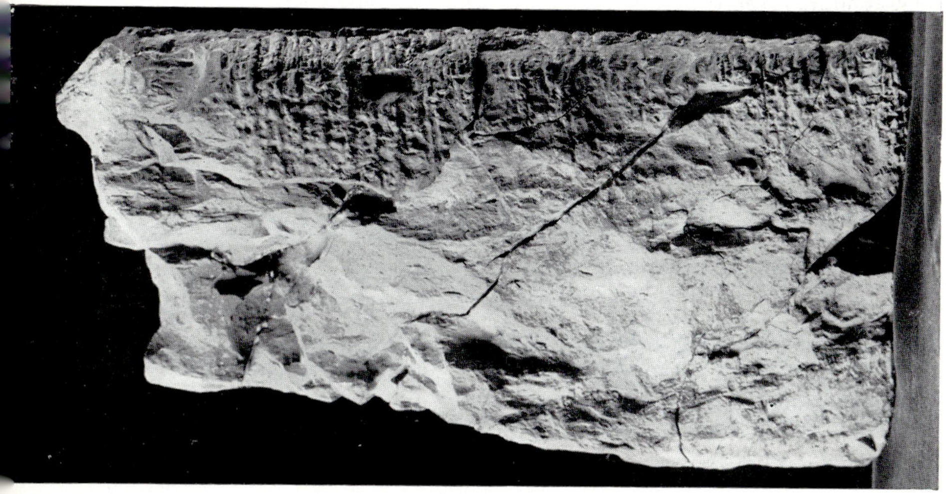

reverse
CBS 13394

observe

obverse

reverse

CBS 8321

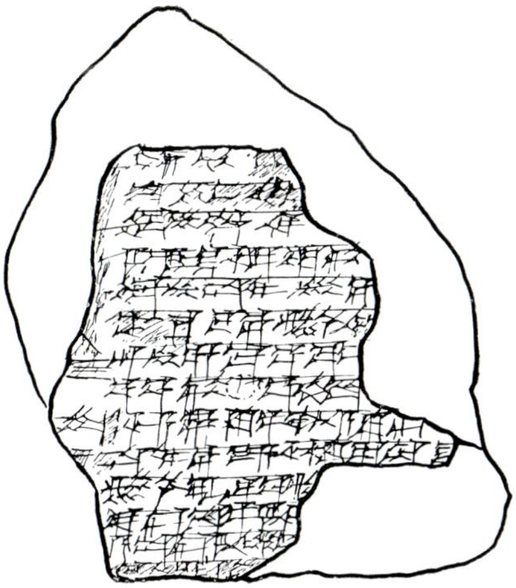

obverse

Ni 4137

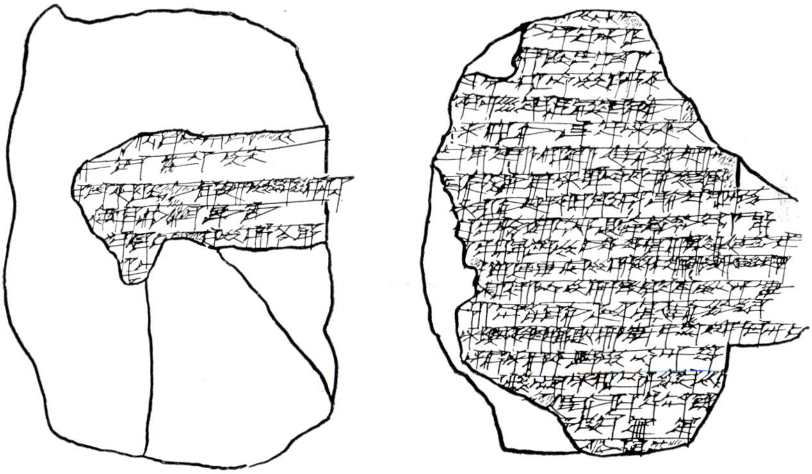

obverse reverse

Ni 4587

right edge

reverse
CBS 15205

obverse

63. á-še ama-ugu-mu ír-mu igi-zu-šè na-an-gul-e
64. nin$_9$-mu balag-di-ad-dùg na-....
65. níg-ag-šu-ḫul-dug$_4$-ga-mu ír-ra ḫa-ra-nı-ib-bé
66. dam-mu du-lum-mu ANŠE^{x}KÁR-LU- ? ḫa-ra-nı-ib-pàd-pàd-dè
67. nar-sìr-zu-e nam-tar-gig-ga-mu(?) gu-gim ḫa-ra-si-il-e
68. dingir-mu kalam-e [1]) u$_4$ ba-zalag mà-ar u$_4$ ma-ku$_{10}$-ku$_{10}$
69. u$_4$-zalag-ga u$_4$ -dùg á-gim ....
70. ír a-nir šà-sìg ḪUR-BAD-a šà-mà mu-un-gá-g[á] [2])
71. du-lum-e dumu-ír-pàd-da [3])-gim šu mu-un-dul-dul-e
72. nam-tar-ra šu-ba igi mi [4])-ni-... [5]) zi-mu mi-ni-tùm-tùm
73. su-mà á-sìg-níg-ḫul-gál-[e a mi-ni]-ib-tu$_5$
74. a-rá-mà níg [6])-gig-ga-b[i ...-mà(?) níg(?)-ḫul(?)]-dím-ma-bi
75. .... -šag$_5$-ga igi ....-lá(?)-lá(?)-e
76. .... MI-nu-gar-ra ....-ge
77. ....-bı-nu-me-en ....
78. .... TUR-bi-nu-me-e[n] ....
79. ....-[g]im mu-ra-....
80-81. .... (Approximately 2 lines destroyed)
82. .... DU ....-an..
83. ....-i(?)
84. ....-sìg-ge-e[n]
85. .... sag(?) mu-íl
86. ....-[t]ùm-tùm
87. ....
88. ... GAR ....-en [7])
89. .... mi-ib-DU
90-94. .... (Probably 5 lines destroyed)
95. .... [n]u(?)-še$_8$-š[e$_8$]
96. dingir-mu za-e [a]-a-ugu-mu-me-en igi-mu ?-....
97. áb-zi-gim(!?) arḫuš-a šà-ne-ša$_4$ á-nun ḫ[é]-....
98. en-na-me-[šè] èn-mu nu-tar-re-en ki-mu nu-kin-[k]in-en
99. gud-gim ? -ši-ib-zi nu-mu-ra-ab-zi-gi-i[n].
100. ús-zi nu-mu-ub-díb-bé-en

---

[1]) So A and C; B: *kalam-ma*.
[2]) So A; C: [*mu-u*]*n*-DU-DU.
[3]) So B; A and probably C have -*še*$_8$- for -*pàd-da*-.
[4]) So A; in C, the traces do not point to *mi*-.
[5]) So A; B seems to omit *igi mi-ni*- .... .
[6]) So B; C omits *níg*-.
[7]) Between lines 88 and 89 there seem to be traces of an inexplicable separating line.

101. mi-ni-ib-bé-ne šul-gal-an-zu-ne inim-zi-si(?)-sá(?)
102. u$_4$-na-me dumu-nam-tag-nu-tuku ama-a-ni nu-tu-ud [1]
103. DÙL la-ba-DI erín-nam-tag-nu-tuku ul-ta nu-gál-la-àm
104. dingir-mu ku$_6$-lam-ma níg-sag(?)-bi-šè mu-da-ab-sù-da-mu
105. níg-búr-ra .. -bi igi-zu-šè mà-e bí-ag-a-mu
106. guruš na-a[n]-šeg$_6$-gá kù-zu-a inim-ḫi-li-a ḫé-ni-ne
107. u$_4$-nu-zalag(?) á-mà ná-a-mà igi-zu-šè ḫa-ba-ab-dib-bé-en
108. nu-kug ? nu-zalag-zalag-mu-NE uru(?) DI-ba ḫa-ba-tag-ge-en
109. u$_4$-íb-ba ? -ši-ib-dù-a-zu inim-ḫi-li-a ḫé-ni-ne
110. u$_4$-TÚG(?) mu-. . .-GÍR-GÍR-ba-zu e-ne ḫúl-la ḫu-mu-dug$_4$
111. dingir-mu ... nam-tag-mu igi-mu ù-mi-zu
112. ká-. . .-ka ku$_6$-lam-ma-bi dil-bad-bi ga-àm-dug$_4$
113. guruš-me-en KA-TAR-nam-tag-mu igi-zu-šè ga-si-il
114. ukkin-e sa(?)-KU [2] im-dugud [3]-gim ḫu-mu-ub-šèg-šèg(?)-e(?)
115. dag-zu ama-šà-ne-ša$_4$-mu .... ḫé-ni-. . .
116. šul-me-en ARḪUŠ šà-ne-ša$_4$ .... kù-zu ḫé-im-. . .
117. [guruš ....] zi IM(?) ....-gi$_4$-gi$_4$
118. [sizkur-sizkur-a-ra-zu-ni]
[dingir-ra]-ni giš ba-an-tuku[-àm]
119. [ír-a]-nir-gál-i-si-iš-lá-[a-ni]
šà-dingir-ra-na mu-un-ši-[ḫun]
120. inim-zi-inim-kug-ga-dug$_4$-ga-ni-a
dingir-ra-ni šu ba-an-ti
121. guruš(!?)-e inim a-ra-zu-a mi-ni-in-zu-àm
122. ? -kug ? su-dingir-ra-na ka-zal-le-éš ...
dingir-ra-ni inim-ḫul-gál-ta šu-ni ba-ra-an-BU
123. .. šà-sìg-ge-dam BI-nu-me-en-na(?) gú in-da-lá-e
124. [á]-sìg-nigín-e á mu-ni-tál-la líl-la im-mi-in-sìg
125. ... LU- ? -ag-gim mu-un-sì-ga sug-ge$_4$ im-mi-in-kú
126. [nam]-tar-ra DI-a-na mu-un-gál-la KA^x ? mu-na-an-ag
127. [gur]uš(?)-a(!?) du-lum-ma-ni ḫúl-la mi-ni-in-tu
128. .. ^{d}udug-sig$_5$(?) KA-e en-nu-un-ag maškim mu-un-da-an-tab
129. .. ^{d}lama-^{d}lama igi-šag$_5$ mu-na-an-sì
130. [guruš-e] nam-maḫ-dingir-ra-na zi-dè-eš-š[è im-me]
131. .... mi-ni-ib-è .... bí-zu(!?)-zu [4]

---

[1]) So D; A: *nu-un-tu-ud.*

[2]) So D; B: SIG$_7$.ALAM for *sa*(?)-KU.

[3]) So D; B: *im-dugud*^{mušen}

[4]) This is probably the last line of the poem; the line in C which follows this line probably begins a new composition.

TRANSLATION [1]

1. Let a human being utter constantly the exaltedness of his god,
2. Let a man praise artlessly the words of his god,
3. Let the inhabitant of the straightforward land moan(?),
4. In the house [of] s[on]g let him interpret(?) .. to his (female) companion (and) his friend,
5. Soothe [his(?) he]art,
6. Bring forth ...., utter ....,
7. Measure out(?) ....,
8. Let his lament soothe the heart of his god,
9. (For) a human being without a god would not obtain food.

10. The(?) man—he uses not his strength for evil in (?) the place of deceit,
11. (Yet(?)) ..., sickness, bitter suffering ..d him,
12. ..., fate, .. brought .. close to him,
13. Bitter ... confused(?) its(?) .., covered his ..,
14. .... placed an evil hand on him, he was treated as .... .

15. .... of his god,
16. .... in his ...., ... he weeps(?),
17. .... he directed a ... ,
18. Speaks [tearfully] to him of his suffering ... ,
19. .... in(?) his .. wrath,
20. ..s .... .

21-25. (Approximately 5 lines destroyed)
26. "I am a man, a discerning one, (yet) who respects(?) me prospers(?) not,
27. My righteous word has been turned into a lie,
28. The man of deceit has covered me (with) the Southwind, I (am forced to) serve him,
29. Who respects(?) me not has shamed me before you.

---

[1] For the benefit of scholars who are not cuneiform specialists, it may be useful to stress the fact that the Sumerian literary texts still pose serious difficulties to the translator, particularly in matters lexical, and that translations of them therefore should not be quoted and cited with the readiness and assurance that may be justifiable, for example, in the case of Hebrew and Greek texts. The translation offered in this study, the best the writer could muster, is far from definitive, and the student of comparative religion should use it with reasonable care and caution.

30. You have doled out to me suffering ever anew,
31. I entered the house, heavy is the spirit,
32. I, the man, went out to the street, oppressed is the heart,
33. With me, the valiant (?), my righteous shepherd has become angry, has looked upon me inimically,
34. My herdsman has sought out evil forces against me who am not (his) enemy,
35. My companion says not a true word to me,
36. My friend gives the lie to my righteous word.

37. The man of deceit has conspired (?) against me,
38. (And) you, my god, do not thwart him,
39. You carry off my . .,
40. The wicked has conspired (?) against me,
41. Angered you, stormed about, planned evil.

42. I, the wise, why am I bound to the ignorant youths?
43. I, the discerning, why am I counted among the ignorant?
44. Food is all about, (yet) my food is hunger,
45. On the day shares were allotted to all, my allotted share was suffering.

46. The brother (?) . . . quarrelled, planned [evi]l,
47. [He . . s] my . . . .,
48. . . . .,
49. Raises up . . . .,
50. Carries off . . . .,
51. Writes on clay . . . . the wise . . .,
52. Seeks out the . . . of (?) the journey,
53. Cuts down like a tree the . . of the road,
54. . . . [. . s] the supervisor,
55. . . . [. . s] the steward.

56. My god, [I would stand] befo[re yo]u,
57. Would speak to you, ..., my word is a groan,
58. I would tell you about it, would bemoan the bitterness of my path,
59. [Would bewail] the confusion of . . . . .

60. Let the wise . . in (?) my plans, lament will not cease,
61. I . . . to my friend,
62. I . . . to my companion.

63. Lo, let not my mother who bore me cease my lament before you,
64. Let not my sister [utter] the happy song and chant,
65. Let her utter tearfully my misfortunes before you,
66. Let my wife voice mournfully (?) my suffering,
67. Let the expert singer bemoan my bitter fate.

68. My god, the day shines bright over the land, for me the day is black,
69. The bright day, the good day has .. like the ..,
70. Tears, lament, anguish, and depression are lodged within me,
71. Suffering overwhelms me like one who does (nothing but) weep,
72. (The demon of) fate in its hand ..s me, carries off my breath of life,
73. The malignant sickness-demon bath[es] in my body,
74. The bitterness of my path, the e[vil] of [my(?) ..],
75. ..s the kindly (?) ....,
76. ..s the unsettled (?) .....

77. I who am not the .. of the .. ..,
78. I who am not the .. of the .. ..,
79. [L]ike .... I .. before you,
80-94. (Largely destroyed)
95. .... I(?) weep not (?).

96. My god, you who are my father who begot me, [lift up(?)] my face,
97. Like (?) an innocent cow, in pity (?) .... the groan,
98. How long will you neglect me, leave me unprotected?
99. Like an ox, ...,
100. (How long) will you leave me unguided?

101. They say—the valiant (?) sages—a word righteous (and) straight-forward:
102. 'Never has a sinless child been born to its mother,
103. .... a sinless workman (?) has not existed from of old.'

104. My god, the .. of destruction which I have ..d against you,
105. The .. of .. which I have prepared before you,
106. Let them not .. the man, the wise (?); utter, (my god), words (?) of (?) grace (?) upon him (?),
107. (When(?)) the day is not (yet) bright(?), in my .., in my .., make me walk before you,

108. My impure (and(?)) my lack-lustre .. — touch(?) their ...,
109. Utter(?) words(?) of(?) grace(?) upon him(?) whom you ..d on(?) the day of(?) wrath,
110. Whom you ..d on(?) the day ... — pronounce joy upon(?) him.

111. My god, now that you have shown(?) me my sins ...,
112. In the gate of ..., I would speak ....,
113. I, the man, would confess(?) my sins before you.

114. May you rain(?) upon the assembly ... like a cloud,
115. May you .. in(?) your chamber(?) my groaning mother(?) ....,
116. Me, the valiant(?), may you .. in(?) wis[dom(?) my] groaning ..."

117. [To(?) the man] .... [he an]swers,
118. [His prayers and petitions] his god heard,
119. [The weeping, la]mentation and wailing which filled [him], [soothed] the heart of his god,
120. The righteous words, the artless words uttered by him, his god accepted,
121. The words which the man prayerfully confessed,
122. Pleased(?) the ...., the flesh(?) of his god, (and) his god withdrew his hand from the evil word,
123. .. which oppresses the heart, ... he embraces,
124. The encompassing sickness-demon, which had spread wide its wings, he swept away(?),
125. The ..., which had smitten him like a ..., he dissipated,
126. The (demon of) fate, who had been placed (there) in accordance(?) with his sentence(?), he turned aside(?),
127. He turned the [m]an's(?) suffering into joy,
128. Set by him the .. good(?) .. spirit (as a) watch (and) guardian,
129. Gave him .. the tutelary genii of friendly mien.
130. [The man uttered] constantly the exaltedness of his god,
131. Brought forth ...., made known .....

COMMENTARY

Lines 1-9. The word *guruš* (line 2), rendered by "man" throughout this study, approximates in semantic range the Hebrew גֶּבֶר. For the rendering "moan" of *gu-gim—si-il* (line 3), cf. lines 58 and 67. The restoration of the first part of line 4 is, of course, doubtful; for *usar*, cf. *Indogermanische Forschungen* 60, p. 116. The restoration of the text of line 5 is very doubtful. In line 7 the verb may be a compound such as *á—ág* "to commission" or *ki—ág* "to love." In line 8 the literal meaning of the first complex seems to be "his in the mouth placed wail."

Lines 10-25. The translation assumes that lines 9 and 10 are not parallel in meaning in spite of surface indications to the contrary; it further assumes that *ḫul—gá-gá* is a causative, the object of which is *á-ni* (in spite of the unexpected *-ba-e-*); and that the *lul* of *ki-lul-la* (seemingly for *ki-lul-la-ka*) is to be rendered by its primary meaning "deceit." Other interpretations are, of course, possible. Perhaps even the verb is positive rather than negative, i.e., the word division should perhaps be *ḫul-la ba-e-gá-gá*. For line 17, cf. "Enmerkar and the Lord of Aratta", line 441. For the suggested restoration of "tearfully" (line 18), cf. lines 65-66.

Lines 26-55. In line 26, *á-zu*, if the restoration is correct (cf. line 29), seems to mean literally "the strength knower." For *šu-kin—díb* (line 28), cf. *JAOS* 69, p. 214. In line 29 *-pe-lá-* seems to be for the more usual *pe-el-lá*. A more literal translation of *ù-mu-un-tu-re-en* (line 31) and *um-è-en* (line 32) would be "I, having entered" and "I, having gone out." In line 33 the word "valiant" attempts to render *šul*; note, however, the rendering "youth", or perhaps better "fellow", for it in line 42. In lines 33 and 34, if the words "shepherd" and "herdsman" refer to the king, the poet seems to be thinking of the sufferer as a man who had been close to the royal court. The rendering of lines 37 to 41 is quite doubtful; the grammatical analysis assumed for the several verbal forms is obvious from the translation, but may turn out to be quite erroneous (note moreover that the "conspired" of lines 37 and 40 is no more than a guess based on the context). In line 46 the traces do not point to *-mu* following *šeš*, as might perhaps have been expected. For the approximate meaning of *in—dúb*, cf. for the present the comment to proverb 29 in "Forty-eight Proverbs and Their Translation" in *Compte Rendu de la Troisième Rencontre Assyriologique Internationale Organisée ... par le Groupe François Thureau-Dangin* (p. 80).

Lines 56-95. In line 56, a verbal form such as *ga-mu-ši-gub* is probably to be restored. In lines 61 and 62 it is difficult to get at the meaning intended for the verbal forms since the context is not clear. In line 64 a verbal form such as *na-[an-ab-bé]* is probably to be restored.

In line 66 the unintelligible third complex may parallel the *ír-ra* of the preceding line. In line 69, we might expect a phrase such as "has been carried off" to have ended the line (cf. lines 174-175 of the "Ur Lament"), but then the *á-gim* is hard to explain in the context. In line 72, *nam-tar-ra* is rendered as if it read *nam-tar-re*.

Lines 96-116. In line 96, a verbal form such as *ḫé-ib-íl-en* might perhaps be expected. In line 97, the reading *arḫuš-* is by no means certain; cf. line 116. In line 99, it is difficult to make a reasonable guess at the meaning of the complexes following *gud-gim*. For *ús-zi—díb* (line 100), cf. *ZA* 47, p. 190. In line 101 note the interesting and unusual word-order. The first part of line 103 is difficult to analyse; the assumed word division is a guess only. Lines 104-110 are so difficult that it might have been wiser to leave them untranslated altogether. The *ḫé-ni-ne* of lines 106 and 109 is probably for *ḫé-ni-in-e*(*-en*). In line 107, the usual meanings of *á* and *ná* do not seem to go well with the verb "walk." In line 110, the verb is rendered as if it read *ḫu-mu-dug$_4$-ge-en*. In line 112, it is difficult to fit the usual meanings of the second and third complexes into the context. In line 113, the rendering "confess" for KA-TAR—*si-il* is no more than a guess (note the rather unexpected position of KA-TAR); for a discussion of KA-TAR—*si-il*, cf. *AfO* IX 278 ff. In line 114 note the interesting variant SIG$_7$.ALAM for *sa*(?)-KU. The meaning of this and the following two lines is quite obscure and the attempted renderings might have been better omitted altogether.

Lines 117-to end. The translation assumes that the sufferer's prayer ended with line 116 and that line 117, which is difficult to restore, begins the concluding passage which describes the man's deliverance from his suffering. In line 119, the *-ši-* of the verb seems to be instead of an expected *-na-*. In line 123, the meaning of BI-*nu-me-en-na*(?) is obscure, and its grammatical relationship to the rest of the sentence uncertain. In line 124, "swept away" for *líl-la im-mi-in-sìg* is no more than a guess, and so too is "turned aside" for KA^x? *mu-na-an-ag* in line 126; for *sug-ge$_4$—kú* (line 125) on the other hand, cf., for example, line 279 of the "Ur Lament." In line 126, the *-ra* of the first complex is unnecessary if the translation is correct. In lines 128 and 129, the initial words are difficult to restore in spite of the relatively clear context. Line 131 might be expected to parallel and extend the statement made in line 130.

DIE KRISE DES RELIGIÖSEN GLAUBENS BEI KOHELET

VON

AARRE LAUHA
Helsinki

Den Gedankeninhalt des Buches Kohelet hat man oft durch Bedingtheiten des Milieus erklären wollen: im Buch ist entweder der griechische oder der orientalische Einfluss erkennbar. Auf diesem Wege der Beurteilung gelangt man jedoch kaum zu einer endgültigen Entscheidung, denn die eigentliche Problematik und Lebenshaltung Kohelets entzieht sich einer so äusserlichen und geradlinigen Auslegung. Es handelt sich darin vor allem um eine strukturelle Eigenschaft der Persönlichkeit und um eine bestimmte Verhaltungsweise der Religion gegenüber.

Zum Verständnis des Predigers ist es gut, seine Problematik und seine Lösungen mit denen des Buches Hiob zu vergleichen. Es zeigt sich nämlich deutlich, dass der Ausgangspunkt beider Verfasser ungefähr der gleiche ist. Um so mehr fällt es auf, dass die Entwicklung der Gedanken und die Schlussfolgerungen ganz verschieden sind und das Endergebnis Kohelets in gewisser Weise im Gegensatz zu dem des Hiob steht.

Die Veranlassung zu den beiden Büchern ist die Krise, in die das traditionelle, schematische Glaubensdenken beide Schriftsteller geführt hat. Die altisraelitische Lebensauffassung setzt eine religiös-sittliche Harmonie zwischen dem inneren und äusseren Geschehen voraus [1]). Wenn die Seele des Menschen heil und gerecht ist, so herrscht auch in seinem ganzen äusseren Leben *b^erākā* und *šālōm*. Dem entsprechend zeugen Unglück und Misserfolg für die Schuldhaftigkeit des davon Betroffenen. Diese adäquate Wechselbeziehung zwischen dem religiös-sittlichen und dem physisch-materiellen Geschehen gründet sich darauf, dass Jahwe gerecht ist und die Gerechtigkeit aufrechterhält. Somit ist die Verwirklichung der Gerechtigkeit

---

[1]) JOHS. PEDERSEN, *Israel I-II*², København 1934, p. 262 ff.; JOH. LINDBLOM, *Boken om Job och hans lidande*, Lund 1940, p. 101 ff.

ein göttlicher Grundsatz alles Daseins. Wenn nun andrerseits eine gesunde Seele ihrer Beschaffenheit nach handeln kann und der Mensch damit fähig ist, seinen sittlichen Willen zu verwirklichen, ist alles Geschehen rational zu verstehen und die ganze Lebenseinstellung ist optimistisch. Auf Grund dieser klaren Weltbetrachtung war es den Weisheitslehrern leicht, geradlinige Lebensgesetze vorzulegen und diesen angepasste praktische Lebensanleitung zu erteilen [1]).

Die Realität des Lebens aber hat sowohl dem Verfasser des Buches Hiob als auch dem Prediger diese geradlinige Theorie zerbrochen. Das Axiom, dass Untadelhaftigkeit den Segen zum Lohne erhält, hat sich nicht als stichhaltig erwiesen. Die Beobachtung der Tatsachen und die erfahrenen Enttäuschungen haben beiden Verfassern die Grundlagen des gesamten Seins fraglich werden lassen.

Der Verfasser des Buches Hiob nimmt die Frage nach Gottes Gerechtigkeit so persönlich und schwer, dass seine ganze Existenz davon abhängt. Hiob fühlt sich unschuldig. Wenn seine Leiden durch den Gedanken der Vergeltung erklärt werden, wird der Glaube an Gottes Gerechtigkeit erschüttert. Gott, der die Quelle aller Gerechtigkeit sein sollte, zerbricht selbst die ethische Weltordnung. Er, auf dem der Bund beruht, hält ihn nicht, obgleich der andere Partner ihn gehalten hat [2]). Elihu sah die Sache richtig, als seiner Meinung nach Hiob „seine Seele für gerechter hielt denn Gott" (xxxii 2). Als dem Hiob Gott in seinem Tun gewalttätig, ungerecht und willkürlich erschien, war auch das ganze Leben sinnlos und willkürlich, dem Sein war jeder Grund entzogen. Diese Sinnlosigkeit alles Bestehenden, die Hiob in seinem Schicksal — ja an seinem eigenen Leibe — erfährt, erfüllt ihn mit Bitterkeit und führt ihn an die äussersten Grenzen der Hoffnungslosigkeit und des Unglaubens. Mit der ganzen Leidenschaft seiner Seele fordert er sein Recht. Das Problem des Buches Hiob ist nicht nur das Problem des Gottesbildes, sondern das des persönlichsten Gottesglaubens.

Dieselbe Krise finden wir im Buch Kohelet. Wenn der Prediger, nach dem er des Lebens Mühen und Freuden erfahren und das Weltgeschehen geprüft hat, zu seinem pessimistischen Schlussergebnis kommt und alles als Eitelkeit bezeichnet, liegt diesem nicht nur ein allgemeines Gefühl der Ermüdung zu Grunde, dass alles — Arbeit

---

[1]) Über die rationale und optimistische Art der alttestamentlichen Weisheit s. WALTHER ZIMMERLI, "Zur Struktur der alttestamentlichen Weisheit", *ZAW* (1933), p. 177 ff.

[2]) PEDERSEN, *a. a. O.*, p. 269 und 283 ff.

und Genuss, Reichtum und Armut, Weisheit und Torheit, Leben und Tod — seinen ewigen Kreislauf geht und dass man darin keinen vernünftigen Sinn finden kann, sondern den Grundgedanken bildet die erschütternde Feststellung, dass die Gerechtigkeit im Leben nicht Stand hält und somit allem Geschehen der *sittliche* Inhalt fehlt.

Der Prediger sieht die Ungerechtigkeit in der Gesellschaft. „Und weiter sah ich unter der Sonne: an der Stätte des Rechtes, da war der Frevel, und an der Stätte der Gerechtigkeit, da war die Bosheit" (iii 16). Dem Fehlen der sozialen Gerechtigkeit hatten auch die Propheten ihre Aufmerksamkeit zugewandt, aber für sie bedeutete dieser Mangel eine Aufforderung zum Protest, einen Aufruf, Gottes Gerechtigkeit hervorzuheben und für diese im menschlichen Gemeinschaftsleben zu kämpfen. Für den Prediger dagegen bedeutet die Feststellung der Ungerechtigkeit nur eine Konstatierung der Tatsache [1]). „Ich wandte meinen Blick auf all die Unterdrückungen, die unter der Sonne geschehen. Siehe da die Tränen der Unterdrückten, dieweil sie keinen Tröster haben, und die gegenüber ihren Drängern kraftlos sind, dieweil sie keinen Rächer haben. Da pries ich die Toten, die längst dahin sind, vor den Lebenden, die noch weiter leben müssen, und höher als die beiden den, der gar nicht ins Dasein tritt, der nicht zu sehen braucht das üble Geschehen, das unter der Sonne geschieht" (iv 1 f.). Die grausame Wirklichkeit hat dem Prediger den Glauben an die Kraft und den Sieg der ethischen Lebensgesetze zerbrochen. Er vermag nicht mehr, das Vorhandensein einer gerechten Vergeltung anzuerkennen. „Da sind Gerechte, die trifft ein Geschick, das dem Tun der Frevler entspricht. Da sind Frevler, die trifft ein Geschick, das dem Tun der Gerechten entspricht" (viii 14, vgl. viii 10). Die ganze ererbte sittliche Grundlage ist zerstört, es gibt nur ein hoffnungsloses Chaos. „Eins aber ist, das allen zukommt, nämlich *ein* Geschick: dem Gerechten und dem Gottlosen, dem Reinen und dem Unreinen, dem Opfernden und dem, der nicht opfert. Wie der Gute, so der Sünder, wie der Schwörende, so der, der nicht schwört" (ix 2). Diese Beobachtungen über die indifferente Gleichgültigkeit des Weltgeschehens gegen die sittliche Vergeltung haben die Zweifel des Predigers verursacht und ihn in einen verhängnisvollen Widerspruch zu der traditionellen Anschauungsweise gebracht [2]).

---

[1]) KURT GALLING, "Prediger Salomo", *Handb. z. AT*, Tübingen 1940, p. 63.

[2]) JOHS. PEDERSEN, "Scepticisme israélite", *Revue d'Histoire et de Philosophie religieuses* (1930), p. 347 ff.

Das Chaos der sittlichen Grundlagen führt ihn innerlich zu einem weltanschaulichen Bankrott, so dass auch sein religiöser Glaube in eine gefährliche Krise gerät. Gott verliert seine sittliche Wesensart und damit seine Stellung als Erhalter des Bestehenden, als Quelle der Gerechtigkeit und Lebenskraft. Kohelet kommt keineswegs dazu, Gottes Existenz zu leugnen, aber die zuversichtliche Lebensgrundlage, die Gott so kennzeichnend für die alttestamentliche Frömmigkeit bedeutet, findet er in ihm nicht. Es lässt sich nicht beweisen, dass Gott den Gerechten liebt und den Gottlosen hasst [1]). Einer ist ihm wohlgefällig, ein anderer nicht — irgendeine sittliche Qualifikation übt hierbei keinen Einfluss aus (ii 26). „Der Mensch erfasst nicht das Werk, das Gott tut, weder Anfang noch Ende" (iii 11, vgl. viii 17 und xi 5). Gott ist ein ferner, unbegreiflicher Despot, ein willkürliches Wesen. „Gott ist im Himmel, du aber auf Erden" (v 1). Die Religion wird zum Fatalismus, der Glaube zur Unsicherheit (vgl. auch iii 14). Die Grundlage der traditionellen, geradlinigen religiös-sittlichen Lebensdeutung ist aufgelöst. Die Problematik des Predigers ist fürwahr die gleiche wie bei Hiob: die Problematik des Gottesbildes und des Gottesglaubens. Aber die Stellung zum Problem, seine Behandlung und das Ergebnis sind verschieden. Der Prediger hat sein Problem zu einem „philosophisch"-weltanschaulichen an Stelle eines religiösen gemacht [2]). Es brennt ihm nicht die existenzielle Schmerzhaftigkeit der Frage auf der Seele, die Hiobs Kampf Inständigkeit und tragische Grösse gibt. So gelangt jeder der beiden Schriftsteller zu einer ganz verschiedenen Lebenshaltung.

Als Hiob durch die rationale Theodizee in eine Sackgasse getrieben wird, gibt er sich damit nicht zufrieden. Die drei Freunde vertreten das starre Vergeltungsdogma und der vierte versucht das Problem zu lösen, indem er Hiobs Leiden als Gottes erzieherische Tat auslegt. In einem sind jedoch die Freunde derselben Ansicht, dass nämlich Hiobs Schicksal und Gottes Gerechtigkeit miteinander in Übereinstimmung gebracht werden können. Sie finden eine verstandesmässig anzuerkennende Erklärung für Hiobs Schicksal [3]).

---

[1]) H. L. Ginsberg, *Studies in Koheleth*, New York 1950, p. 4.

[2]) H.-J. Blieffert, *Weltanschauung und Gottesglaube im Buch Kohelet*, Rostock 1938, p. 14 f.

[3]) "Ein in sich widerspruchloser Gott, ein rein rationaler Gott — das war, was die Freunde haben wollten." Joh. Lindblom, "Die Vergeltung Gottes im Buche Hiob", *In piam memoriam Alexander von Bulmerincq*, Riga 1938, p. 94.

Aber diese Lösung nimmt das Buch Hiob nicht an. „Ihr habt nicht recht von mir geredet", sagt Gott (xlii 7). Kein rationales Schema reicht aus, den verborgenen Gott zu erklären.

Und doch bleibt das Buch Hiob nicht in Verzweiflung und Bitterkeit stecken. Als keine theoretischen Erklärungen den Verfasser aus der Sackgasse hinausführen, erkämpft er einen anderen Ausweg, um eine Antwort auf das schmerzliche Fragen seiner Seele zu finden. Dieser andere Weg ist zentral religiös: er *erlebt* den lebendigen Gott, und diese persönliche Begegnung mit Gott ist die Lösung des Problems [1]). „Vom Hörensagen hatte ich von dir vernommen, nun aber hat mein Auge dich geschaut. Darum bekenne ich mich schuldig und ich bereue in Staub und Asche" (xlii 5 f.). Solange er Gott nicht begegnet war, waren Gott und sein Tun ein theoretisches Problem. Nun aber ist alles anders. Hiob hat keine rationale Antwort erhalten; aber allein die Tatsache, dass Gott eine persönliche Verbindung mit ihm einging und zu ihm sprach, war eine grössere Wirklichkeit als die Verzweiflung des Menschen und seine unbeantworteten Fragen. In seinen entscheidenden Worten berührt Gott nicht die Leiden Hiobs, sondern er spricht von seiner Allmacht, die in den Wundern der Schöpfung und in ihrem Beherrschen zu sehen ist. Aber durch diese Rede Gottes geht Hiob ein neues Licht auf. Des allmächtigen Gottes Gedanken sollen seine eigenen Geheimnisse bleiben. Der Seele genügt die Anrede des lebendigen Gottes, seine Gegenwart, die irrationale Gewissheit, dass er nicht verlässt. Diese Lösung ist der reinste Ausdruck des *religiösen* Verhaltens, desselben, das den Psalmisten sprechen lässt: „Wenn ich nur dich habe, so frage ich nichts nach Himmel und Erde. Wenn mir gleich Leib und Seele verschmachtet, ist Gott doch allzeit mein Fels und mein Teil" (Ps. lxxiii 25 f.). Die Seele gibt sich zufrieden, obgleich die Fragen theoretisch ungelöst bleiben. Und was am wichtigsten ist: es handelt sich nicht um eine müde Resignation, sondern um den sieghaften Ausgang eines gigantischen Kampfes. Auch über Hiobs Kampf kann man als Motto die Worte setzen: „Ich lasse dich nicht, du segnest mich denn." Der Gottesglaube ist auf neue Weise erstarkt, real und zu einer das ganze Leben tragenden positiven Kraft geworden. Gott und seine Gerechtigkeit ist nicht mehr eine Lehre und ein Schema, sondern erlebte Wirklichkeit, gleichzeitig furchterregend

---

[1]) Walther Eichrodt, "Vorsehungsglaube und Theodizee im AT", *Festschrift Otto Procksch*, Leipzig 1934, p. 67.

und beglückend. In der Entscheidung des Buches Hiob feiert der alttestamentliche Gottesglaube seinen Triumph.

Gerade hierin liegt bei Kohelet der Unterschied. Als der Konflikt zwischen dem traditionellen Glauben und den Zweifeln den Verfasser in eine weltanschauliche Krise führt, kämpft er nicht zäh für seinen Glauben, sondern gibt nach. Er begnügt sich damit, in seiner Sackgasse zu bleiben und als aussenstehender Beobachter seine Betrachtungen anzustellen. Damit gelangt er auch nicht zu einem sieghaften Durchbruch. Das Ergebnis ist ein fruchtloser Skeptizismus. An Stelle der unbedingten religiösen Klarheitsforderung im Buche Hiob steht hier ein müder intellektueller Pessimismus. Obgleich somit die Problemstellung in beiden Büchern von derselben Voraussetzung ausgeht, ist bei Kohelet nicht dieselbe Inständigkeit des inneren Kampfes da, die Gott gleichsam zu antworten herausfordert. Wenn der Prediger die Sinnlosigkeit des Weltlaufes und seine sittliche Gleichgültigkeit feststellt, erhebt er keinen leidenschaftlichen Widerspruch sondern findet, dass der Mensch nichts anderes tun kann, als sich dem unentrinnbaren Geschick zu fügen. „Nicht kann er rechten mit dem, der stärker als er ist" (vi 10).

Da der Kampf um religiöse Klarheit unausgefochten bleibt, wird die Lebenshaltung Kohelets auch sonst in gewisser Weise gleichgültig. Wenn er *alles* Tun als eitel bezeichnet (i 14), erweist der Textzusammenhang, dass sein Wort ausdrücklich auch den Kampf für sittliche Ideale einschliesst. Es ist ja doch so: „Gekrümmtes lässt sich nicht strecken, Fehlendes nicht hinzutun" (i 15, vgl. vii 13). Nicht nur persönlich ist alles eitel, sondern überhaupt haben alle Lebenswerte eine Inflation erlitten. Es lohnt sich nicht, sich zu ereifern oder anzustrengen, denn das Leben wird doch nicht besser und erhält weder Sinn noch Wert. Wenn dem Leben so der tiefere Inhalt fehlt und wenn man auf das geistige Ringen um Klarheit verzichtet, muss man sich damit zufriedengeben, das zu geniessen, was das alltägliche Leben einem bieten kann, die kärgliche physische Glückserfahrung. „Siehe, was ich gesehen habe als das Beste, was schön ist: dass einer isst und trinkt und sich's gut sein lässt in all seiner Mühe, mit der er sich müht unter der Sonne" (v 17, vgl. iii 13). Freilich ist das trügerisch und klein, aber im einförmigen Ablauf der Eitelkeiten doch etwas, das Farbe und Freude hat (ix 7 ff.). Verglichen mit dem riesenhaften Geistesringen des Buches Hiob wirkt dieser kleinliche Hedonismus beinahe als Negation der wahren

Werte. An Stelle der unbedingten inneren Wahrheitsforderung begegnet uns hier ein Achselzucken.

Aber Kohelet führt seinen Gedankengang nicht folgerichtig zu Ende. Er hat nicht die Unerbittlichkeit, alle Brücken hinter sich abzubrechen, in offenen Aufruhr überzugehen und den vollständigen moralischen Nihilismus zu verkünden. Obgleich der traditionelle Glaube in seiner Seele Bankrott erlitten hat und der für das Alte Testament typische sittliche Eifer fehlt, bricht er äusserlich nicht die Beziehung zum geistigen und geistlichen Erbe seines Volkes ab. Innerlich zerrissen ergibt er sich einem müden Kompromiss mit den alten Formen. Besonders betrifft das seine Beziehung zur Moral. Obwohl er sich nicht mehr die traditionelle religiöse Lehre aneignen kann, versteht er doch, dass das menschliche Zusammenleben ohne moralische Sitten nicht aufrecht zu erhalten ist. Deshalb hält er es für notwendig, im gewohnten Stil der Weisheitsliteratur eine konventionelle Anweisung der praktischen Lebenskunst zu erteilen, da das Leben nun ein für allemal so zu nehmen ist, wie es eben ist (z.B. vii 2 ff.). Diese Lebensweisheit und Lehre ist sehr immanent und utilitaristisch, wenn man sich auch darin formal auf Gott beziehen kann. Der ethische Kampf ist nicht ein zitterndes *coram Deo*. Man kann vor Gottes Forderungen kalkulieren und um sie feilschen, je nach dem, wie es klug und vorteilhaft ist (v 4 f.). Wenn die sittliche Forderung nicht mehr absolut ist, ist die Schuldhaftigkeit des Menschen vor Gott kein Grund zur Verzweiflung [1]). Mit Recht hat man gesagt, dass die Wirklichkeit der Sünde für Kohelet ihre eigentliche Schwere und Qual nicht mehr hat und dass die Begriffe *ṣaddīq* und *rāšāʿ* ihres existenziellen Anspruchs beraubt sind [2]).

Wenn man die Haltung Kohelets mit der Hiobs vergleicht, genügt es nicht, auf Verschiedenheit der äusseren Verhältnisse hinzuweisen. Natürlich kann der historische Hintergrund ein ganz anderer gewesen sein, und vermutlich ist in Hiobs geistiger Umgebung der traditionelle Glaube stärker gewesen als beim Prediger, der offensichtlich unter dem Einfluss der hellenistischen, alte Anschauungen auflösenden Strömungen gelebt und daher gewagt hat, seine Zweifel auszusprechen [3]). Aber zuletzt geht der Unterschied darauf zurück, dass es sich um zwei verschiedene Menschentypen handelt.

Für Hiob ist die Frage nach Gott das einzige Zentrum von allem,

---

[1]) Blieffert, *a. a. O.*, p. 41 f.

[2]) Kurt Galling, "Kohelet-Studien", *ZAW* (1932), p. 291.

[3]) Pedersen, "Scepticisme israélite", p. 363.

die erschütterndste Wirklichkeit des Lebens. Einerseits ist Gott das furchterregende *tremendum*, andrerseits die Voraussetzung der Existenz, die Kraft der Seele und der Anreger des Lebens, *fascinosum*, ausserhalb dessen und ohne den nichts ist, das dem Dasein Wert und Inhalt geben könnte. Auch in seiner Verzweiflung sich an Gott klammernd und allem zum Trotz beharrlich in den Kern des Gottesglaubens eindringend findet Hiob die religiöse Lösung, die Glaubensentscheidung und siegt. In dieser seiner theozentrischen Haltung und in seinem persönlichen schmerzvollen Kampf ist Hiob der typische *homo religiosus*.

Für den Prediger ist das Gottesproblem nicht die einzige Wirklichkeit. Gott bedeutet für ihn nicht den Mittelpunkt, von dem aus alle Dinge und Werte bestimmt werden. Seine Fragen und Urteile sind anthropozentrisch und eudaimonistisch. Oft beurteilt er das Tun und das Geschehen danach, welcher Nutzen dem Menschen daraus erwächst [1]). Wenn die Haltung so ist, dass dem Leben das einzig Wichtige fehlt, ist es begreiflich, dass dem Prediger beim Auftreten von Zweifeln auch die Glut des persönlichen Kampfes fehlt. Er weicht zurück und begnügt sich mit einem Kompromiss. So gleitet er von der religiös-existenziellen Linie ab in eine dem Alten Testament fremde uninteressierte Blasiertheit. Der Horizont verengt sich, alles wird zum Überdruss. Zum Ziel des Strebens wird die eigene kleine Bequemlichkeit. So bleibt Kohelet auch in seinen Zweifeln auf halbem Wege stehen. Er ist nicht bereit, sein Selbst preiszugeben, um sich zum Prometheus-Trotz zu erheben und die Schemata, in die er sich innerlich nicht mehr einfügen kann, offen zu zerbrechen. Das Glaubensproblem ist für ihn nicht persönlich zwingend. Er ist nach der Beschaffenheit seiner Seele und nach seiner Haltung der säkularistische Mensch, dem die religiöse Leidenschaft und der absolute Gottesanspruch fehlen.

Weil der Verfasser des Buches Hiob unablässig um die Glaubensentscheidung eifert und streng an der religiösen Problematik festhält, der Prediger aber von der religiösen, theozentrischen Fragestellung auf die menschlich-weltanschauliche, „philosophische" Linie übergeht, gelangen beide Schriftsteller, obgleich sie denselben Ausgangspunkt haben, zu ganz verschiedenen Lösungen — oder vielleicht

[1]) Es ist kennzeichnend, dass eines der gewöhnlichsten Spezialwörter des Predigers *jitrōn*, "Gewinn", "Vorzug", ein Wort ist, das nirgends anders im AT sich findet; ausserdem kommen bei Kohelet noch andere Derivata vom Stamme *jtr* vor.

muss man sagen: der eine von ihnen gelangt zur Lösung, der andere bleibt in der Ausweglosigkeit. Die Aufgabe des Prediger-Buches in dem biblischen Kanon scheint somit etwa die zu sein, die Hoffnungslosigkeit und Unhaltbarkeit der säkularistischen Lebenshaltung aufzudecken und dadurch indirekt die lebendige Gottesrealität und die Unumgänglichkeit eines persönlichen Glaubenskampfes zu verkünden.

WISDOM IN THE OLD TESTAMENT PROPHETS

BY

JOHANNES LINDBLOM

Lund

'Wisdom' and 'wise men' as a special phenomenon in human society were well known to the Israelite prophets. In particular the prophets were cognizant of the existence of Wisdom among foreign peoples, e.g. the Edomites (Jer. xlix 7; Ob. 8), the Phoenicians (Ezech. xxviii; Sach. ix 2), the Egyptians (Jes. xix 11 ff.), the Babylonians (Jes. xliv 25, xlvii 10; Jer. l 35, li 57), the Assyrians (Jes. x 13), the gentiles as a whole (Jer. x 7). This idea of the existence of Wisdom in a special sense among foreign peoples accords with a common opinion among the ancient Israelites. In 1 Reg. v 10 f. it is said of Solomon's wisdom that it surpassed the wisdom of all the children of the East and that of all Egypt. Job and his friends, thought of as paragons of wisdom, originated from Edom or other countries in the East. Agur (Prov. xxx 1) and Lemuel (Prov. xxxi 1) were foreigners. The wise men of Egypt were widely renowned (Gen. xli 8; Ex. vii 11). So were the wise men of Persia (Esth. i 13, vi 13). The Ishmaelites, the Sabeans, and the Arabs had the reputation of being searchers for, and lovers of, wisdom (1 Reg. x 1; Bar. iii 23).

Sometimes the wise men are identified with the high officials in a kingdom (Jes. xix 11), sometimes they form a special class among the leaders of society, alongside the high officials, the diviners, and the warriors (Jer. l 35 f.), the high officials, the governors, the prefects, and the warriors (Jer. li 57), the soothsayers and the diviners (Jes. xliv 25).

The wise among the foreign peoples are occasionally spoken of as remarkable and important personalities. It was realized that the wisdom of the pagan nations was one of the causes of their political and commercial power. When in Ezech. xxviii 3 it is said that the wisdom of the prince of Tyre was superior to the wisdom of Daniel, a paragon of wisdom according to an old tradition, possibly going back to Ugaritic mythology, this assertion is not entirely ironical, but includes a certain measure of appreciation.

Wisdom was one of the privileges which appertained to Primeval Man in Paradise (Ezech. xxviii 12 f.). Wisdom was a gift belonging to kings and had its origins in ancient ages (Jes. xix 11). This was in accord with both general Israelite tradition and Egyptian or Babylonian tradition. The contents of the Book of Proverbs are ascribed to King Solomon. The same is true of the Book of Ecclesiastes and the Book of Wisdom. A collection of Solomonic proverbs is said to have been made by the men of King Hezekiah (Prov. xxv 1). Another collection is ascribed to King Lemuel (Prov. xxxi 1). From Egypt we have King Amen-em-het's advice to his son and successor, the instruction of a hereditary prince for his son, a collection of counsels given by a king to his son Meri-ka-Re, etc. Ptah-hotep, who instructed his son on the actions and attitudes which make a successful official of the state, was a vizier of King Izezi [1]). In Babylonia Wisdom was first revealed to the primeval kings. In the Assyro-Babylonian story of Ahiqar this Ahiqar is described as a wise scribe and secretary of the king, and called father of all Assyria [2]). Words of kings and other prominent men, and the utterances of the ancestors of a distant past were regarded as particularly authoritative. 'Cover up the word of a king with the veil of the heart' [3]) is an admonition that expresses a leading principle of ancient wisdom. This fully explains the utterance in Jes. xix 11.

However, compared with Yahweh's wisdom and true prophecy, the wise among the peoples are naught in the eyes of the prophets: they are nothing but brutes and blockheads. When Yahweh's judgment comes upon the gentiles, all their wisdom will be put to shame. The wise men will stand there as fools. In such a connection pagan wisdom becomes an object of biting scorn to the prophets.

Do the prophets know a definite class in Israelite society which represents wisdom in a special sense? We are not concerned here with passages which refer to men and women distinguished by ability and skill in technical practice. Deutero-Isaiah speaks of workmen clever in constructing idols (*ḥārāš ḥāḵām*, Jes. xl 20). So does the interpolator in Jeremiah when he describes the idols as work by clever men (*maʿᵃśēh ḥᵃḵāmîm*, x 9). Ezekiel speaks about skilful men (*ḥᵃḵāmîm*) whom Tyre used as sailors (xxvii 8) and re-

---

[1]) J. B. Pritchard, *Ancient Near Eastern Texts relating to the Old Testament*, Princeton 1950, p. 412 ff.

[2]) *Ibid.*, p. 427 ff.

[3]) Ahiqar, Aram. text, vii, Pritchard, p. 428 f.

pairers of leaks (xxvii 9). Women able to perform ritual wailing and other ceremonies connected with mourning and death are called 'wise women' (*ḥᵃkāmôṯ*, Jer. ix 16). Whether the expression *ḥᵃkam ḥᵃrāšîm* in Jes. iii 3 means men clever in magic acts or skilful artisans in general is not fully clear. At any rate the reference is to practical ability.

The following passages require a closer examination.

Isaiah speaks of those who are wise (*ḥᵃkāmîm*) in their own eyes, and prudent in their own sight (v 21). He does not think here of 'the wise' as a special group in the nation. People wise in their own eyes are all those who have rejected the guidance of Yahweh and his words through the prophet and acted according to their own ideas and their own plans. Such an attitude was characteristic of the leaders of the people. A good example is King Ahaz, who in his embarrassment during the Syro-Ephraimitic war would not follow the advice of Yahweh's prophet, but trusted in his own political calculations. Of such a conceited wisdom Isaiah says that it will perish and keep itself hidden when Yahweh's punishment comes upon the people (xxix 14).

In Jeremiah the matter is more complicated. We begin with the passage xviii 18. The enemies of Jeremiah are setting about a persecution of the prophet. They are plotting to have him condemned and killed. The motivation of this scheme is expressed in the following words. 'For the teaching in the law shall not perish from the priests, nor counsel from the wise, nor the word from the prophets'. These words are to be understood as alluding to utterances of the prophet wherein he had announced doom upon three different groups and their activities. The priests and the prophets do not need any explanation. But who are the 'wise', whose counsel shall not be put to shame? Counsel, *'ēṣāh*, is also in Jes. xix 11 and Jer. xlix 7 connected with wisdom and the wise in the special sense. Alongside the priests and the prophets 'the wise' must form a special class. It is difficult to deny that this passage indicates that there was in the time of Jeremiah a definite group in the nation, designated as 'wise men', which was identical with those with whom we are familiar through the Wisdom literature. Against the opinion that 'the wise' are here identical with the Torah teachers in Jer. ii 8 and viii 8 f. [1]) is the fact that *'ēṣāh* is never used of the teaching in the

---

[1]) So P. Volz, *Der Prophet Jeremia*, 2nd ed. Leipzig 1928 and W. Rudolph,

Torah [1]), whereas it is a favourite term in the Wisdom literature to describe the instruction of 'the wise' [2]). Consequently Jeremiah had announced doom upon these three categories: the priests, the representatives of Wisdom in the special sense, and the prophets. Now his enemies would take vengeance. Through the killing of Jeremiah and the triumph of his antagonists it would be clearly demonstrated that his prophecy was wrong and abortive, and that the cause of the priests, the wise and the prophets was right.

The wise as a special category are also mentioned in Jer. ix 22 f. Yahweh says, 'The wise may not boast of his wisdom, nor may the strong warrior boast of his strength, nor may the rich boast of his riches. He who will boast may boast of his understanding and knowledge of me' [3]). Alongside the warriors and the rich, the wise are here thought of as a definite class which the prophet blames for its interest in rational wisdom at the sacrifice of the true knowledge of God.

In Jer. viii 8 f. *ḥᵃḵāmîm* denotes a quite different category. While in the foregoing passages the term *ḥāḵām* stands undetermined, it is here connected with the law: 'We are wise, and Yahweh's Torah is with us.' Of this Torah the prophet says that it is a falsification made by the scribes, *sōfᵉrîm*. I agree with the commentators who maintain that the falsified Torah is Deuteronomy and other written laws contrary to the older oral tradition, focused, according to Jeremiah, in the Decalogue [4]). Thus 'the wise' are people who have devoted themselves to the study of these laws and present themselves as instructors of the people in questions pertaining to the law and the application of its rules in practical life. It seems as though the emergence of this class of wise coincided with the appearance of Deuteronomy. They call themselves 'wise'. This designation is dependent on the claim of Deuteronomy itself to contain the true wisdom (iv 6).

Jeremia, in Eissfeldt, *Handbuch zum Alten Testament*, Tübingen 1947; cf. O. S. Rankin, *Israel's Wisdom Literature*, Edinburgh 1936, p. 6.

1) Only in one biblical passage is *ʿēṣāh* connected with the Torah, namely Ps. cxix 24: Thy testimonies are my delight and my counsellors, *ʾanšē ʿᵃṣāṯî* But here the expression is purely figurative.

2) On this term in the Wisdom literature and its significance, see further W. Zimmerli, "Zur Struktur der alttestamentlichen Weisheit", *ZAW* 51 (1933), p. 177-204 (esp. p. 182 ff.).

3) The authenticity of this passage is somewhat doubtful Volz rejects it, while Rudolph defends it The ideas here expressed are not un-Jeremianic. The difficulty lies in the placing of the word.

4) So, recently, Rudolph in his commentary.

The prophet upbraids them for having rejected Yahweh's word, i.e. the words of the true prophets [1]).

One day Yahweh's doom will come upon them. Then their wisdom will be of no help to them. I think that 'the wise' in this passage are identical with the *tōfᵉsē hattôrāh*, those who handle the law in ii 8, of whom it is said that they did not know Yahweh. They stand here beside the priests, the shepherds, i.e. the political leaders, and the prophets.

Thus, three groups are to be distinguished in this passage: the scribes, who have composed the laws, the wise, who give instruction in the law and its application in practical life, and finally the prophets, who preach Yahweh's words [2]). In earlier times there existed no intimate relation between the Torah and 'the wise' as representatives of Wisdom in the special sense. A change came about in post-exilic times. The Torah was then regarded as the epitome of all Wisdom and the standard of Wisdom; and the teaching in the Wisdom schools manifestly also included instruction in the principles and commands of the law [3]).

Though 'the wise' as a definite class in Israelite society are not often mentioned in the prophetic literature, it is a fact that there existed Wisdom and 'wise men' in the time that the great prophets were at work. Then the question arises whether traces of the ideas of the Wisdom teachers are to be found in the preaching of the prophets. Of course, there is a great difference between 'the wise' and the prophets as to their way of thinking. In the preaching of the prophets everything was centred in the relation between God and man. Sin and doom, conversion, forgiveness, and salvation were the chief ideas of that which the prophets had to announce. Wisdom deals with the

---

[1]) Thus, this word may not be used, as is sometimes done, to throw light upon passages such as Jes. xxix 14 and Jer. xviii 18; against RANKIN, *op cit.*, p. 6; cf. also RUDOLPH, *op. cit.*, p. 107.

[2]) Thus, I cannot agree with the scholars who maintain that 'the scribes' and 'the wise' in Jer. viii 8 f. are identical. So for instance H. RANSTON, *The Old Testament Wisdom Books and their Teaching*, London 1930, p. 13. Nor can I agree with RUDOLPH, who comments: "Seine (referring to the law) Hüter sind die Priester, die hier—eben als Verwalter der Tora—Weise und—als Aufzeichner der Tora—Schreiber heissen." The relation between 'the wise' and *sōfᵉrîm* in ancient Israel is obscure and calls for a thorough investigation.

[3]) See further J. FICHTNER, *Die altorientalische Weisheit in ihrer israelitisch-jüdischen Ausprägung*, Giessen 1933, p. 79 ff., and "Zum Problem Glaube und Geschichte in der israelitisch-jüdischen Weisheitsliteratur", *Theologische Literaturzeitung* 76 (1951), cols. 145 ff.

ways and methods which lead to well-being, success and happiness (*šālôm*) in human life. Wisdom is knowledge of these rules and obedience to them in everyday life. The preaching of the prophets was theocentric, the teaching in the Wisdom schools was anthropocentric. Reference has rightly been made to the Wisdom literature as the documents of Israel's humanism [1]), and to the anthropocentric-eudaemonistic starting-point of Wisdom [2]). The prophets had principally the people, the nation in sight; 'the wise', the individual man. In spite of these differences, it is conceivable that the prophets may occasionally have taken up some ideas from Wisdom. It is a well known fact that the prophets were open to influences from other domains, for instance cultic life, popular poetry, and so on. We are entitled to speak of such influences from Wisdom when, in the sayings of the prophets, we meet with words and thoughts which are alien to the prophetic thought-world in general, but characteristic of the doctrines of Wisdom [3]).

In Wisdom Yahweh is the originator of all wisdom, He is wise and He bestows wisdom on man [4]). Now it is said in some prophetic passages that Yahweh is wise.

In Jes. xxxi 1 f. the prophet calls down a curse on the heads of the political leaders of the people, who go down to Egypt for help. Of these political leaders the prophet said in v 21 that they were wise in their own eyes. Alluding to the imagined wisdom of these men—which has nothing to do with Wisdom in the narrower technical sense—the prophet says that Yahweh also is wise, i.e. He directs the course of historical events in accordance with divine and eternal principles.

In Jer. x 12 (li 15) Yahweh manifests Himself as wise by means of creation and His wonderful activities in the universe. The passage

---

1) Rankin, *op. cit.*, p. 3. E. C. Burleigh, "The Influence of Hebrew Wisdom Literature upon Early Christian Doctrine", *Australian Biblical Review* 1 (1951), p. 78.

2) Zimmerli, *op. cit.*, p. 203.

3) Nothing indicates that any one of the prophets belonged to the Wisdom class. Fichtner maintains that this was the case with Isaiah (*Theologische Literaturzeitung* 74 (1949), cols. 75 ff.), but his arguments are not convincing.

4) Some examples: Prov. ii 6, viii 22 ff.; Iob ix 4, xi 6, xii 13, xxviii, xxxii 8, xxxvii 16, xxxviii 36 f.; Sir. i 1, xv 18; Bar. iii 32; Sap. vii f., ix 9; cf. Ps. civ 24. Cf. P. van Imschoot, "Sagesse et esprit dans l'ancien testament", *Revue biblique* 47 (1938), p. 23 ff. Also in the pagan Wisdom literature Wisdom had its origin in the Gods; see H. Gressmann, *Israels Spruchweisheit im Zusammenhang der Weltliteratur*, Berlin 1925, p. 53; H. Ringgren, *Word and Wisdom*, Lund 1947, p. 128 ff.

x 1-16 does not belong to the authentic prophecies of Jeremiah, but is a composition by a prophetic personality of the exilic period [1]). The same idea is met with in Jes. xl 12 ff., 28. Now the essential attributes of Yahweh in the prophets are holiness and power, love and mercy, wrath and righteousness, but not wisdom, while in the Wisdom literature wisdom is one of the most characteristic qualities of Yahweh. In the Wisdom schools it was taught that Yahweh created the world in His wisdom, and by means of His wisdom sustained all things. Prov. iii 19 f.: 'The Lord by wisdom founded the earth, by reason He established the heavens. By His knowledge the depths are broken up, and the clouds drop down dew.' Iob xxxvii 16: 'Do you know the balancings of the clouds, the wonders of the one perfect in knowledge?' xxxviii 37: 'Who counts the clouds by wisdom? And who tilts the waterskins of the heavens?' Sir. xlii 21: 'The mighty works of His wisdom He has ordained. Nothing can be added unto them or diminished from them; and He has no need of any counsellor.' On the whole, the creation of the universe and the wonders of nature are a favourite topic in Wisdom. To cite instances would be superfluous. In view of such passages we may take it for granted that the few passages in the prophets where reference is made to Yahweh's wisdom in creation are influenced by Wisdom.

The passage Jes. xxviii 23-29 falls into the same category. Here Yahweh's wisdom reveals itself in the order that the farmer observes in his agricultural actions: 'This also comes from the Lord of hosts, whose counsel is wonderful, whose wisdom is great.' The parable itself and the terms *'ēṣāh* and *tûšiyyāh* verse 29, connected with Yahweh, indicate influence from the Wisdom schools.

Wisdom belongs to Yahweh, but also to the Messianic king. In Jes. xi 2 it is said about the ideal king of the future that Yahweh's spirit shall rest upon him, the spirit of wisdom and understanding (*rûᵃḥ ḥoḵmāh ûḇînāh*). Wisdom is here the ability to act according to what the circumstances demand, here thought of as a divine endowment. Wisdom in this sense is a qualification pertaining to a king, particularly in his capacity of a judge, in accordance with the ideal of a king in the ancient East. Solomon was given a wise and understanding heart (1 Reg. iii 12, v 26). A divine wisdom was in him to do judgment (iii 28). David had wisdom like the wisdom of God's angel (2 Sam. xiv 20). Joshua as chief of the Hebrew tribes was filled

[1]) So RUDOLPH in his commentary, p. 65.

with the spirit of wisdom (Deut. xxxiv 9; cf. further Prov. viii 15, xvi 10, xx 26; Sir. x 1 ff.). Then the wisdom of the Messianic king has nothing to do with the technical wisdom of the Wisdom schools.

In many passages of the prophetic scriptures wisdom or understanding (*ḥokmāh, bînāh, tᵉbûnāh*) and their opposite, foolishness or imprudence (*nᵉbālāh* and synonyms), are connected with the momentous idea of the knowledge of Yahweh, *daʿaṯ yahweh* [1]). Wise and prudent is he who possesses *daʿaṯ yahweh*, foolish and imprudent is he who does not have *daʿaṯ yahweh*. This combination of *daʿaṯ yahweh* and wisdom is clearly expressed e.g. in Jer. iv 22: 'My people is foolish, they do not know me, they are sottish children, and have no understanding; they are wise to do evil, but to do good they have no knowledge.' It is unnecessary to give here an analysis of the idea *daʿaṯ yahweh* as comprising the right knowledge of Yahweh's essence, His ways and His will as well as the right relation to Him and obedience to His commands. It suffices to state the frequent recurrence in the prophets of this manner of speaking which is of course genuinely prophetic and has nothing to do with the doctrines of the Wisdom teachers [2]).

It is a well known fact that Wisdom had a predilection for discussions of questions pertaining to individual reward and retribution. The pronounced individual religion, for instance in Jeremiah and Ezekiel, is not in itself a symptom of influence from Wisdom; it is a product of a necessary inner development in Israelite religion; but there are several passages in the prophetic literature which deal with the different lot of the righteous and the unrighteous in a manner typical of Wisdom.

In Jer. xii 1-3,5 the problem is intimately connected with Jeremiah's personal experiences. Comparing his own sufferings with the success of his adversaries, he was tempted to doubt Yahweh's righteousness. Jeremiah's discussion with Yahweh has its roots in a concrete situation in the personal life of the prophet and has hardly anything to do with the more general argumentation which is usual in the Wisdom literature.

In Jer. xvii 5-8, xvii 9-10 and xvii 11 the situation is different.

---

[1]) For the notion *nāḇāl, nᵉḇālāh*, see J. PEDERSEN, *Israel, its Life and Culture, I-II*, London & Copenhagen 1926, p. 429 ff. and 539.

[2]) ZIMMERLI has rightly seen the difference between 'wisdom' and *daʿaṯ oahweh, op. cit.*, p. 183, while in RANSTON's treatment there is a serious confusion, *yp. cit.*, p. 19.

The first passage varies in general terms, and in using the framework of curse and blessing, the usual topic of the difference between the righteous and the unrighteous man, so characteristic of Wisdom. The second word expresses the idea of God as one who searches the heart and tries the reins (very common in Wisdom). Finally, the third word with its comparison between the partridge on her eggs and him who gathers ill-gotten goods, has the character of a proverb similar to hundreds in the Wisdom literature. Nothing in the whole passage is suggestive of Jeremiah's mode of expression. It surely originates from the collector of Jeremiah's revelations, who was under the influence of the Wisdom schools.

Jes. iii 10-11 expresses the same idea as Jer. xvii 5-8, though in a less poetical form: 'Happy the righteous! for well shall they fare. For the fruit of their deeds they shall eat. Woe to the wicked! ill shall they fare. For the work of their hands shall be paid back to them.' Here, too, we trace the hand of a collector familiar with the ideas and the diction of 'the wise'.

Jes. xxvi 7-10 contains a reflection concerning the just and the wicked man, appropriate in the psalm of thanksgiving xxvi 1-14. The late composer of the so-called Apocalypse of Isaiah (for which I have used the term 'cantata') made use of different literary categories, and, *inter alia*, was influenced by Wisdom [1]).

Mal. iii 14-18 is likewise coloured by the ideology of Wisdom. Those who are at present in doubt as to Yahweh's righteousness will at some time in the future recognize the difference which prevails between the righteous and the wicked, between those who serve God and those who do not serve Him.

Wisdom embraced rules for a happy and successful life, but also knowledge in different domains of human erudition, such as it was conceived in the ancient oriental world. King Solomon is presented as a perfect prototype of wisdom. He was a master in knowing and composing proverbs and poems of various kinds; he possessed, furthermore, a comprehensive knowledge of the world of nature. He could speak about trees and herbs as well as about beasts, birds and fishes (1 Reg. v 9 ff.) [2]). According to the descriptions of oriental

---

[1]) See further J. LINDBLOM, *Die Jesaja-Apokalypse. Jes. 24-27*, *Lunds universitets årsskrift*, N. F. 1: 34, 3, Lund & Leipzig 1938, p. 40 ff.

[2]) In an article entitled "Die Weisheit Salomos" in *Kleine Schriften zur Geschichte des Volkes Israel II*, München 1953, p. 90 ff., A. ALT maintains that there existed in ancient Israel "eine besondere Gattung der Naturweisheit", the pattern of which

wisdom in Bar. iii 2 f., 'the wise' were also *mythologoi*, i.e. tellers of stories, fables and legendary lore. One of the outstanding characteristics of the Wisdom Literature is its predilection for metaphors and comparisons of different kinds. In particular the Book of Job also contains many fine observations in the field of nature. The stories and fables are few in the canonical Wisdom-writings. However, there are reasons for believing that the oral teaching of 'the wise' was more diversified, and made a more extensive use of parables, allegories, similes, and stylistic devices. The story of Ahiqar contains abundant material of this sort.

The prophetic literature is, as we know, rich in parables, allegories, proverbial expressions, comparisons, similes, metaphors. It is natural to suppose that the prophets in this respect were influenced by Wisdom. I refer for instance to the parable of Nathan, the allegory of the vineyard in Jes. v, the parable of the farmer, illustrating the wisdom of Yahweh, in Jes. xxviii, the many allegories in Ezekiel, similes like that of the baker in Hos. vii 4 f., of the axe, the saw, and the staff in Jes. x 15, of the horses and the plougher in Am. vi 12, and the long series of similes in Am. iii 3-6 [1]).

The prophetic scriptures are also rich in proverbs and proverbial expressions. A few examples: the sour grapes and the children's teeth set on edge (Jer. xxxi 29; Ezech. xviii 2); 'as the mother, so her daughter' (Ezech. xvi 44); 'every jar shall be filled with wine' (Jer. xiii 12); 'can one break iron from the north and brass?' (Jer. xv 12); 'what has the straw to do with the wheat?' (Jer. xxiii 28); 'can prey be taken from a warrior or a tyrant's captives be rescued?' (Jes. xlix 24) [2]).

In respect of style and stylistic devices, the rhetorical question is very characteristic of the Wisdom literature. It is likewise typical of the diction of the prophets. Sometimes influence from the language of the cult is obvious: Mich. vi 6 f.; Hagg. ii 10 ff.; Mal. i 7, but in other passages the question has a more didactic aim: Jes. x 15; Jer. xxiii 28; Ezech. xv 2 ff.; Am. iii 3-8, vi 12, ix 7; Mal. i 6, ii 14 f., 17, iii

---

is to be found in Egypt and Mesopotamia. This kind of 'wisdom' must, says Professor ALT, be strictly distinguished from what he calls "menschliche Lebensweisheit".

[1]) See further Jer. xvii 11; Hos. vii 16, viii 9, xiii 3; Am. iii 12; Hab. ii 5. Other examples in LINDBLOM, *The Servant Songs in Deutero-Isaiah*, ***Lunds universitets årsskrift***, N. F. 1: 47, 5, Lund 1951, p. 75-93.

[2]) See further Jes. lxv 8; Jer. viii 4; Ezech. xi 3.

7 f., iii 13 f. It is likely that in such cases the prophets are influenced by the methods of the Wisdom teachers [1]).

In some descriptions of prophetic visions the vision is displayed in the form of a dialogue between God or an *angelus interpres* and the prophet according to this scheme: what seest thou? . . . and I said . . .' This is the case in two visions of Amos, the vision of the plummet (vii 7 f.) and the vision of the summerfruit (viii 2). We have examples of the same mode of expression in Jer. i 11 f., 13, xxiv 3; Sach. v 1 f. Surely we have to do here with a fixed stylistic form. It seems likely that behind this form of question and answer lies the normal didactic method in the teaching of 'the wise' [2]).

The formal structure of the prophecies of Amos against the nations in Am. i-ii is keenly debated. I am convinced that these prophecies form a coherent composition and that the pattern of this composition is the tribal poem which in my opinion was a clearly distinguishable genre in ancient Hebrew poetry [3]). Here the Israelite tribes are replaced by the foreign pagan nations and Israel, possibly also Judah, at their side. But there is one thing more that demands an explanation, I mean the reiterated formula 'for three transgressions and for four'. On the whole, numbers play an important rôle in the prophetic books, e.g. Jes. xvii 6; Jer. xv 3, xxxvi 23; Hos. vi 2; Am. iv 8, v 3, vi 5. In the Wisdom literature from the Book of Proverbs to Pirqe Aboth this peculiarity is still more striking; and, in particular, the type used in Am. i-ii is very frequent in the instruction of 'the wise', where it obviously served a didactic aim. I have noted the following examples: *one* and *two* Iob xxx 14, *one* and *two* and *three* Sir. xxiii 23, *two* and *three* Iob xxxiii 29; Sir. xxiii 16, xxvi 28, l 25; Ahiqar vi (Aram. text) [4]), *two* and *three* and *four* Prov. xxx 15-16; Sir. xxvi 5, *three* and *three* Sir. xxv 1-2, *three* and *four* Prov. xxx

---

[1]) Some examples: Prov. i 22, vi 27, xvii 16, xx 9, xxx 4; Eccles. i 3, iii 21, vii 14, viii 1; Sir. x 9. In the Book of Job this mode of expression is very common. For the stylistic peculiarities of Wisdom, see further J. SCHMIDT, *Studien zur Stilistik der alttestamentlichen Spruchliteratur*, *Alttestamentliche Abhandlungen* XIII, 1, Münster i. W. 1936, p. 56 ff.; J. HEMPEL, *Die althebräische Literatur*, Wildpark-Potsdam, 1930, p. 49 ff. W. BAUMGARTNER in *Theologische Rundschau* 5 (1933), p. 274, points to the connection of the 'question' with the riddle, *ḥîḏāh*.

[2]) For the colloquy form in the Wisdom schools, see L. DÜRR, *Das Erziehungswesen im Alten Testament und im antiken Orient*, *Mitteilungen der vorderasiatisch-ägyptischen Gesellschaft* 36, 2 (1932), p. 72 f.

[3]) Cf. LINDBLOM, "The Political Background of the Shiloh Oracle" in *Supplements to Vetus Testamentum*, Vol. 1, Leiden 1953, p. 78 ff.

[4]) The formula runs here: 'two things . . . and the third'.

18-19, 21-23, 29-31; Sir. xxvi 5-6, *six* and *seven* Prov. vi 16; Iob v 19, *seven* and *eight* Eccles. xi 2, *nine* and *ten* Sir. xxv 7-11.

Thus, there is no ground for seeking the pattern of the formula in question in the cult; it evidently originates in the teaching of 'the wise'. In other respects, too, Amos shows acquaintance with popular stylistic forms; see for instance the dirge in v 2 (cf. v 16 f.).

In order to draw attention to their words the prophets sometimes use the method of reiteration and concatenation of ideas and phrases. I think of passages such as Hos. xi 23 f.: 'It shall come to pass on that day, I will answer, saith the Lord, I will answer the heavens, and they shall answer the earth; and the earth shall answer the corn, and the wine, and the oil, and they shall answer Jezreel.' Some other passages of the same type are Jes. lxv 13-14; Jer. xv 2 f., li 20-23; Am. iii 3-6. Such enumerations are much appreciated by the Wisdom teachers, for didactic reasons, of course, that their disciples might learn their words by heart. Sir. xix 13-15 runs: 'Question a friend; perhaps he did not do it; or if he did, so that he will not do it again. Question your neighbour; perhaps he did not say it; or if he did, so that he may not repeat it. Question a friend, for often there is slander, and you must not believe everything that is said.' Other examples Eccles. iii 1-9; Sir. xxv 13-14, xl 18-26, xlii 1-5 [1]).

From a terminological point of view it is noteworthy that the term *mûsār* ('discipline'), which appears in countless passages in the Wisdom literature, is a favourite word in Jeremiah, especially in the combination *lāḳaḥ mûsār*: ii 30, v 3, vii 28, xvii 23, xxxii 33, xxxv 13. It seems that Jeremiah and his disciples had special contact with the Wisdom school.

In later times we hear of special houses of instruction (Sir. li 22). For earlier times we have to think that, as has always been the habit in the Orient, wise men gathered round themselves disciples who, in freer forms, made use of their instruction. In this personal instruction certain methods and devices were developed which are also reflected in the Wisdom books and occasionally were taken up by the prophets to draw attention to their words. Such instruction is probably implied in Jes. li 4: 'Each morning he wakens my ear to hear as disciples do.' [2]).

---

[1]) Paronomasia, alliteration and such matters are to be found in the prophetic books as well as in the Wisdom writings (G. Boström, *Paronomasi i den äldre hebreiska maschallitteraturen*, Lund & Leipzig 1928), but I think the prophets use them simply as poetical forms, not specially in dependence on Wisdom.

[2]) See further Dürr, *op. cit.*, p. 106 ff.

Among the latest additions to the prophetic books there are some passages which contain pious reflections made by readers manifestly dominated by the ideology and phraseology of Wisdom. There is, for instance, the ending of the Book of Hosea: 'Who is wise, so that he understands these things? prudent, so that he perceives them? for the ways of the Lord are right, and the just walk (in safety) in them, but the transgressors stumble in them.' The terminology as well as the idea of the different lot of the righteous and the unrighteous are both very typical of Wisdom. The influence of Wisdom thought is also evident in the addition Jer. x 23-25: 'Man's way is not his own; it is not in man's power how he walks and directs his steps', etc. For this idea compare e.g. Prov. xx 24: 'A man's steps are directed by the Lord, how, then, can any man understand his way?' The same is true of Jes. ii 22: 'Cease from man, whose breath is in his nostrils. At what is he to be estimated?' The feebleness and worthlessness of man is a favourite theme in the Wisdom literature. Finally, the passage Jes. iii 10-11 must be included in the same category. Here, too, we trace the hand of a man belonging to the Wisdom school. The passage contains a rather trivial reflection concerning retribution: with the righteous it shall be well, for they shall eat the fruit of their deeds, but woe to the wicked for they shall be rewarded according to their works.

The results of this investigation can be summarized in the following way:

1) The prophets are well acquainted with Wisdom among foreign, pagan peoples and speak about it in traditional terms.

2) The prophets are cognizant of the existence of 'wise men' as a definite class in Israel, too, though they do not often mention it.

3) Wisdom is in some measure appreciated by the prophets, but when wisdom is opposed to the divine word through the prophets it becomes an object of scorn and condemnation.

4) Certain features of the teaching in Wisdom circles are taken up by the prophets. Particular mention may be made of the idea of God's wisdom manifested in the creation and in nature, and the problem of individual retribution.

5) The style of the prophets also shows influence from the instruction of 'the wise'. Here we may point out the abundant use of parables, allegories, similes, metaphors, proverbial expressions, rhetorical questions, dialogues, reiterations of phrases and ideas, numbers and enumerations.

6) Several late additions in the prophetic books originated in the Wisdom circles.

PSALMS AND WISDOM

BY

SIGMUND MOWINCKEL

Oslo

I

The present paper was prepared as a lecture to be given in Manchester at the invitation of Prof. H. H. ROWLEY which, however, was prevented by unfavourable circumstances. Now it is presented as a token of admiration and friendship.

The interpretation of the Biblical Psalms that forms the basis of this paper is my conviction that not only psalm poetry as such, but also the great majority of the psalms transmitted to us are true cultic poetry [1]). Psalm poetry as such has sprung from the temple cult. Even the psalms transmitted to us, perhaps more than 140 of the 150 of the Psalter, have not only been used as cult-psalms, but have also been composed for that purpose. The real psalm poets are the temple singers and temple poets, the "sons of Qorah" and of "Asaph", etc. [2]), and their purpose is not to express the subjective experiences and emotions of the individual poet, but to serve the congregational cult. Accordingly we have in principle to distinguish between the Ego of the psalm and the poet [3]). The speaking Ego is the representative of the congregation—very often the king—or of the single member of the congregation in general, Everyman who was in the situation that he had to perform a cultic or ritual act to which belonged the recitation of a psalm—a lamentation or a thanksgiving song.

This being the case, a problem arises when we find in the Psalter some poems which do not seem to have been composed for cultic use. The problem in psalm exegesis is not the cultic psalms, but the non-cultic ones.

---

[1]) See the present writer's *Offersang og Sangoffer*.

[2]) See the writer's *Psalmenstudien VI*, *Die Psalmdichter*.

[3]) Cf. the writer's remarks in *HUCA* XXIII, 1 1950/51, p. 217 ff.

II

The point of departure for dealing [1]) with this problem may be the circumstance that these few psalms show many characteristic similarities to the wisdom poetry of the learned men, the *sopherim*, the scribes—as late Jewish psalmography does as a whole [2]). And our thesis is that in this case we have to do with a psalmography that has originated in the circles of the "wise men", the learned leaders of the "wisdom schools". We shall try to demonstrate in short the relations of this "learned psalmography" to the older patterns of form and content and to the wisdom literature.

Scholars have often distinguished too sharply between the different "classes" of the "intelligentsia" in ancient Israel: priets, prophets, scribes, wise men, etc., as if they really were sharply defined social and functional "classes". The borders between them were, however, rather fluctuating. Several prophets are said to have come from priestly families; the majority of prophets formed an official class of cult functionaries [3]); the psalm poets as a rule belonged to the temple singers; Levites gradually became interpreters of the law (cp. Neh. viii 7 f.), the scribes were also the "wise men", *ḥak̠åmim*.

To the temple personnel belonged even scribes; see Neh. xiii 13; Jer. xxxvi 5 f., 10 f. The historical nucleus of the tradition about Solomon being the author of "proverbs" and other "poetry of wisdom" (1 Reg. iii 9, v 9 ff.; Prov. i 1 ff., x 1, xxv 1; Eccl. i 1, xii 9 f.) is probably just that he was the one who founded the school for scribes in Jerusalem and introduced there the international poetry of wisdom of the Orient [4]). For, along with the teaching of foreign languages, this kind of literature belonged to the special

---

[1]) This has rightly been demonstrated by H. LUDIN JANSEN, *Die spätjüdische Psalmendichtung, ihr Entstehungskreis und ihr "Sitz im Leben"*. Cf. my review in *Norsk Teologisk Tidsskrift* (1938), p. 236 ff. BEGRICH's opposition in *Svensk Exegetisk Årsbok* III (1938), p. 126 ff. is in my opinion not valid.

[2]) At somewhat greater length I have treated the problem in a paper in *NTT* 51 (1950), p. 1 ff.

[3]) See the writer's *Psalmenstudien III. Kulturprophetie und prophetische Psalmen*; A. R. JOHNSON, *The Cultic Prophet in Ancient Israel*; A. HALDAR, *Associations of Cult Prophets among the Ancient Semites*; MOWINCKEL, *Offersang og Sangoffer*, p. 308ff.

[4]) Cf. H. GRESSMANN in *ZAW* 42 (1924), p. 272 ff; W. BAUMGARTNER, *Israelitische und altorientalische Weisheit*; J. FICHTNER, "Die altorientalische Weisheit in ihrer israelitisch-jüdischen Ausprägung" (*BZAW* 62); T. E. PEET, *A Comparative Study in the Literatures of Egypt, Palestine, and Mesopotamia* (*Schweich Lectures*, 1931), p. 99 ff.; B. GEMSER, "Die Sprüche Salomos" (*HBAT* 16), p. 5 f.; C. H. GORDON, *The Living Past*, p. 133.

professional education of the "scribes". It belonged to the "schools for scribes" [1]). Here Solomon took up the traditions from the great empires as well as from the courts of Canaanite princes. The schools for scribes, and the art and culture they represented, were an international phenomenon [2]). There is every reason to believe that the school for scribes in Jerusalem, as elsewhere in the Orient, was closely connected with the temple; this is apparent from the very fact that the "wisdom literature" of Israel was considered to belong to the canonical writings.

The guilds of scribes and temple singers and poets were closely connected. A metaphor like that of Ps. xlv 2: "My tongue is like the pen of a ready writer (properly: quick writer)" seems to indicate that the poet is proudly aware of being a master of the noble art of writing. It is not unreasonable to suppose that the teaching of that part of the professional knowledge of the temple singers, which was made up of psalmography, would also take the form of learning to copy earlier psalms.

At any rate it was these "*learned writers*" that gradually became the "scribes" of New Testament times, who took in hand the collection and handing down of the Psalter. Even the headings and their learned interpretations of them are indications of this. The author of the poem of wisdom about Job knows perfectly well the different species of composition in psalmography [3]). We shall see that psalmography was cultivated in the circle of learned scribes far down throughout the ages.

From of old these "learned" or "wise" men used to cultivate a special kind of literature, "the poetry of wisdom", which was cultivated all over the Orient, and had a common, markedly international, character, in Egypt, Babylonia and Canaan. Characteristic of its form is the "saying", the proverb and the exhortation, and the contents are moralistic and didactic; it aims at practical wisdom of life, not least so for the "scribes" themselves, who have intercourse with kings and great men, and travel in foreign countries, and have to do with the affairs of the realm and with all sorts of people. But practical wisdom of life—even if it has a utilitarian character—has always a

---

1) See GRESSMANN, *op. cit.*, p. 291 ff.

2) Cf. GRESSMANN, *op. cit.*, p. 295. The expression "quick writer" *sopher måhir* Ps. xlv 2 is an old Canaanite term which has been adopted in Egyptian terminology. See also W. F. ALBRIGHT, in *The Jewish People, Past and Present I*, p. 36.

3) Cf. MOWINCKEL, *Diktet om Ijob og hans venner*, p. 115 ff.

religious basis; the true "wisdom" is "the fear of God", that is the deepest motive of morality. As this morality and this poetry are international and related to social position and profession, they also have a general and rational character. What they will teach the reader are the—from the point of view of the ancient Orient—universal human virtues, and they speak with preference of the "deity" in general, whereas the more national aspect of religion, expressing itself, for instance, in the name Yahweh for God, becomes less prominent. This does not prevent it from being adapted to the national religion of Israel; nor are the later learned men prevented from finding that the highest "wisdom" has been revealed in the law of Yahweh.

Now we see that not a few psalms have been marked by the wisdom poetry with regard to substance as well as form. This becomes apparent for instance in the testimonies of the thanksgiving psalms and their exhortations to the congregation, in which the tone, in the nature of the case, is didactic. Naturally these passages will have the form of a "proverb", a wise saying (*måšål*). This becomes prominent in the psalms, in which suffering and the justice of Yahweh are felt to be a problem, on which the author is pondering and which he is trying to solve; even in this case it is especially the thanksgiving psalms, such as for instance Ps. lxxiii, which have the character of a "problem psalm". The psalmists have learnt from the learned men, and the learned men have learnt from the psalmists: when they are speaking of the greatness and wisdom and justice of God, they often do so in the form of a hymn, just as their instruction about the "two roads", the road of virtue and the road of vice, not infrequently has the form of the blessing or the cursing word.

The learned men were also traditionalists; they joined in caring for the ancient holy traditions, the laws and the sayings of the prophets and the traditions of the temple, among the latter of psalmography. In proportion as the importance of "Yahweh's law" increased in Judaism, their own importance likewise increased as guardians of law tradition and law interpretation, and of religious life in general. They thought of themselves as the inheritors both of the prophets and of the psalmists. They became psalmists too, and to the ancient cultic poetry was added a later, private, learned psalmography.

III

In spite of the didactic character of the "learned psalmography", which will be demonstrated more in detail below, it has one essential thing in common with genuine psalmography: these poems are and will be considered as *prayers*. They will, as every real psalm, speak to God, even if they often are speaking to men as well. And the origin of this new sort of poetry must be seen against the background of the Jewish view of prayer.

Prayer is the most spontaneous outcome of piety—of the relationship to God. Even in Israel there always more or less existed free, instantaneous prayer, independent of the temple service [1]). And the more the relationship to God became a personal matter of the individual, the more prayer would be a regular part of life in God. We notice how a personal relationship of prayer would grow into being among the prophets as a result of the personal problems forced upon them through their calling [2]). Even the later disciples of the prophets and the learned collectors of the tradition were pious people. And in proportion as the law and the scriptures became the standards and sources of religious life in Judaism, piety was, in fact, to a certain degree detached from the temple cultus, and found much of its nourishment in the synagogue and in the lecture room (the school) of the learned men. And, like the prophets of old, so even the learned rabbis were supposed to be men of prayer. Both synagogue and private life had their prayer life, which gradually in turn assumed established forms. Thus we know that in Jewish times pious people thought it the proper thing to have three fixed hours of prayer daily; this custom is taken for granted in the legends of Daniel [3]).

In the nature of the case, the forms and motives of free prayer would actually to a great extent be determined by the fixed traditional style of the regular service. In the psalms the pious would find expressions for what they themselves had to say, and to a great extent they would learn from them what it was proper to say and what ought to be said to God. The influence of psalm style on the "free" prayers to be found in O.T. may be demonstrated step by step. We see it already in the short prayers in Amos and Isaiah, and

---

[1]) Cf. i.a. Gen. xxiv 12 ff., xxxii 10 ff. See A. WENDEL, *Das freie Laiengebet im vorexilischen Israel* (though much of the matter given by him belongs to the ritual and cultic sphere).

[2]) Especially to be seen in Jeremiah. Cf. H. W. HERTZBERG, *Prophet und Gott. Eine Studie zur Religiosität des vorexilischen Prophetentums*; W. BAUMGARTNER, "Die Klagegedichte des Jeremia" (*BZAW* 32).

[3]) Dan. vi, 11, 14. Cf. E. SCHÜRER, *Geschichte des jüdischen Volkes im Zeitalter Jesu Christi II*[1], p. 350, n. 40. Cf. also Index s.v. "Gebet".

quite distinctly in the lamentations and prayers of Jeremiah [1]); likewise in the influence of the hymn style on the sayings of Deutero-Isaiah, and the personal hymnal exclamations sometimes to be found with him [2]).

This non-cultic prayer, which was originally free with regard to occasion, time and place, but on which fixed limits were gradually imposed, and which, at any rate as far as form and substance were concerned, was largely dependent on tradition, affords *one condition of a non-cultic psalmography*. There is another step thence to conscious psalmography. Jeremiah did not compose psalms, but he poured out his heart in guided words in the sacral psalm style, and he included these prayers in his other sayings because, in addition to the answers received from God, they made part of his message to his people. Still more obviously the "hymns" of Deutero-Isaiah are circumlocutions of the message, even if no doubt his own heart is engaged in them; that he sometimes puts the hymn in the mouth of Yahweh himself (Jes. xlv 8) testifies to the fact that he did not want it to be looked upon as poetry, as a "meditation of his heart" (Ps. xix 15).

On the other hand we find that the latest, anonymous prophets, who were learned collectors rather than original prophets in the old sense of the word, do not infrequently burst into the jubilant hymn to be sung by the saved, when the great "turning of destiny" has taken place, or they sing it already for their own part [3]).

IV

So among the learned and inspired collectors of the holy traditions of the ancients a *cultus-free psalmography* also came into being.

They were men of prayers and they were officially inspired "*pneumatics*". To be able to pray rightly, to make a doxology or a prayer with the proper content and in the proper form, was considered not only evidence of piety, but also proof of the inspiration which the wise claimed for themselves and were conscious of possessing (Sir. xv 10, xxxix 5 f.). It was just these wise men who took over and further developed the estimate of the psalmists of prayer and psalm as being the true and acceptable sacrifice; a man like Jesus Sirach no

---

1) See BAUMGARTNER's book (above, n. 2).

2) Jes. xlii 10-13, xliv 23, xlix 13 lii 9 f. Hymnical motifs: xl 22-24b, 28b-31, xliv 25-28, xlv 18, xlvi 10 f.

3) Jes. xii, xxiv 15 f., xxv 9, xxvi 1 ff., xxvii 2 ff.

longer has any real understanding of the offering of animals [1]). Thus they started to think it a pious work, acceptable to God, to compose a psalm, especially if a person had been delivered from disaster or danger, and perhaps also to recite it in the circle of disciples; then the latter would learn at the same time something of this pious art ("wisdom").

The way the learned estimated the psalm is brought out by their conception of the pious of the past. The later writers of sagas and legends every now and then make their persons recite a psalm or a psalm-like prayer, both when relating their disasters and their deliverance; this is the case with Hannah, king Hezekiah, the prophet Jonah, Ezra and Esther, Daniel and his friends, king Manasseh, and Tobit and Judith [2]); even in the burning furnace the three friends of Daniel are said to have recited a psalm.

Sometimes the teachers of wisdom include such psalms in their writings; this is not infrequently the case with Jesus Sirach, whose mode of composition, even in other respects, gives evidence of being largely influenced by the psalm style [3]). It aims at teaching and edifying the reader, that is to say, at being used for private edification, preferably in the lecture room.

Here we are face to face with a learned psalmography, which is not derived from the temple singers, but is of a truly private nature, and which has no longer any direct relation to the cultus.

Of course, this does not exclude the possibility that several of these learned men may have been Levites, belonging to the families of singers. Nor that among this private poetry there may also have been psalms destined for use in the cultus. Perhaps this especially applies to the thanksgiving psalms, which seem to have been the particular favourites of the "wise". Among the thanksgiving psalms of the Psalter we find so much of personal experience coupled with such manifold varieties of and departures from the old style pattern, that we cannot help asking if this or that psalm has not been composed by the very individual who has been saved, even though, according to the liturgical notes of the heading, it has been used on cultic occasions, and then probably also composed for such use. This especially applies to Ps. lxxiii, the problem and situation of which are

---

[1]) Sir. xxxii 6 f. Cf. STADE-BERTHOLET, *Biblische Theologie d.A.T.*, p. 178 f.

[2]) 1 Sam. ii; Jes. xxxviii. Or. Man.; Tob. xiii; Judith xvi. See below § 6.

[3]) Sir. xlii 15 ff., xxxix 12 ff., li 1 ff. etc. See BAUMGARTNER in *ZAW* 34 (1914), p. 169 ff.

certainly typical and in so far universally valid, but in which they have found such personal expressions that there seems to be no reason for a distinction between the "ego" of the worshipper and that of the author [1]). If Ps. xxxiv was composed for cultic use, much the same thing seems to be the case here.—We might think, therefore, that it had become usual among the pious wise men that the person who had been saved had better himself compose the thanksgiving psalm to be recited at the sacrificial feast—if he was at all able to do so, which again means: if he was a "wise" and "learned" man. It was both a natural expression of his feelings, and it was considered evidence of particular piety to honour the Lord in such a way.

In addition to the above mentioned psalms in stories and books of wisdom, we have had handed down to us from late Jewish times a whole collection of such psalms, the so-called *Psalms of Solomon*.

The learned psalmist often had a twofold object for his poem. First of all it was meant to be a pious work: to honour God by praising and thanking him for his great works and his benefits, and to call upon him in such a way, when in distress and tribulation—and to do so in inspired verses. That is what the author of Ps. l makes Yahweh himself impress upon the pious man: "Call upon me in the day of trouble—I will deliver thee, and thou shalt honour me" (l 15).

We do not know much about the way this calling upon God and thanksgiving were performed. As we have seen, it is just possible that the person who brought a thank-offering would even on some occasions recite his private thanksgiving psalm in the circle of relations and friends at the thank-offering feast. And from Sirach's book of wisdom we may at any rate infer that such poems were recited before the students of the schools of wisdom, in the circle gathered around the teacher. And this brings us to the second object: that of teaching young people the art of calling upon and praising the Lord in inspired "songs of wisdom" [2]). But then this is the true religious

---

[1]) Cf. *HUCA* XXIII 1, p. 228 ff.

[2]) On the connection between the "school" and the "wisdom psalm", see LUDIN JANSEN, *op. cit.* In *Acta Orientalis* XV (1937), "Die Jüdischen Weisheitspsalmen und ihr Sitz im Leben", P. A. MUNCH has also tried to give a picture of the life in the school. His hypothesis of regular daily "school devotion" cannot be proved by what is said in Jer. Meg. iii 1 of Rabbi Nehemiah's custom. MUNCH overestimates the polemical traits in Pss. Sal., and does not do full justice to the personal religious element even in the "instruction psalms", as he labels one of his typological groups ("Gattungen"); so, e.g., when he thinks that Sirach's purpose in his thanksgiving psalm (Sir. li 13 ff.) was to "enlist pupils" for the school, *op. cit.*, p. 135.

element: the poet wants to share his religious experiences with the young people, bear witness to them, and through this personal example admonish them to walk in the right way.

V

It looks as if some of these non-cultic poems were included in the Psalter; this may perhaps be the case with psalms like nos i, xxxiv, xxxvii, xlix, lxxviii, cv, cvi, cxi, cxii, cxxvii.

Characteristic of the latest psalmography is, in the first place, that it tries on the whole to keep to the old paths and to adhere to the *old rules of composition*, but that it is not done intelligently. As the poets would no longer compose poetry for a definite cultic occasion, the preservation of the modes of composition was no longer supported by their "place in life", as it used to be, and the different modes and motives were *mixed up*. Therefore we may speak of a *dissolution of the style*. This is particularly marked in what Jewish opinion held most skilful, viz., *alphabetic psalms*, in which every line—the (period) ("bicolon")—starts with a new letter in alphabetic sequence; here sometimes elements of composition from nearly all ancient species of poetry are mixed up, according as the initial would call up by association one characteristic catchword or another.

In the second place this poetry is more or less influenced by the style and contents of the *poetry of wisdom*. The psalm becomes more or less a didactic poem. Even the old thanksgiving psalm tended that way [1]). A prominent feature of this type of psalm was the worshipper's testimony *coram publico* of the salvation he had experienced, wherefore he now will "Confess Yahweh's name before his brethren". In such a "testimony" something of a desire to win other people for God is always included; it is a "witness" in the religious sense of the word: do as I have done and turn to Yahweh in distress, then you will be saved! I know it for I have experienced it myself!—Thus the testimony to some extent assumes the nature of an *admonition*, whether it calls the person blessed, who confesses his sins and obtains forgiveness and is healed from illness and impurity, or straightway invites others to follow the example of the worshipper (Ps. xxxi 24, xxxii 6 f., xxxiv 6 ff., cxxiv 8).—Here the style and ideas of the "poetry of wisdom" are likely to have made themselves felt; for even the latter

[1]) Cf. *Offersang og Sangoffer*, p. 290 ff.

has for its object exhortative religious and moral instruction, where the teacher (father) often refers to his own experience as a guarantee of the truth of his words. When now in the thanksgiving psalms the experience is expressed in a general sentence (Ps. xxxvii 35 f.), or in the form of a blessing (Ps. xxxii 1 f.), or through direct admonition in the imperative (Ps. xxxiv 4-9), or by inviting others to take a lesson from what has been (Ps. xxxiv 12 ff.), all this is a result of influence from the poetry of wisdom. Consequently the thanksgiving psalm may become chiefly instructive and approximate to the didactic poem, as is the case with Ps. xxxiv.

In the later "learned psalmography" this didactic tendency becomes much more prominent. The form becomes that of the admonition or warning of the proverbs and of the instructive statement of the latter as to how different kinds of people will fare in this world. A favourite subject is the instruction about the *destinies of good and evil people*, as in Pss. i and cxii, and more or less successful attempts at proving that the Jewish dogma of retributive justice holds good: that piety will be rewarded and ungodliness punished in this life on earth, if not until untimely death shall overtake the ungodly—that is the thought in which the author of Ps. xlix takes comfort.

In this way the psalm receives the character of a *theodicy*: the author wants to prove that God has acted rightly. Therefore it often leads to a *hymnal element* in the style; we get a kind of didactic hymn, like Pss. lxxviii and cv. The material is then usually derived from the *history* of Israel [1]), and the intention is to testify to the faithfulness of Yahweh and the breaking of the covenant by the people, proving the justice of punishment and disaster. Such a didactic hymn may develop into a downright "*hymnal legend*", a synopsis of the holy history in the style of a hymn, as is the case with Pss. lxxviii and cv. There is a line to be drawn from the liturgies in connection with the renewal of the covenant (Ps. lxxxi, xcv) [2]) *via* the prophetic exhortation of a psalm like Ps. l to a hymnal legend like Ps. lxxviii.—But history may also provide the material for a confession of sins and a prayer for restoration on the part of the congregation, and thus result in a *historical penitential psalm*, like Ps. cvi.

In the background of the discussions about the justice of God is to be perceived the *religious division of the congregation* as a result of

---

[1]) Cf. A. LAUHA, *Die Geschichtsmotive in den alttestamentlichen Psalmen.*
[2]) Cf. *Offersang*, p. 156 ff.

the progress of the ideals of *law religion*. The psalmists side with the strict adherents to the law—for they belonged to the "scribes"—and look upon others as sinners and apostates. And as these worldly-minded would generally hold power in the Jewish province, the authors would put the matter as if piety and lowliness on one side were at variance with power and riches and ungodliness on the other; sometimes they seem to identify those who were in power in the province with the pagan oppressors. When a pious person is affected by personal tribulation, and particularly such as have to do with the difference between rulers and ruled, "rich" and "poor", then the problem about the unequal apportionment of the good things of life and about the "ungodliness" and "worldliness" of those in power would become a big issue. Then the pious person may have reason to "fear", namely that God will fail him, and that the doctrine of retributive justice will not hold good (xlix 6, 16) [1]). Then he will comfort himself and his fellow-believers by stating that at all events riches will come to an end in death (Ps. xlix, xxxvii); face to face with death all are alike; but for all that he will maintain that the ungodly mighty ones will end in disaster, whereas the pious and humble and lowly will be saved from all dangers (Ps. xxxiv, xxxvii) [2]). Even the experiences of these poets culminate in such a personal religious confidence (xlix 16). Sometimes a personal occasion of the problem as well as of its solution shines distinctly through; for instance, Ps. xxxiv is most likely meant to be a thanksgiving psalm on deliverance from some distress; see the personally felt and hinted hymnal introduction and especially verses 5 and 7; cf. also verses 16-21; the same thing may apply to Ps. xxxvii; see verses 39 f. Incidentally, both psalms may have been composed for use in the cultus. None of these psalms gives expression to the solution of the problem and the comfort based on the hope of eternal life and the belief in a resurrection and a personal life to follow on death; as yet the belief in resurrection was no part of Jewish religion [3]).

---

[1]) MUNCH deletes these verses (*ZAW* 55, p. 44 f.), STAERK only v. 16, but VOLZ (*ZAW* 55, [1938], p. 236 ff.) rightly says that that is to delete the very point of the psalm.

[2]) M. LURJE "Studien zur Geschichte der sozialen und wirtschaftlichen Verhältnisse im israelitisch-jüdischen Reiche" (= *BZAW* 45), and MUNCH (*loc. cit.*) will interpret these psalms in terms of the "class strife", and thus fail to see the personal religious problem.

[3]) Neither Ps. xlix (against VOLZ in *ZAW* 55) nor xvi 10 nor lxxiii 24. 26 speak of a life after death; see *Offersang*, p. 240 ff. In *Horae Soederblomianae I* 1, p. 21 ff. LINDBLOM tries to demonstrate that the point in Ps. xlix is the con-

Ardour for the Law sometimes finds vent in a *hymn to the Law of Yahweh*, to which is now attributed nearly all the power-filled and saving qualities, for which the hymn used to praise Yahweh himself. This is the case in Ps. xix, where the author, in connection with an ancient hymn to the sun, celebrates the law of Yahweh as the outstanding work of his creation, the outcome of his "righteousness", and the truly enlightening and life-giving sun of men, and ends with a prayer that this poem of his may be acceptable to God and secure to himself protection against the designs and temptations of the demons (*zedim*) [1]). The same love for the Law is seen in a great many hymnal "motivations of the prayer" in Ps. cxix. The value of the Law, because it enlightens the ignorant and admonishes the faltering, is particularly emphasized. In psalms of prayer, and in laments in acute or permanent distress, the author will plead his ardour for the Law as a motivation of his prayer, and ask for more enlightenment in order to keep the commandments; this is very conspicuous in Ps. cxix.—But otherwise the influence of law religion on psalmography is not very discernible [2]).

One may ask how we shall then explain that such private poetry was included in the collection of cult psalms transmitted to us, or was even used in the official worship of the temple.

We have already seen how closely the "scribes" and the "learned" originally were connected with the temple staff, especially with the singers and the temple prophets, and how the learned gradually became the guards of the spiritual and literary traditions of the temple. There is every reason to think that they also became the last collectors of the psalms transmitted to us and the redactors of the canonical Psalter [3]). So there at least remains the possibility that

---

fidence that the rich ones will be taken away in "der summarischen eschatologischen Katastrophe", whereas the pious ones will be saved; but this seems to me incompatible with the very personal form of vers 16. Ps. xlix does not speak of the general eschatological judgment, but of God's judgment over every single man through the end which he takes, good or evil.

[1]) See the writer's *Psalmenstudien I. Åwän und die individuellen Klagepsalmen*. To what extent the present writer has modified his rather one-sided view in *PsSt. I* the reader may see in *Offersang*, p. 198 f., 251, 254 ff.—As for Ps. xix, cf. *Offersang*, p. 101.

[2]) If the expression "nomistic psalms" means psalms in which the typical Jewish form for "nomism" is a fundamental feature—which seems to be the true meaning of the word—then it is an exaggeration when H. Birkeland (*Die Feinde des Individuums in der israelitischen Psalmenliteratur*, p. 280 ff.) calls Pss. xxv, lxxxi, cxvi, cxliii and xxxii "nomistic psalms".

[3]) See *Offersang*, p. 466 ff.

some poems of their own have been included in the collection, which were never ritually used, such as Ps. i or cxxvii.

As for the thanksgiving psalms it is more easy to show how this *may* have happened. There is evidence for the custom of writing a thanksgiving psalm on a votive stela or on leather and placing it or laying it down "before Yahweh" in the temple [1]). In just such a way personal thanksgiving psalms like Ps. lxxiii and xlix, or xxxiv and xxxvii, and perhaps also a mixed supplicatory and laudatory psalm like cxix, may have been deposited as a votive and memorial gift to Yahweh and a testimony to future generations, and on a later occasion have been included in the treasury of psalms transmitted to us, the handing down of which was the function of the temple singers and the temple poets. In this way we can imagine that some of them may also have come to be used ritually in the cult.

VI

It is this learned, non-cultic psalmography which is followed up by the post-canonical, late Jewish psalmography.

We meet with two main types of the latter: poetry put into the mouths of the persons appearing in the *legendary stories*, and free, *independent poetry*.

The former group, to be found in the additions to the book of Daniel, in Judith and Tobit (Dan. ii 20-23; G iii 26-45; iii 52-9; Jud. xvi 2-18; Tob. xiii), are related to the poetry of biblical authors: Hannah's hymn of thanksgiving (1 Sam. ii 2 ff.), the prayer of Jonah (Jon. ii 1 ff.), the thanksgiving psalm of King Hezekiah (Jes. xxxviii 9 ff.), and so on (see above). They are anthems of praise of the power of God and of his protection of his pious ones and doxologies of the God of the fathers, who will some day restore his people. In the main the old hymnal style has been retained, partly with an eschatological element.

The latter group is found partly in Sirach, partly in the so-called Psalms of Solomon.

Alongside the real "words of wisdom" and exhortative and didactic poems on the pattern of wisdom, Sirach also composed psalms in the traditional psalm style [2]), but with recognizable elements

---

1) See *Offersang*, p. 294 f.

2) See BAUMGARTNER, *ZAW* 34, p. 161 ff.

from the ideas and forms of "wisdom"; a great deal of space is taken up by reflections. We find hymns in the I-form, having the greatness of Yahweh in nature for their subject, or speaking of Yahweh's wise and just rule of the world. At other times to his didactic poem are added hymnal motifs, which, in a more or less pure hymnal style, speak of God's judgment of the proud, or of his glorious revelation in nature, his wise ordering of the universe, and his loving kindness and his mercy in forgiving sins (x 14-18, xvi 18 f., xvi 26-xvii 24, xvii 29 f., xviii 1-7, xxiii 19 ff., xxxix 12-35, xlii 15-xliii 23). — Sirach avails himself of the hymnal style in a new way, when using it for a poem of homage to the pious patriarchs and kings and prophets of old (xliv 1-l 20). Elements from the poetry of wisdom sometimes make themselves felt in the style and in the didactic note.—The object is twofold: partly to give personal expression to the piety of the author and make him acceptable to God, partly to teach the disciples the proper fear of God and give them the proper knowledge of the character and the work of God.

The thanksgiving psalm of Sirach (li 1-12), evidently on a concrete occasion, has a more personal note: that of thanking for the help of God in the dangers to which the calumny of mighty enemies had exposed him. The style is the traditional one, in general terms. The "promise" of doxology, with which it ends according to traditional custom, has evidently been fulfilled by his composing this psalm and reciting it before his colleagues and disciples in the school of wisdom.

Sirach often speaks of prayer as well; he especially mentions prayer for help in illness, for forgiveness of sins and for healing (xxv 21, xxxviii 9). And sometimes we even meet with personal prayers from him. The prayer aims at the power of appropriate and seemly mode of expression, at becoming upright, humble and pure in thought and wishes (xxii 27-xxiii 6), that is to say, such virtues as were particularly important in the profession of a teacher of wisdom. That he also had the welfare of the people sincerely at heart may be seen from the prayer for the re-establishment of Israel (Hebr. text xxxvi 1-27), on the pattern of the national psalm of lamentation and the congregational prayer [1]). Even in the circle of the teachers of wisdom the hope for the future was lively. When Sirach approaches this subject, we also become aware of the influences from the prophetic style and from the promises of the cultic oracles; here these

[1]) See *Offersang* ch. vi (p. 192-226).

expressions are used to preach the faith by which the Jewish congregation lived.

VII

In the *Psalms of Solomon* we find elements from practically all the old psalm types. These 18 psalms were composed between the years 63 and 40 B.C. They have an actual historical background in a definite historical situation; it is the fall of the Maccabeans and the conquest of Palestine by Pompey which have occasioned most of these prayers and lamentations and confessions of sins and reflections, and the expressions of confident hope which they also contain—in spite of the hard chastening of the Lord, which has fallen even upon the pious, who are co-responsible and have to suffer for the joint sins of leaders and people.

The species of composition are here in the main the old classical ones—no new types have developed—but characteristic of them all is that the elements of reflection and "wisdom" are much stronger. It is characteristic also that the species of composition are much more mixed up, without any rules, than in the biblical psalms. It is very difficult to classify this late Jewish psalmography according to "species" ("Gattungen"), and such attempts are apt to become mechanical. But we constantly come across the old primary forms.

As to the form, the two groups "I-psalms" and "We-psalms" are both represented. But as for the content, there is no sharp limit between them. The poets identify themselves with their people, or more correctly, with the strict adherents of the Law, with the ideal congregation, and speak as its exponents. In fact, they played a leading part within the pious congregation. But often we meet their personal relation to the problems, and they speak in their own name, "I". They feel the concern of the true congregation as their own concern, and know that all true Israelites agree with them, both in their feeling of being "just", and in their confession of sins. They feel and express what every true Jew ought to feel and express.

Not all of these 18 psalms show the same clear connection with the historical background; some of them may be older than 63 B.C. So, for example, Ps. Sal. v, a hymn of praise with motifs from the thanksgiving psalm.

The typical mixture of hymn of praise and of wisdom poetry we find in Ps. Sal. x, the benediction of the man "whom the Lord remembers with reproving and whom He restrains from the way of evil with strokes". Cf. Ps. Sal. vi, the benediction over "the man whose heart is fixed to call upon the name of the Lord", and who experiences the blessings of the prayer—possibly meant as a thanksgiving psalm.—The well known *mashal* pattern: the ways of the just and of the ungodly, is the theme of Ps. Sal. iii; cf. Ps. i and cxii. It begins as a hymn of praise, "for good is a psalm to God from a glad heart". But the praise is more of an indirect kind, and soon takes the form of a didactic admonition. When the righteous stumbles, he acknowledges God's righteousness and 'searches His houses to remove all iniquity (done) by him in error", and he can do so because he knows that "they that fear the Lord shall rise to life eternal". The ungodly "curses his birthday", and "add sins to sins".—Of the same type is Ps. Sal. xiv.

At all events, Ps. Sal. xv and xvi are private thanksgiving psalms, the latter obviously inspired by the biblical Ps. xxxii.—In the thanksgiving psalm xiii, the political events are re-echoed; the poet thanks God because he has been saved from the catastrophe that has befallen the sinners. Contrary to the classical psalms, the poet speaks more of the fall of his antagonists, the "sinners", than of his own salvation; cf., however, Ps. lxxiii. Here the didactic style is obvious.

Some of the poems, for example, Ps. Sal. iv and xii, take us into the midst of the strife between the "ungodly" rulers and the pious circles. Here as a rule the form and style of the psalm of lamentation are used. The "lament" has the form of a description of the evil deeds and words of the "sinners", the "enemies" of the poet and his fellow-believers; thought and expression are influenced both by the rebukes of the prophets, and by the description of the wicked in the wisdom literature. The prayer is to the effect that God may remove and destroy the sinners; as in the biblical psalms, this prayer often takes the form of a curse. As in the classical style, the prayer ends by expressing "the confidence of being heard", for "the Lord's (word) is salvation for his servant Israel for ever".—To the apostrophe of the wicked man as "introitus", Ps. Sal. iv 1, cf. Ps. lii.

In other poems the catastrophe of 63 B.C. is the actual background. Ps. Sal. i is a penitential psalm of lamentation. Jerusalem confesses her sins, the sins of the dynasty and the ruling classes, and describes the catastrophe ("the lament").—In Ps. Sal. viii the poet himself expresses the confessions on behalf of himself and his people. The description of the calamities is mingled with religious reflections. The poem is a mixture of congregational psalm of lamentation in I-form and reflections; the disaster raises the problem of the common responsibility and of God's justice. "I thought upon the judgements of God since the creation", and (I) have now seen, that God is just; the pious have no other escape than God's own mercy upon which they set their hope.

The poet in Ps. Sal. ii has already seen the disgraceful end of Pompey in 48 B.C., and takes this as the beginning of God's hearing their prayers. This inspires him to a thanksgiving psalm. But still God's hand is heavy upon them; what has happened is not only a just punishment, but also a profanation of God's own city and temple. And so he has to put forth his lament and pray for salvation. From the point of view of "Gattung" and style, the poem is a mixture of lament and thanksgiving psalm, with reflections upon the religious problem.

An important place in the ideas of these poets was the *eschatological hope*, but still in the old nationalistic-political intra-mundane form. Ps. Sal. xvii is built up after the pattern of the psalm of lamentation and supplication. It starts with the confession of faith in "the Lord, our king for ever and ever", "our hope". How long shall we still wait upon him and the fulfilling of his promises? "But for our sins, sinners rose up against us". Then follows the lament, a description of all the disasters that have befallen them from the time before the rule of the Maccabees unto the present day, with confession of their sins. Then the prayer: "Behold, O Lord, and raise up unto them their king, the son of David, at the time which Thou seest that he may reign over Israel Thy servant"! The prayer includes a long description of the blessings that Messiah will bring to his people, and ends with the confidence of being heard. Here the influence from prophetic style and ideas is very prominent, and the expression of the confidence becomes a confession of the Messianic faith of the poet and his circles.

Very interesting is Ps. Sal. xi. It is composed after the pattern of Ps. lxxxii and lxxxv: first a description of the expected salvation in prophetic style, and then the prayer that the salvation may (soon) come. The original connection of this pattern with the promises and prayers at the great annual festival is quite clear [1]). The poet is obviously conscious of this liturgical model. But his definite ideas of the salvation are taken from Deutero-Isaiah. The point of the poem

---

[1]) See *PsSt II* p. 67 ff., 77, 160 f, *Offersang* p. 159 ff.

is the prayer for the coming salvation. The poet has resolved to begin with the description of the salvation just because these learned and "wise" poets felt themselves the heirs of the prophets. He wishes to inform the faithful that the salvation will come. But he also wishes to remind God of his promises; the first part of the poem is also a "motif of confidence": may God hear those who trust in Him and His promises!

VIII

The subjects treated are much the same both in the poems in the legendary stories and in the free poetry.

A prominent part is played by lamentations over disasters which have befallen the congregation, over pagan oppression and the licentiousness of ungodly people, and then there are prayers for the help of Yahweh, for deliverance and re-establishment. So the national hope for the future finds expression here; Jewish eschatology may be said to be the basis of this psalmography. It goes without saying that lamentations and prayers are expressed in the style of the psalm of lamentation. But the reflections and thoughts concerning the problem of retributive justice and God's rule of the world occupy much space. A leading emotion is the deep consciousness of sin and contrition on the part of the pious.

Sometimes the confidence of faith finds expression in direct prophecy, in a mixture of hymnal and prophetic psalm style.

Most of these poems have a personal character with a speaking ego. Sometimes, therefore, the poem in question is evidently meant to be the concrete confession of sins and penitential prayer or thanksgiving psalm for salvation which an individual has experienced. They very plainly testify to the conception prevailing in the circle of learned men, that such a prayer in the style of a psalm, recited before colleagues, was to be considered a pious work alongside cultic and ritual measures. And that its strongholds were the very circles of learned men can be seen amongst other things from the fact that Sirach has included a great many such personal poems in his book of wisdom.

But in spite of the I-form, the psalm will as a rule give expression to the emotions and thoughts and wishes of the whole circle and of the congregation. The author is conscious of being the spokesman of the congregation of pious people, of the "righteous" in general. He confesses what they all confess, he speaks in the name of "Jerusalem", he prays for the salvation which is the joint belief and hope of the congregation, for the re-establishment of Israel, the coming of Messiah. This psalmography has nothing to do with the cult. It is "private". But it is not popular, it is "learned". It is written in Hebrew, the language of the learned. It demonstrates knowledge of the thoughts and the style forms of the *ḥakåmim* as well as of the old psalm poetry. It belongs to the "school", to the circles of the "wise" and pious men, men of the type of Jesus b. Sirach, whose psalmography shows the closest relationship to the psalms of Solomon.

IX

Finally we also have to point to examples of psalmography which lived on among the first congregation of Jewish Christians: the *anthems of praise of Zacharias and Mary* in the gospel of Luke [1]. Their religious and ideological background is the eschatology of the Jewish congregation, now realized by the coming of the Messiah Jesus, and their stylistic pattern is ultimately the "enthronement psalms" in their eschatological aspect [2]. Here the rejoicings over the salvation already experienced through the very coming of Jesus-Messiah find expression in the ancient style of the epiphany psalm [3]; the hope for the future is being actualized through the new experience that in Christ God has again come to his people, and has created salvation and founded his kingdom for all future time.

Here, however, we have no longer to do with the poetry of a learned school, as in Sirach or the Psalms of Solomon. As contrasted with the psalms of Sirach, there does not here seem to be any strict metre; verses and hemistichs are of unequal length; the constituting element of the metrical structure is here in fact the "thought rhyme", the "parallelism" between the two hemistichs and the grouping of "distichs" ("bicola") two by two into short stanzas. What has been preserved of the traditional composition of the psalms is the hymnal style and note and the eschatological contents, which are finally based on the complex of ideas of the epiphany. That is what has now become new personally experienced reality to these authors. There-

---

1) Cf. H. GUNKEL, "Die Lieder in der Kindheitsgeschichte Jesu bei Lukas", *Festgabe für A. v. Harnack*, p. 43 ff.; H. SAHLIN, *Der Messias und das Gottesvolk. Studien zur protolukanischen Theologie*, p. 159 ff., 286 ff.

2) See *Offersang*, p. 183 ff., 186 ff., 189.

3) See *Psalmenstudien II. Das Thronbesteigungsfest Jahwäs und der Ursprung der Eschatologie*; *Offersang og Sangoffer*, p. 118-191.

fore these psalms, in a way different from that of the poetry of the Psalms of Solomon as well as of Sirach, are practically made up of hymnal-eschatological terms from the Old Testament: now the old promises given to the fathers in the Scripture have been turned into reality, and the authors are praising God for it. These psalms have not been composed out of the experiences of individuals only, but the individuals are speaking as members of the first Christian congregation; the author is speaking in the names of all the others ("we"), and what he has experienced is typical of them all. The starting-point of these psalms is the very faith and experience they have all had when joining the congregation, and which they are re-experiencing and praising there, when the congregation is gathered round the experience of salvation in Jesus Messiah.

The psalm tradition, kept alive by the learned psalmography in certain learned circles, is here reborn in a new and fresh way—in spite of all dependence on old patterns—in the Christian congregation, as an expression of something simultaneously experienced in the present and at the same time an object of hope for the future and of faith. In the assembly of the congregation, where anybody who "hath a psalm" (1 Cor. xiv 26; cf. verses 15-17) recites it to the edification of all, even these psalms sprang into life. Psalmography has returned to its original home: in the cultic assembly of the congregation, in the divine service.

DIE BEWÄHRUNG VON SALOMOS „GÖTTLICHER WEISHEIT"

VON

MARTIN NOTH

Bonn

Die bekannte Erzählung vom „salomonischen Urteil" in 1 Reg. iii 16-28 dient nach ihrem Schlusssatz als Erweis dafür, dass „göttliche Weisheit" in Salomo war (V. 28), nachdem Salomo bei der nächtlichen Traumtheophanie auf der „grossen Kultstätte" [1]) von Gibeon sich von Gott „Weisheit", und zwar speziell richterliche Weisheit, erbeten und daraufhin auch zugesagt erhalten hatte (1 Reg. iii 4-15). Das salomonische Urteil machte die Tatsache der „göttlichen Weisheit" in Salomo in „ganz Israel" öffentlich bekannt und anerkannt. Das Thema der Weisheit Salomos steht breit sogleich im Anfang der überlieferten Salomogeschichte, die nur in 1 Reg. iii 1-3 einige — übrigens literarisch nicht einheitliche und teilweise sekundäre — Notizen vorausschickt, um dann eben zunächst zum Thema der Weisheit Salomos überzugehen.

Literarisch und sachlich unabhängig von den Erzählungen in 1 Reg. iii 4-28 tritt innerhalb der Salomoüberlieferung der Gegenstand der Weisheit Salomos noch einmal in 1 Reg. v 9-14 auf [2]). Diesem letzteren Stück hat A. Alt eine grundlegende Untersuchung gewidmet [3]); in dieser wird einleuchtend und m. E. abschliessend gezeigt, dass es sich hier um eine „Naturweisheit" handelt, die nach der Art der aus dem alten Ägypten und dem alten Zweistromland bekannten „Listenwissenschaft" die Gesamtheit der Erscheinungen der sichtbaren und auch der unsichtbaren Welt zusammenzufassen und zu klassifizieren sich bemühte und die — das wäre vielleicht das

---

[1]) Zur Bedeutung des Wortes במה vgl. jetzt A. Schwarzenbach, *Die geographische Terminologie im Hebräischen des Alten Testamentes* (1954), p. 12 ff.

[2]) Von dem sporadischen sonstigen Auftreten dieses Gegenstandes in der Salomoüberlieferung, z. B. in der Erzählung vom Besuch der Königin von Saba in 1 Reg. x 1 ff., kann hier abgesehen werden.

[3]) A. Alt, „Die Weisheit Salomos", *ThLZ* 76 (1951), p. 139-144 = *Kleine Schriften zur Geschichte des Volkes Israel*, II (1953), p. 90-99.

Neue und Besondere bei Salomo — diese Zusammenfassungen und Klassifizierungen in die poetische Form von „Sprüchen" und „Liedern" zu bringen sich anschickte [1]). Es ist klar, dass diese Naturweisheit einen anderen Typus von „Weisheit" darstellt als die richterliche Weisheit, von der in 1 Reg. iii 4-28 die Rede ist. Nachdem die Überlieferung mit der Gestalt Salomos einmal die Erscheinung exemplarischer königlicher „Weisheit" verbunden hatte, ist dann in verschiedener Weise konkret diese Weisheit Salomos dargestellt worden.

Es ist nicht leicht, das überlieferungsgeschichtliche und chronologische Verhältnis zwischen 1 Reg. iii 4-28 und 1 Reg. v 9-14 zu bestimmen. Fest steht zunächst nur, dass beide Stücke in der deuteronomistischen Darstellung der Salomogeschichte enthalten waren; und wahrscheinlich ist darüber hinaus, dass sie auch bereits in dem vom Deuteronomisten zitierten „Buch der Salomogeschichte" (1 Reg. xi 41) gestanden hatten. Denn als vordeuteronomistisch sind beide ziemlich sicher anzusprechen. Für 1 Reg. v 9-14 ist das schon aus dem Umstand zu erschliessen, dass hier die Weisheit Salomos als „Naturweisheit" gedacht ist, Salomo also als Repräsentant eines Typs von Weisheit erscheint, der nach allem, was wir wissen, schon zur Zeit des Deuteronomisten in Israel ganz hinter dem Typ der Lebensweisheit in den Hintergrund getreten war. Im übrigen ist schon formgeschichtlich die Eigenart des Abschnitts 1 Reg. v 9-14 sehr schwer zu bestimmen. Um eine volkstümliche Erzählung handelt es sich offenbar nicht; dazu fehlt es zu sehr an einem bestimmten anschaulichen Inhalt. An eine Herkunft aus den amtlichen Königsannalen aber wird man auch schwerlich denken dürfen trotz der in v 12 mitgeteilten Zahlen für die „Sprüche" und „Lieder" Salomos; denn allgemeine und zusammenfassende Urteile über den König ohne erkennbaren Zusammenhang mit konkreten Einzelvorgängen aus seiner Regierungszeit sind kaum in den offiziellen Annalen aufgezeichnet worden. Man muss fragen, ob wir es bei 1 Reg. v 9-14 überhaupt mit einer ursprünglich selbständigen literarischen Einheit zu tun haben und nicht vielmehr nur mit einer allgemeinen Einleitung zu einem uns nicht mehr sicher bekannten literarischen Stück. Von da aus gesehen erscheint die Vermutung von

---

[1]) Alt, *a. a. O.*, p. 140 bezw. p. 91 f. erinnert mit Recht an einige Spuren solcher in poetische Form gefassten Naturweisheit in den Büchern Hiob und Proverbien.

ALT [1]), es könnte sich um die Einführung zu einer „von Salomo selbst oder in seinem Auftrag bei Hofe verfassten Sammlung von Weisheitssprüchen und -liedern" handeln, immerhin erwägenswert, wozu nur zu bemerken wäre, dass ebenso gut eine nachträglich dem Salomo zugeschriebene Sammlung von Weisheitssprüchen und -liedern in Betracht zu ziehen wäre [2]). Damit ist zugleich gesagt, dass zeitlich dieser Abschnitt nicht mehr mit auch nur einiger Sicherheit festzulegen ist. Allzuweit herunter bis in die zeitliche Nähe des Deuteronomisten wird man wohl nicht gehen dürfen mit Rücksicht auf den hier in Erscheinung tretenden Typ der Naturweisheit. In diesem Rahmen aber wird man mit ALT a.a.O. die Frage nach Zeit und Herkunft offen lassen müssen.

Ähnliches gilt aber auch für 1 Reg. iii 4-28. Dieser Abschnitt besteht aus zwei Einheiten, die aber doch zusammengehören. Denn die Erzählung vom salomonischen Urteil gibt sich besonders in ihrem Schlussvers (V. 28) als Beweis für die in der Traumoffenbarung von Gibeon dem Salomo zugesprochene „Weisheit"; und die Geschichte von der Traumoffenbarung lässt etwas über die Auswirkung der dem Salomo gegebenen Weisheit erwarten. Ja, mit der Betonung der Sorge Salomos, dass er fähig sein möge, das Volk Jahwes zu „richten", scheint die Geschichte von der Traumoffenbarung geradezu auf die Erzählung vom salomonischen Urteil hin formuliert zu sein. Gleichwohl kann sie nicht ausschliesslich als Einleitung zu der Erzählung vom salomonischen Urteil verfasst worden sein; denn in der Rolle, die Gibeon als Stätte der Gottesoffenbarung spielt, enthält sie ein selbständiges Element, das aus der Erzählung vom salomonischen Urteil nicht ableitbar ist. Man wird also in der Mitteilung einer Gottesoffenbarung an Salomo in Gibeon ein besonderes Überlieferungsstück unbekannter Herkunft sehen müssen, das zu einer auf die Erzählung vom salomonischen Urteil hinführenden Geschichte literarisch ausgestaltet worden ist. Der Komplex 1 Reg. iii 4-28 ist nun sicher vordeuteronomistisch. Zwar finden sich in V. 4-15 offenkundig deuteronomistische Wendungen, aber sie stehen in deuteronomistischen Zusätzen zum ursprünglichen Bestand, wie hier nicht genauer ausgeführt zu werden braucht. Allein schon die Nennung der „grossen Kultstätte" von Gibeon, auf der Salomo auch noch Opfer darbringt (V. 4), beweist, dass die

---

[1]) ALT, *a. a. O.*, p. 139 bezw. p. 90.

[2]) Allenfalls könnte in 1 Reg. v 9-14 die allgemeine Einleitung zu der Geschichte vom Besuch der Königin von Saba vorliegen.

Grundlage der Geschichte vordeuteronomistisch ist. Dazu kommt dann noch das Verhältnis von iii 4 ff. zu ix 1 ff. In ix 1-9 liegt ein durchweg deuteronomistisches Stück vor, das auf die Geschichte von der Traumoffenbarung in Gibeon zurückweist und als ein Gegenstück zu dieser Geschichte verfasst worden ist und dabei geflissentlich keinen Ort nennt, an dem die zweite Gottesoffenbarung an Salomo statthatte, das also jedenfalls die Geschichte von der Traumoffenbarung in Gibeon als schon vorhanden und gegeben voraussetzt. Für die zeitliche Ansetzung von 1 Reg. iii 4-28 bleibt nun die ganze Spanne zwischen Salomo und dem Deuteronomisten als Möglichkeit offen. Mit Rücksicht auf die Verarbeitung des Überlieferungselements von einer Gotteserscheinung an Salomo in Gibeon, das nicht nach einer späten Konstruktion aussieht, sondern auf irgend eine noch lebendige Tradition der Salomozeit zurückzugehen scheint, wird man auch in diesem Falle nicht gern zeitlich allzuweit heruntergehen wollen.

Nach alledem lässt sich also nicht einmal das zeitliche Verhältnis der beiden Stücke 1 Reg. iii 4-28 und 1 Reg. v 9-14 zueinander auch nur einigermassen bestimmen. Die beiden Überlieferungen von der richterlichen Weisheit Salomos und von der Naturweisheit Salomos stehen für uns also nebeneinander als zwei verschiedene Ausführungen des Themas von der Weisheit Salomos, ohne dass sich eine Prius für die eine der beiden Ausführungen ergäbe. Dass später vielleicht schon das „Buch der Salomogeschichte" und dann jedenfalls der deuteronomistische Geschichtsschreiber die erstere bevorzugt und sogar an die Spitze der ganzen Salomoüberlieferung gestellt hat, während die letztere an wenig betonter Stelle im Zusammenhang mit den Nachrichten über den Glanz und Reichtum des salomonischen Königtums steht, besagt höchstens für eine jüngere Einschätzung dieser beiden Typen von Weisheit etwas, aber nichts für die alte Überlieferungsgeschichte des Themas von der Weisheit Salomos. Umgekehrt wird man freilich auch nicht die knappe, notizenartige Form von 1 Reg. v 9-14 gegenüber der erzählerischen Ausführlichkeit und überlieferungsgeschichtlichen Zusammengesetztheit des Doppelabschnitts 1 Reg. iii 4-28 im Sinne grösserer Ursprünglichkeit und höheren Alters verstehen dürfen, da 1 Reg. v 9-14 nicht eine originale, selbständige Einheit zu sein scheint.

In 1 Reg. v 9-14 wird ausdrücklich auf die internationalen Zusammenhänge jener Naturweisheit hingewiesen, von deren besonders glücklicher und erfolgreicher Pflege und Weiterbildung durch Salomo die Rede ist. Auch die im salomonischen Urteil sich bewährende richterliche Weisheit Salomos hatte in der Weise, in der von ihr erzählt wird, internationale Zusammenhänge. Das wird zwar nicht erwähnt — es hätte ja berichtet werden können, dass Salomo als weiser Richter alle anderen Könige übertraf [1]) —, es ergibt sich aber aus der Tatsache, dass Volkserzählungen von erstaunlich weisen richterlichen Entscheidungen sehr weit verbreitet und wahrscheinlich von Volk zu Volk gewandert sind und dass speziell Anekdoten sehr ähnlichen Inhalts wie die Geschichte vom salomonischen Urteil sich in mannigfachen Varianten im Erzählungsgut der Völker finden. H. GRESSMANN hat vor längerer Zeit einmal das bekannte Material an Parallelen zu 1 Reg. iii 16-28 zusammengestellt [2]). Sie stammen aus dem vorderen Orient, aus Indien und China. Alles, was GRESSMANN beibringt, ist allerdings erst aus erheblich jüngerer Zeit bezeugt als die alttestamentliche Erzählung; aus dem alten vorderen Orient sind Seitenstücke zur Geschichte vom salomonischen Urteil bis jetzt nicht bekannt. Gleichwohl ist nicht damit zu rechnen, dass etwa in 1 Reg. iii der Ausgangspunkt für das sich weit verbreitende Erzählungsmotiv zu suchen sei. Schon GRESSMANN hat darauf hingewiesen [3]), dass die Einführung von zwei Dirnen, die beide annähernd gleichzeitig einen Sohn geboren hatten, als ein vermutlich sekundäres Element in der Ausgestaltung des Erzählungsmotivs zu betrachten sei und dass man es für wahrscheinlich halten müsse, dass es sich in der ursprünglichen Form um zwei Frauen eines Mannes gehandelt habe, für die ein lebender Sohn zugleich die bevorzugte Stellung der Mutter des Erben und der vom Manne „geliebten" Frau bedeutete oder jedenfalls bedeuten konnte. Im Alten Testament wäre also mit Rücksicht auf das üble Verhalten der einen der beiden Frauen die Geschichte aus dem Milieu des Hauses eines Mannes mit mehreren rechtmässigen Gemahlinnen in das Milieu eines Dirnenhauses verlegt worden, und zwar für beide Frauen, da ja die Erzählung notwendig das gleiche äussere Erscheinungsbild für beide Frauen voraussetzte, das die Entscheidung des Streitfalles so schwer machte. Wir müssen danach annehmen, dass die Geschichte vom

---

[1]) Eine solche Bemerkung findet sich tatsächlich in 1 Reg. x 23 (vgl. auch iii 12), aber eben nicht in dem Stück vom salomonischen Urteil selbst.

[2]) H. GRESSMANN, „Das salomonische Urteil", *Deutsche Rundschau* 130 (1907), p. 212-228.

[3]) So GRESSMANN, *a. a. O.* und *Die älteste Geschichtsschreibung und Prophetie Israels, Die Schriften des Alten Testaments in Auswahl* II 1 ([2]1921), p. 198; vgl. auch H. GUNKEL, *Das Märchen im Alten Testament* (1921), p. 145 f.

salomonischen Urteil aus wanderndem Erzählungsgut aufgenommen und in Einzelzügen vom alttestamentlichen Erzähler umgebildet worden ist. Ihre Herkunft ist auf Grund des vorhandenen Materials kaum noch sicher zu ermitteln. Da aus Indien Parallelen bekannt sind, die in dem genannten Punkte die vermutete ursprüngliche Form bieten, hat GRESSMANN und haben nach ihm andere Indien als Heimat angenommen. Diese Möglichkeit ist nicht völlig auszuschliessen, da es sehr alte geschichtliche und wirtschaftliche Beziehungen Indiens zum vorderen Orient gegeben hat; aber ein Beweis ist für sie nicht zu erbringen, weil die indischen Parallelen erst für so viel spätere Zeit nachzuweisen sind und damit gerechnet werden muss, dass nach Indien die Geschichte von anderswoher eingewandert ist. Man muss sich also damit abfinden, dass ihre Herkunft nicht mehr zu ermitteln ist; wahrscheinlich aber bleibt, dass ihr Ursprung nicht im Alten Testament zu suchen ist, dass sie vielmehr vom alttestamentlichen Erzähler aus dem wandernden Erzählungsgut aufgenommen wurde, dass es sich also wie bei der Naturweisheit so auch bei der richterlichen Weisheit Salomos um ein „internationales" Phänomen handelt.

Was nun inhaltlich an der Erzählung vom salomonischen Urteil bemerkenswert ist, ist die „profane", „aufgeklärte" Einstellung des Ganzen. Darin steht diese Erzählung den Nachrichten über die Naturweisheit Salomos in 1 Reg. v 9-14 sehr nahe. Zwar wird abschliessend das salomonische Urteil als Erweis „göttlicher Weisheit", die in Salomo war, bezeichnet (V. 28), ebenso wie die Mitteilungen über die Naturweisheit Salomos mit der Bemerkung eingeleitet werden, dass Gott dem Salomo „Weisheit und sehr viel Verständnis gegeben" habe (1 Reg. v 9); aber im Grunde handelt es sich in der Substanz dieser Überlieferungen um „Weisheit Salomos". Beim salomonischen Urteil wird gar nicht mit anderen Möglichkeiten der Aufklärung des zunächst dunklen Sachverhalts gerechnet. Das alte israelitische Recht hatte solche Möglichkeiten vorgesehen. Natürlich gibt es in diesem Recht keinen Rechtssatz, der speziell den der richterlichen Entscheidung Salomos vorgelegten Sonderfall im Auge hätte. Doch musste nach altisraelitischen Begriffen dieser Fall zum Gebiete der Eigentumsvergehen gehören; und zwar handelte es sich um den besonderen Tatbestand, dass eine Person eine andere des Diebstahls beschuldigt hatte, diese andere aber den Diebstahl geleugnet hatte und keine Zeugen vorhanden waren, die zur Aufklärung hätten beitragen können. Es gab kasuistische Rechtssätze, die hier anwendbar waren, die zwar konkret für andere Objekte des

Diebstahls oder auch der Veruntreuung formuliert waren, die aber in der Rechtsprechung sinngemäss auf entsprechende Fälle angewandt werden konnten und gewiss auch angewandt worden sind und die auch im vorliegenden Falle hätten Anwendung finden können. In Ex. xxii 9, 10 findet sich die Bestimmung: Wenn jemand seinem Nächsten einen Esel oder ein Rind oder ein Stück Kleinvieh oder sonst ein Tier zur Aufbewahrung gibt und dieses stirbt oder sich ein Glied bricht oder, ohne dass jemand es sieht, weggetrieben wird, so soll ein Eid bei Jahwe zwischen ihnen beiden geschworen werden, ob er (der Aufbewahrer) nicht etwa seine Hand nach der Sache seines Nächsten ausgestreckt hat, und sein Besitzer soll (den Eid) annehmen; er (der Aufbewahrer) braucht dann keinen Ersatz zu leisten. Es hätte nahe gelegen, die Angelegenheit der beiden Frauen in der Geschichte vom salomonischen Urteil in analoger Weise durch einen Eid aufzuklären. Geschah das nicht, weil von den beiden Dirnen nicht zu erwarten war, dass sie die mit einem Schwur ausgesprochene Selbstverfluchung ernst nehmen würden, weil sie vielmehr leichtfertig schwören würden in ihrem eigenen Interesse? Wenn eine solche Erwägung etwa im Hintergrunde der Erzählung gestanden haben sollte, so würde man jedenfalls schon nicht mehr mit einer objektiven Wirkung der eidlichen Selbstverfluchung gerechnet haben, wie sie doch nach der ursprünglichen Auffassung mit der Eidesleistung verbunden war. Es hätte aber nach altisraelitischem Rechte auch noch eine andere Möglichkeit der Ermittlung des Sachverhalts gegeben. Unmittelbar vor dem soeben angeführten Rechtssatz stehen im Bundesbuch die Bestimmungen (Ex. xxii 7, 8): Wenn der Dieb (der aus einem Hause anvertrautes Gut gestohlen hat) nicht gefunden wird, so soll der Besitzer des Hauses (da er nicht nachweisen kann, dass das anvertraute Gut aus seinem Hause gestohlen worden ist) vor die Götter treten, ob er nicht etwa seine Hand nach der Sache seines Nächsten ausgestreckt hat. Bei jedem Falle von Unterschlagung, handle es sich um ein Rind, einen Esel, ein Stück Kleinvieh, einen Mantel oder sonst um irgend etwas abhanden Gekommenes, wenn er (d.h. der Eigentümer des Verlorenen) sagt: Das ist es!, soll die Sache der beiden vor die Götter kommen; wen dann die Götter für schuldig erklären, der soll seinem Nächsten doppelten Ersatz leisten [1]). Hier ist also im Falle einer ungeklärten

---

[1]) Auf die literarischen und rechtsgeschichtlichen Probleme der angeführten Sätze aus dem Bundesbuch braucht hier nicht eingegangen zu werden; in jedem

Eigentumsangelegenheit, in der Behauptung gegen Behauptung steht, ein Gottesurteil vorgesehen. Wie das Gottesurteil herbeizuführen wäre, wird nicht gesagt; in anderen Zusammenhängen weiss die alttestamentliche Überlieferung von der Durchführung von Gottesurteilen zur Ermittlung von Schuldigen zu berichten, sei es durch eine magisch wirkende Probe mit den einer Schuld verdächtigen Personen (vgl. Num. v 11 ff.) oder durch ein Losverfahren (vgl. Jos. vii 14 ff.; 1 Sam. xiv 38 ff.). An diese sakralen Möglichkeiten der Aufklärung eines unbekannten Tatbestandes denkt die Erzählung vom salomonischen Urteil anscheinend überhaupt nicht mehr; in ihr kommt alles an auf die grosse Weisheit des menschlichen Richters, der in einem besonders schwierigen Falle der Rechtsfindung doch noch einen Weg findet, um die Schuldfrage zu klären. Zwar ist diese Weisheit eine „göttliche Weisheit", d.h. ein Geschenk Gottes, wie alles, was ein Mensch hat, von Gott gegeben ist; aber sie ist doch nun „in" Salomo, sie ist sein Besitz, mit dem er wirken kann, und sie erübrigt ein „Befragen" Gottes in Einzelfällen der Rechtsfindung.

Das entspricht nun durchaus dem allgemeinen Charakter der „Weisheit", sei sie nun Naturweisheit oder richterliche Weisheit oder auch schlichte Lebensweisheit. Es ist bemerkenswert und muss ausdrücklich festgestellt werden, dass im Alten Testament der Begriff der „Weisheit" nur sehr selten und nur in ganz bestimmten Wendungen und erst ziemlich spät mit Gott in Verbindung gebracht wird. Dass Gott „weise" sei, wird nur ein einziges Mal im Alten Testament ausgesagt, und zwar an einer Stelle (Jes. xxxi 2), an der diese Aussage offensichtlich ironisch gemeint ist. Der Prophet spricht in einem „Wehe"-Ruf von denen, die nach Ägypten hinabgehen, um über ägyptische Waffenhilfe zu verhandeln, auf die sie sich verlassen wollen, die aber dabei nach Jahwe nicht fragen; dieser aber — so fährt der Prophet fort — ist „auch weise" und wird die Machenschaften der auf ihre politische Klugheit so stolzen Judäer zunichte machen. Die Meinung ist offenbar die: Wenn die Judäer so weise zu handeln glauben, so ist jedenfalls Jahwe „auch weise", er ist es erst recht und noch mehr [1]). Hier wird das Wort חכם durch die Übersetzung „weise" gar nicht ganz treffend wiedergegeben;

Falle handelt es sich um Satzungen altisraelitischen, der Substanz nach vorsalomonischen Rechtes.

[1]) Die auf diese Aussage folgenden beiden Worte in Jes. xxxi 2 sind leider textlich nicht in Ordnung und nicht mehr sicher wiederherzustellen.

man sollte besser übersetzen „klug", ja vielleicht sogar „schlau". Zwar wird im Ugaritischen von dem Gotte El huldigend die durchaus ernst gemeinte Aussage gemacht, dass er „weise" (*ḥkm*) sei (51 iv 41; 51 v 65; ʿnt v 38; vgl. auch 126 iv 3 GORDON, *Ugaritic Handbook*). Aber im Alten Testament hat man jedenfalls in der früheren Zeit Hemmungen gehabt, das Prädikat „weise" auf Gott anzuwenden, weil mit ihm allzu sehr der Gedanke an menschliche Klugheit verbunden war. Die feierliche neutestamentlich-paulinische Prädikation Gottes als des „allein Weisen" (Röm. xvi 27) und der „im Geheimnis waltenden göttlichen Weisheit" (1 Kor. ii 7) könnte kaum im Alten Testament stehen und geht schwerlich auf alttestamentliche Auffassungen zurück. An einigen gerade ziemlich alten alttestamentlichen Stellen wird der Stamm חכם im Sinne von „Schlauheit", „List", ja „Verschlagenheit" gebraucht. Nach 2 Sam. xiii 3 machte ein „sehr weiser" Freund des Davidsohnes Amnon diesem einen verschmitzt ausgedachten Vorschlag, wie er zur Erfüllung seiner heissen Liebe zu seiner Halbschwester Thamar würde kommen können; und nach Ex. i 10 J beschlossen der Pharao und die Ägypter, sich Israel gegenüber „weise zu verhalten" (חכם hitp.), d.h. sie zu überlisten. Es ist nach alledem fraglich, ob man gut tut, den hebräischen Stamm חכם besonders hinsichtlich seiner älteren Vorkommen, durchweg mit „weise" wiederzugeben. Diese Wiedergabe trifft die Sache nicht ganz genau. THOMAS MANN hat einmal auf Grund des Gebrauchs der Worte „weise, Weisheit" in der deutschen Bibelübersetzung die Bemerkung gemacht, dass „Weisheit eine ins Schelmische gesteigerte Klugheit" sei [1]). Er hat damit treffend zum Ausdruck gebracht, dass der Begriff „Weisheit" in der deutschen Bibelübersetzung nicht ganz und jedenfalls nicht immer das bezeichnet, woran im Deutschen bei diesem Begriff gedacht zu werden pflegt; denn nach deutschem Sprachgebrauch müsste man den zitierten Satz eher dahin umkehren, dass „Klugheit eine ins Schelmische gesteigerte Weisheit" sei.

Es ist nach alledem so, dass im Alten Testament bei dem Begriff „Weisheit" — diese nun einmal eingebürgerte Übersetzung wird dabei trotz des soeben Gesagten beibehalten — zunächst an menschliche Findigkeit, Geschicklichkeit, Klugheit [2]) zu denken ist; und in dieser Sphäre bewegen sich auch die alttestamentlichen Erzählungen

---

[1]) THOMAS MANN, *Joseph und seine Brüder* (Stockholmer Gesamtausgabe), p. 1976.

[2]) Noch in späten alttestamentlichen Quellen wird die Geschicklichkeit eines Handwerkers als „Weisheit" bezeichnet (Ex. xxviii 3 P. u. ö.).

von Salomos Weisheit. Es ist die Sphäre des Menschen und nicht die Gottes. Von Gott sagt man, dass er „weise macht", „Weisheit lehrt", „Weisheit gibt", so wie er beispielsweise auch „reich macht", „Reichtum gibt" [1]). Es sind im allgemeinen ziemlich junge Stücke der alttestamentlichen Literatur, in denen in dieser Form von der menschlichen Weisheit als einer Gabe Gottes die Rede ist (Ex. xxviii 3; xxxi 3, 6, xxxv 31, 35, xxxvi 1, 2; Ps. li 8, cxix 98; Iob. xxxv 11, xxxviii 36; Prov. ii 6; Eccles. ii 26; Dan. i 17, ii 21, 23; vgl. auch Ps. xix 8, wo vom „Gesetz Jahwes" gesagt wird, dass es „weise macht"). Die ältesten alttestamentlichen Aussagen darüber, dass Gott Weisheit gibt, sind diejenigen, die sich auf die Weisheit Salomos beziehen (vgl. ausser den schon erwähnten Stellen in 1 Reg. iii und v noch 1 Reg. v 26; x 24). Von der Weisheit Gottes selbst in dem Sinne, dass sie ein Besitz, ein Vermögen Gottes sei [2]), ist nur sehr selten und wiederum nur in ziemlich späten Stücken des Alten Testaments die Rede, und zwar speziell mit Bezug auf Gott als Schöpfer, der alles „mit Weisheit" geschaffen hat (Ps. civ 24; Iob xxxviii 37; Prov. iii 19); nur ganz selten wird in diesem Sachzusammenhang determiniert von „seiner (= Gottes) Weisheit" gesprochen (Jer. x 12; li 15). Erst im Danielbuch wird in einem allgemeineren Sinne die Weisheit als ein Besitz Gottes bezeichnet (Dan. ii 20; vgl. auch v 11). Älter sind einige Stellen, die nicht Gott selbst, sondern der Umgebung Gottes „Weisheit" zuschreiben. Hier kommt vor allem 2 Sam. xiv 20 in Betracht, wo die exemplarische Weisheit des „Gottesboten", des „Gottesengels" genannt wird; und vielleicht darf in diesen Sachzusammenhang auch die sehr singuläre Aussage von Jes. xi 2 gestellt werden, nach der der „Geist Jahwes", mit dem der messianische König ausgestattet werden soll, u.a. als ein „Geist von Weisheit" zu verstehen ist. An dieser Stelle ist allerdings zugleich an die richterliche Weisheit gedacht, die ein König haben soll, wenn er ein rechter König sein will. Endlich sind noch die beiden Stellen zu nennen, an denen allgemein die Weisheit in Beziehung gesetzt

---

[1]) Vgl. das Nebeneinander von Weisheit und Reichtum u.a. als Gaben Gottes in der Salomogeschichte von 1 Reg. iii 11 ff.

[2]) In 1 Reg. iii 28 ist von der „Weisheit Gottes" in dem Sinne die Rede, dass sie eine Gabe Gottes ist. Dazu ist zu stellen auch die merkwürdige Formulierung von Esr. vii 25: „die Weisheit deines (= Esras) Gottes, die in deiner Hand ist". Mit der „Weisheit" ist hier das Gesetz(buch) gemeint, ähnlich wie in Deut. iv 6 das Israel gegebene Gottesgesetz als Quelle der „Weisheit" Israels bezeichnet wird, die es vor anderen Völkern auszeichnet. Auch in Esr. vii 25 handelt es sich also bei der „Weisheit Gottes" um die von Gott gegebene Weisheit.

wird zu der himmlischen Welt, zu der „Ratsversammlung" Gottes (Iob xv 8; Prov. xxx 3 [1])).

Damit ist die Reihe der alttestamentlichen Stellen, die die Begriffe „weise", „Weisheit" in irgend eine Beziehung zu Gott setzen, aber auch schon zu Ende. Ihr steht die sehr lange Reihe der Stellen gegenüber, an denen die „Weisheit" auf Menschen bezogen wird. Es ist ganz deutlich, dass man im Alten Testament nur sehr zögernd das Prädikat der „Weisheit" Gott zugesprochen hat, dass man abgesehen von ganz späten Stellen gelegentlich die Schöpferweisheit Gottes ausgesagt, im übrigen aber an einer Reihe von Stellen die Weisheit nur so zu Gott in Beziehung gesetzt hat, dass sie als eine Gabe Gottes gepriesen wurde wie andere Gaben Gottes auch, die von Menschen empfangen werden; auch dies letztere vorwiegend in späten Stücken der alttestamentlichen Literatur. In der Salomoüberlieferung allerdings taucht, und zwar sowohl in dem Abschnitt über die richterliche Weisheit wie in dem über die Naturweisheit Salomos, schon verhältnismässig früh die Bezeichnung der Weisheit Salomos als einer Gabe Gottes auf; denn es ist kaum angängig, nur um dieser Aussage willen die beiden genannten Abschnitte stark herunterzudatieren, wenn anderweitige Argumente dafür nicht vorliegen. Vielmehr ist anzunehmen, dass trotz des schon ziemlich frühen Auftretens der Gedanke, dass zu den Gaben Gottes die menschliche Weisheit gehöre, im Ganzen des alttestamentlichen Glaubens verhältnismässig wenig Gewicht hatte, so dass er weiterhin nur sporadisch erscheint, bis er erst in später, nachexilischer Zeit sich etwas häufiger meldet.

Dass die Überlieferungen von der Weisheit Salomos, und zwar speziell die Erzählung von der Bewährung von Salomos richterlicher Weisheit, kaum sehr späten Datums sind, dafür spricht die Tatsache, dass sie in ihrer oben besprochenen „profanen" Haltung merkwürdig eng verwandt sind mit anderen alttestamentlichen Überlieferungen, die die Zeit und Person Salomos betreffen und die aller Wahrscheinlichkeit nach auch literarisch nicht sehr viel jünger sind als die Zeit, von der sie handeln. So wie die Naturweisheit Salomos im Zusammenhang mit der altorientalischen „Listenwissenschaft" nach der Überlieferung ein erstaunlicher und überragender Erweis aufnehmender und ordnender menschlicher Erkenntnis war, so bewährte sich im Richterspruch Salomos menschliche Klugheit und Findigkeit, die die

[1]) Mit קדשים sind in Prov. xxx 3 offenbar die Wesen der himmlischen Umgebung Gottes gemeint.

älteren sakralen Möglichkeiten der Rechtsfindung in schwierigen und ungeklärten Fällen entbehrlich machte. An diese Möglichkeiten scheint in 1 Reg. iii gar nicht mehr gedacht zu werden; alles kommt hier darauf an, dass ein menschlicher Richter kraft der ihm innewohnenden „Weisheit" einen Weg findet, einen wegen des Fehlens von Zeugen dunklen Fall so aufzuklären, dass die getroffene richterliche Entscheidung allgemein einleuchtet. In ähnlicher Weise tritt auch anderwärts menschliches Vermögen, sei es auch ein von Gott gegebenes Vermögen, an die Stelle des Gebrauchs bestimmter alter sakraler Möglichkeiten. Die Überlieferung vom Aufstieg Davids in 1 Sam. xvi 14-2 Sam. v 10 weiss zwar noch davon zu berichten, dass David gelegentlich „Jahwe befragte", wenn es um eine bestimmte Entscheidung ging. Als er hörte, dass die Philister die Stadt Kegila bekämpften, „fragte er bei Jahwe an", ob er gegen die Philister ziehen solle, und erhielt von Jahwe eine positive Antwort, die dann noch einmal auf eine erneute Anfrage hin wiederholt wurde, nachdem die Gefolgsleute Davids trotz der ersten Orakelantwort Bedenken angemeldet hatten (1 Sam. xxiii 1-4); und nach der Katastrophe Sauls „fragte" David wiederum „bei Jahwe an", ob er nunmehr in eine der Städte von Juda hinaufziehen solle, und nachdem er eine bejahende Antwort erhalten hatte, fragte er weiter, wohin er ziehen solle (2 Sam. ii 1, 2). In den beiden genannten Fällen wird nicht gesagt, auf welche Weise die göttliche Orakelantwort ermittelt wird. Hingegen wird in 1 Sam. xxiii 9-12 und xxx 7, 8, wo es sich ebenfalls um Orakelanfragen Davids ähnlicher Art handelt, erzählt, dass der Priester Ebjathar mit dem Ephod herbeigeholt wurde, um Frage und Antwort mit Hilfe seiner Orakelmöglichkeiten zu vermitteln. In derselben Überlieferung vom Aufstieg Davids steht aber doch auch bereits die breit ausgeführte Erzählung von 1 Sam. xx, nach der die Frage, ob David in der Umgebung Sauls verbleiben oder aber angesichts der Missgunst Sauls fliehen solle, nicht mehr durch eine Orakelanfrage entschieden wird, sondern durch ein zwischen David und Jonathan verabredetes menschlich kluges Verfahren der Erprobung Sauls und der Benachrichtigung Davids. Noch mehr spielt in der Überlieferung von der Thronnachfolge Davids (2 Sam. vii, ix-xx; 1 Reg. i, ii) die menschliche Klugheit an Stelle der Gottesbefragung eine Rolle. Schon in der Angelegenheit eines etwaigen Tempelbaus in Jerusalem fragt David nicht bei Jahwe an, sondern legt nur seine Erwägung dem Hofpropheten Nathan vor, der seinerseits daraufhin zunächst von sich aus eine ermutigende Antwort gibt, dann allerdings in der gleichen Sache dem David ein Gotteswort zu überbringen hat, das die Dinge definitiv entscheidet [1]). In 2 Sam. xiv 20 wird seitens der Frau aus Thekoa David gespriesen als ein Mann mit so grosser Weisheit, dass diese Weisheit zu vergleichen ist mit „der Weisheit des Gottesboten" und darin besteht, „alles zu wissen, was auf Erden vorgeht". Ein so weiser König bedarf der Gottesbefragung kaum noch, besonders dann, wenn er auch noch so kluge Ratgeber hat, wie jener Ahitophel war, dessen „Ratschlag, den er in jener Zeit zu geben pflegte", „sowohl bei David wie bei Absalom" so viel galt, „wie wenn man das Gotteswort befragte", d.h. auf irgend eine Weise sich ein Gottesorakel geben liess (2 Sam. xvi 23). Wenn gleichwohl Absalom dem Rat dieses Ahitophel nicht folgte, so bedeutete das für ihn Unheil und Untergang (2 Sam. xvii 14). Die befremdliche Tatsache aber, dass Absalom den Rat Ahitophels verwarf, beruhte auf einer Wirkung Jahwes, der durch eine solche Lenkung eines menschlichen Entschlusses den Geschichtsverlauf so führte, wie es seinem Willen entsprach. Auch dieser Zug, dass Jahwe durch die Vermittlung von menschlichen Entschlüssen die Geschichte bestimmt, gehört zu den Eigenarten der hier in das Auge gefassten alttestamentlichen Literatur. Er findet sich wieder in der Erzählung über Ahia von Silo und Jerobeam (1 Reg. xi *29-39; xii *1-31; xiv 1-18) [2]), nach der die göttliche Absicht und Ankündigung, dass Jerobeam König von Israel werden sollte, dadurch verwirklicht wurde, dass Rehabeam in der entscheidenden Verhandlung mit den Israeliten in Sichem unter der Wirkung einer göttlichen „Fügung" dem unklugen Rat seiner jungen Ratgeber folgte und entgegen dem besseren Rat erfahrener Leute den Israeliten eine schroffe Antwort gab (1 Reg. xii 15).

In alledem spürt man die geistige Luft der salomonischen Zeit. Es ist nicht wahrscheinlich, dass erst eine späte Überlieferung diese im einzelnen verschiedenen und in mehreren literarischen Quellen auftretenden, aber in der Grundlage übereinstimmenden Züge zusammengetragen habe für die Erzählungen über die spätdavidisch-salomonisch-nachsalomonische Zeit. Vielmehr haben wir es offenbar zu tun mit der Atmosphäre dieser Zeit, wie sie wirklich war [3]).

---

[1]) Das Phänomen des inspirierten „Propheten", der ungefragt ein Gotteswort überbringt, ist eine Sache für sich, auf die hier nicht genauer einzugehen ist.

[2]) Vgl. dazu M. Noth, *Oudtestamentische Studien* 8 (1950), p. 35 ff.

[3]) Vgl. G. v. Rad, *Der Heilige Krieg im alten Israel* (1951), p. 39 ff., 49 f.

WISDOM AND IMMORTALITY

BY

JOHS. PEDERSEN

Copenhagen

In the writings of the ancient Orient we sometimes find expressions of wonderment at man's position in creation. In the instruction for the Egyptian king Merikare by his father it is said: "Well directed are men, the cattle of the god. He made heaven and earth according to their desire, and he repelled the water-monster. He made the breath of life (for) their nostrils. They who have issued from his body are his images. He arises in heaven according to their desire. He made for them plants, animals, fowl, and fish to feed them. He slew his enemies and injured (even) his (own) children because they thought of making rebellion. He makes the light of day according to their desire, and he sails by (?) in order to see them. He has erected a shrine around about them, and when they weep he hears. He made for them rulers (even) in the egg, a supporter to support the back of the disabled. He made for them magic as weapons to ward off what might happen and dreams by night as well as day. He has slain the treacherous of heart among them, as a man beats his son for his brother's sake. For the god knows every name" [1]).

Here we see the whole creation produced for the sake of man. A suggestion of this thought may be found in Gen. ii 18 f., according to which the animals were created for the purpose of being a helpmeet for man; but the basic idea in the O.T. is the related one that man is to rule over the other creatures. It is stated indirectly in Gen. ii 19 f. through the fact that man named the animals, and expressly in Gen. i 28. This place apart gives man a position as a kind of intermediate being between the divine world and the rest of creation. It creates a strong tension in the view of man's position, which is stated with impressive clearness in Ps. viii: "When I consider thy heavens, the

---

[1]) J. A. WILSON in J. B. PRITCHARD, *Ancient Near Eastern Texts* p. 417, with some differences from ERMAN, *Die Literatur der Aegypter*, 1923, p. 118 f.

work of thy fingers, the moon and the stars, which thou hast set up, what is man, that thou rememberest him, a son of man, that thou takest care of him? And yet thou hast let him lack little to be a God, and hast crowned him with glory and honour. Thou madest him have dominion over the works of thy hands, thou hast put all things under his feet ..."(Ps. viii 3 ff.).

This kinship with God is, in the passage quoted from the Wisdom-book of Merikare, expressed in the thought that human beings have issued from the god's body as his images. In other places it is said that the god (Khnum) formed man out of clay. The same idea is expressed in another way in Assyro-Babylonian myths. According to *Enuma Elish*, Tablet VI, human beings were created as a link in the rearrangement of the world of the gods which was made after the great fights between the gods that ended in Marduk, according to the gods' choice, killing Tiamat and subduing those gods who had joined her. After the gods had been divided and had had their provinces allotted to them, and the making of the cosmos had been started, Marduk planned the creation of a savage-man (lullu) out of blood and bone, and on Ea's advice this was taken from Kingu, who had been put on the throne by Tiamat, as he was the one who was most responsible for the rebellion of the gods. Thus man was formed from the blood of a rebellious god who was sacrificed in order that the other gods might obtain servants to maintain their temples and cult: "May he (the god) shepherd the black-headed ones ... To the end of days, without forgetting, they shall proclaim ... May he establish for his fathers the great food-offerings; their support they shall furnish, shall tend their sanctuaries. May he cause incense to be smelled, ... their spells, a likeness on earth of what he has wrought in heaven. May he order the black-headed to re [vere him] (?). May the subjects ever bear in mind their god, and may they at his word pay heed to the goddess. May food-offerings be borne (for) their gods and goddesses. Without forgetting let them support their gods. Their lands let them improve, build their shrines, let the black-headed wait on their gods" [1]). Inversely, the human beings were, of course, supported by the gods.

In another Babylonian myth the idea of man's creation from clay mixed with blood from the slain god is supplemented by the idea of a birth at which the mother-goddess Mama plays the principal part.

[1]) *Enuma Elish*, Tab. VI 107-120, transl. by E. A. SPEISER in PRITCHARD, *op. cit.*, p. 69.

The birth takes place through fourteen wombs, out of which seven of the male sex and seven of the female sex are born [1]).

In Gen. i 26-28 man's special position is expressed by the statement that he was created in God's image, male and female He created them, the purpose of man's creation being that he is to have dominion over the earth and to subdue other creatures. In Gen. ii the God Yahweh formed man out of the moist soil and breathed into his nostrils the breath of life, after which he put him into the mythical garden in order to dress and keep it. The animals were created for the man's sake, and his dominion over them is expressed by the fact that he named them.

Thus man's divine kinship was described in ancient Egypt, Assyro-Babylonia, and Israel partly by his being formed by a god's blood, partly by his being created in the god's image, just as the son is begotten in his father's image (Gen. v 3). There is nothing remarkable in this, the view of life of the ancients being what it was. Everything alive, human beings, animals, plants, wood, stone, etc., may through a cult come to participate in holiness, which is the sphere of the divine, and the divine is the intensified spiritual power which underlies all forms of life. An Egyptian myth even says that Ptah "is in every body and in every mouth of all gods, all men, [all] cattle, all creeping things, and (everything) that lives, by thinking and commanding everything that he wishes" [2]).

The fact that man is set apart among all creatures as a descendant of the gods, is in the nature of things due to his mental powers, his power to comprehend and "make counsel", which is expressive of his wisdom, through which he approximates to the gods. This intermediate position creates a dramatic element in the relation between gods and human beings, which on the one hand is due to man's craving for more, on the other hand to the gods' zealous maintenance of their absolute superiority. There is undoubtedly an idea in the fact that, according to the Babylonian myth, it is a rebellious god from whose blood man has been formed, just as in an Egyptian myth (The Dragon and the Creation) it says that "mankind originated as the tears of the creator-god" [3]).

From the three areas mentioned here we have also narratives to the effect that the gods planned to exterminate human beings because of

[1]) *Ibid.*, p. 99 f.
[2]) Wilson in Pritchard, *op. cit.*, p. 5a.
[3]) Wilson in Pritchard, p. 6b.

their rebelliousness. Thus the Egyptian myth about Re, who, after consulting the oldest gods, made the goddess Sekhmet slaughter human beings until Re himself stopped her by a ruse [1]). In the Assyro-Babylonian world we find the same theme in the Atraḫasis myth about the destruction of mankind by a flood as well as by drought, and in the section about the flood in the Gilgamesh epic. The god Enlil has tired of the human beings' clamour and uproar [2]), just as Yahweh has in the Israelite account [3]). The human beings, who had been created in order to serve the gods, behaved as if they were independent. This brings us to the point of this small sketch written in honour of a man to whom Old Testament studies and Old Testament scholars owe so much, viz., what ancient Oriental primeval myths teach us about the question of God and man in comparison with Israelite ones. In this connexion the Assyro-Babylonian myths, which mainly have a Sumerian basis, are of special interest. We shall first consider the Gilgamesh epic. Gilgamesh was a king and therefore had a greater share in the divine than other men— two parts of him were god, one part was man; his predominant qualities were wisdom (*nimequ*) and strength. When, after doing great deeds, he saw his friend Enkidu dead, he considered how he might escape death and said to the god: "Let me not see the death which I ever dread" (Tab. X 2, 13). He received the answer that "when the gods created mankind, death for mankind they set aside, life in their own hands retaining" (3,3-5). Nevertheless, after superhuman efforts he succeeded, with the assistance of Utnapishtim, in getting hold of a plant whereby a man may regain his life's breath. "Its name shall be 'Man becomes young in old age'. I myself shall eat it and thus return to the state of my youth" (Tab. XI 282-284). But shortly afterwards, when he was bathing in a well, a serpent carried off the plant. Then Gilgamesh returned to Uruk, and the spirit of Enkidu, which Ea helped him to raise from the nether-world, could give him no delightful description of the order of that world. The lesson of the great epic is that even the man who attains the highest degree of wisdom and strength, thus obtaining the greatest share in the divine, is subject to the law of death. Shamash was right when he said to Gilgamesh: "The life thou pursuest thou shalt not find" (Tab. X 1,8). This view was not rendered void by Utnapishtim's fate.

---

1) *Ibid.*, p. 10 f.
2) The Atrahasis myth, *ibid.*, p. 104.
3) Gen. vi 5 ff., 13; cf. xviii 20.

Utnapishtim was "the wise", too. He built his ship on the advice of Ea, who disclosed to him some part of the gods' secret decision. When the flood raged and the creatures were being exterminated, Ishtar repented of her share in the decision, and a large number of the gods, especially the earth gods, wept with her. They could not do without mankind, and when Utnapishtim made offerings to them after the flood, the gods flocked like flies round the offering. Ea then blamed Enlil for not having contented himself with chastising the human beings, so that they were not exterminated, but were only checked in their presumption (Tab. XI 176 ff.). Enlil then was appeased and made Utnapishtim and his wife into gods, who settled "far away, at the mouth of the rivers" (Tab. XI 189-195), beyond the waters of Death, as appears from the narrative about Gilgamesh's journey [1]). It is not clear from the narrative how the continuation of mankind was secured, but the idea must be that it took place through Utnapishtim in spite of his isolation. Gilgamesh calls Utnapishtim his father (Tab. IX 3,3). But the question of the immortality of man is rejected, Utnapishtim being admitted to the world of gods. He himself assumes that this is something which will not be repeated (XI 197 f.). The Hebrew narrative about the flood does not touch on this problem, as Noah, because of his righteousness, is saved as founder of a new generation. But the background of the flood is the same here as in the East. Gods' sons mixed with human women, and in this way a generation arose which was marked by a presumption which carried mankind beyond the bounds that might be tolerated by the gods.

The dramatic element in the relation between God and mankind is expressed more intensely in polytheism than in monotheism because it may be represented as a play between gods representing the various elements of existence. We have seen this in the myth of the flood, in which the great goddess takes the initiative in condemning the extermination, and in which Ea, man's creator god, saves Utnapishtim by a ruse from destruction. But in another myth, which is particularly instructive as regards the question dealt with here, it stands out clearly, viz., in the Adapa myth [2]), the contents of which are as follows: Ea, the wise god in Eridu, created Adapa as a perfect human being, gifted with wisdom, but without immortality, and Adapa was in charge of the whole of the cult in the temple of Eridu.

---

[1]) Assyrian version II, 27, 29; see Pritchard, p. 91.
[2]) Transl. Pritchard, p. 101-103.

While he was sailing at sea in order to catch fish, the south wind suddenly rushed out over the calm water and made the boat capsize, so that Adapa went down into the "house of the fish". He uttered a curse on the south wind, through which its wing was broken, and it did not blow for seven days. When Anu, the god of heaven, noticed this, he called his messenger Ilabrat, and learnt from him what had happened, after which he gave orders for Adapa to be brought to him. Ea then instructed Adapa about the journey. He was to go up with tousled hair and dressed in mourning. At Anu's gate he would meet the two gods Tammuz and Gizzida, and when they asked him for whose sake he wore these signs of mourning, he was to say: "For two gods who have disappeared". Then they would ask the names of these, and he was to answer: "Tammuz and Gizzida"; then they would help him. This came to pass. When the two gods heard how greatly they were mourned, they looked smilingly at one another. Adapa was then brought before Anu, who asked him why he had broken the wing of the south wind. Adapa told him why, and Tammuz and Gizzida then went up and spoke for him. Anu was appeased, but said, "Why did Ea disclose the heart of the heaven and the earth to a worthless (?) human, rendering him distinguished and making a name for him? As for us, what shall we do about it?" He then gave orders for bread of life and water of life to be brought to him; but Ea had also been prepared for this, and had told Adapa that he would be offered bread of death and water of death and that he was to refuse this offer, whereas he might accept the offer for a garment and oil with which to anoint himself. Adapa obeyed this order. Anu then asked Adapa why he had not accepted the bread and water of life, and Adapa told him what Ea had said. Then Anu laughed loud, sent Adapa back to earth again, and glorified the priesthood of Eridu.

Myths are not dogmas but narratives which describe the work of gods and characterize their mutual relations and their relation to creation. Myths about the same things therefore need not be homogeneous. In the myth just summarized, Ea by his wisdom wins the game before the god of heaven. He creates a perfect and wise man to found his own cult in Eridu. In *Enuma Elish*'s account, too, mankind was created with wisdom to perform the cult. The conflict with Anu arose when man, during his activities for the benefit of Ea, insulted the god of heaven by paralyzing the south wind. Ea makes sure that Anu does not annihilate his masterpiece, who worships him, by means of the stratagem with the two gods, a feature which undoubtedly contains a touch of humour. Anu does not destroy Adapa, but he cannot, on the other hand, approve of the possibility that this creature, poor in relation to the gods, should have so great wisdom, and he tries the expedient of giving him eternal life; for in this way he would, as Utnapishtim, be made a god, and the problem would be solved. But there Ea again thwarts him. He does not want to lose the leader of his cult by the latter's admission to the world of gods, and he tricks Adapa into refusing the food and drink which would have given him immortality. Man was on the point of becoming a god, but was defrauded of it by the god who had created him.

Thus these myths are expressive of the flickering relation between God and man. Man is related to the gods, a relation which appears in his wisdom. This is especially evident in the great man, the king, but there is no unmixed joy in this among the gods. The kinship would be complete if man were also given immortality. He has been close to immortality, but still, he did not obtain it, and if he did so, he would no longer be human.

The present author has elsewhere tried to point out that it is the same problem which is treated of in the narrative of the Fall in Gen. iii [1]), although in a completely different form. Even though there is a reference to several divine beings in the Israelite narrative, there is only one acting god, who has created man with woman as his helpmeet to dress and keep the garden into which they have been put. There is no mention of any cult, but of a demand for obedience, consisting in a prohibition from eating of the tree of the knowledge of good and evil, from the fruits of which man might thus acquire wisdom. No grounds for the prohibition are given, but the prohibition is reinforced by a threat of immediate death after eating, a threat which is not, however, carried into effect. When the serpent, who is well informed, discloses the true facts, woman's curiosity is aroused, she and the man eat of the fruit and Yahweh says that now "man is become as one of us, to know good and evil". In order to prevent them from eating also of the tree of life which is in the garden, he sends them forth from the garden and sets guards at the entrance.

In this narrative it is not a god who outwits another, but man who, almost accidentally, secures wisdom by getting behind the god's

---

[1]) In the *Festschrift* to S. MOWINCKEL.

stratagem [1]), and this entails as a consequence that the god bars the road to immortality. We may ask whether man could know the animals in the garden and have dominion over them without possessing the intellectual faculty which gives a "knowledge of good and evil", but such questions are beside the purpose of the narrative. Its moral is that it would have been in accordance with the divine plan that man did not display any independence, but in filial obedience lived completely under the divine rule, so that the distinction between him and the divine world was a sharp one. But the transgression of this system led to the same result as in the other Eastern myths, viz., that man stands in the world with a strength and wisdom which closely connect him with the divine world, but that his craving for immortality cannot be satisfied, however close to its fulfilment he has been. Here is the boundary between God and man.

In Egypt, conditions were different. Man's share in the divine was there concentrated in the king much more than was the case in Mesopotamia. The king was identified with the god Re, but as he was also a human being, he could with particular strength attend to the cult of the gods on behalf of men. As early as the time of the pyramids care is taken that the deceased king is preserved and enabled to continue life in the hereafter, and the idea of a hereafter extends to more and more comprehensive groups of the people [2]).

The point of view expressed in the myths mentioned above is not, however, exhaustive as regards the view of the dead, at any rate not in ancient Israel. There was constantly a doublesidedness also in the view of the dead and the divine world. In certain ways they formed a transition to the latter [3]).

The approaches to a belief in an individual resurrection found in the O.T. are due to a demand for the accomplishment of justice. When the idea of immortality spread in Hellenistic times, this was found to be a consequence of the fact that man was created in the image of God. "For God has created man to immortality and formed him in the image of his own nature" (Sap. ii 23), but a distinction is made between the righteous, who are in God's hand (iii 1), and the

---

1) A suggestion of a related idea is found in Iob xv 8.

2) Cf. ERMAN, *Die Religion der Ägypter*, 1934, p. 207-94. In his important book *Kingship and the Gods*, 1948, H. FRANKFORT stresses the divine character of the Pharaoh in relation to that of Babylonian kingship. But the position of the Pharaoh in performing the cult towards the gods shows that he also acts on behalf of man.

3) See the author's *Israel*, III-IV, p. 486 ff.

ungodly, "for those who do not take heed of wisdom and discipline are unhappy, their hope is worthless, their efforts are in vain, and their works are unserviceable" (iii 11).

In Judaism the idea of resurrection became prevalent. As "righteousness" became decisive of fate in the hereafter, considerations of wisdom receded into the background, and a continued eternal life was no longer thought to displace the boundary between God and man.

ROYAL WISDOM

BY

NORMAN W. PORTEOUS

Edinburgh

The Hebrew king's day seems to have begun early, if we may judge by the statement in 2 Sam. xv that, when Absalom wished to play the demagogue and capture the ear of would-be plaintiffs at the royal court of final appeal in Jerusalem, he had to rise betimes so as to catch them at the gate on their way into the city from the country. It is clear from the argument which Absalom is able to use that the system had not been working too well. David had not been practising sufficiently the art of devolution, though there was far more business to be transacted than he could satisfactorily tackle single-handed. That he did, however, on occasion give close personal attention to even small matters of private concern is shown by the extraordinarily interesting story of the wise woman of Tekoa in 2 Sam. xiv, not to speak of the parable of Nathan in ch. xii which was ostensibly addressed to the king in his capacity as judge.

In exercising this judicial role David makes it clear that, as regards one of his functions, he is standing in lineal descent from the charismatic *shōphᵉtim* of the pre-monarchic period, who in addition to their warlike activities had certain judicial functions to fulfil. We are thus provided with what must be very nearly contemporary evidence that the Davidic monarchy, in replacing the old amphictyonic council, which had not been forgotten in spite of the intervening years of the kingdom of Saul, carried on the judicial tradition which had been associated with it. This is further made clear by David's transfer to his new capital of Jerusalem of the ancient palladium of the tribes, the ark of God [1]).

What is of particular interest for the purpose of the present study is the evidence the narratives give us of the extent to which the administration of justice depended on the individual judgment of the

---

[1]) 2 Sam. vi; Ps. cxxxii.

king. Even if we discount the element of flattery in the words which the wise woman of Tekoa addresses to the king—'My lord the king is like the angel of God [1]) to discern good and evil' (xiv 17):

'My lord has wisdom like the wisdom of the angel of God [1]) to know all things that are on the earth' (xiv 20)—it is clear that it was not out of place to attribute to him some kind of charismatic endowment for the carrying out of his judicial duties. The administration of justice in Israel, as elsewhere in the ancient east, does not seem to have rested on the basis of statutory law codes [2]). The codes we possess may conceivably, when promulgated, have had a propagandist value or, more probably, are descriptive of a legal tradition with a view to stabilizing law or guiding inexperienced judges. The elders who transacted legal business at the gate of village or town were guided, not by a binding code, but by local precedents handed down orally and constantly supplemented. A certain number of cases would find their way to the royal court in Jerusalem. It is clear that a great deal depended for the successful working of the system on the native shrewdness of the judges. For the decision of the hard cases which came before the king there was need for more than ordinary insight. The wise woman of Tekoa, as we have seen, credits David with superhuman wisdom, and it apparently consists not only in the skill to decide hard cases but in 'knowledge of all things that are on the earth'. Even though the language is extravagant and the wise woman may have had her tongue in her cheek, it cannot have sounded altogether absurd.

This association of David with the supreme judicial function appears in Ps. cxxii 5 in which the Psalmist looks back to the time when the royal tribunal was set up and David on occasion heard cases himself. In Jes. xvi 5, in a poem which describes a flight to Zion of refugees from Moab, we read that

> 'then a throne will be established in steadfast love
> and on it will sit in faithfulness
> in the tent of David
> one who judges and seeks justice
> and is swift to do righteousness.'

---

[1]) Cf. 2 Sam. xvi 23, where the counsel of Ahithophel on which both David and Solomon relied is compared to the oracle of God.

[2]) See the important article, "Ancient Oriental and Biblical Law", by GEORGE E. MENDENHALL, in *The Biblical Archaeologist*, xvii (1954), p. 26-46.

The reference to 'the tent of David' may indeed be a gloss, but the words are nevertheless significant for the tradition embodied in them.

It seemed worth while emphasizing what is said about David in view of the more legendary character of the evidence about Solomon. As will be pointed out presently, the belief that kings were specially endowed with wisdom was common in the ancient east, and it is important to notice that this quality was recognized in David before the monarchy began to conform more closely to the usual oriental pattern, as it did under Solomon. David still stood near to the people, unlike his son who had been born in the purple.

It was with Solomon in particular, however, that Jewish tradition connected the idea of wisdom [1]), so much so that later books of wisdom, both canonical and extra-canonical, were attributed to him. The story was that he had received it as a gift from Yahweh on a night which he had spent 'incubating' at the high place in Gibeon. The words attributed to Solomon in response to the divine offer enshrine a noble view of the burden of kingship [2])—'Thy servant is in the midst of thy people whom thou hast chosen, a great people, that cannot be numbered or counted for multitude. Give thy servant therefore an understanding mind to govern thy people; that I may discern between good and evil; for who is able to govern this thy great people?' The faculty of discernment for which he asks is precisely that which is attributed to David by the wise woman of Tekoa. The story of Solomon's judgment which follows immediately purports to give a concrete example of the wisdom with which Solomon is endowed in answer to his prayer.

There is, however, another type of wisdom with which Solomon is associated in the tradition and which, we are told, God had put into his mind [3]). We are told [4]) that 'God gave Solomon wisdom and understanding beyond measure, and largeness of mind like the sand on the sea-shore, so that Solomon's wisdom surpassed the wisdom of all the people of the east, and all the wisdom of Egypt'. We read too of his proverbs and his songs and of his interest in the curiosities of nature. Gerhard von Rad has recently [5]) drawn attention to what he calls not inappropriately the humanism of the age of Solomon.

[1]) I Reg. ii 6, iii 28, v *passim*, x *passim*; 2 Chron. ix *passim*; I Reg. xi 41; 2 Chron. i *passim*. Cf. Sap. vii-ix.

[2]) I Reg. iii 8 f.

[3]) I Reg. x 24.

[4]) I Reg. iv 29.

[5]) *Der Heilige Krieg im alten Israel*, p. 39-42.

It seems to have been at this time that Israel began to become acquainted with international wisdom and to draw upon its lore [1]). This would doubtless first become manifest in court circles where the opportunities for foreign contacts were greatest and where there would be the leisure to cultivate the things of the mind. VON RAD thinks, however, that it would not be very long before a certain 'democratization' of wisdom took place. Rhetoric, literature and music began to be cultivated as arts, and men are found taking an enquiring interest in the phenomena of the world around them and in the history of the recent, and even of the dim and distant, past.

A developing culture, of course, especially when it is heavily indebted to alien borrowings, can experience loss as well as gain. It is important in this connection to notice that wisdom in Israel continued to mean not only the cultivation of the mind and the development of intellectual interests, but the endowment of the individual for the necessary tasks of life. Wisdom of this second kind was felt to be particularly necessary as equipment for royalty in view of the increasingly complicated rôle the king had to play. No elaboration of rules of procedure could take away from the personal responsibility for difficult decisions which was laid upon the king who occupied David's throne and who, therefore, stood in a covenantal relationship with a God of righteousness and justice.

It is no doubt true that, as GADD maintains, the Code of Deuteronomy takes up a rather negative attitude to the king and that in the account in 1 Reg. 'even the judgments of Solomon are not recorded with any purpose of displaying him as a father of his people' [2]). The Code of Deuteronomy was clearly not a royal manifesto but was accepted by the king as a warning to the dynasty and people. On the other hand, we must not forget that the Books of Kings edited under Deuteronomic influence laid repeated emphasis on the importance of the Davidic dynasty, and the evidence of the royal psalms must be taken seriously [3]). There were certainly those in Judah who made it their business to remind the king of his covenantal responsibility for the righteous government of his people.

The connection between the kingship and the proper regulation of human life is, of course, not confined to Israel. In Egypt we have

[1]) Cf. O. S. RANKIN, *Israel's Wisdom Literature*, p. 6, 14.

[2]) C. J. GADD, *Ideas of Divine Rule in the Ancient East*, p. 44-5.

[3]) I Reg. ii 33, 45, viii 66, ix 5, xi 12 f., 32, 34 f., xv 4; 2 Reg. viii 19, xix 34, xx 6; Pss. lxxii, lxxxix, cxxxii. Cf. 2 Sam. vii 8 ff., xxiii 5; Jer. xxxiii 21; Jes. lv 3.

the evidence of the accession hymns. In the hymn celebrating the accession of Mer-ne-ptah we read [1]):

'Be glad of heart, the entire land! The goodly times are come! A lord—life, prosperity, health!—is given in all lands, and normality has come down (again) into its place: the King of Upper and Lower Egypt, the lord of millions of years, great of kingship like Horus: Ba-en-Re Meri-Amon—life, prosperity, health!—he who crushes Egypt with festivity, the son of Re, (most) serviceable of any king: Mer-ne-ptah Hotep-hir-Maat—life, prosperity, health!

'All ye righteous, come that ye may see'. Right has banished wrong. Evildoers have fallen (upon) their faces. All the rapacious are ignored. The water stands and is not dried up: the Nile lifts high. Days are long, nights have hours, and the moon comes normally. The gods are satisfied and content of heart. (One) lives in laughter and wonder. Mayest thou know it.'

It can be seen from this one example alone that the Pharaoh is thought of as a divine being who maintains the harmonious order of nature and human life. IVAN ENGNELL, who quotes the above hymn and another concerning the enthronement of Ramesses IV [2]), comments: 'The king is identical with the high god and hereby with the universal order, with Cosmos, that he upholds by virtue of his functioning in the ritual .... His chief task is not to be executive king—earthly king, but law-king—sky-god.' This is something very different from the function of the Davidic king who was charged with an executive task to ensure the obedience of his people to the God who had a claim upon them and had made a covenant with David and his descendants. In Hebrew thought God is transcendent above the world of His creation, and man's duty is not to attain harmony with the world in which he finds himself but to obey the will of the transcendent God [3]). This is man's dignity and it is the dignity of the king as a representative man that he is called upon to help his people to meet their covenanted obligations.

---

[1]) Quoted from *Ancient Near Eastern Texts* (ed. J. B. PRITCHARD), p. 378.

[2]) *Studies in Divine Kingship in the Ancient Near East*, p. 13-15. ENGNELL quotes these hymns from A. ERMAN, *The Literature of the Ancient Egyptians* (trans. A. M. BLACKMAN), p. 278-280. Cf. H. GRESSMANN, *Altorientalische Texte zum Alten Testament*, p. 25.

[3]) Cf. H. FRANKFORT, *Kingship and the Gods*, p. 342 ff.; G. E. WRIGHT, *The Old Testament against its Environment*, p. 63, 68; W. EICHRODT, *Man in the Old Testament* (Engl. transl.), p. 15, 25, 47 f. (German original: *Das Menschenverständnis des Alten Testaments*, p. 13, 23, 46).

The situation in Mesopotamia was somewhat different from what it was in Egypt. As a general rule the king was not deified. He had moreover a very considerable executive function as representative of his people and he seems to have dealt with a great variety of matters both important and trivial. The king was divinely ordained to his task of maintaining an order which was according to the will of the gods. Once again as in Egypt the object of government was to maintain man's harmony with this order. There were times when much of a king's work consisted in consulting the omens and through them ascertaining the inscrutable will of the gods [1]). There is nothing here which is really parallel to the position of the Hebrew king who was charged with maintaining a covenantal relationship with God which antedated the monarchy. Nevertheless, for what he had to do—and his duties were many and various—the king in the Mesopotamian lands was credited with wisdom and understanding. ENGNELL has conveniently collected [2]) a number of references of this kind concerning such kings as Gudea, Šamšu-iluna, Hammurabi, Esarhaddon, Nebuchadrezzar, Nabonidus, along with a parallel set of references which prove that similar terms were applied to the kings as to the gods.

That the conception of the duty of the king towards the weak members of society was recognized in Ugarit is shown by the words of Keret's son addressed to his father [3]):

'Hearken, I pray thee, Keret the noble.
List and incline thine ear.
. . . .
Thou hast let thy hand fall into mischief.
Thou judgest not the cause of the widow,
  Nor adjudicat'st the case of the wretched;
  Driv'st not out them that prey on the poor;
Feed'st not the fatherless before thee,
  The widow behind thy back,
Having become a brother of the sick-bed,
  A companion of the bed of suffering,
Descend from the kingship—I'll reign;
  From thine authority—I'll sit enthroned.'

There is no appeal here, however, to a divine covenant. Yassib, Keret's son, seems to have thought all this up himself! 'Yassib sits

---

[1]) Cf. GADD, *op. cit.*, p. 39.
[2]) ENGNELL, *op. cit.*, p. 189-91.
[3]) Quoted from PRITCHARD, *op. cit.*, p. 149.

in the palace and his inward parts do instruct him.' One suspects that he was interested in matters of justice as much as Absalom was.

The particular concern of the present study is to suggest that, alongside of what has been called the 'democratization' of wisdom into the prudence which should govern ordinary human life in all its variety, there continued in Israel the conviction that wisdom was required in quite a special way by those who were charged with the duty of government and that this eventually had important theological consequences.

In the prologue to the Book of Proverbs [1]) in which Wisdom is personified we find her declaring:

'I have counsel and sound wisdom, (תּוּשִׁיָּה)
  I have insight, I have strength.
By me kings reign,
  And rulers decree what is just;
By me princes rule,
  And nobles govern the earth.'

That of course is a general statement and need not be regarded as referring specifically to Israelite kings, but it does occur in that part of the Book of Proverbs which contains Israel's most distinctive contribution to the conception of Wisdom. It is perhaps significant that in the Wisdom of Ben Sira the author, addressing "my son", says of the search for Wisdom [2]):

'Enquire and search, seek and find,
  And take hold of her, and let not go of her;
For at last thou wilt find her rest,
  And she will be turned into delight for thee;
And her net will become for thee a stay of strength,
  And her bonds robes of gold.
An ornament of gold is her yoke,
  And her fetters a cord of blue.
With glorious garments shalt thou array thyself,
And with a crown of beauty shalt thou crown
  thyself with her.'

That is to say, he who finds wisdom is entitled to wear royal robes. In another place in the same book [3]) it is said that

'The wisdom of a poor man lifteth up his head
And causeth him to sit among princes.'

---

[1]) viii 14-16.
[2]) vi 27-31.
[3]) xi 1.

We may further compare a passage in the Book of Proverbs [1]):

'The beginning of wisdom is this: get wisdom,
and whatever you get, get insight.
Prize her highly (?), and she will exalt you;
She will honour you if you embrace her.
She will place on your head a fair garland;
She will bestow on you a beautiful crown.'

Wisdom herself is regarded as royal in Prov. viii 23, if we may accept RINGGREN's translation [2]):

'I was installed from everlasting,
From the beginning, at the origin of the earth.'

His translation seems to be supported by Ps. ii 6.

The Book of Wisdom has interesting things to say about the connection of Wisdom and kingship [3]):

'The desire for Wisdom leadeth unto a kingdom.'
'If, therefore, ye delight in thrones and sceptres,
ye rulers of the peoples,
Honour Wisdom, that ye may reign for ever.'

And still more appositely:

'The multitude of wise men is the salvation of the world,
And a prudent king is the stay of his people.'

The evidence given above for a persistent belief in Israel in the close connection between Wisdom and royalty would not be complete without a reference to the fact that the 'Messianic' figure described in Jes. xi 2, who in ch. ix 6 has been named פֶּלֶא יוֹעֵץ 'a wonder of a counsellor', is to receive the spirit of wisdom —

'The spirit of the Lord shall rest upon him,
The spirit of wisdom and understanding,
The spirit of counsel and might,
The spirit of knowledge and the fear of the Lord.'

The endowment of wisdom is evidently intended to fit him for his judicial function which is described in what immediately follows. The king who is to come is to perform perfectly the task which was laid upon the Davidic king. Although the words used to describe the coming king are different, there is a clear reference back to Jes. xi in Jer. xxiii 5—'Behold, the days are coming, says the Lord, when

[1]) iv 7-9.
[2]) H. RINGGREN, *Word and Wisdom*, p. 99-100, 143.
[3]) vi 20 f., 24.

I will raise up for David a righteous Branch, and he shall reign as king and deal wisely (וְהִשְׂכִּיל probably, have success) and shall execute judgment and righteousness in the land.'

With the 'Messianic' figure of Jes. xi we may contrast the king of Tyre of Ezech. xxviii, who arrogates wisdom to himself. He considers himself wise as a god, and the prophet represents the Lord God as saying to him:

'You are indeed wiser than Daniel;
no secret is hidden from you;
by your wisdom and your understanding
you have gotten wealth for yourself,
and have gathered gold and silver
into your treasuries;
by your great wisdom in trade
you have increased your wealth.
And your heart has become proud in your wealth —
therefore thus says the Lord God:
"Because you consider yourself
as wise as a god,
therefore, behold, I will bring strangers upon you,
the most terrible of the nations;
and they shall draw their swords
against the beauty of your wisdom
and defile your splendour."' (verses 2-7)

And later:

'You were the signet [1]) of perfection,
full of wisdom
and perfect in beauty
Your heart was proud because of your beauty;
you corrupted your wisdom for the sake of your splendour
(verses 12, 17)

In a valuable passage in his book *Revelation in Jewish Wisdom Literature*, ch. v, J. Coert Rylaarsdam points out that in the Book of the Wisdom of Solomon we have a very clear identification of Wisdom with the Spirit, actions which are attributed to the Spirit in the Old Testament being now attributed to Wisdom. We see this especially in ch. x, in which certain events of the Exodus period which are elsewhere credited to the Spirit are now credited to Wisdom. Rylaarsdam adds [2]): 'The Wisdom of Solomon also transfers to Wisdom the rôle formerly played by the Spirit in the special capacity

[1]) Better 'pattern'.
[2]) *Op. cit.*, p. 113.

of judges, leaders and kings'. All this is very important in view of the other fact that, beginning with the Wisdom of Ben Sira xxiv, Jewish conservative thought was identifying Wisdom with the written Torah and even crediting the Torah with royal status [1]). The Wisdom whose product is

'the book of the covenant of God Most High,
the Law which Moses commanded as an heritage
for the assemblies of Jacob' (verses 19-23)

declares:

'In the high places did I fix my abode
and my throne was in the pillar of cloud.' (verse 4)
'Likewise in the beloved city He caused me to rest,
And in Jerusalem [2]) was my authority'. (verses 11 f.)

There is a noble side to this identification of the Mosaic Law with Wisdom. EDWYN BEVAN calls it [3]) a 'challenge to the pretensions of any foreign culture'. 'The Hebrew sage feels vividly that this Law handed down among his people is no mere code of a single small race, not even merely of the earth, but the incarnation, if one may say so, of a cosmic principle and akin to the stars. He feels Israel to be the centre of all things, the eventual heir of the ages' [4]).

Yet there is a danger here which must be frankly recognized. It is the great merit of the Book of the Wisdom of Solomon that, as RYLAARSDAM has pointed out [5]), alongside this identification of Wisdom with the written Law, it helped to keep the concept of Wisdom as something fluid, vital and contemporaneous.

Before we pass to the New Testament it should perhaps be mentioned very briefly that our theme links up with the conception of the

---

[1]) W. D. DAVIES, *Paul and Rabbinic Judaism.*, p. 168 ff.

[2]) O. S. RANKIN, in *The Origins of the Festival of Hanukkah*, p. 252 ff., speaking of the conjunction of the terms Σοφία and Αἰών in mystic thought about the time of St. Paul, goes on: 'Among the results of the spread of the Aion-concept in the West was the rise of the belief in the ever-enduring sovereignty of Rome, the city and the Empire (*aeternitas imperii*), and finally even of the Emperor himself as representative of the Empire. It would not seem to be a further stage of development, but only a more thorough application of prevalent ideas, when Constantine, in transferring the "*aeternitas*" conception to his new capital, has the great Basilica dedicated to 'Ἁγία Σοφία.'

RANKIN compares all this with the anticipation in the Wisdom of Ben Sira xxiv where Wisdom, here, as we have seen, equated with the Law, represents Yahweh's sovereignty in Jerusalem.

[3]) *Jerusalem under the High Priests*, p. 41.

[4]) *Op. cit.*, p. 60. Quoted also by DAVIES, *op. cit.*, p. 149.

[5]) *Op. cit.*, p. 117 f.

Primeval Man (*Urmensch*). There may not be general agreement with A. Bentzen when he declares [1]) that the first man in Gen. i 24-28 is represented as the first King of the world who is commissioned to 'rule' over all the living creatures of the earth. It is interesting, however, to notice that in Ps. viii, which gives, one might say, a poetical version of Gen. i, the psalmist says to God of his creature man:

> 'Thou hast made him little less than God,
> and dost crown him with glory and honour.'

In Ezech. xxviii, to which reference has already been made, we seem to have an allusion to a variant of the Genesis account and we have seen there the linking of royalty and wisdom. In the Slavonic Book of Enoch, otherwise called 'The Book of the Secrets of Enoch' [2]), we read that the Lord says to Enoch: 'I created man ...... and I placed him on earth, a second angel, honourable, great and glorious, and I appointed him as ruler to rule on earth and to have my wisdom, and there was none like him on earth, of all my existing creatures'.

Coming now to the New Testament we find a very complicated situation. Into all the tangled issues involved it would obviously be impossible to enter here. W. D. Davies has devoted an interesting chapter of his volume *Paul and Rabbinic Judaism* [3]) to considering the use which St. Paul makes of the conception of the Divine Wisdom in working out his Christology. He argues that it was his thought of Christ as a New Torah replacing the Old that enabled him to transfer to Christ the attributes of pre-existence and creativeness which the Torah had acquired in Jewish thought from its identification with Wisdom. In the previous chapter [4]) Davies crosses swords with C. H. Dodd [5]) who had interpreted the phrase νόμος τοῦ Χριστοῦ as νόμος τοῦ πνεύματος τῆς ζωῆς ἐν Χριστῷ 'Ιησοῦ, and explained it as 'an immanent principle of life like the Stoic Law of nature, but determined by the Spirit of Christ.' Davies—and he admits that Dodd elsewhere has said much the same thing—wishes to preserve a place for the normative authority of the teaching of Jesus and thinks that 'it is possible to make too much of the contrast between Pauline

---

1) A. Bentzen, *Messias Moses Redivivus Menschensohn*, p. 12 f. Eng. transl. *King and Messiah*, p. 17 f.

2) R. H. Charles, *Apocrypha and Pseudepigrapha of the Old Testament*, ii, p. 449; G. N. Bonwetsch, *Die Bücher der Geheimnisse Henochs*, p. 28 f. Cf. R. Bultmann, in *ΕΥΧΑΡΙΣΤΗΡΙΟΝ*, ii, p. 22 f.

3) Ch. 7, The Old and the New Torah; Christ the Wisdom of God, p. 147 ff.

4) *Op. cit.*, p. 144 f.

5) *The Bible and the Greeks*, p. 37.

Christianity as a religion of liberty and Judaism as a religion of obedience'. We may agree. At the same time it would be a mistake to forget the spontaneity of that Spirit of Wisdom which was to be the first of the endowments of the 'Messiah' of prophetic expectation. The teaching of Jesus who fulfilled that expectation has a normative function, but it must be interpreted in such a way as does not involve the bondage of the letter.

St. Paul in 1 Cor. i 24 describes Christ as the power and the wisdom of God in opposition to both Jews and Greeks who severally sought after power and wisdom of a very different kind. Ὁ Λόγος ὁ τοῦ σταυροῦ, which is defined as Χριστὸς ἐσταυρωμένος, is the divine wisdom which for all its seeming weakness is stronger than all human wisdom. The section ends (verse 31) with the words: 'Let him who boasts boast of the Lord'. What St. Paul means by that must be understood in the light of the original prophetic passage (Jer. ix 23 f.) from which he is quoting and which he abbreviates without fundamentally changing its meaning—'Let not the wise man glory in his wisdom, let not the mighty man glory in his might, let not the rich man glory in his riches; but let him who glories glory in this, that he understands and knows me, that I am the Lord who practice kindness, justice and righteousness in the earth; for in these things I delight, says the Lord'. In the Cross of Christ St. Paul sees the ultimate evidence for the divine activity in the world of Him 'Whom God made our wisdom, our righteousness and sanctification and redemption' (verse 30). The wisdom of God manifests itself, not in some esoteric doctrine which is addressed to the intellect of initiates of some secret cult, but in action, God's supreme action in Christ on the Cross. Here is indeed a transvaluation of values. Yet we can see that, in doing what He did, Christ is fulfilling the prophecy of Jes. xi 2-4, though in carrying out the task of judge He takes the consequences of sin upon Himself [1]).

It must finally be asked whether there is ground for believing that Jesus Himself made any claim to be the Divine Wisdom or whether St. Paul is merely drawing conclusions for himself.

It is possible that in Matth. xi 19 (= Luke vii 35) both Jesus and John the Baptist are described as the children of Wisdom. But the Matthean version of the *logion* is variously reported, the evidence being divided between ἔργων (works) and τέκνων (children),

[1]) Cf. Romans viii 34.

though the Lucan version has only the latter reading. In Matth. xii 42 (= Luke xi 31) Jesus declares that 'The queen of the South will arise at the judgment with this generation and condemn it; for she came from the ends of the earth to hear the wisdom of Solomon, and behold, something greater than Solomon is here'. It might be legitimate to conclude that the meaning of this *logion* is that in Solomon was the royal wisdom with which God endowed a king and which aroused the wonder even of a royal personage, but that in Jesus is manifested the Wisdom of God in person. That is not said in so many words, but Jesus at least here lays claim to a wisdom superior to that of Solomon by virtue of His personal superiority to Solomon.

It is with this saying in mind that we must turn to the passage Matth. xi 25-30 which is paralleled in Luke x 21 f., though the important verses 28-30 in Matthew's version do not appear in Luke at all. This famous *pericope* has been the subject of endless discussion into the intricacies of which it is impossible to enter here. If it were permissible to take the whole of the passage in Matthew as representing authentic words of Jesus, then, inasmuch as the concluding section apparently echoes the words of Wisdom in Sir. li, there would be ground for holding that Jesus is consciously identifying Himself with Divine Wisdom, but emphasizing the truth that there is a Wisdom intended, not for those who think themselves wise, but for the childlike in heart, a Wisdom moreover which is itself gentle and lowly and which, unlike the Wisdom which the Jews have identified with the Law, does not lay heavy burdens upon men.

EDUARD NORDEN, in his book *Agnostos Theos*, and, following him, TOMAS ARVEDSON, in his book *Das Mysterium Christi*, have carried out an elaborate form-critical study of the whole passage, and have come to the conclusion that it is built up on a *schema* which is common to Jewish, Christian and Hellenistic, in particular Hermetic, writings. NORDEN, in view of the evidence which he presents in the most elaborate way, denies the authenticity of the passage, but believes that some Christian thinker has set himself to use the *schema* to contrast Christ with the Oriental-Hellenistic saviour gods (θεοὶ σωτῆρες) and, in so doing, has done substantial justice to Christ Himself. ARVEDSON goes further and regards the passage as coming to us from a Christian esoteric mystery cult in which Christ is presented to His worshippers as a Saviour God. One difference between NORDEN's interpretation of the passage and that of ARVEDSON should be noted. The former understands the words πάντα μοι παρεδόθη ὑπὸ τοῦ πατρός μου as referring to παράδοσις or tradition, the handing down of knowledge, which is then defined in the words that follow. ARVEDSON, on the other hand, takes the words to refer to the handing over of royal power to Christ and claims that we have here an enthronement formula. He points to parallels to this declared relationship between Father and Son in the accounts of the Baptism and the Transfiguration [1]) where we have the royal adoption formula which recalls Ps. ii 7 and Jes. xlii 1, and adduces evidence from the Passion and Resurrection narratives and from sundry ancient liturgies. ARVEDSON is convinced [2]) that we have here the meeting and mingling of royal and wisdom ideologies. The royal Messiah is represented as the Wisdom of God.

This is not the place to discuss at length the vexed question of the authenticity of these words attributed to Christ. It may, however, be pointed out that they belong in all probability to the Q Source, though the omission in Luke's version of the *logion* of the third section as we have it in Matthew does cast a certain doubt on the origin of Matth. xi 28-30. Quite apart, however, from the question of authenticity, it is a little difficult to believe with ARVEDSON that a fragment of the liturgy of a Christian mystery cult could have found its way into the Source Q and from it been taken over by two of the Synoptic Gospels. Moreover, the resemblance of the middle section of the *logion* (Matth. xi 27 = Luke x 22) to what we have in the Fourth Gospel [3]) (John vii 28 f., viii 54 f., x 14 f.), instead of leading us to question the authenticity of the Synoptic *logion*, should be taken in connection with what ANTON FRIDRICHSEN has lately written of the Fourth Gospel [4]). 'The Gospel of St. John, full as it is of the ideas and language of the Beloved Disciple and of his circle, is an authentic historical testimony to Christ .... Confronted with the problem of "St. John and the Synoptics", we do not think it valid to brand the Gospel of St. John as an historically inferior product of the mysticism and speculation of a later age. The Synoptists and St. John alike present us with a portrait of Jesus which is ultimately derived from personal observation, experience and impression .....

---

[1]) Cf. the elaborate study of the Transfiguration by H. RIESENFELD, *Jésus Transfiguré*, in which the enthronement motif is emphasized.

[2]) Cf. RINGGREN, *op. cit.*, p. 124, 142 f.

[3]) Cf. C. H. DODD, *The Interpretation of the Fourth Gospel*, p. 166.

[4]) *The Root of the Vine: Essays in Biblical Theology*, by ANTON FRIDRICHSEN and other members of Uppsala University, p. 57 f.

The two portraits of Jesus must stand independently. *But they must be viewed together*. Then we shall see one consistent historical reality'. These are wise and weighty words. They embolden us to accept the Synoptic *logion* we have been considering as an authentic utterance of Jesus and so to claim that Jesus did indeed think of Himself as fulfilling and, in his own royal way, combining the rôles both of the King-Messiah and of the Divine Wisdom. We may perhaps be allowed to apply to the present context words of S. A. Cook [1]): 'There was no mere synthesis of existing ideas, but a movement "from outside", as it were, which took only what it needed and moulded it to a new purpose'.

The Logos speculation which appears in the Prologue to the Fourth Gospel undoubtedly stands in some kind of relation to the Jewish Wisdom speculation. That, however, is too large a subject to discuss here and has been deliberately excluded from consideration. The limited purpose of this present study has been to suggest that the judicial wisdom (with its practical as opposed to speculative slant) attributed to David and Solomon and the 'Messiah' of Jes. xi is fulfilled in the One who by His very presence in the world was a judgment upon it and who, by His life, death and resurrection, founded a Kingdom in which the righteousness of God finds expression. Perhaps it is for this reason that the commandment 'You shall love your neighbour as yourself' is called by St. James (ii 8) the royal law, βασιλικὸς νόμος. The ultimate revelation of the Divine Wisdom which is seen in the love of Him who, having loved His own, loved them to the end, — St. Paul calls this 'the foolishness of God'—is matched in loving and understanding response by the ultimate democratization of that same Wisdom when men, under the easy yoke of Christ, fulfil towards their neighbours the royal law, the law of liberty. Not many wise, perhaps, as the world counts wisdom, but the Wise Men of old knew where to find the incarnate Divine Wisdom, and it may be that all speculation will ultimately come to rest there too.

---

1) S. A. Cook, *The Old Testament: a Reinterpretation*, p. 211.

SOLOMON AND THE BEGINNINGS OF WISDOM IN ISRAEL

BY

R. B. Y. SCOTT
Montreal

The traditional connection of the name of Solomon with books of Hebrew wisdom and poetry raises a series of related problems. It is quite out of the question that the king was in fact the composer of the whole book of Proverbs, of Ecclesiastes and Wisdom, of psalms canonical and extra-canonical: how then did his name come to be attached to them? If—as appears likely—the ultimate origin of this literary convention is the statement of 1 Reg. v 12 that "he uttered three thousand proverbs, and his song(s were) a thousand and five" [1]), what reliance can be placed on this claim? Does it mean no more than that Solomon was credited with these accomplishments because wisdom literature and poetry flourished at his court and under his patronage [2])? Are the accounts of Solomon's superlative wisdom and fame a legendary embellishment of history? If so, what was the historical basis of these accounts, and when and why did the embellishment take place? How is this picture of Solomon's wisdom as intellectual brilliance and literary productivity to be related to the quite different interpretation of it—as discernment to render justice—in the famous story of the dream at Gibeon?

Many scholars seem to accept almost at its face value the story in 1 Reg. v 9-14 of Solomon's superlative literary gifts and fame, and hence have no difficulty in regarding him as the earliest patron, and indeed the fountain-head, of Israelite wisdom. EISSFELDT, for example, speaks of the "ganz richtig festgehaltenen Tatsache, dass Salomo an seinem Hof die Weisheitsdichtung gepflegt hat und auch selbst auf

---

1) LXX "five thousand".

2) R. EISLER draws attention to the parallel claim of Ashurbanipal to have written the tablets of his library; *AJSL* 42 (1926), p. 73, note 1. He says that Nabû gave him wisdom, and he acquired the arts of reading and writing; cf. D. D. LUCKENBILL, *Ancient Records of Babylonia and Assyria*, ii, secs. 767, 934, 986.

diesem Gebiet sehr fruchtbar gewesen ist" [1]). Similarly BAUMGARTNER in his 1951 survey of recent studies in the Wisdom Literature comments that "there is now again more disposition to treat seriously the ascription of both (Prov. x 1—xxii 16 and xxv—xxix) to Solomon" [2]). Most historians of Israel and commentators on the Wisdom books allow a greater or lesser degree of historical substance to the Solomonic tradition [3]), but there remains considerable scepticism about the antiquity and reliability of the more extravagant accounts of Solomon's wealth and wisdom. CAUSSE calls these "le mirage salomonien", and H. WHEELER ROBINSON says of Solomon's "posthumous reputation for wisdom" that "it is not easy to decide just where the historic Solomon ends and the legendary accretions begin" [4]). SKINNER, who accepts the tradition of Solomon's wisdom as substantially historical, nevertheless acknowledges that the description of it in 1 Reg. v 9-14, "with its backward look to the shadowy personages of a hoary antiquity .... can hardly have come from an ancient source" [5]). ALBRIGHT infers that Solomon's literary production, of which "nothing seems to have been directly preserved, ... was more prolific than inspired" [6]).

---

[1]) O. EISSFELDT, *Einleitung in das Alte Testament*, p. 527.

[2]) W. BAUMGARTNER, in *The Old Testament and Modern Study* (ed. H. H. ROWLEY), p. 213.

[3]) Cf. *inter alia*, E. SELLIN, *Geschichte des israelitisch-jüdischen Volkes*, i, p. 197; ii, p. 179; C. F. KENT, *History of the Hebrew People*, 13th ed. (1916), p. 184-187; R. KITTEL, *Geschichte des Volkes Israel*, 2nd ed. (1909), p. 231-232; A. T. OLMSTEAD, *History of Palestine and Syria*, p. 341; J. SKINNER, *I and II Kings* (Century Bible), p. 97; O. S. RANKIN, *Israel's Wisdom Literature*, p. 6; B. GEMSER, "Sprüche Salomos", *HAT*, p. 2; W. BAUMGARTNER, *TR* N.F. 5 (1933), p. 270; H. M. ORLINSKY, *Ancient Israel*, p. 85; E. SELLIN, *Einleitung in das Alte Testament*, 8th ed. (1950), ed. L. ROST, p. 156; W. A. IRWIN, in *The Interpreter's Bible*, p. 179. This view is stated more tentatively by T. H. ROBINSON, *History of Israel*, i, p. 242; M. NOTH, *Geschichte Israels*, (2nd ed. 1954) p. 200-201; H. R. HALL, *Ancient History of the Near East*, 7th ed. (1927), p. 433; and A. ALT, *TLZ* (1951), p. 139-144.

[4]) A. CAUSSE, *BZAW* 66, p. 148 ff.; H. WHEELER ROBINSON, *History of Israel*, p. 69-70.

[5]) J. SKINNER, *op. cit.*, p. 97. Cf. also I. BENZINGER, "Die Bücher der Könige", *KHAT*, p. 23-24; H. MEINHOLD, *Die Weisheit Israels*, p. 6; W. O. E. OESTERLEY, *ZAW* N. F. 4 (1927), p. 17; R. H. PFEIFFER, *Introduction to the Old Testament*, p. 383, 645; J. A. MONTGOMERY, ed. H. S. GEHMAN, "The Books of Kings", *ICC*, p. 107, 129; A. BENTZEN, *Introduction to the Old Testament*, 2nd ed. (1952), ii, p. 172. It is striking that J. FICHTNER, "Die altorientalische Weisheit in ihrer israelitisch-jüdischen Ausprägung", *BZAW* 63 (1933) does not seem to mention Solomon's name, except in the title of Sap. Sol.!

[6]) W. F. ALBRIGHT, *From the Stone Age to Christianity* (1940), p. 224.

I

The traditional connection of the name of Solomon with Israelite gnomic literature rests on two biblical foundations: the descriptive narratives in 1 Reg. v 9-14 and x 1-10, 13, 23-24; and the titles in Prov. i 1, x 1 and xxv 1 [1]). The ascription to him of Ecclesiastes and Wisdom, like the fantastic developments of later Jewish and Muslim legend, is based unquestionably on these passages and supplies no independent evidence. In fact, the title in Prov. i 1 (or, more exactly, in i 1-6) [2]), is itself dependent on x 1 and xxv 1, as is clearly shown by the inclusion also in the book of sections credited to other authors [3]). This biblical evidence must be examined closely to see if it merits the confidence or the scepticism with which it has been viewed by different scholars. Before this is done, we may note certain general considerations of historical probability which appear to support the biblical tradition.

In the first place, it seems unlikely that the focusing of Wisdom on Solomon, as of the Law on Moses and the Psalms on David, could be entirely without foundation. Though, as ELMSLIE says, "one suspects that the King's reputation for sagacity may have been enhanced by his royal estate, and that .... we see him through the haze of grandeur, ... the tradition of his wisdom stands, and like all firm traditions has a basis in fact" [4]). The basis in fact may have been far removed from the fanciful accounts given in 1 Reg. v and x, but "there must have been some reason for connecting wisdom with Solomon in this way" [5]).

The reason may well have been the known connections of the king with the Egyptian court, where wisdom literature had flourished since the days of the Middle Kingdom or before [6]). "That the practice of wisdom found a home at Solomon's court is made the more likely", says BAUMGARTNER, "by the latter's strong leaning toward the Egyptian monarchy" [7]). GEMSER argues further that the deliberate cultivation of Wisdom in Jerusalem began with Solomon's estab-

---

[1]) The writer of Eccles. assumes the Solomonic tradition, and poses as the king though without mentioning his name.

[2]) Cf. R. H. PFEIFFER, *op. cit.*, p. 645.

[3]) xxii 17-xxiv 22, and xxiv 23-24, to "the Wise"; xxx 1-33 to Agur ben Jakeh, and xxxi 1-9 to king Lemuel.

[4]) W. A. L. ELMSLIE, *Studies in Life from Jewish Proverbs*, p. 71.

[5]) W. O. E. OESTERLEY, *The Book of Proverbs*, p. xxii.

[6]) Cf. J. B. PRITCHARD, *Ancient Near Eastern Texts*, p. 412-424.

[7]) BAUMGARTNER, *op. cit.*, p. 213; cf. *TR* N.F. 5 (1933), p. 270.

lishment of a corps of officials on the pattern of the Egyptian court, whether or not the king himself engaged in literary composition [1]). ALT's argument is more substantial; noting the remarkable fact that the subject matter of the proverbs attributed to Solomon in 1 Reg. v 13 is the non-human natural world, whereas in the book of Proverbs it is human life and experience, ALT suggests that so unexpected a representation must have had firm roots in credible sources utilized by the editors of Kings. The analogy of the encyclopaedic nature-wisdom of Egypt and Mesopotamia, and the fact that in Egypt at least this was a living phenomenon at that time—as witness the Onomastikon of Amenope—lend support to the tradition [2]). The same may be said of VON RAD's view that the Joseph story, with its interest in Egypt and its portrait of the hero as exhibiting the qualities prized by "the older wisdom", is a product of a kind of *Aufklärung* under the early monarchy [3]).

Certainly it must be acknowledged that the assertions of 1 Reg. v 9 ff. and x 1 ff. that Solomon (or his court) was famous for developing Wisdom on the Egyptian model are not, on general historical grounds, improbable. It must be pointed out, however, that the Pharaoh's daughter was only one of Solomon's many wives, even if the principal one. This marriage, even with the dowry provided by Pharaoh and the private palace provided by Solomon [4]), is a slim basis for speaking of the latter's "strong leaning toward the Egyptian monarchy" in culture as well as in politics. The gods to whom his wives are said to have turned away Solomon's heart in his old age [5]) were not gods of Egypt. They did, however, include gods of the Sidonians, with whom, through Hiram of Tyre, Solomon's relations are much better documented than are his relations with Egypt [6]). The influence of Egypt, says OESTERLEY, "might have been indirect, through the Phoenicians, or direct, through the friendly relations between the royal houses". But OESTERLEY goes on to say, "While

[1]) B. GEMSER, "Sprüche Salomos", *HAT*, p. 2. Cf. H. GRESSMANN, *ZAW*, N.F. I, p. 282; SELLIN, *op. cit.*, ii, p. 197; 1 Reg. iv 1-6.

[2]) A. ALT, "Die Weisheit Salomos", *TLZ*, 76, p. 139-144.

[3]) G. VON RAD, *Josephgeschichte und ältere Chokma*, Congress vol., Copenhagen S.V.T. I (1953), p. 120-127. MAX WEBER, *Ancient Judaism*, p. 199, adds that "the short story of Joseph .... indicates .... relations to the temple priesthood of Heliopolis, the main seat of Egyptian wisdom".

[4]) 1 Reg. ix 16, 24, iii 1.

[5]) 1 Reg. xi 5, 7, 33.

[6]) Cf. 1 Reg. v 15-32, vii 13-14, ix 10-14, 26-28, x 11, 22.

the possibility is recognized, it must be held to be improbable that at this period the Israelites were influenced by Egyptian religious or literary thought; for the soil was not yet sufficiently receptive" [1]).

II

The only evidence which directly links the name of Solomon with the introduction of Wisdom literature in Israel consists, as already noted, in the narratives of 1 Reg. v and x, and in the titles in Prov. x 1 and xxv 1. [2]). The latter, in fact, would be meaningless apart from the existence of some such tradition of Solomon's wisdom as is presented in the former, though not necessarily so extravagantly stated. PFEIFFER remarks that the "Book of the Acts of Solomon" mentioned as a source in 1 Reg. xi 41 "was based partly on folk tales and the writer's fancy" [3]). The romantic and fanciful elements are clearly those which have to do principally with Solomon's proverbial glory and wisdom. Yet it is on these passages alone that the repute of Solomon as founder and patron saint of the Wisdom literature in Israel ultimately depends.

The key passage is 1 Reg. v 9-14, where Solomon's wisdom is defined as intellectual superiority and universal knowledge, surpassing the traditional lore of Egypt, of the desert Arabs and of the Edomites [4]), and resulting in the production of three thousand proverbs and vast numbers of songs. While these six verses have a certain completeness in themselves, the story of the Queen of Sheba in x 1-10, 13 is their natural sequel. A third short passage, x 23-25, lays emphasis on a feature common to all three,—the universal fame of the king's superlative wisdom. In these two passages in chapter x this wisdom of Solomon is linked in the exuberant description with material prosperity and magnificence as its natural counterparts. Since these additional features appear also in iv 20, v 1, 4-5, and since v 10-11, 14 so closely resemble x 23-24, and v 6 resembles x 26, it is natural to associate the accounts of Solomon's political supremacy in iv 20, v 1, 4-5 with those of his world famous wisdom in v 9-14.

---

[1]) W. O. E. OESTERLEY, *ZAW* N.F. 4 (1927), p. 16-17.

[2]) Chron. adds no independent information of value; the narrative of 1 Reg. v 9-14 is ignored. On the important differences between the M.T. and LXX in 1 Reg. 1-11, see below.

[3]) PFEIFFER, *op. cit.*, p. 383.

[4]) On Heman and Ethan as Edomite sages, cf. R. H. PFEIFFER, *ZAW* N.F. 3, p. 14.

In other words, it seems that the claim that the king was supreme among contemporary sages on the international scene, and was the author of thousands of proverbs and songs, is but one element in a cycle of folktales of the glory of Solomon.

It is noteworthy that, when the theme of the king's wisdom as encyclopaedic knowledge is resumed in x 1-10, 13, in the story of the Queen of Sheba, it is once more associated with a description in superlative terms of Solomon's wealth and magnificence. Chapter x 23-24, furthermore, repeats the thought and language of v 14; especially if we read in x 24, with LXX, "all the kings of the earth". There is something quite distinctive about the picture of people and queens coming from the ends of the earth to Solomon's presence to "hear his wisdom" [1]), and also about the intimate association in these stories of wealth and wisdom as characteristic of his glory [2]), The bliss of his subjects, the far extent of his dominions, the power of his chariot force, the superlativeness and fame of his intellect, the incomparable splendour of his court, the vast size of his harem,—all this in manner and conception is of one piece. It is surely significant that such extravagant descriptions of royal magnificence are found elsewhere in the Bible only in Esth., Dan. i-vi, and Chron. The pomp and splendour of courts and palaces are the subjects of midrashic tales in Esth. and Dan. i-vi, and in these pictures the wise men at the royal court are a frequent feature [3]). The Chronicler makes a fabulous character of David, as this folklore in the first Book of Kings makes of Solomon: David musters armies of fantastic size; like Solomon, his fame is world wide, and his riches—including three thousand talents of Ophir gold—are enormous [4]).

The extent of this element of folklore in the account of Solomon's reign in the first Book of Kings is a point to be considered. It has often been noted that the extravagant statements in iv 20, v 1, 4-6, about the extent and prosperity of Solomon's kingdom, disrupt the sequence and alter the tone of their context. The LXX preserves, as a sequel to iv 7-19, a shorter text in a more natural order,—v 7-8, 2-3. This is followed by a shorter form of M.T. v 4 [5]), which in turn introduces the "wisdom" passage, verses 9-14, with which we are

[1]) Cf. v 14, x 1, 8, 24.
[2]) Cf. v 1, 4-6, 9-14, x 4-7, 23-25, xi 1, 3.
[3]) Cf. Esth. i 13, vi 13; Dan. i 4, 20, v 11-12, etc.
[4]) 1 Chron. xii 23-37, xiv 17, xxix 3-5.
[5]) A clear case of homoioteleuton, *pace* MONTGOMERY, *op. cit.*, p. 132.

chiefly concerned. The verses intruded in M.T. into this shorter text, i.e., iv 20, v 1, 4-6, clearly belong with v 9-14 [1]). In chapter x, verses 1-10, 13-15, 20b-25, 27 are of the same genre [2]). In addition, the words "And Solomon son of David reigned over Israel and Judah in Jerusalem", which occur at the beginning and the end respectively of the LXX insertions at ii 35 and ii 46b, and which have no exact counterpart in M.T., may belong to the folktale cycle [3]).

The literary and linguistic affinities of this material are with post-exilic, rather than with pre-exilic, writings. In addition to the general impression of lateness created by the grandiose imagination of the writer or writers, and the parallels already noted with Esth., Dan. i-vi and Chron., there is more precise linguistic evidence to the same effect:

iv 20, v 15—"*Judah and Israel*" (in this order, as designation of the whole people); elsewhere only in 2 Chron. xvi 11, xxv 26, xxviii 26, xxxii 32.

iv 20—"*eat, drink, and rejoice*" (the verbs *ʾḵl, šṯh śmḥ*, thus co-ordinated); elsewhere only in Eccles. viii 15; cf. Eccles. ii 24, iii 13; Esth. ix 17-19, 22.

v 1, 4, x 1, 24, 25—Aramaizing use of participle for finite verb, with or without *hāyâ*.

v 4—"*beyond the river*"; the reference clearly is to the area *west* of the Euphrates, as sixteen times in Esr.-Neh. and not elsewhere. (In Jos. xxiv 2, etc., the reference is to the area *east* of the Euphrates).

v 9—"*understanding*" (*tᵉḇûnâ*); a word found chiefly in Prov. and rare in pre-exilic writings.

v 9—"*largeness of mind*" (*rōḥaḇ lēḇ*); the closest parallel is the late Ps. cxix 32. *lēḇ* with the meaning "mind, intelligence" is commonest in Prov.

v 11—"*be wise*" (*ḥāḵam*); almost all the twenty-seven occurrences of this verb are post-exilic.

---

[1]) Of this material only v 4ac appears *here* in LXX; however, iv 20, v 1ac, 4, 5 (plus "eating and drinking"), 6, 1ab are found in the long insertion which follows ii 46b in LXX. The inclusion of v 6 with the legendary material may be questioned on account of its obvious dependence on the annalistic record in x 26; but *all* the folklore elements may be said to be imaginative developments of a more sober tradition.

[2]) Note that x 26 is in LXX followed by the equivalent of v 1a.

[3]) Apparently as its opening sentence. In the first instance it follows a composite verse, ii 35a, 46c, 35b. In the second instance it replaces iii 1 which, *in M.T.*, follows directly on ii 46c. The form of the sentence is related to xi 42, iv 20 and v 5.

v 11—"*Ethan, Heman, Calcol, Darda*"; proper names found elsewhere only in 1 Chron. ii 6 and derived psalm titles (Pss. lxxxviii and lxxxix).

v 13—"*trees*"; BURNEY [1]) remarks that the plural use is mostly late or poetical.

x 2, 10, 25—"spices" (*beśāmîm*); of the twenty-five occurrences of this word outside this chapter, twenty-two are in "P", Cant., Esth. and Chron.

x 3—Nip'al of *'lm*, of hidden knowledge, is found again only in "P", Iob, Eccles. and the Chron. parallel.

x 8—"*happy*!" (*'ašrê*); commonest in late Pss. and Prov.

x 15—"*governor*" (*peḥâ*); of twenty-three occurrences outside this passage, at least nineteen are post-exilic.

The internal evidence that these accounts of Solomon's wisdom and glory are legendary and late is supported by several indications that they were not part of the original Deuteronomic edition of the Book of Kings. The textual disorder which accompanies the appearance of this material in 1 Reg. v, already noted [2]), is exemplified further where it appears again in chapter x. The first part of the story of the Queen of Sheba, x 1-10, interrupts the continuity of ix 28—x 11-12, and similarly the last named verses separate x 1-10 from its conclusion in x 13. In the LXX textual tradition ix 15, 17-22 have been transferred to follow x 22; x 26 is a variant of M.T. v 6, and is followed by the equivalent of v 1a. It is of interest that the parallel in 2 Chron. ix 25-26 agrees at this point with the LXX of Kings. Evidently the text of Kings was still fluid when the Old Greek translation was made. The disorder noted may be due to the insertion of the folklore material at different points in existing parallel textual traditions. In both M.T. and LXX this material is patently intrusive [3]).

A fundamental difference in viewpoint between the midrashic tales of Solomon's glory and the Deuteronomic context in which they are now found lies in the interpretations given of the king's traditional wisdom. Three distinct interpretations appear, of which the second is consequent upon the first, and the third upon the second. These are:

---

1) *Op. cit.*, p. 52.

2) LXX includes v 9-10 in the apparently miscellaneous matter inserted after ii 35; and also, in a second long insertion after ii 46b, all of iv 20-v 6 together with v 9 (abbreviated) and some other material.

3) Cf. MONTGOMERY, *op. cit.*, p. 126 (commenting on iv 20-v 14) "a *pot-pourri* of material bearing on the reign, much of it duplicated in cc. 9 and 10. Evidently Heb. Kings early underwent transformations".

1) Wisdom as *the ability of the successful ruler*. This occurs in two contexts in the narratives of Solomon's reign, 1 Reg. ii 1-2, 5-9 and v 15-26. In the first of these the moribund David speaks of his son as "wise" in the unspecialized sense of "competent, knowing what to do", like Joseph in Gen. xli 33, 39, and able rulers in general [1]). The Deuteronomic intrusion in ii 3-4 makes it clear that the remainder of ii 1-9 belongs to a pre-Deuteronomic introduction to the story of the summary executions in ii 28-46. In any case, the "wisdom" spoken of has nothing to do with the making of proverbs, nor is it unique with Solomon, even in degree.

The second passage, v 15-26, also shows marks of the intrusion of editorial material, verses 17-19, 21, into a pre-Deuteronomic narrative which reads consecutively without the interpolated speeches. The editorial verse 21 clearly echoes the Deuteronomic language of the speeches in Solomon's dream (iii 5-15), and the word "wise" here takes its colour from that earlier passage. On the other hand, "wisdom" in v 26, as the context makes clear, is the competence in negotiation and administration which marks the successful ruler. It is to be noted that it is *this kind of wisdom* which is said to have been promised to Solomon; apparently a reference back to the source underlying the present account of the dream which is in distinctively Deuteronomic language [2]).

2) Wisdom as *the insight to distinguish right from wrong*, with the resulting *ability of a judge to render true justice*. This is one particular quality of a successful ruler, and so may be seen as the special emphasis of the Deuteronomic editor. He has made it the theme of his rewriting of the dream story, and has appended as an illustration of such judicial wisdom the old folktale of the two mothers [3]). The translation "govern" for *lišpōṭ* in iii 9 is too broad; that the particular capacity to judge justly is in question is clear from the specifications in verses 9 and 11, as well as from the concluding words of

---

[1]) Cf. F. Brown, S. R. Driver, C. A. Briggs, *Hebrew and English Lexicon of the Old Testament*, p. 314. It is possible but less likely that the meaning here is "shrewd, cunning".

[2]) Montgomery, *op. cit.*, p. 107, agrees with Kittel that the incident of the dream at Gibeon "is in origin an early, practically contemporary story", but assigns its present form to late editors. C. F. Burney, *Notes on the Hebrew Text of the Books of Kings*, p. 28-32, demonstrates conclusively that in its present form the story is thoroughly Deuteronomic in tone and style.

[3]) Montgomery, *op. cit.*, p. 109, cites a close parallel from Indian lore, and notes that Gressmann has assembled twenty-two such parallels.

the appended illustration. It is all the more curious that this aspect of royal wisdom is not referred to again after chapter iii.

3) Wisdom as *intellectual brilliance and encyclopaedic knowledge*, especially of the world of nature other than man. This picture of Solomon's wisdom as given in v 9-14, and x 1-10, 13, 23-24, is the basis of his repute as founder of the Wisdom literature. If the Deuteronomic editor who composed the speeches in Solomon's dream had intended to include in the subsequent narrative these pictures of the king as the supreme sage of mankind, he could hardly have restricted his definition of wisdom to the rendering of true justice. But, on the other hand, the legend could easily have developed from the words of Yahweh's promise in the dream, iii 12-13: "I give you a wise and discerning mind, ... also .... both riches and honour, so that no other king can compare with you".

One notable characteristic of the Deuteronomic editing of the material concerning Solomon's reign is the composition of speeches in the editor's distinctive style [1]). It is therefore important that the speech of the Queen of Sheba in x 6-9 does not resemble the other speeches in this regard, although x 9 seems to be patterned on Hiram's benediction in v 21 [2]). The Deuteronomic editor and his sources show no acquaintance with the legendary material, whereas the latter at almost every point can be recognized as an imaginative development of the promise in iii 12-13 of wisdom, riches, and honour beyond compare.

A further piece of evidence that the passages which thus glorify Solomon are post-Deuteronomic interpolations is the fact that the definitely Deuteronomic editorial and source material does *not* glorify the king unduly, except as builder of the Temple and as displaying judicial wisdom. Only once, in the language of the dream at the commencement of his reign, is it said that Yahweh was pleased with him. On the other hand, Solomon is admonished and warned

---

[1]) Cf. ii 3-4, iii 6-14, v 3-5, 7, vi 12-13, viii 14-30, 46-61, ix 3-9.

[2]) *yᵉhî bārûḵ* is found elsewhere only in Prov. v 18; Ru. ii 19 (Jer. xx 14 is not a real parallel); *ḥāpēṣ b*, followed by infin. does not appear in any Deuteronomic context; *nāṯan* for "set" (on a throne) is not used elsewhere in Kings, contrast 1 Reg. ii 24; the fem. infin. cstr. of *ʾhḇ* is used once thus in Deut. vii 8, but contrast Deut. iv 37, etc.; to "love Israel forever" *sounds like* Deut., but apparently is not found there; *śîm lᵉmeleḵ* (cf. *nāṯan lᵉmeleḵ*, 2 Chron. ix 8) is in contrast to the *Hip̄ʿil* of *mlḵ* used in the Deuteronomic prayer at iii 7. In contrast to these many differences in a single verse it should be observed how closely the language of Hiram's benediction in v 21 resembles that of the prayer in iii 6-9.

repeatedly, in anticipation of his defection from Yahweh [1]). The rebel Jeroboam is even promised the legitimate succession upon the same conditions as Solomon. The narrative of Rehoboam's disastrous meeting with the northern tribesmen at Shechem (a calamity which the editor regards as divinely ordained), reflects not only on the young king but on his father.

Again, the law of the kingship in Deut. xvii 14-20 unquestionably forbids a later monarch to pattern himself on Solomon. These verses imply that it was Solomon's misfortune (and perhaps his excuse?) that he did not have available a copy of the law of Moses for study. The king is commanded to be literate, and there is not the slightest suggestion that Solomon was remembered for his wisdom as well as for his horses, his wealth and his wives. All this is hard to reconcile with knowledge by the Deuteronomic writers of the lavish adulation of Solomon's wisdom found in 1 Reg. v 9-14. In fact it must be asserted unequivocally that this passage and its portrait of Solomon as the wisest of men and the author of proverbs of encyclopaedic wisdom is late and largely imaginary. It is a quite insufficient foundation for the far-reaching conclusions with respect to the Wisdom literature which have been built upon it.

III

The second piece of biblical evidence upon which rests the traditional connection of Solomon with Wisdom writings is found in the titles of collections of proverbs at Prov. x 1 and xxv 1. The bodies of material which follow these headings—Prov. x 1 - xxii 16, and xxv 1 - xxix 27—are the only writings to which Solomon's name is attached which have the slightest claim to be dated before the Exile, let alone in the early monarchy [2]). It is therefore important to decide what weight can be laid on the descriptions of these collections as "proverbs of Solomon", and what is meant by the reference to the literary activities of "the men of Hezekiah".

The phrase "Proverbs of Solomon", like the phrase "Psalms of David", is of so indeterminate meaning as to be valueless as evidence of authorship. It may be simply a conventional term for proverbs

---

[1]) ii 3-4, iii 14, vi 11-13, ix 3-9, xi 1-40.

[2]) Eissfeldt, *op. cit.*, dates Eccles. in the 3rd cent. B.C.; Prov. i-ix in the 4th or 3rd; Cant. in the 3rd; Sap. Sol. and Pss. Sol. in the 1st cent. The titles of Pss. lxxii and cxxvii are obviously late inferences from the content of each.

of a particular type (cf. "a Miltonic Ode") or of a historic era (cf. "Elizabethan poetry") known familiarly by a famous name associated with it [1]). At the same time it must be admitted that ascription of authorship (whether justified or not) is the most probable meaning, if only because the post-exilic folktale in 1 Reg. v 9-14 claims this specifically. Since the title in xxv 1 appears to *look back* to Hezekiah's age, it does not prove that the ascription of proverbs to Solomon was a convention as old as, or older than, Hezekiah.

The added information, however, that the collection beginning with xxv 1 consists of proverbs "which the men of Hezekiah king of Judah *brought forward*" [2]), is interesting and probably significant. BARNES sees here "strong evidence not lightly to be set aside" that the tradition of Solomon's authorship of collections of proverbs was accepted in the days of Hezekiah [3]). This is a possible explanation, though, as noted already, the heading may mean no more than that these proverbs were "Solomonic" in some general sense. More important is the mention of Hezekiah's scribal establishment. Since no tendentious purpose can be suspected in the mentioning of the otherwise unknown "men of Hezekiah", this is first-rate evidence that an organized literary wisdom movement existed at Hezekiah's court and under his patronage. The king's men *transcribed*, *published*, or *carried forward from tradition* a collection of maxims which, *in this later editorial title*, are designated "proverbs of Solomon". There is a double ambiguity: just as the phrase may *or* may not indicate authorship, so it may *or* may not imply that the association of proverbs with the name of Solomon existed before Hezekiah's time. The significant point is that such an association did exist *at that time*, when a literary wisdom movement and a court scribal establishment were to be found at Jerusalem under royal patronage.

It is a remarkable fact—particularly remarkable if Solomon had been in fact the founder and patron of Wisdom literature in Israel—that

---

1) Cf. SELLIN-ROST, *op. cit.*, p. 157; S. R. DRIVER, *Introduction to the Literature of the O.T.*, 9th ed. (1913), p. 407.

2) *Hipʿil* of *ʿtq*; A.V. "copied out"; R.S.V. "copied"; PFEIFFER, *op. cit.*, p. 645, "collected". The lexicons of BROWN, DRIVER and BRIGGS and of KÖHLER and BAUMGARTNER propose the meaning "transcribe", as in late Heb.; this meaning does not occur elsewhere in the O.T. The only other appearances in the O.T. of this verb. in Hipʿil, viz., Gen. xii 8, xxvi 22; Iob ix 5, xxxii 15, support for this context in Prov. the meaning "bring forward", i.e., "bring forward from the past", "transmit", "transcribe".

3) W. E. BARNES, *The First Book of Kings* (Camb. Bible), p. 38.

"the wise" as a class or profession do not once appear *during or after* Solomon's reign, until the time of Isaiah and Hezekiah. Then they come on the scene quite definitely, are recognized as leaders of society in Jeremiah's time, and, like Solomon himself, are credited with collections of proverbs [1]). It is true that, earlier, two female soothsayers are mentioned and called "wise women", but there is no indication that they had anything to do with literary wisdom. It is true, also, that the quotation of folk proverbs in the early histories points to a popular gnomic tradition stretching far back into the past [2]). But there is nothing whatever in the records to suggest the continuous existence since the time of Solomon of a school of literary wisdom in Israel [3]). As has been shown, the fabulous tales of Solomon's own wisdom are of little, if any, historical worth.

This is not to suggest for a moment that the traditions of Solomon's glorious reign had no foundation in fact. Quite the contrary! It was a period of remarkable social and political development, of economic organization and expansion, of centralized power, court life, and international relations. Above all there were the great building enterprises of palaces and temple and chariot cities, visible evidences of Solomon's power and glory remaining to later generations. It is no wonder that tales of that glory were kept alive through the long centuries after that glory had departed [4]). A selection of them—in a post-exilic form—were inserted into the Deuteronomist's account of Solomon's reign. A pre-exilic form of the same tales of Solomon's glory and wisdom may have come from the scribal school of Hezekiah.

Hezekiah was the first king since Solomon who could claim to be the sole Israelite monarch. Several lines of evidence suggest that he set out to foster a national revival, taking Solomon as his model. In particular, he became a patron of wisdom literature, more effective

---

[1]) Jes. v 21, xxix 14, xxxi 2; Jer. viii 8-9, ix 23, xviii 18; Prov. xxii 17, xxiv 23.

[2]) 2 Sam. xiv 2, xx 16; 1 Sam. x 12, xxiv 14; 1 Reg. xx 11, etc.

[3]) The one possible exception to this categorical statement is the Joseph story with its "wisdom" characteristics, as von Rad has pointed out; see above, p. 274. It is debatable how much older than the eighth century the Joseph story is; in any case it is not nearly as old as Solomon's reign.

[4]) Noth, *op. cit.*, p. 187-188, identifies the "Book of the Acts of Solomon" (1 Reg. xi 41) as containing the factual material on the reign, and distinguishes from this "noch einige Anekdoten, wie sie offenbar über Salomo noch lange im Umlauf waren. Diese Anekdoten haben Salomos Reichtum und Weisheit zum Gegenstand".

though less famous than his predecessor. As GEMSER says, commenting on Prov. xxv 1, "Der Regierung Hiskias, also der Zeit Jesajas, ist ein solches Unternehmen, das die Schätze der Tradition sichern wollte, wohl zuzutrauen. Die assyrische Bedrohung Judas und die Abwendung der Gefahr, die Berührung mit den grossen Kulturmächten der Zeit und die nationale Wiedergeburt — das alles hatte zur Folge, dass sich das Volk auf seine geistigen Güter besann, und das um so mehr, als nach dem Falle Samariens .... Juda das Erbe des Nordreichs antrat" [1]).

Although since 722 most of the territory of northern Israel had been organized as an Assyrian province, at least part of the tribal lands of Benjamin was under Hezekiah's control [2]). If the account in 2 Chron. xxx of the invitation to the northern tribes to resume the practice of pilgrimage to Jerusalem is substantially true, the intended result would be as much political as religious (as Jeroboam I had foreseen long before). The editor of Kings credits Hezekiah with military prowess, though he gives but one example of it [3]). The Chronicler, on the other hand, concludes his account of the crisis of 701 with the assertion that the Lord similarly saved Hezekiah from *all* his enemies. He adds that (like Solomon!) Hezekiah had peace on all sides, received tribute and universal admiration, and possessed riches and honour and treasuries and store-houses and cities [4]). Most important of all in the eyes of this writer were Hezekiah's measures to cleanse the temple and restore the full glories of worship; here the comparison with Solomon becomes quite specific,—"since the time of Solomon .... there had been nothing like this in Jerusalem" [5]).

The restricted interests of the Chronicler are perhaps responsible both for the extravagant language used about Hezekiah's power and glory, and for his omission of any reference to certain other parallels to the Solomonic tradition of which we hear in the prophecies of Isaiah [6]). This evidence is much more important than the Chronicler's

---

[1]) GEMSER, *op. cit.*, p. 73.

[2]) Cf. SELLIN, *Geschichte*, i, p. 268-269, citing Micah's addresses to Judah as "Jacob" and "Israel". Cf. Mich. iii 9-12.

[3]) 2 Reg. xx 20, xviii 7-8. Perhaps the revolt against Assyria was thought to have been successful, in view of xix 21-37. The editor's text could hardly have included xviii 14-16, which is omitted in the parallel text in Jes. xxxvi.

[4]) 2 Chron. xxxii 22-23, 27-29; cf. 1 Reg. v 1, 4, 14, x 21-25. Hezekiah's wealth is testified to also in Jes. xxxix.

[5]) 2 Chron. xxix 3-36, xxx 13-27.

[6]) The records of Hezekiah's reign in 2 Reg. xviii-xx consist chiefly of excerpts from an earlier Book of Isaiah. Apart from this Isaianic material, 2 Reg. tells us

because it is contemporary, but also because it is *incidental*, i.e., it is not coloured in order to highlight a theme. Three interrelated features which appear in Isaiah's picture of Hezekiah's reign recall three similarly interrelated features of the Solomonic tradition: (i) intercourse with Egypt, with resulting strong Egyptian political and cultural influence on the Jerusalem court; (ii) unusual prominence in the scene of horses and chariots as the basic military arm, and as a symbol of glory; (iii) the power and influence at court of organized "Wisdom"; in this case not so much in the person of the king [1]) as in "the wise" as a professional group, and in the person of court secretaries like Shebna [2]). The first two of these are of interest chiefly as further evidence that Hezekiah may have thought of himself as reviving through imitation the ancient glories of Solomon. The third bears more directly on the thesis of this paper.

It is altogether to be expected that the political and economic expansion of Hezekiah's reign should have been paralleled in the cultural sphere. This showed itself in religious expansion, iconoclastic reform, and measures to restore the prestige of the temple. It is evidenced also in the literary developments of which there are many indications, and particularly in the new prominence in Israel of literary Wisdom. The religious and the literary movements may, indeed, have been closely associated, particularly if BENTZEN is correct in surmising that a scribal school was installed in the temple at Jerusalem, as at Mari and elsewhere [3]). BENTZEN also refers with approval to the suggestion of NYBERG that the end of the eighth century was a time when oral traditions were being fixed in writing as a result of the realization—following the catastrophe to Samaria—that Israel's traditions were in danger of perishing.

The most concrete piece of evidence for this literary renaissance is, of course, the reference in Prov. xxv 1 to the literary undertaking of the "men of Hezekiah" [4]). PEROWNE recalls the view of SAYCE

---

only of the king's iconoclasm, his rebellion against Assyria (with no details), his Philistine conquests, and his feats of hydro-engineering.

[1]) Though A. COHEN, *The Proverbs*, p. 166, comments on the "fine style" of Hezekiah's message in 2 Reg. xix 3. The fact that the king here originates, or quotes, a proverb, is also of interest. There seems no reason to question that this contemporary record reproduces Hezekiah's words with substantial accuracy.

[2]) For (i), cf. Jes. xix 1-15, xx 1-6, xxx 1-7, xxxi 1-3, xxxvi 4-10. For (ii), cf. Jes. ii 7, xxii 18, xxx 16, xxxi 1-3, xxxvi 8-9. For (iii), cf. Jes. v 21, xxix 14, 15-16, xxx 1, xxxi 2, xxii 14, xxxvi 3, 22.

[3]) BENTZEN, *op. cit.*, p. 171-172; ii, p. 173.

[4]) This use of the word "men" in the sense of "professional servants", "fol-

that this title points to the existence of a royal library at Jerusalem, and Hezekiah has even been called "a Jewish Ashurbanipal" on the basis of it [1]). Although it is too much to claim that the attribution to Hezekiah in Jes. xxxviii 9 of the following psalm establishes his authorship, the very fact that his name could be attached to it shows that he was associated in the popular mind with literary activity. Unlike Moses, David and Solomon, moreover, Hezekiah did not move in the mists of remote antiquity. He is the *only* pre-exilic king after Solomon whose name has literary associations, and these are with both psalmody and wisdom writings.

The evidence, indeed, is quite sufficient to show that the reign of Hezekiah was a time of literary activity in Judah. It is the most probable time for the bringing together of northern and southern historical traditions, prophetic records and psalm collections. The reference in Prov. xxv 1 to Hezekiah's scribal school as engaged in the collection and publication of proverbs is only one of several indications that the Wisdom movement had become influential both in culture and in politics. Jes. v 21 tells us that self-styled "wise men" and sceptics are in positions of authority. In the oracles of Isaiah found in xxix 13-14, 15-16, xxx 1-5 and xxxi 1-3 the prophet makes it plain that "the wise" are a coherent party influential at court, working for a calculated pro-Egyptian political policy which ignores the prophet's call to trust in Yahweh. Very pointedly Isaiah threatens disaster, since those who rely on horses and chariots do not consult Yahweh, "though *he too* is wise!".

It is striking, too, how Isaiah pours his scorn on the wise men of Egypt on whom their opposite numbers in Judah modelled themselves: "How can you say to Pharaoh, I am a son of the wise, a son of ancient kings?" [2]) Is it unlikely that these "wise men" of Judah also claimed an inheritance going back to "ancient kings", and thus built on the tradition of Solomon's success as a ruler the legend of his accomplishments as a sage?

The close relationships of nascent Israelite literary wisdom in this

---

lowers" (cf. "David's men", 1 Sam. xxiii 3, 5; "Abner's men", 2 Sam. ii 31) tells against the emendation in 1 Reg. x 8 of "happy are thy men!" to "happy are thy wives!" (with LXX). The latter would be an incongruous remark in the circumstances; no oriental would suggest that Solomon maintained his harem in order to admire his wisdom.

[1]) T. T. Perowne, *Proverbs* (Camb. Bible) p. 156; E. Sellin, *Introduction to the O.T.* (tr. W. Montgomery), p. 209; cf. Bentzen, *op. cit.*, ii, p. 173.

[2]) Jes. xix 11.

period with the ancient wisdom tradition of Egypt are demonstrated by the evidence of direct dependence in at least one instance. It is now generally agreed that the section entitled "the words of the wise" in Prov. xxi 17 — xxiv 22 is directly or indirectly dependent upon "The Instruction of Amen-em-opet", an Egyptian literary work of 1000-600 B.C. [1]). Possibly there is some significance in the fact that this section of Proverbs is separated by only one small collection (xxiv 23-34) from the collection attributed to "the men of Hezekiah" (xxv—xxix). "Dass die spätere Königzeit den Amen-en-ope als Lehrmeister gehabt hat, ist jetzt über allen Zweifel sicher bewiesen", concludes SELLIN-ROST [2]).

The familiarity in Isaiah's time, not only of wisdom as an organized social phenomenon, but of gnomic literary forms, is evident from that prophet's own use of these. In Jes. xxviii 23-29, the Parable of the Farmer, the oracle is in the manner of the Wisdom teachers. The form of address recalls Prov. v 1 and xxii 17; and the rhetorical questions Iob xv 2-3. For the dependence of human upon Divine wisdom, cf. Iob xii 7-26; Prov. viii. Again, in Jes. xxxii 1-8 the prophet promises the fruits of royal justice and the discomfiture of the fool and the knave; for the matter we may compare Jes. xi 1-9, but the manner is that of Prov. viii 15-21 and xvi 10-15. Just as in Jes. v 1-7 the prophet adopts the rôle of the singer of vintage songs, so here he takes the role of the wisdom teacher. In each case it must have been because the respective figures were thoroughly familiar to his audience.

Two minor pieces of evidence may be appended in support of the thesis that Hebrew literary Wisdom received its first great impetus as a result of Hezekiah's efforts to renew the vanished glories of Solomon. The first is the prominence at court of the professional scribe, Shebna. In Jes. xxii 15-19 he is royal chamberlain, and is denounced for the pride which he exhibited in the possession of "splendid chariots", and the preparation for himself of a princely "tomb on the height" [3]). Clearly such a man was in a position of power. Even when (apparently) in xxxvi 3 he has yielded the superior

---

[1]) Cf. PRITCHARD, *op. cit.*, p. 421; W. O. E. OESTERLEY, *ZAW* N.F. 4 (1927), p. 16 ff.; BENTZEN, *op. cit.*, ii, p. 172-173; H. H. ROWLEY, *Growth of the Old Testament*, p. 141; R. H. PFEIFFER, *Introduction to the Old Testament*, p. 648.

[2]) *Op. cit.*, p. 156.

[3]) The interesting possibility that this tomb has been identified is discussed by N. AVIGAD, *Israel Exploration Journ.*, iii, p. 137-152.

office to Eliakim, as Isaiah predicted would happen, Shebna the scribe is still one of the principal royal ministers.

Finally, there is a further reflection arising from the law of the kingship in Deut. xvii 14-20, which has already been discussed in another connection [1]). It is a well known principle of law that a practice is not forbidden by law unless the situation demands it, i.e., unless the practice exists or the act has been done. Whom did this law have in mind, when it forbade the king to pattern himself on Solomon, unless it be Hezekiah? The Deuteronomic code was almost certainly formulated in the 7th century, after Hezekiah's reign. This law, however, could hardly have had in mind Hezekiah's successor Manasseh, who imitated and surpassed Solomon only in his cruelty and oppression.

IV

We seem now to be in a position to answer the questions raised in the opening paragraph of this paper, if not with full assurance, at least with a high degree of probability. Though general historical considerations do not preclude, but rather favour, the connection with Solomon of the origins of literary wisdom in Israel, the ostensible biblical evidence for this in the first Book of Kings is post-exilic in date and legendary in character. The legend is based on the promises which, in 1 Reg. iii 12-13, accompany the Deuteronomic editor's interpretation of Solomon's wisdom as judicial discernment.

The first real impact of Egyptian Wisdom on Israel, with evident results in Hebrew literary production, seems to belong to the reign of Hezekiah. This is suggested by Prov. xxv 1, supported by the other lines of evidence which have been enumerated above. If "proverbs of Solomon" were so called before this time, there is no substantial evidence to show when and how this came about. The reason may lie in the existence of popular tradition based on Solomon's known relations with Egypt, and on the visible remains of his magnificent buildings. In any case, the tradition seems to have been cultivated deliberately by Hezekiah as part of his grandiose plans to restore the vanished glories of Solomon's kingdom, for in Hezekiah's reign appear the first clear evidences of Hebrew Wisdom as a significant literary phenomenon.

---

[1]) See above, p. 281.

TEXTUAL AND PHILOLOGICAL NOTES ON SOME PASSAGES IN THE BOOK OF PROVERBS *)

BY

D. WINTON THOMAS

Cambridge

I 4: לְנַעַר דעת ומזמה

Parallelism with לִפְתָאיִם in the first half of the verse might lead us to expect לִנְעָרִים. The plural has indeed the support of the Tg. and Pesh. (טלאי, ܠܛܠܝܐ), and is read by some scholars [1]). Possibly לנער here is an abbreviation (לנער' for לנערים). In cases where the masculine plural is abbreviated in the M.T., only the final *mêm* as a rule disappears, while the *yôdh* remains [2]). The disappearance of both consonants is, however, not unknown [3]).

I 11: נארבה לְדָם נצפנה לנקי חִנָּם.

The emendation of חִנָּם into חֵרֶם "net" [4]) is unnecessary. The verb נצפנה is parallel in meaning to נארבה —both mean "lurk" [5])—and חִנָּם is used here, as elsewhere [6]), of groundless hostility or attack. The adoption of תָּם "perfect" [7]) for דָּם also seems difficult to justify, since the phrase ארב [ל]דם occurs elsewhere in Proverbs (e.g., i 18, xii 6), and moreover דם has the support of the ancient versions.

---

*) The following abbreviations are used throughout: BEER = G. BEER in KITTEL, *Bibl. Hebr.*; BDB = BROWN-DRIVER-BRIGGS, *A Heb. and Engl. Lex. of the O.T.*; EHRL. = A. B. EHRLICH, *Randglossen z.d. Hebr. Bibel*, vol. VI; FRANK. = W. FRANKENBERG, *Die Sprüche*; GEMS. = B. GEMSER, *Sprüche Salomos*; TOY = C. H. TOY, *A Critical and Exegetical Commentary on the Book of Proverbs* (Intern. Crit. Comm.); WILD. = G. WILDEBOER, *Die Sprüche*.

1) E.g., N. SCHLOEGL, *Rev. Bibl.* ix (1900), p. 520.

2) For examples see F. PERLES, *Anal. zur Textkritik des A.T.*, 1895, p. 29; R. GORDIS, *The Song of Songs*, p. 94 f.

3) See PERLES, *op. cit.*, p. 28 f.

4) So BEER, *ad loc.* FRANK., p. 21, supplies רֶשֶׁת "net" as object of נצפנה. LXX (ἀδίκως), Tg. (מגן), Vulg. (*frustra*) support the M.T.

5) For the intransitive meaning of צפן, see BDB, p. 860.

6) *Ibid.*, p. 336.

7) E.g., by TOY, p. 19; WILD., p. 3; GEMS., p. 14.

The text seems to express the mounting glee of the blood-seekers (חטאים) as they contemplate, in a crescendo of delight, their groundless attack on those who have done nothing to deserve it. The sense may be brought out thus —

"Let us lie in wait for blood!
Let us lurk—for the innocent!!
Though we have no cause against them!!!" [1])

I 17: כי־חנם מְזֹרָה הרשת

The word מזרה has been explained in several different ways—as ptcp. Pu. of זרה "scatter" [2]); as ptcp. pass. Qal of מזר "spread out" (read as מְזוּרָה) [3]); and as ptcp. Pu. of זור "draw tight" [4]). The proverb is sometimes taken to mean that it is to no purpose that a net is spread out in the sight of a bird, for the fowler will gain nothing, since the bird will take fright and avoid the net [5]). Ehrlich [6]), however, following Rashi, argues, with much probability, that מזרה here refers to the sprinkling of a net with grain as bait. Rashi's comment is as follows—כי העופות הרואות חטים וקטניות מזורים על הרשת חנם הוא בעיניהם שאינם מכירים על מה היא נזרת ויורדין בה ואוכלין "When the birds see wheat and small grain strewn upon the net, to no purpose is it in their eyes, because they do not realize why it is strewn with grain, and so they alight upon it and eat." The birds, that is to say, are lured on by the bait and caught in the net, even though the net was baited in full sight of them—they see the bait prepared, but it is to no purpose, for they do not see the danger, and so meet their death [7]). Neither Rashi nor Ehrlich, however, indicate how the meaning "strewn with grain" for מזרה is obtained. This

---

1) For the use of חנם in connection with blood shed without good cause, see especially 1 Sam. xxv 31, 1 Reg. ii 31. Pesh. here has ܒܢܟܠܐ "deceitfully".

2) So, e.g., BDB, p. 280.

3) So Beer *ad loc.*; L. Köhler and W. Baumgartner, *Lex. in Vet. Test. Libros*, p. 266, 510; Ges.-Buhl, *Hebr. u. Aram. Handwörterb.*, 16th ed., p. 206, 412.

4) G. R. Driver, *Biblica* 32 (1951), p. 173, who thinks the root מזר is also possible. Frank., p. 22, reads פרושׂה "spread"; cf. Toy, p. 20. The versions render as follows-LXX ἐκτείνεται; Tg. פריסא; Pesh. ܦܪ̈ܝܣܢ; Vulg. *jacitur*; Pal. Syr. ܡܬܦܫܛܝܢ "spread" (*A Palestinian Syriac Lectionary*, ed. A. S. Lewis, p. 104).

5) So, e.g., Frank., p. 22.

6) P. 13.

7) Similarly Ibn Ezra—לא יראה הרשת ולא יכחד ממנה עד שינוח בה יראה האוכל שבה ולא הרשת—("the bird) does not see the net and is not afraid of it, until it alights on it; it sees the bait which is on it, but not the net". Cf. further Gems., p. 14; Toy, p. 17; Wild., p. 4.

meaning can be obtained, however, if זרה is given the meaning which ذرى has in Arabic. This Arabic root, which means "winnow", also means "throw, scatter, like as one throws grain for sowing" (ذرا الارض "he sowed the land, scattering the seed") [1]), and ذرة means "corn" [2]). So the net is not "spread", a meaning which זרה seems not to have elsewhere, but "strewn" (with seed). As birds do not see the danger before them, so the wicked, lured on by seeming advantage, do not realise that they "lie in wait for their own blood, lurk for their own lives" (verse 18) [3]).

III 35: וכסילים מֵרִים קלון

The word מרים in this passage has been much emended. J. REIDER, after listing four emendations, proposes yet another, viz., מָרִים, ptcp. plur. Qal from מור = Arabic مار, in the sense "procure" [4]). This attempt to explain מרים as a participle in the plural, agreeing with כסילים [5]), loses sight, however, of the fact that מרים occurs again in an analogous passage, viz., xiv 29, with a singular subject—וקצר־רוח מרים אולת. In this last passage מרים אולת stands as a parallel to רב־תבונה, and מרים should accordingly have a meaning similar to רב "great". The meaning "enhance, increase" (German "steigern") for מרים here has already been suggested [6]), but seems to have found little support. Yet it provides good sense, and may be compared with the English "heighten" in the sense of "intensify, augment". The Tg.'s מסגי "increases" (cf. LXX's ἰσχυρός) has led some commen-

---

[1]) LANE, *Arab. Eng. Lex.*, p. 964.

[2]) HAVA, *Arab.-Engl. Dict.*, p. 228; KAZIMIRSKI, *Dict. arabe-français*, I, p. 772.

[3]) EHRL., *loc. cit.*, thinks that verse 18 refers to the birds mentioned in verse 17. This verse (18) seems clearly to link up, however, with verse 11—the machinations of the sinners recoil upon themselves. Cf. TOY, p. 17; FRANK., p. 22; GEMS., p. 14. BEER's emendation לנפש תם for לנפשתם is accordingly unnecessary.

[4]) *VT* II (1952), p. 124. In this proposal he has been anticipated by B. HALPER, *ZAW* 31 (1911), p. 263 ff. For earlier suggestions, by G. BEER and H. TORCZYNER, see GES.-BUHL, p. 751. G. R. DRIVER has recently withdrawn his earlier suggestion to read וּמְרַיִם כסילים קלון "and the desire of fools is shame(ful)" (*JTS* XXXVIII (1937), p. 403) in favour of מַדָּם "their garment", the verb ינחלו in the first half of the verse being emended to נֶחֱלוּ "they are adorned" (חלה = Arabic *ḥalā* "adorned with fine clothes, jewels"); see *Biblica* 32 (1951), p. 177.

[5]) Similarly MELVILLE SCOTT, *Textual Discoveries in Proverbs, Psalms and Isaiah*, p. 30, who proposes פרים "propagate" (root פרה).

[6]) E.g., by C. SIEGFRIED and B. STADE, *Hebr. Wörterb.*, p. 711, and F. HITZIG, *Die Sprüche*, p. 143.

tators to emend מרים to מַרְבֶּה [1]), but the sense of "increase" can be obtained without difficulty from מרים (ptcp. Hiph. רום "be high") as it stands [2]). The meaning of מרים in iii 35 must, it is suggested, be similar—wise men obtain honour from their fellow men, but fools go on increasing dishonour [3]) for themselves. It is thus only necessary to alter מרים into מְרִימִים (cf. LXX's ὕψωσαν) [4]), unless indeed the singular מרים can be justified [5]).

VI 26: ואשת איש נֶפֶשׁ יְקָרָה תצוד

G. R. Driver's suggestion [6]) that בעד in this verse is a noun meaning "change, exchange, price" helps considerably the proper understanding of כי בעד־אשה זונה עד־ככר לחם—"although the price of a harlot (mounts) up to a loaf of bread". His explanation of יקרה נפש as "costly abundance" seems, however, to depend on the meaning "abundance" given to נפש in Jes. lviii 10 [7]), and this is not altogether certain [8]). May not נפש יקרה here simply mean "a weighty person"? The married woman, who is contrasted with the harlot, makes a person of substance her quarry, since he can keep her in comfort [9]). It would seem at first sight natural perhaps to regard יקרה as an adjective in agreement with נפש· The phrases נֶפֶשׁ־בְּרָכָה "one who blesses" (xi 25), and נֶפֶשׁ רְמִיָּה "one who is idle" (xix 15) suggest, however, the possibility that נפש יקרה may likewise be a case of a construct and a noun in the genitive—"a person of weight". According to some authorities, יקרת in Jes. xxviii 16 is the construct of a noun יְקָרָה [10]), and this word could be read here. It would,

---

1) So Beer, *ad loc.*; Ehrl., p. 81; cf. Toy, p. 302.

2) Vulg.'s *exaltat* supports the consonants of the M.T.

3) קלון is accusative, and not, as BDB, p. 927, subject. The parallelism shows that כסילים is subject.

4) Cf. Tg. and Pesh. (ܢܩܒܠܘܢ ,נקבלון). Vulg.'s *exaltatio* suggests that מרים was taken as a substantive.

5) See Gesenius, *Hebr. Gramm.* (Kautzsch-Cowley), 2nd. ed., p. 145 l.

6) *VT* IV (1954), p. 244.

7) G. R. Driver, *ZAW* 52 (1934), p. 53 f.

8) See W. von Soden, *ibid.*, 53 (1935), p. 291, and Driver's reply, 55 (1937), p. 68 f.

9) For יקר with נפש as expressing a person's value or importance, cf. 1 Sam. xxvi 21, 2 Reg. i 13 f. For a like use in Akkadian, see W. Muss-Arnolt, *A Concise Dict. of the Assyr. Lang.*, p. 90, and F. Delitzsch, *Assyr. Handwörterb.*, p. 240.

10) So J. Fürst, *Hebr. u. Chald. Handwörterb.*, I, p. 541; cf. Gesenius, *Hebr. Gramm.*, p. 422, n. 4.

however, be better to keep the present vocalisation and to compare יְקָרָה with the Aramaic יְקָרָא "honour, cost" [1]).

With תצוד "hunt" in this passage may be compared the use in Arabic of صَيُود, used of a woman "who takes, captures, ensnares, something from her husband" [2]). The heart of the woman whom Koheleth found "more bitter than death" (Eccles. vii 26) is "snares and nets" (מְצוֹדִים וַחֲרָמִים), and the "snares" (מצודות) of the woman who plays the harlot are referred to in Sir. ix. 3. The Tg. [3]) renders Prov. xxiii 28b by וצאידא בניא שברי "and she (i.e. the harlot) ensnares foolish sons".

VII 21: הטתו ברב לִקְחָהּ

In two passages in Proverbs (xvi 21, 23) לֶקַח is commonly taken to mean "persuasiveness, power of persuasion", in a good sense. In this passage the same meaning is generally given to it, but—only here—in a bad sense [4]). It may be wondered, however, whether לֶקַח here may not express more than mere verbal persuasion [5]). Possibly alluring gestures too are included [6]). May לִקְחָהּ be the equivalent of the English phrase "her *taking*, attractive, ways"? An example of the verb לקח in the sense of "allure, attract", by seductive play of the eyes, is found in Prov. vi. 25—"let her (viz., the evil woman) not allure thee (אַל־תִּקָּחֲךָ) with her eyelids". [7]).

X 32: שפתי צדיק יֵדְעוּן רצון

The word ידעון here is sometimes explained as meaning "pay

---

[1]) G. H. Dalman, *Aram.-Neuhebr. Wörterb.*, p. 177; J. Levy, *Chald. Wörterb. über die Targ.* I, p. 343.

[2]) Lane, p. 753. The occurrence of *ṣwd* "hunt" in South Arabic has not been noted in the dictionaries; see K. Conti Rossini, *Chrest. arab. meridionalis epigraphica*, p. 223.

[3]) P. de Lagarde, *Hagiog. Chald.*, p. 137.

[4]) BDB, p. 544. LXX ὁμιλίᾳ; Tg. Pesh. מילהא, ܡܠܬܗ; Vulg. *sermonibus*.

[5]) Toy, p. 155 "with much fair speech".

[6]) Cf. B. Boothroyd, *Bibl. Hebr.* (1810-16), p. 187.

[7]) Tg. for עפעפיו has גבינתהא "her eyebrows"; Vulg. has in mind other signs of invitation—"her nods" (*nutibus illius*). J. Reider's "overpower thee" in the sense of "seize forcibly", the verb לקח being almost synonymous with אחז (*Journ. of Jewish Stud.* III [1952], p. 79) gives to תקחך here a sense of physical compulsion which is out of place in the context. With this verse in Proverbs, cf. Sir. xxvi 9 (LXX).

attention to, care for", a meaning which ידע frequently has [1]). The use of ידע in this sense with lips as subject is, however, as TOY [2]) remarks, strange—צדיק would rather be expected as subject—and he accordingly emends to יַבִּיעוּן "utter", which is thought to have the support of the LXX (ἀποστάζει). Since, however, the LXX translates נבע in xv. 2,28 by ἀναγγέλλει,· ἀποκρίνεται, it is not immediately evident that the Greek translators had יביעון before them in this passage. Moreover, the LXX uses ἀποστάζειν to translate also ינוב in the previous verse. No great reliance can, therefore, be attached to the Greek rendering of ידעון here [3]). If the consonants of the M.T., which have the support of Aq., Theod. and Quinta (γνώσονται) [4]), are retained, two possible explanations suggest themselves. In the first place, יֹדִעוּן "declare" might be read [5]). The second possibility is that the root in question here is not ידע "know", but דעה, cognate with the Arabic دعا "sought, desired, asked, demanded". This root has already been detected in Prov. xxiv 14—possibly also in Hos. vi 3—while the derivative דַּעַת "claim, suit" has been found in Prov. xxix. 7 [6]). If this equation be accepted here, יִדְעוּן must be read for יֵדְעוּן, and the translation will run—

> "The lips of the righteous seek goodwill" (i.e., seek by words uttered to spread goodwill)
> But the mouth of the wicked (seeks) perverse utterances".

That the idea of lips "seeking, desiring" is not alien to Hebrew thought is shown by the phrase אֲרֶשֶׁת שְׂפָתָיו "the desire, request of his lips" (Ps. xxi 3). It is perhaps worth while to ask whether יִרְעֶה in Prov. xv 14, which is parallel to יבקש, should not be read יִדְעֶה [7]) "and the mouth of fools seeks (desires) folly".

XIV 8: ואולת כסילים מִרְמָה

The LXX's ἐν πλάνῃ has induced some scholars to emend מִרְמָה

---

1) See, e.g., TOY, p. 219; FRANK., p. 71; WILD., p. 33.
2) P. 219. MELVILLE SCOTT, *op. cit.*, p. 38, emends to יערון "pour out" (root ערה).
3) Cf. HITZIG, *op. cit.*, p. 102.
4) F. FIELD, *Origenis Hexapl.*, II, p. 331.
5) In Prov. i 23 אודיעה is parallel to אביעה.
6) THOMAS in *JTS* XXXVIII (1937), p. 401 f.
7) Cf. LXX γνώσεται = יֵדַע.

to a participle—to מַטְעָה [1]) or מַתְעָה [2]) "leads astray" [3]). It seems preferable, however, to read מְרַמֶּה (ptcp. Pi. רמה "mislead"), which involves only a change in the vocalisation. In verse 25, מִרְמָה should in all probability be vocalised מְרַמֶּה (with the versions) [4]).

XIV 17: ואיש מזמות יִשָּׂנֵא

As it stands, יִשָּׂנֵא appears to mean "is hated" [5]). Toy [6]), however, following the LXX's ὑποφέρει, reads יִשָּׂא—"a man of thought endures", i.e., "bears much without getting angry". Nearer to the M.T. would be יִשְׁנֶא [7]) = יִשְׁנֶה, from שנה = Arabic سنى "become high, exalted in rank", a root which has been discovered in several passages in the O.T. [8]). The meaning of the proverb would then be that the quick-tempered man acts foolishly and thereby loses the respect of his fellow men, whereas the wise man attains high rank, honour, dignity, in the eyes of his fellows.

XV 30: מְאוֹר־עֵינַיִם ישמח־לב

"Light of the eyes" מְאוֹר־עֵינַיִם is sometimes explained as light which beams from the eyes of him who brings good news, and is thought to be equivalent to "good news" [9]). This would seem,

---

1) So Beer, *ad loc.*

2) So Toy, p. 286; cf. Frank., p. 86.

3) Vulg. *errans*. Tg. Pesh. render by substantives (רמיותא, ܛܘܥܝܬܐ).

4) LXX δόλιος; Tg. רמייא; Pesh. ܡܣܩܘܪܐ ܕܠܐ; Vulg. *versipellis*. See Perles, *op. cit.*, p. 66, and Beer, *ad loc.*

5) So English Versions and Vulg.; cf. Frank., p. 88.

6) P. 292; Beer, *ad loc.*, reads יִשְׁאַנֵן. Cf. Gems., p. 50; Wild., p. 43 proposes יִשְׁאַן. The versions, except Theod. and Vulg., understand מזמות in a good sense.

7) For the spelling with *aleph*, cf. יְשֻׁנָּא (Thren. iv 1), יְשֻׁנֶּא (Eccles. viii 1), and generally Gesenius, *Hebr. Gramm.*, 75 rr. Ehrl., p. 79, emends to יִשְׁגֶּא = יִשְׁגֶּה "commit an error".

8) Thomas, *ZAW* N.F. 11 (1934), p. 236 ff., 14 (1937), p. 174 ff.; further J. A. Montgomery, 12 (1935), p. 207 f. J. Reider reads שָׁנִים for שָׁנִים in Hab. iii 2, and translates "exalted ones" (*VT* IV [1954], p. 284). In Prov. v 9 שְׁנוֹתֶךָ, which probably means "dignity" (*ZAW* 14 [1937], p. 174) is translated by Ehrl., p. 27, "dein Glanz". It seems that he had سنى in mind—it can mean "shine, gleam"—though he does not mention it.

9) Wild., p. 47; Toy, p. 316; Frank., p. 95, "good fortune"; Gems., p. 53, "bright eyes are a sign of reviving after weariness".

however, to read too much into the Hebrew phrase. The LXX's rendering of מאור־עינים by θεωρῶν ὀφθαλμὸς καλά, suggesting the reading מַרְאֵה־עֵינַיִם[1], may point the way to a correct understanding of this Hebrew phrase. As is well known, ראה often has the meaning "look at with enjoyment" [2]). Seeing and enjoyment are both implied in the phrase מַרְאֵה עינים [3]) (Eccles. vi 9; cf. xi 9), and in Yoma 74b we find מראה עינים באשה "the pleasure of looking at one's wife" [4]). The meaning required in this verse, if a satisfactory parallel to שמועה טובה "good tidings" is to be obtained, is not, however, the pleasure of looking at something and enjoying it, but something which is seen and enjoyed. Such a meaning can be obtained if we read מָרְאֵה (ptcp. Hoph. construct ראה) "what is seen (and enjoyed) by the eyes". The whole verse may accordingly be translated: —

"A fine sight cheers the mind
As good tidings make the bones fat".[5])

XIX 17: מַלְוֵה יְהוָה חונן דל וגמלו ישלם־לו

"He lends to Yahweh who has pity on the poor, and (Yahweh) will repay him his (good) deed", i.e., whoever treats the poor kindly lays up with Yahweh a treasury of good works; Yahweh becomes his debtor, and will in his own time repay what he borrowed [6]). An interesting parallel to the thought of this proverb occurs in the Babylonian work known as "A Pessimistic Dialogue between Master and Servant". The relevant passage is as follows:—

"Servant, obey me". Yes, my lord, yes. "Bring me at once water for my hands, and give it to me. I will offer a sacrifice to my god".

---

[1]) Cf. Hitzig, *op. cit.*, p. 154. Tg., Pesh., Vulg., as M.T.

[2]) BDB, p. 908. Similarly *re'ya* in Ethiopic; see A. Dillmann, *Lex. Ling. Aeth.*, p. 297.

[3]) BDB, p. 909.

[4]) M. Jastrow, *A Dict. of the Targ., etc.*, II, p. 834; cf. Levy, *Neuhebr. u. Chald. Wörterb. über die Talm. u. Midr.*, III, p. 235.

[5]) For the parallelism between שמח and דשן עצם, cf. Sir. xxvi 13 (LXX). With שמועה טובה here and in xxv 25, cf. שמעת טב in Ostracon IV, line 2, and שמעת שלם in Ostr. II, lines 2 f., and III, line 3, from Lachish; see D. Diringer, in O. Tufnell, *Lachish III (Tell ed-Duweir) The Iron Age*, p. 332 f. Pesh here has ܠܒܐ ܒܣܝܡܐ "a cheerful heart" for שמועה טובה.

[6]) See Frank., p. 112; Toy, p. 375; Wild., p. 57. Cf. Matth. xxv 40.

Offer, my lord, offer. A man offering sacrifice to his god is happy, *loan upon loan he makes* [1]).

XIX 18: וְאֶל־הֲמִיתוֹ אַל־תִּשָּׂא נַפְשֶׁךָ

Toy [2]), who translates "set not thy heart on his destruction", is surely right when he says that "in the family life contemplated by Pr. it is highly improbable that a father would ever think of carrying chastisement to the point of killing his son". But when he thinks of the son, if uncontrolled, as finally suffering "death as the natural (legal or other) consequence of his ill-doing", he fails to see the true force of הֲמִיתוֹ, which is to be taken in a figurative, and not a literal, sense. I have recently suggested that the noun מָוֶת "death" sometimes has a superlative force in Hebrew, like our "deadly dull", "sick to death", and so on [3]), and in this passage the verb המית may be used similarly, possibly as a colloquialism, with a superlative force. When it is said-"Chasten thy son while there is still hope, but have no mind to kill him", הֲמִיתוֹ, literally "to kill him", may accordingly mean no more than "to chastise him excessively" [4]). In English the threat "I will thrash you to death" usually means only "I will give you a very severe thrashing"; and a joke or situation is sometimes described colloquially as "killing" when it creates an unusual degree of amusement. In Prov. xxiii 13 the phrase לֹא יָמוּת may also be used figuratively [5]), with a superlative force—"Withhold not chastisement from thy child, for if thou beat him with the rod,

---

[1]) R. H. Pfeiffer's translation in J. B. Pritchard, *Ancient Near Eastern Texts*, p. 438b. The Babylonian original of the phrase "loan upon loan he makes" is *kip-tu eli kip-tu ip-pu-uš* (S. Langdon, *Babylonian Wisdom*, p. 76). Mr. W. G. Lambert, who has kindly drawn my attention to this Babylonian parallel, informs me that in his opinion the translation "is happy" does not really bring out the sense here of *libba-šu ṭâb*. He thinks that the phrase is used rather in the sense that it bears in business documents, where it is added when a bargain is agreed by both parties, who undertake not to make any claims against the agreement later. The sense is then rather like our phrase "have a square deal".

[2]) P. 376.

[3]) *VT* III (1953), p. 209 ff.

[4]) Tg. Vulg. "to his death" (למיתותיה, *ad interfectionem ejus*). LXX, however, εἰς ὕβριν "to haughtiness", and Pesh. ܠܨܥܪܗ "to his shame". Gems., p. 60, reads חֵמוֹת "anger", translating "do not allow yourself to give way to passion", though he thinks the meaning "kill" is not impossible.

[5]) Toy, p. 433, again thinks of physical death. Boothroyd, *op. cit.*, p. 204, writes: "Here I think we have the figure Litotes, "Withold not correction from a child; But chastize him, *that he may live*".

he will not die!" — לֹא יָמוּת, that is to say, means no more than "he will come to no very great harm" [1]). In English we say that such and such a thing, for example, an unusually strenuous effort "will not kill you", when we mean nothing more than "it will do you no great harm" [2]).

XIX 26: מְשַׁדֶּד־אָב יַבְרִיחַ אֵם

The meaning "assault, maltreat", which is usually given to מְשַׁדֵּד here by lexicographers and commentators, has suggested to some scholars [3]) that the parallel יַבְרִיחַ bears the meaning which بَرَحَ has in Arabic, viz., "molest, annoy, hurt" [4]). H. GRÄTZ [5]), however, retaining the meaning "drives away" for יבריח, seeks to find a parallel to it by emending משדד to מְנַדֵּד "ejects" [6]). If this is the required meaning, it can, however, be obtained from משדד without alteration, for in Ethiopic *sadada* means "expel, eject" [7]).

XXII 4: עֵקֶב עֲנָוָה

The LXX's γενεά "offspring" for עֵקֶב goes back to the Arabic عَقْب "son, offspring" [8]), literally "that which follows, results, issues".

---

1) Cf. Aḥiqar, line 82—הן אמחאנך ברי לא תמות "If I smite thee my son, thou wilt not die" (A. COWLEY, *Aram. Papyri of the Fifth Century B.C.*, p. 215).

2) Cf. my remarks on the similar use of موت in Arabic (*VT* III (1953), p. 222).

3) E.g., C. F. HOUBIGANT, *Notae criticae in universos veteris testamenti libros*, 1777, II, p. 119; cf. EHRL., p. 113. Pesh. ܡܥܝܩ "annoy, grieve". LXX (ἀπωθούμενος), Tg. (מעריק) and Vulg. (*fugat*) give ברח its usual meaning.

4) LANE, p. 181, and derivatives given there.

5) Cited in TOY, p. 382.

6) Cf. TOY, p. 380 f.—"*maltreats* is probably equivalent to *drives away*. The son here seems to be in possession of the property in his father's lifetime; the latter is presumably decrepit, the care of the property falls naturally to the son whose unfilial conduct, though it may be condemned by public opinion, does not come under the cognizance of the law".

7) See DILLMANN, p. 396. For *saddada* "send", *asaddada* "send away, banish", in Amharic, see C. H. ARMBRUSTER, *Initia Amharica, Pt. iii, Amhar.-Engl. Vocab.*, I p. 752 f. For משדד, LXX has ἀτιμάζων; Tg. and Pesh. ביז, ܒܣܪ.

8) LANE, p. 2101; HAVA, p. 486. عَاقِبَة has the same meaning, and أَعْقَب means "left offspring". EHRL., p. 129, reads עֶקֶב (عقب II "auf etwas bedacht sein, darauf Fleiss verwenden").

XXX 16: עֹצֶר רָחַם

I have for a long time wondered whether רחם in the phrase עצר רָחַם usually translated "the barren womb"—"the reference is to the desire of a childless wife for children" [1])—might not refer to the bird רָחָם mentioned in Lev. xi 18, Deut. xiv 17. According to LANE [2]), رَخَمَة (*nomen unitatis* of رَخَم) is the *vultur percnopterus*, "called by some the white carrion-vulture of Egypt, and the neighbouring countries", and is described as "vehemently voracious, and fond of alighting upon carcasses" [3]). In a context whose subject is insatiable voracity, the רָחָם may then not be considered out of place. It was with great interest that I recently came across B. HODGSON's translation of עצר רחם by "the ravenous gier-eagle" [4]). When applied to this bird, עצר, HODGSON thinks, must signify "voracious", and he compares the Arabic عصر *prandium*, *coena* [5]). It is possible to think also of the Arabic عَظِرَ "feel disgust at a thing" (عِظَارَة "indigestion of drink", عَظُور "indisposed through excess of drink") [6]). This word has been suggested to me by Professor A. GUILLAUME, who tells me that he thinks that, though the usual meaning of عظر is "drink too much to one's discomfort", a wider meaning like "gorge" is necessary, seeing that the male locust is nicknamed العظارى [7]). May we then think of a Hebrew word עֹצֶר meaning "voracity"? That עצר רחם here may mean "the voracity of the carrion-vulture" is a possibility only, for the traditional rendering of the phrase is not lightly to be discarded [8]). It seems worth while, however, to recall an interpretation which was at one time current, and which today may be considered not altogether impossible.

---

[1]) TOY, p. 529.
[2]) P. 1059.
[3]) For an illustration of the bird and a further description of it, see H. B. TRISTRAM, *The Natural History of the Bible*, p. 179 f.
[4]) *The Proverbs of Solomon*, 1788, *ad loc.* (the volume is not paginated). Reference is made to HODGSON's interpretation by BOOTHROYD, *op. cit.*, II, p. 212.
[5]) FREYTAG, III, p. 167, gives أَعَاصِير *prandium, coena.*
[6]) HAVA, p. 482.
[7]) See the *Qamus* (*sub* عظر).
[8]) See the references to Arabic and Indian proverbs in TOY, p. 529.

XXX 31: וּמֶלֶךְ אַלְקוּם עִמּוֹ

So many and varied are the interpretations of this obscure phrase which have been offered that it may be useful, without any attempt at a solution, briefly to draw special attention to two points which have hitherto received less notice than they deserve. In the first place, the fact that the first three of the four things that are "stately in carriage, motion" (מיטבי לכת, verse 29) are animals, makes it very probable that מֶלֶךְ in verse 31, if it is original (see below), refers not, as is generally thought [1]), to a human king, but to an animal [2]). Secondly, it may be asked whether אוֹ־תַיִשׁ may not be an explanatory gloss on זַרְזִיר מָתְנַיִם, whose meaning is most uncertain; for the simple conjunction *waw* (ותיש), and not או, would normally be expected. If it be a gloss, then two animals must be recovered from ומלך אלקום עמו. If, however, we read ותיש [3]), the "he-goat" then being in fact a firm member of the quartette of animals, then only one animal is to be looked for in the last member of the verse, which then seems overcrowded. Toy [4]) suggests that מלך may be a corruption of אלקום, or *vice versa*, is it too bold to suggest that in מלך אלקום is to be seen a dittograph [5]) of מֶלֶךְ אֵין לָאַרְבֶּה (verse 27), the last two words אין לארבה being here abbreviated to א׳ל׳ (thus [מלך אל] קום)? We should then be left with the letters קום עמו from which the name of an animal has to be extracted.

XXXI 11: וְשָׁלָל לֹא יֶחְסָר

The word שָׁלָל in the description of the capable housewife has not been adequately explained hitherto. It is customarily translated "gain", a meaning which is given to it in this passage only; everywhere else it means "booty taken in war" [6]). As Toy, for example, says—"the

---

[1]) Most recently G. R. Driver, *Biblica* 32 (1951), p. 194.

[2]) Cf. Toy, p. 537—"the original text referred to the majestic mien and movement of some animal". Melville Scott, *op. cit.*, p. 88, has suggested reading מלך איל קום פעמיו "a king stag that raiseth high its steps". A "queen bee" is called in Latin *rex apium*.

[3]) Cf. Frank., p. 164; Toy, p. 538.

[4]) *Ibid.*

[5]) For examples of vertical dittography, see M. Lambert, *Traité de gramm. hébr.*, p. 102, 105, 113, 119; further, R.-J. Tournay, *Vivre et Penser*, III (1945), p. 232, n. 2.

[6]) So LXX here (καλῶν σκύλων); cf. Tg מתבזא, Vulg. *spoliis*. Pesh. has ܒܙܬܐ

military term came to be employed in a peaceful sense" [1]). Since, however, such a usage is without parallel in Hebrew, another explanation may be advanced. There is an Arabic proverb لا تعدم صنع ثلّة "a clever woman is not without wool" (to spin or weave when she has nothing else to do) [2]). May not שלל לא יחסר be the Hebrew counterpart of this Arabic proverb? If so, the Hebrew phrase may be translated—"and wool (שלל = ثلّة) is not lacking (to her)" [3]). In both the Arabic and Hebrew proverb the capable woman (אֵשֶׁת־חַיִל, verse 10) is thought of as never idle; she is always at her wool [4]). Mention may be made in this connection of a passage in Livy (I, lvii, 9), where it is related how Lucretia, taken by surprise, was found sitting busy at her wool (*deditam lanae*), and gained the prize for womanly virtues [5]) .. So, too, Jerome recommends that a young girl should have as her guardian one who is "not given to much wine, nor in the apostle's words, idle and wordy, but sober, sedate, industrious in spinning wool" [6]). We may recall also the well known epitaph of the beautiful and virtuous Roman matron, Claudia, who "kept to her house, and spun wool" (*domum servavit, lanam fecit*) [7]).

"store, victuals". F. Zorell, *Lex. Hebr. et Aram. Vet. Test.*, p. 852, would seem to be in error in giving the meaning "gain" to שָׁלָל in Sir. xxxvii 6: see R. Smend, *Die Weisheit des Jesus Sirach* (Translation, p. 63; Commentary, p. 328).

[1]) P. 543; cf. W. O. E. Oesterley, *The Book of Proverbs*, p. 283—"that which is acquired by skilful management of the estate, and thus income".

[2]) Lane, p. 346.

[3]) Inserting לה after יחסר, with LXX (ἡ τοιαύτη); cf. Pesh. The word is thus the subject of the verb, and not object, as BDB, p. 341, *et al.*

[4]) Cf. verse 13 of this chapter.

[5]) The passage runs in full as follows: "citatis equis avolant Romam. Quo cum primis se intendentibus tenebris pervenissent, pergunt inde Collatiam, ubi Lucretiam haudquaquam ut regias nurus, quas in convivio luxuque cum aequalibus viderant tempus terentes, sed nocte sera deditam lanae inter lucubrantes ancillas in medio aedium sedentem inveniunt. Muliebris certaminis laus penes Lucretiam fuit" (*Livy Bks. I and II, Loeb Class. Library*, p. 198). I am indebted to Mr. H. St J. Hart for this reference.

[6]) *Sancti Eusebii Hieronymi Epistulae* (*Corpus Scriptorum Ecclesiasticorum Latinorum LVI*) *recensuit* Isidorus Hilberg, Pt. iii, Letter cxxviii, p. 16, lines 19 ff. The passage runs: "sit ei magistra, comes, paedagoga, custos non multo vino dedita, non iuxta apostolum otiosa atque verbosa, sed sobria, gravis, lanifica et ea tantum loquens quae animum puellarem ad virtutem instituant".

[7]) *Corp. Inscr. Lat.*, I. 2, 1211 (last line); cf. VI. 3, 15346.

HIOB XXXVIII UND DIE ALTÄGYPTISCHE WEISHEIT

VON

GERHARD VON RAD

Heidelberg

Über die dichterische Grossartigkeit der Gottesrede Iob xxxviii f. sind sich die Ausleger seit je einig; aber in der Bestimmung der spezifischen Form, in der diese Rede einhergeht, sind wir seit der Begründung der Gattungsforschung durch GUNKEL noch nicht weitergekommen. Dass man sich mit dieser Aufzählung der Schöpfungswunder thematisch in der Nähe der Hymnen befindet, ist klar. Auch in formaler Hinsicht hat man gemeint, die Frageform von Iob xxxviii f. mit den rhetorischen Fragen in Verbindung bringen zu können, die sich nicht selten in den Hymnen finden [1]). Aber der Fragestil der Hymnen ist doch ein ganz anderer: er ist zwar auch rhetorisch, aber in den Hymnen ist der anbetende Mensch selbst der Fragende, hier aber ist er der Gefragte. Ausserdem verbietet schon die Tatsache, dass Iob xxxviii f. überhaupt nur aus Fragen besteht, von vornherein, diese Einheit als einen Hymnus zu bezeichnen. Wir müssen versuchen, dem Problem von einer ganz anderen Seite beizukommen.

Das von Sir ALAN H. GARDINER herausgegebene und kommentierte Onomastikon des Amenope ist bekanntlich ein wissenschaftlich enzyklopädisches Werk gewesen, es war eine „Lehre über alles von Ptah Geschaffene, über den Himmel mit seinem Zubehör, über die Erde und was in ihr ist". Von da geht das Werk — immer nur in der Aufzählung von blossen Substantiven oder kurzen Wortverbindungen — zu anderen Gegenständen über, zu Personen, Ämtern, Berufen, Stämmen, ägyptischen Städten u.s.w. Das Werk, soweit es erhalten ist, umfasst 610 Gegenstände [2]). Uns interessiert hier nur der Beginn der Aufzählung, denn es könnte doch vielleicht nützlich sein, einmal die Aufzählung der kosmologischen und meteorologischen Dinge bei Amenope mit der in der Gottesrede

---

[1]) GUNKEL-BEGRICH, *Einleitung in die Psalmen* (1933), p. 54 f.

[2]) A. H. GARDINER, *Ancient Egyptian Onomastica* (1947). Für Beratung in ägyptologischen Fragen habe ich Herrn Privatdozent Dr. FECHT zu danken.

Iob xxxviii zu vergleichen. Diese Gegenüberstellung kann billigerweise erst bei Iob xxxviii 12 einsetzen, denn in den Versen 4-11 ist von Jahwes Weltschöpfung die Rede und noch dazu in der unägyptischen Vorstellung vom Chaosdrachenkampf. Das Onomastikon verzichtet aber in seinem ersten Teil auf alle theologischen oder mythologischen Hintergründe und beschränkt sich auf die dürre Aufzählung der kosmischen Gegebenheiten. So kann sich also für diesen ersten Teil der Gottesrede bei Amenope keine Entsprechung finden. (s. p. 264).

Wie ist nun die Abfolge der Phänomene bei Amenope einerseits und bei Iob xxxviii 12 ff. andrerseits zu beurteilen? Von einer genauen Entsprechung kann gewiss keine Rede sein. Die Entsprechungen setzen erst bei Amenope Nr. 12 ein und sind auch da ohne rechte Genauigkeit. Allerdings bei der Aufzählung der meteorologischen Phänomene — Schnee, Hagel, Winde — also bei Amenope Nr. 12-23 und bei Iob xxxviii 22-29 kommen sich doch beide Texte recht nahe. Dasselbe gilt auch von den Gestirnen, wenngleich sie bei Amenope sinnvoll am Anfang aufgeführt sind, während sie bei Hiob fast wie eine Interpolation die Aufzählung der meteorologischen Erscheinungen unterbrechen (Iob xxxviii 31-32). Man kann also gewiss nicht behaupten, dass in Iob xxxviii das Onomastikon des Amenope literarisch benutzt sei; trotzdem muss doch wohl eine Beziehung zwischen beiden Texten bestehen. Es kann ja ein anderes Onomastikon gewesen sein, das der Dichter der Gottesrede „benutzt" hat. Das Ramesseum-Onomastikon enthielt z.B. Listen von Pflanzen, Mineralien, Vögeln, Fischen und Vierfüsslern [1]). Iob xxxviii f. beschränkt sich demgegenüber auf die Aufzählung von Himmelserscheinungen und lässt abrupt in xxxviii 39-xxxix 26 eine Liste von Tieren folgen. Auch diese Reihe ist wegen der dazwischen genannten Vögel gewiss nicht ursprünglich. Aber ist das denn bei einer Dichtung anders zu erwarten? Bei Hiob ist ja das Ganze durch den Übergang zu einer freien Satzbildung stilistisch so aufgelockert, dass sich für einen Dichter allenthalben Assoziationen boten, denen er nachgehen konnte. Unter diesem Gesichtspunkt muss man sich vielmehr wundern, wie streng auch in der Dichtung der Aufzählungsstil immer noch eingehalten ist. Erst in der zweiten Hälfte der Gottesrede lässt der Dichter die Zügel lockerer und gibt sich freieren Schilderungen hin.

---

[1]) GARDINER, *a. a. O.*, p. 7 ff.

omastikon des menope

. Himmel
. Sonne
. Mond
. Stern
. Orion
. Grosser Bär
. Pavian
. "Der Starke"
. Sau
. Sturm
. Orkan
. Morgendämmerung
. Dunkelheit
Sonne
. Schatten
. Sonnenschein
Sonnenstrahlen
Tau
. ?
Schnee (?)
Regensturm (?)
Urwasser
"Flut" (Nil)
Fluss
Meer
Welle
Meerartiger See
See
Brunnen
Bassin (?)
Bewässerungsanlage
"Wasser"
Teich
Vorderseite
Bückseite
Brunnen
Wasserdurchbruch
?
Flussufer
?
Wasserlauf
Stelle zum Wasserschöpfen
Flüsschen
Flut
?
Strom
Wasserloch
?
Ufer
?

Hiob xxxviii

12. Morgen
13. Morgenröte
16. Meer
    Urflut
17. Unterwelt
    Dunkel
18. Erde
19. Licht
    Finsternis
22. Schnee
    Hagel
24. "Wind"
    Ostwind
25. Regenguss
    Gewitterwolke
28. Regen
    Tautropfen
29. Eis
    Reif
31. Plejaden
    Orion
    Hyaden
32. Bär
    Löwin
34. Wolken
    Wasserguss
35. Blitz
36. Ibis
    Hahn
37. Wolken
    Himmelsschläuche
39. Löwe
    Junglöwe
41. Rabe

Hiob xxxix

1. Steinbock
   Damhirschkuh
5. Zebra
9. Büffel
19. Pferd
26. Falke

Sirach xliii

1. Firmament
   Himmel
2. Sonne
6. Mond
9. Sterne
11. Regenbogen
13. Blitz
14. Wolken
15. Gewölk
    Hagel
16. Südwind
17. Wirbelwind
    Sturm
    Wettersturm
    Reif
19. Eis
22. Regen
    Tau
23. Rahab
25. Walfisch

Psalm cxlviii

1. Himmel
3. Sonne
   Mond
   Sterne
4. Himmel
   Himmelsozean
7. Drachen
   Urflut
8. Feuer (Blitz?)
   Hagel
   'Eis' (LXX)
   Sturmwind
9. Berg
   Hügel
   Fruchtbaum
   Zedern
10. Wilde Tiere
    Haustiere
    Kriechtiere
    Vögel
11. König
    Völker
    Beamter
    Richter
12. Jungmann
    Jungfrau
    Greis
    Bursche

Hymnus der drei Männer

59. Himmel
60. Himmelsozean
61. (Engel)
62. Sonne
    Mond
63. Sterne
64. Regen
    Tau
65. Luft
66. Feuer
    Hitze
67. Frost
    Kälte
68. Tau
    Schnee
69. Eis
    Kälte
70. Reif
    Schnee
71. Nacht
    Tag
72. Licht
    Finsternis
73. Blitz
    Wolken
74. Erde
75. Berg
    Hügel
76. Gewächse
77. Quelle
78. Meer
    Flüss
79. Seeungeheuer
80. Vögel
81. Vierfüssler
    Wild
82. Mensch
83. Israel

Da unsere Beweisführung vielleicht noch auf schwachen Füssen steht, ziehen wir zu ihrer Stützung noch einen anderen Text heran, den Schöpfungshymnus Sir. xliii 1 ff. Die Formen der Aussagen sind hier gegenüber dem monotonen Fragestil von Iob xxxviii f. viel beweglicher und mannigfaltiger; trotzdem kann doch kein Zweifel sein, dass sich auch diese Dichtung an ein ihr vorgegebenes Schema hält. Hier ist das Schema — beginnend bei den Gestirnen und von da wiederum zu den mannigfachen meteorologischen Phänomenen fortschreitend — vergleichsweise noch deutlicher erkennbar als in Iob xxxviii f. Dabei brauchen wir uns aber auch bei diesem Beispiel über den Grad der Abhängigkeit keiner Täuschung hinzugeben. Es kann natürlich keine Rede davon sein, dass die beiden hebräischen Texte direkt im literarischen Sinn von einem ägyptischen Onomastikon abhängig sind. Aber dies kann immerhin behauptet werden, dass solche enzyklopädischen Werke auch nach Israel gekommen sind und dass man es auch in Israel gelernt hat, die kosmischen und meteorologischen Phänomene, aber auch die Tierwelt derart wissenschaftlich aufzureihen. Die Weisen, wohlbewandert in aller gelehrten Literatur, standen dann vor der nicht allzuschweren Aufgabe, bei der Herstellung ihrer Lehrdichtungen diesem von der damaligen Wissenschaft längst sanktionierten Schema entlang zu gehen und die nüchternen Reihen in Dichtungen umzusetzen. Der Vorgang in Sir. xliii 1 f. ist also grundsätzlich der gleiche wie in dem πατέρων ὕμνος Sir. xliv-xlix. In dem einen Fall handelt es sich um die Umdichtung einer gelehrten historischen Vorlage, im anderen um die einer gelehrten naturwissenschaftlichen.

Als nächstes Beispiel führen wir Ps. cxlviii an. Er beginnt mit der Aufforderung zum Lobpreis Jahwes. Die ersten, die ihn preisen sollen, sind die Himmlischen. Sie stehen bekanntlich ausserhalb des enzyklopädischen Bereiches der Onomastika. Aber kaum ist der Hymnus von den überirdischen Wesen zu den kosmologischen und meteorologischen Phänomenen übergegangen (3 ff.), so folgt er sofort dem herkömmlichen wissenschaftlichen Schema, das ihn wieder wie das Onomastikon des Amenope von den Gestirnen über die meteorologischen Erscheinungen herunter auf die Erde führt. Dieser letzte Teil ist uns hier besonders interessant, weil er stofflich erheblich über Iob xxxviii f. und Sir. xliii hinunterführt. Dieser Teil ist freilich viel summarischer; er zählt weniger Einzelheiten auf (wie noch im meteorologischen Abschnitt), sondern mehr Arten: Fruchtbäume, Wild, Haustiere, Kriechtiere und Vögel. Diese Abfolge erinnert an das Ramesseum-Onomastikon, das in dem fast ganz unleserlichen Anfang Pflanzennamen und Flüssigkeiten enthalten hat, um dann zu Vögeln, Fischen und Vierfüsslern überzugehen [1]). Dagegen entspricht in unserem Psalm 11 f. ziemlich genau der Disposition des Amenope-Onomastikon, das nach der Abhandlung vom Himmel, dem Meteorologischen und der Erde zum König übergeht und von da zu anderen Ämtern und Berufen. Mit Vers 12 (Jungmannen, Jungfrauen, Älteste, Burschen), sind wir zu dem Abschnitt gekommen, den GARDINER mit „types of human being" überschrieben hat, und hier ist die Berührung mit dem Onomastikon besonders schlagend.

Der entsprechende Passus bei Amenope sieht folgendermassen aus:

295. Mann
296. Junger Bursche
297. Alter Mann
298. Frau
299. Junge Frau
300. Verschiedene Personen
301. Knabe
302. Kind
303. Junge
304. Mädchen

Es lohnt sich, zuletzt noch einen Blick auf den „Gesang der drei Männer im Feuer" (Dan. iii 52-90 LXX) zu werfen [2]). Sein Alter ist schwer zu bestimmen; sicher war er ursprünglich eine selbständige Dichtung und ist nicht erst ad hoc als Zusatz zu Daniel gedichtet worden. Er kann aus der gleichen Zeit wie Ps. cxlviii stammen, dem er sehr ähnlich ist. Keinesfalls ist er eine Nachdichtung von ihm, denn er bewahrt Ps. cxlviii gegenüber durchaus seine Eigenart. So ist es interessant, dass er den Himmelserscheinungen und den Bergen und Hügeln eine kurze Aufzählung der irdischen Wasser und ihrer Arten folgen lässt (Quellen, Meer, Fluss in Vers 77 f.). Der Passus wäre an sich nicht weiter auffällig, wenn nicht das Onomastikon des Amenope gleicherweise eine — nur wieder viel detailliertere — Aufzählung der irdischen Gewässer enthielte (Nr. 23-33), in der u.a. auch Meer, Fluss und Brunnen genannt wird. Andrerseits findet sich in dem Hymnus einiges, das nicht in dem ägyptischen Schema enthalten gewesen sein kann (z.B. Vers 61 die Engel, Vers 79

---

1) GARDINER, *a. a. O.*, p. 37.

2) Vgl. die formgeschichtliche Analyse bei C. KUHL, „Die drei Männer im Feuer", *BZAW* 55 (1930), p. 90-100.

die Seeungeheuer). Wir geben den Text in einer Übersetzung nach der Textausgabe von RAHLFS ohne in kritische Einzelerörterungen einzutreten (dass die Verse 68-69 als Interpolation verdächtig sind, hat schon ROTHSTEIN gesehen) [1]).

Die hier angeschnittenen Fragen drängen nun freilich nach manchen Seiten weiter. Zunächst müssten natürlich Einzelheiten aufs Korn genommen werden. Es wäre festzustellen, an welchen Stellen etwa das von Israel übernommene Schema infolge von landschaftlichen oder klimatischen Bedingtheiten abgeändert oder erweitert worden ist. Es wäre weiter die Reichweite dieses Schemas im Bereich der alttestamentlichen Hymnik abzugrenzen. Vor allem aber wäre die theologische Seite der Sache zu erwägen, dass Israel auch diese nüchterne Wissenschaft zum Lobpreis seines Gottes ausgestaltet hat [2]).

Wir kehren noch einmal zu unserem Ausgangspunkt, zu Iob xxxviii f. zurück, denn die Frage nach der eigentümlichen Stilform der Gottesrede ist ja noch offen geblieben. Diese Kette von Fragen, sagten wir oben, kann nicht hymnisch verstanden werden; wir haben ja auch keine Hymnen, die nur aus rhetorischen Fragen bestehen. Könnte nicht auch diese seltsame Stilform, die in Israel einmalig zu sein scheint, auf irgend eine Weise der altägyptischen Weisheit entlehnt sein? Wenden wir uns einmal der berühmten Streitschrift zu, in der der Beamte Hori über seinen Kollegen — er heisst auch Amenemope — herfällt, um ihn literarisch zu vernichten. Dieses Dokument, das wir nach der einzigen vollständig erhaltenen Handschrift Papyrus Anastasi I zu nennen gewohnt sind, stammt aus der Zeit Ramses' II. (1301-1234), also gerade aus jener Zeit der Spätblüte, in der die altägyptische Weisheit auch in Israel wirksam geworden ist. Von der umfangreichen Schrift interessiert uns hier nur der berühmte Syrienabschnitt, der zur Erkenntnis der historischen Geographie des vorisraelitischen Palästina wichtig geworden ist.

---

[1]) KAUTZSCH, *Apokryphen und Pseudepigraphen* I, p. 182.

[2]) Nachträglich macht mich mein Assistent KL. BALTZER auf eine Reihe in 4 Esra vii 39 ff. aufmerksam: „nicht Sonne, nicht Mond, nicht Sterne, nicht Wolken, nicht Donner, nicht Blitz, nicht Wind, nicht Regen, nicht Nebel, nicht Dunkel, nicht Abend, nicht Morgen, nicht Sommer, nicht Frühling, nicht Hitze, nicht Winter, nicht Eis, nicht Frost, nicht Hagel, nicht Wetter, nicht Tau, nicht Mittag, nicht Nacht, nicht Glanz, nicht Dämmerung, nicht Helle . . ." Interessant ist die Reihe deshalb, weil sie zeigt, dass in Israel solche Aufzählungen auch ausserhalb der poetischen Verkleidung zur Hand waren. — Die Frage nach dem Verhältnis von Gen. i zu diesen Reihen bedarf einer besonderen Prüfung.

Hier nämlich — und merkwürdigerweise nur in diesem Unterabschnitt (von xviii 9-xxviii 1) — stossen wir auf ganz ähnliche rhetorische Fragen, und zwar dergestalt, dass fast der ganze Abschnitt als eine einzige Folge solcher Fragen stilisiert ist. „Bist du nicht zum Chattiland gegangen und hast du das Land Upi nicht gesehen?" — so beginnt die Reihe; „belehre mich doch über Berytos", „wo ist der Weg nach Aksaph"? „Belehre mich doch auch über den Berg User? Wie ist sein Gipfel ..." „Bist du nicht zum Lande Tachsi gekommen?" [1]) Das sind nur wenige Beispiele. Es mögen im Ganzen etwa 50 solcher Fragen sein. Und nun vergleiche man damit die Fragen in Iob xxxviii f.: „Belehre mich" (3bβ), „wo warst du?" — du weisst es ja" (5a) — „hast du geboten?" (12) „bist du gekommen?" (16a, 22a) „— sind dir aufgetan"? (17a) — „hast du gesehen"? (17b, 22b) — „hast du erkannt"? (18a) — „wo geht der Weg zu?" (19, 24a) u.s.w. Es bedarf wohl keiner weiteren Erörterung, dass wir es hier wie dort mit der gleichen Stilform zu tun haben. Wie eng beide Texte gattungsmässig zusammenhängen, sieht man besonders an dem „belehre mich", das bei Hiob einmal, bei Anastasi I dreimal vorkommt; vor allem aber auch an den Phrasen „bist du nicht zu .... gekommen?", „wo ist der Weg zu?", Fragen, die in der Streitschrift real gestellt sind, während sie bei Hiob auf die Kammern des Schnees (22) oder die Pforten der Finsternis (17) bezogen nur bildlich verstanden werden können [2]).

Die Stilform der ironischen Frage in der Gestalt, wie sie uns in der Streitschrift und in der Gottesrede des Buches Hiob entgegentritt, ist nun zweifellos eine rein literarische Erscheinung. Aber die Frage ist doch berechtigt, ob sie das schon immer war. Ist es nicht denkbar, ja sogar naheliegend, dass diese Form der rhetorischen Frage — oder sagen wir genauer der katechetischen Frage — ursprünglich einen sehr realen Sitz im Leben hatte und also erst sekundär zur literarischen Stilform geworden ist? Wir befinden uns doch bei der Weisheit sowieso schon im Bereich der Schule, der lehrhaften Unterweisung derer, die zur Laufbahn der höheren Beamten bestimmt sind. Betrachten wir unter diesem veränderten Gesichtspunkt noch

---

[1]) Übersetzung nach A. ERMAN, *Die Literatur der Ägypter*, p. 286 ff. und J. B. PRITCHARD, *Ancient Near Eastern Texts*, p. 477 f.

[2]) Der zeitliche Abstand zwischen dem Hiobdichter und dem Verfasser des Pap. Anastasi I ist wohl gross. Aber gerade diese weisheitlichen Stilformen hatten eine ausserordentliche Lebenskraft. Die Berufssatire, schon im Ägypten des Mittleren Reiches beliebt, findet sich noch bei Sirach (xxxviii 24 ff.).

einmal einige der Fragen des Papyrus Anastasi I: „Belehre mich über den Berg User? Wie ist sein Gipfel"? „Wie ist Byblos beschaffen"? „Wo ist der Litanifluss"? „Wie überquert man den Jordan"? „Wie geht man bei Megiddo vorüber"? „Setze mich auf den Weg nach Hamat"! „Wenn man nach Adummim geht, wohin kehrt man da das Gesicht"? „Wieviel Meilen sind von Raphia nach Gaza"? Muss man nicht annehmen, dass das einmal echte Schulfragen waren? So sind die jungen Beamten, die künftigen „Provinzialgouverneure" wirklich in der Geographie der Ägypten benachbarten Länder eingeübt und in ihr examiniert worden [1]). Man denke nur an das „Komm heraus, dass du geprüft werdest", das die Reihe der Fragen eröffnet und an das „Antworte schnell", das sie abschliesst. Dagegen kann man dasselbe natürlich nicht von den Fragen der Gottesrede behaupten; bei ihnen handelt es sich nurmehr um eine literarisch-dichterische Form.

Übersehen wir alles bisher Dargelegte, so enthält nun aber unser Ergebnis über Iob xxxviii noch eine störende Frage. Wir sahen, dass Iob xxxviii f. hinsichtlich der Abfolge der kosmologischen und naturkundlichen Phänomene einem vorgegebenen Schema entlang geht, das letztlich der ägyptischen Wissenschaft entstammt, wie sie in den Onomastiken niedergelegt ist. Wir sahen weiter, dass die Frageketten der Gottesrede ihre genaue Entsprechung in den satirischen Fragen des Pap. Anastasi I haben, die ihrerseits wieder auf den katechetischen Fragestil zurückgehen, der zu der Unterweisung in den altägyptischen Beamtenschulen gehört hat. Aber ist das denn einleuchtend, dass Iob xxxviii f. formgeschichtlich zugleich auf zwei ganz verschiedene Formen zurückgeht, so dass sich der Dichter der Gottesrede zugleich an das Onomastikonschema und an den satirischen Fragestil sollte angelehnt haben? Was hat ein wissenschaftliches Onomastikon mit einer satirischen Streitschrift zu tun? Vielleicht doch sehr viel! Wir brauchen ja nur zu fragen, woher denn dieser Hori alle die Kenntnisse hat, mit denen er in diesem Abschnitt seinen Kollegen so selbstgefällig schulmeistert? Auf welcher Grundlage werden denn die Weisheitslehrer ihren Unterricht erteilt haben, wenn nicht eben auf der ihrer eigenen gelehrten Werke, also in diesem

[1]) Eine besondere Frage ist, ob auch das „bist du nicht gekommen", das „hast du nicht betreten" usw. zu den wirklichen Schulfragen gehört hat. Hat der Lehrer den Unterricht durch die Fiktion des Augenscheins des Schülers belebt? Vielleicht aber gehören diese Fragen schon auf das Konto der literarischen Abwandlung dieser Stilform.

Falle ihrer Onomastika? Das Onomastikon des Amenope bringt ja in einer besonderen Passage (Nr. 250-270) eine Liste von palästinischen Namen und zeigt uns, wie etwa eine solche Vorlage der Streitschrift ausgesehen haben könnte [1]). Die Annahme, der Verfasser der Streitschrift brilliere mit seiner Palästinakenntnis aufgrund einer persönlichen Autopsie hat nur dann etwas für sich, wenn man das Werk nach Stil und Inhalt für das ausschliessliche literarische Eigentum dieses Hori hält. Macht man sich aber klar, dass er den Lehrbetrieb der Beamtenschulen kopiert und parodiert und dass er seinen Kollegen wie einen Schüler katechisiert, so liegt die Annahme viel näher, dass auch er dabei solchen listenartigen Vorlagen entlang geht. Der strikte Beweis dafür lässt sich nach Lage der Dinge am Text schwerlich führen; aber schon GARDNER hat diesen Teil der Streitschrift mit den Onomastiken in Verbindung gebracht [2]). Eine genaue Untersuchung dieses Textes auf mögliche Vorlagen, auf die Gruppierung der Lokalitäten hin, liegt ausserhalb des Rahmens dieser Skizze. Eine solche Analyse würde, gerade weil sie in der Aufzählung der Namen auf Brüche und Sprünge stossen würde, die Annahme einer Verwendung vorgegebener Listen noch besonders nahelegen. Müssen wir nicht gerade diese Literatur immer noch mehr in ihrer Konventioniertheit sehen, d.h. als ein Arbeiten mit Vorlagen, so dass also der persönliche Anteil des Verfassers sowohl hinsichtlich des Stiles wie des Inhaltes immer noch kleiner ist, als wir denken? Hätte der Verfasser der Streitschrift seinen Kollegen nicht über dessen geographische, sondern über seine kosmologischen und meteorologischen Kenntnisse katechisiert, so hätten wir eine exakte Parallele zu Iob xxxviii [3]).

---

[1]) A. ALT, *Syrien und Palästina im Onomastikon des Amenope = Kleine Schriften zur Geschichte des Volkes Israel* I, p. 231 ff.

[2]) GARDINER, *a. a. O.*, p. 4, Anm. 1.

[3]) Auf die Heranziehung der babylonisch-assyrischen Listen (L. MATOUŠ, *Die lexikalischen Tafelserien des Babylonier und Assyrer* [1933]) konnte verzichtet werden, weil die Anordnung der Gegenstände dort eine ganz andere ist. Der charakteristische Weg vom Himmel über die Gestirne zu den meteorologischen Phänomenen und von da zur Erde findet sich nur in Ägypten und in den davon abhängigen israelitischen Texten. Auch die Listen von Ras Schamra bieten hierzu kein Vergleichsmaterial.

Vielleicht hilft die Kenntnis von diesen Zusammenhängen auch zu einer gerechteren Würdigung der Onomastiken und ihrer Abzweckung. Die Annahme, diese Aufzählungen seien nur zur Erlernung der Orthographie in den Schreiberschulen abgefasst (ERMAN, *a. a. O.*, p. 240 f.) unterschätzt die wissenschaftlichen Ambitionen dieser Werke. Es ist ja kaum denkbar, dass die israelitischen Weisen ihren Lehrdichtungen orthographische Lehrbücher zugrunde gelegt haben.